Blocking Patents in European Competition Law

International Competition Law Series

VOLUME 90

Editor

In its series editor, Alastair Sutton, Kluwer is fortunate to engage and benefit from the experience and expertise of one of the world's outstanding authorities on European Union and international economic law.

Introduction

In their efforts to regulate competition in an increasingly complex business environment, competition authorities face a daunting task. The European Commission and Courts, as well as national courts and legislatures, policymakers, and regulators, are constantly proposing, enacting, reviewing, and enforcing new legal measures, often addressing novel situations. Every industry and service is affected.

Contents/Subjects

With many titles currently available and new ones appearing regularly, the series' coverage includes detailed analyses of relevant legislation and case law in major global trading jurisdictions, defences used in cases involving the digital network economy, state aid cases, enforcement methodologies and a great deal more.

Objective & Readership

The purpose of Kluwer's International Competition Law Series is to follow the ever-changing contours of this dynamic area of the law, keeping the practice in sharp focus so that practising lawyers (including in-house counsel) and academics can be assured of the most up-to-date guidance and sources, in the widest possible range of applications.

The titles published in this series are listed at the end of this volume.

Blocking Patents in European Competition Law

The Implications of the Concept of Abuse

Angelika S. Murer

Wolters Kluwer

Published by:
Kluwer Law International B.V.
PO Box 316
2400 AH Alphen aan den Rijn
The Netherlands
E-mail: international-sales@wolterskluwer.com
Website: www.wolterskluwer.com/en/solutions/kluwerlawinternational

Sold and distributed by:
Wolters Kluwer Legal & Regulatory U.S.
7201 McKinney Circle
Frederick, MD 21704
United States of America
E-mail: customer.service@wolterskluwer.com

DISCLAIMER: Reprint of the dissertation submitted to the University of Zurich by Angelika Murer and adopted by the Faculty of Law of the University of Zurich, represented by Dean Prof. Dr. Thomas Gaechter, on December 2, 2020.

ISBN 978-94-035-3814-3

e-Book: ISBN 978-94-035-3815-0
web-PDF: ISBN 978-94-035-3820-4

to David
without whom I would neither have dared
nor made it through writing this book

Table of Contents

List of Abbreviations

Art.	Article
AAC	Average Avoidable Costs
AB WTO	Appellate Body of the World Trade Organization
Abs.	*Absatz* (ger. paragraph)
ACE	Angiotensin-Converting Enzyme
ACEIs	Angiotensin-Converting Enzyme Inhibitors
AD	*Anno Domini* (in the year of the Lord)
ADME	Absorption, Distribution, Metabolism and Excretion
AEC-test	As-Efficient-Competitor-Test
AEUV	*See* TFEU
AG	Advocate General of the ECJ
API	Active Pharmaceutical Ingredient
ARC	German Act Against Restraints of Competition (in German: GWB)
ATC Classification/ATC System	Anatomical Therapeutic Chemical Classification System
ATC	Average Total Costs
AVC	Average Variable Costs
BBl	*Bundesblatt* (medium of publication of the Swiss government)
BGB	*See* GCC

BGH	*Bundesgerichtshof* (German Supreme Court)
BoA	Board of Appeal of the EPO
BSK	*Basler Kommentar* (legal commentary originating from Basel, Switzerland)
BVerfGE	*Bundesverfassungsgerichtshof* (German Supreme Court for Constitutional Matters)
cit.	cited as
cl.	clause
Co.	Company
COPD	Chronic Obstructive Pulmonary Disease
Corp.	Corporation
CT	Connecticut
D.C. Cir.	United States Court of Appeals for the District of Columbia
DOJ	US Department of Justice
e.g.	*exempli gratia* (for example)
EC	European Commission
ECHR	European Convention of Human Rights
ECJ	Court of Justice of the European Union
ECLI	European Case Law Identifier
ECLR	European Competition Law Review
ECSC	European Coal and Steel Community
ECtHR	European Courts of Human Rights
ed.	edition
ed./eds	editor/editors
EEA	European Economic Area
EEC	European Economic Community
EIPR	European Intellectual Property Review
EMA	European Medicines Agency
EPC	European Patent Convention (in German: EPÜ)
EphMRA	European Pharmaceutical Market Research Association
EPO	European Patent Office
EPUE	European Patent with Unitary Effect
EPÜ	*See* EPC
esp.	especially

et al.	*et alii/et aliae/et alia* (and others)
etc.	*et cetera* (and so forth)
EU	European Union
EuR	*Zeitschrift Europarecht* (journal)
EUV	*See* TEU
FDA	Federal Drug Administration
f./ff.	*et seq./et seqq* (and the following page/pages)
fn./fns	footnote/footnotes
FRAND	Fair, Reasonable and Non-discriminatory
FS	*Festschrift* (compilation in the honour of a professor)
FTC	Federal Trade Commission
GATT	General Agreement on Tariffs and Trade
GBTs	General Business Terms
GC	General Court
GCC	German Civil Code (in German: BGB)
ger.	German for
GrCh	*Charta der Grundrechte der Europäischen Union*/Charter of the Fundamental Rights of the European Union (also referred to as the Charter)
GRUR	*Gewerblichen Rechtsschutz und Urheberrecht* (journal)
GRUR Int.	*Gewerblichen Rechtsschutz und Urheberrecht, Internationaler Teil* (journal)
GWB	*See* ARC
Habil.	*Habilitationsschrift* (ger. Habilitation Thesis)
HTS	High-Throughput Screening
i.a.	*inter alia* (among others)
i.e.	*id est* (that is to say)
ICJ	Imperial Court of Justice (Supreme Court of the German Reich from 1879 till 1945)
IIC	International Review of Intellectual Property and Competition Law

Inc.	Incorporated Company
INNs	International Nonproprietary Names
IP	Intellectual Property
JZ	*Juristen Zeitung* (journal)
KG	*See* SCA
KZR	*Registerzeichen für Verfahren über Beschwerden und Revisionen in bürgerlichen Rechtsstreitigkeiten in Kartellsachen beim Bundesgerichtshof* (index for competition law cases with the German Federal Supreme Court)
MA	Massachusetts
MarkenR	*Markenrecht* (ger. Copyrights Law)
MMR	*MultiMedia und Recht: Zeitschrift für Informations-, Telekommunikations- und Medienrecht* (journal)
MN	Minnesota
MR-Int.	*Medien und Recht International* (journal)
MüKo	*Münchener Kommentar* (legal commentary originating from Munich)
NBER	National Bureau of Economic Research
NCE	New Chemical Entity
NME	New Medical Entities
No	Number/Numbers
NVwZ	*Neue Zeitschrift für Verwaltungsrecht* (journal)
NY	New York
NZZ	*Neue Zürcher Zeitung* (Zurich based newspaper)
OECD	Organisation for Economic Co-operation and Development
OS	Operating System
Para./Paras	Paragraph/Paragraphs
PatA	Swiss Patent Act
PatG	*Patentgesetz* (German Patent Act)
PC	Personal Computer
PCT	Patent Cooperation Treaty
PPI	Proton Pump Inhibitor
R&D	Research and Development

RCA	Radio Corporation of America
RDP	Regulatory Data Protection
SCA	Swiss Cartel Act (in German: KG)
SCID	Studies in Comparative International Development
Sec.	Section
SEP	Standard Essential Patent
SIEC test	Significant Impediment to Effective Competition Test
6th Cir.	Court of Appeals of the 6th Circuit
SME	Small- and Medium-Sized Enterprise
SPC	Supplementary Protection Certificate
SSO	Standard-Setting Organisation
TEC	Treaty Establishing the European Community (renamed into TFEU)
Techn. Univ.	*Technische Universität* (ger. Technical University)
TEEC	Treaty of Rome (1957)
teilw.	*teilweise* (ger. partly)
TEU	Treaty on European Union (2007) (in German: EUV)
TFEU	Treaty on the Functioning of the European Union (in German: AEUV)
TRIPS	Agreement on Trade-Related Aspects of Intellectual Property Rights
UK	United Kingdom
Univ.	University
US	Originating from the United States of America
USA	United States of America
USPTO	United States Patent and Trademark Office
UWG	*Bundesgesetz gegen den unlauteren Wettbewerb* (Swiss Federal Act Against Unfair Competition, UCA)
v.	versus
Virg.	Virginia

WHO	World Health Organization
WIPO	World Intellectual Property Organization
WiSt	*Wirtschaftswissenschaftliches Studium* (journal)
WTO	World Trade Organization
WUW	*Wirtschaft und Wettbewerb* (journal)
ZaöRV	*Zeitschrift für ausländisches öffentliches Recht und Völkerrecht* (journal)
ZEuS	*Zeitschrift für Europarechtliche Studien* (journal)
ZfRV	*Zeitschrift für Europarecht, internationales Privatrecht und Rechtsvergleichung* (journal)
ZGE	*Zeitschrift für geistiges Eigentum* (journal)
ZGR	*Zeitschrift für Unternehmens- und Gesellschaftsrecht* (journal)
ZWeR	*Zeitschrift für Wettbewerbsrecht* (journal)

Acknowledgements

Illustration by Prof. em. Dr. iur. E. Murer, Christmas 2016

'Silence, PhD student at work.' Before starting my PhD, I could not have imagined that unsorted thoughts pushing to be heard, arranged in order and written down could make you want to shout in one second, cry in the next and dance in the next but one and that entering an office where a PhD student is at work is walking a tightrope. This roller-coaster ride is a test of stamina, not only for the PhD candidate but also for all the people embarking on the journey with her.

My first and most important thanks go to my Doktorvater Prof. Dr. iur. Andreas Heinemann who helped me navigate through the ups and downs of writing a PhD thesis by not only encouraging, questioning and challenging me but also supporting my own quests, even though they sometimes led to dead ends. On top of that, his office door was always open and he lent an ear whenever I needed one. I could not have asked for more. Andreas, I am very grateful for the opportunity you gave me. The possibility to learn from you, profit from your immense knowledge and even working together in your department was a great chance.

I also owe big thanks to Prof. Dr. iur. Dipl.-Biol. Herbert Zech who provided his great expertise and rendered the second opinion on my PhD thesis despite his tight schedule.

A big part of why I loved writing this book was my team at the chair of Prof. Heinemann at the University of Zurich. Prof. Dr. iur. Damiano Canapa, Dr. iur. Patricia Hager, Dr. iur. Dorota Paczoska Kottmann, MLaw Beat Althaus, MLaw Nicola Müller, MLaw Robin Landolt and Dr. iur. Giulia Meier – I am grateful for having worked with all of you. I dearly miss our discussions, excursions, lunches, dinners, apéros and so on. Thank you all for your energy, passion and personality. Without you, our offices would not have felt a little like home. Special thanks go to Damiano and Patricia. The two did not only encourage me to join the team while I was finishing my master but also supported me through the writing process of the PhD thesis and even reviewed my manuscript. I could not have asked for more, and I am thankful for the memories and friendship we share. Furthermore, the endless weekends of writing would not have been this pleasant without Dorota joining me. Thank you for sharing the loneliness and toughness of these days. In addition, I could not have asked for a more encouraging and supporting colleague to share my office with than Nicola. The clarity and precision of your thoughts were always inspiring and sharpened my writing and thinking while finalising the book.

During my PhD, I also had the opportunity to join the Berkman Centre for Internet and Society of the Harvard Law School as an independent visiting researcher and the University of Helsinki as a LERU exchange student. For these amazing opportunities and the efforts needed to make them happen, I owe gratitude to Prof. Dr. iur. Urs Gasser and his team at the Berkman Centre as well as Prof. emer. Rainer Oesch, Dr. iur. Juha Vesala and their team at the University of Helsinki.

Of course, this book would not have been possible without the support of numerous friends outside the University. I shall not list you all, but thank each of you for providing shoulders to cry on, raising glasses to celebrate and above all being sympathetic for my situation. Special thanks are due to RA Dr. iur. Oliver Kaufmann who supported my project from the start, always lent me an ear and even reviewed my manuscript in the end. Furthermore, I would like to thank Raffaela and Anna for their professional inputs and RAin Dr. iur. Sarah Leins for her support during the whole project, including organising the stay at the Berkman Centre.

Finally, I would never have been able to take on such an endeavour without my family. First, Erwin who did not only gift me with the splendid drawing at the top but also guided me through the ups and downs of writing a PhD thesis. I really got simmered through these years, as you predicted once. The second goes out to the women, Grosi and Grossmami, you showed me at an early age that women own a place in the workforce too and above all, Mami, you always provide a home to come back to, even if everything else falls apart. Knowing this gave me the confidence and power to keep on pushing myself to the limit and beyond. Papi, without you teaching me that success has to be earned and that quitting is rarely the best option, I would not have made it past the finish line. Ladina, knowing that you always have my back and had it through this journey meant a lot. Last but not least, I owe you David more thanks than I could say, for enduring my hot and cold temper during writing, for the moments of silence, for the long talks, for critical questions, for reading my manuscript, for calming me down and pushing me when I needed it.

Zurich, 31 August 2021

'When the strict field of intellectual property rights has been exceeded, it is necessary to return to the principle that is known as freedom.'[1]

1. Geiger, IIC 2004, 272.

Introduction Subject, Purpose and Method

CHAPTER 1

Subject and Purpose

I SUBJECT

1 Patents are man-made privileges granted to inventors for providing society with knowledge. Patents in theory incentivise innovation by granting time-limited exclusivity to the inventor.[2] One could consequently assume that a patent holder seeks patent protection to start marketing their invention via a marketable product or licence. Yet, numbers obtained from Europe draw a different picture. According to the PatVal Study – a survey that was completed in 2005 and based on data from a large sample of EPO (European Patent Office) patent applicants – a total average of at least 36 per cent of all European patents in the sample remained unexploited for industrial or commercial purposes.[3]

2 There are in fact numerous reasons for patent holders to refrain from using their patents. Some are based on specific characteristics of the invention itself. For example, there are situations when a market for the invention cannot be identified or when the expenditure needed to develop a marketable product is too large to be profitable. On other occasions, invention-specific characteristics are not the reason for the patents being left commercially unexploited. Rather microeconomic factors such as lacking assets for the exploitation or lacking plans to develop a final marketable product are decisive.[4] On yet other occasions, unused patents are simply applied for only strategic reasons. This might be the case when the applicant is striving to secure leeway for further research and commercialisation projects or simply to block competitors from marketing the patented technology.[5]

2. *See i.a.*: BENTLY ET AL., 397 f.; LEVIN ET AL., Brookings Papers on Economic Activity, 783 ff.; OSTERRIETH, para. 17.
3. GAMBARDELLA/GIURI/MARIANI, 51; *see also*: TORRISI ET AL., Research Policy 2016, 1374 f.
4. VOLKMANN, 208 ff.
5. *See*: GIURI ET AL., 18 ff.; *infra* at Part II, Chapter 6, section II.

3 By granting patents, the legislator intervenes in the market, as it is believed that the market itself would not provide a sufficient level of innovation. Patents constitute interference into competition granted with the intent to foster innovation.[6] Unused patents therefore prima facie challenge the legitimacy of the patent system because their suitability to foster innovation is called into question. Consequently, if a patent is applied to be used for blocking purposes only (blocking patent), the question arises whether this amounts to an abuse of patent law. As MACDONALD holds: 'The real pirates are not those who steal innovation from patent owners, but those who steal the system of encouraging innovation from the public.'[7]

4 Owing to the influence of patents on competition, blocking patents raise concerns about not only patent law but also competition law. Individual authors have asked whether a dominant undertaking could be abusing its dominant position in the sense of Article 102 of the Treaty on the Functioning of the European Union (TFEU) by applying for a blocking patent.[8] The grounds for such an argument, on the one hand, is the idea that the mere acquisition of an exclusive right – either in the form of an application or through a transaction from a former right holder – influences the market structure and residual competition. In market structures characterised by the presence of a dominant undertaking, residual competition is already weakened and therefore susceptible to impediments, especially if originating from the dominant undertaking itself. On the other hand, patents as property rights provide their holder with exclusionary power and allow the prevention of others from using the patented technology. Patents thus convey advantages in competition which can be used to hamper competitors.

5 Patent strategies have been subject to quite a few decisions by the EU courts and the Commission in recent years[9] as well as in other jurisdictions worldwide.[10] However, there has not yet been a leading case for patent filing strategies apart from the *AstraZeneca* case on the acquisition of a supplementary protection certificate.[11] The focus of the legal discourse has been on the refusal of patent holders to license the patent, licensing terms (fair, reasonable and non-discriminatory, so-called FRAND terms) or patent settlements and pay-for-delay agreements.

6 Abusive behaviour involved with patents can be divided into three broad categories. The first category consists of cases where the right holder instrumentalises proceedings by authorities. This category includes all cases where a right is claimed to which the

---

6. *See infra* at Part I, Chapter 3, section II.
7. MACDONALD, Information Economics and Policy 2004, 153.
8. HEINEMANN, in: MATTHEWS/ZECH, Research handbook on intellectual property and the life sciences, 150; HAEDICKE, in: HAEDICKE/TIMMANN, Patent law, paras 160 ff.; ZECH, ZWeR 2011, 326 f.; in 1948, *see*: HEINE, GRUR 1948, 170.
9. The most recent example in the EU is the case of *Servier* and its blockbuster perindopril, which was decided by the Commission and the GC, and is now on appeal at the ECJ. GC, *Servier v. Commission*, T-691/14.
10. *See* i.a. in the USA: UNITED STATES SUPREME COURT, *Walker Process Equipment Inc v. Food Machinery & Chemical Corp*, 382 US 172, 1965, 174.
11. *See infra* at paras 334 ff.

claimant is not entitled under the law. This is when a patent holder seeks to apply for a patent that does not meet the patentability requirements or delivers misrepresentations to the authorities. The second category consists of cases where the patent holder executes a right provided for by law. The most important examples are cases of refusal to license. The third category consists of cases where the patent is part of a standard and the patent holder agrees to certain conduct in a FRAND commitment, but later breaks the commitment.[12] Even though the patent holder by refusing a licence or demanding unfair licensing terms executes a legally granted right, the distinguishing factor in these cases is the existence of a commitment. The contravention is therefore related to a factor exogenous to patent law, while the conduct under the first and second categories instrumentalises mechanisms and privileges provided by the patent law and therefore involves endogenous factors.[13] For this reason, FRAND cases are not part of this book and insights from FRAND cases are not used as comparison during the analysis.

7 Following the Pharmaceutical Sector Inquiry of the Commission and the proceedings in the case of *Boehringer Ingelheim*,[14] it became clear that the acquisition of patents might fall into the first two categories.[15] Fundamentally, the dominant undertaking's acquisition of the blocking patent shortens the supply on the technology market, as inventing around and therefore providing an alternative to the already patented technology becomes more difficult. As a result, the supply on the vertically integrated product market is also shortened, as competitors are deprived of the opportunity to market a competing substitute.

II PURPOSE

8 This book aims to answer the question of when and how an application for a blocking patent can amount to an abuse of a dominant position under European Union (EU) competition law or more precisely under Article 102 TFEU. The evaluation will provide characteristics of potentially abusive and non-abusive behaviour regarding applications for blocking patents. The focus will be on the application for patents

12. Through commitments, members of standardising organisations declare licensing their patents on FRAND terms. After making such statements, the ECJ holds the patent holder obliged to license the technology to any third party requesting it and willing to accept FRAND terms. Even more so, the patent holder is obliged to make an initial offer. In the context of FRAND commitments, infringement actions for dominant undertakings are even more restricted and reflect the concerns of the legislator with respect to the limited room for competition. On the one hand, the technology patented in a standard essential patent (SEP) is necessary to launch a product. A prohibition of the use thereof thus automatically excludes the competitor from the market. On the other hand, the FRAND commitment mirrors a legitimate interest of third parties to receive access to the technology on FRAND terms. *See*: ECJ, *Huawei v. ZTE*, C-170/13, paras 63 ff. and 71.
13. A dichotomy between endogenous and exogenous contraventions can also be found in: Pedrazzini, in: Brügger, FS Troller, Der Rechtsmissbrauch im Patentrecht, 207 ff.
14. *See infra* at paras 357 ff.
15. *See*: Schröter/Bartl, in: von der Groeben et al., Kommentar EU-Recht, Article 102, para. 315.

(originary acquisition) rather than on the acquisition of patents through legal transactions (secondary acquisition). Secondary acquisitions will, however, be discussed based on the findings for originary acquisitions.

9 Influenced by the US and European models which existed in the Member States of the EU when drafting the treaties, Article 102 TFEU is based on abstract wording.[16] Because of this vagueness, both EU court practice and legal doctrine had to develop an understanding of the core elements from the roots. The focus of this book is on the term 'abuse' itself (Part V). Since the establishment of the provision, it has proved especially difficult to develop the boundaries of the abuse as an offence. Owing to the difficulties associated with the abstract provision, case law has been built on creating case groups, without providing an analysis of the core of the legal term 'abuse'.[17] The concept 'competition on the merits' known from literature and court practice, which describes the desired form of competition, has proved to be prone to errors when distinguishing between desired and undesired forms of competition based on judicial methodology.[18]

10 In an intermediate step, this book aims to provide a justiciable definition of abuse, which allows abuses of dominance to be determined based on established legal methods and known figures in law. It must be kept in mind, however, that this book proposes an abuse concept, which has not yet been tested in practice.

16. *See*: FUCHS/MÖSCHEL, in: IMMENGA/MESTMÄCKER 2018, Article 102, para. 2.
17. *See infra* at Part IV, Chapter 12.
18. *See infra* at Part V, Chapter 14, section IV.3.

CHAPTER 2
Method

I THE SOURCES OF EU COMPETITION LAW

11 Competition law holds a special status within EU law which is justified through its dedication to granting undistorted competition[19] in an internal market, thus its institutional importance (*see* Protocol 27 TFEU). This is reflected in the systematic integration of Articles 101-106 TFEU into EU constitutional law. Different regulations, directives and notices of the Commission flank these competition law articles of the TFEU. Despite their non-binding character, directives and notices provide important guidelines for the interpretation of competition law and illustrate the understanding of the law by the Commission, which is also reflected in its decisions. However, the directives and notices are not necessarily consistent with the interpretation by the General Court and the European Court of Justice (hereinafter 'Court of Justice', in footnotes referred to as ECJ). Notices and directives therefore do not take precedence, but in the manner of soft law factually influence the interpretation of the law, while decisions of the Commission bind Member States de facto.[20]

12 As an instrument to facilitate competition, an interpretation of competition law cannot be conducted in isolation from scientific economic findings about markets and competition. Doctrinal changes in economic theory therefore often influence the interpretation of competition law. The influence of scientific movements is shown in the interpretation of EU competition law, especially in the activities of the Commission.[21] Economic findings thus influence the case law and also the results of this book. Therefore, this book starts with a brief discourse on competition as an economic concept (Part I, Chapter 3) as well as the system of law bound to guarantee its functioning, including intellectual property in general and patent law in particular (Part

19. For early case law *see*: ECJ, *National Panasonic v. Commission*, C-136/79, para. 20.
20. ACKERMANN, in: RIESENHUBER, Europäische Methodenlehre, para. 11, with further references.
21. ACKERMANN, in: RIESENHUBER, Europäische Methodenlehre, para. 21.

I, Chapter 4). Yet, it must be acknowledged that, as ULLRICH holds, competition law aims at ensuring compliance with other statutory conditions and not changing them.[22] This book will therefore hold back on analysing positive and negative aspects of the presented concepts of competition. The explanations will primarily be to display the difficulties of policymakers as well as legal practice in complying with the current understanding of competition as a regulatory object.

II INTERSECTION BETWEEN PATENT AND COMPETITION LAW: CONSEQUENCES FOR THE ANALYSIS

13 Doctrinal changes occur with respect to not only the understanding of competition in both economics and law but also the justification of patent laws and, more importantly, the relationship between patent and competition law. Answers to questions at the intersection between patent and competition law have to be evaluated against the background of the specific understanding at the time of the analysis. Current academic discussions tend to lay emphasis on which field dominates.[23] This book aims to respect the fundamentals of both fields of law without such emphasis. Consequently, the subject of the book will be approached from two relevant starting points; first, blocking patents as a special category of unused patents (Part II) and, second, the abuse of a dominant position (Parts IV and V). To start, this book takes a closer look at the development of the relationship between patents and competition law (Part I, Chapter 4, section II).

III APPROACHING 'ABUSE'

14 In interpreting EU law, the decisions of the Court of Justice are of groundbreaking importance. Development and interpretation of the law are based on the process of adjudication. Therefore, only the Court of Justice delivers authoritative interpretations of the treaty. Interpretations delivered by the European Commission (hereinafter 'Commission'/EC) within regulations only serve as administrative interpretations, though providing an important insight into the practice of the Commission and often influencing the courts.[24] As in other jurisdictions, the interpretation of EU law is bound to interpretative principles and is not structureless. As a guardian of the law, it is the Court of Justice's task to interpret the law of the Union and to supervise its application (Article 19(1) of the Treaty on European Union (TEU)).

15 The approach to abuse within this book starts with an analysis of previous case law on the abuse of a dominant position and patenting (Part IV, Chapter 12). However, the answers will not be arrived at by merely forming a new case group based on relevant factors acknowledged as decisive by the courts in comparable situations. Such a

22. ULLRICH, in: SCHRICKER/DREIER/KUR, Geistiges Eigentum im Dienst der Innovation, 92 f.
23. *See infra* at Part I, Chapter 4, section II.2.
24. *See supra* at para. 11

method would be operating with known elements that fit with previous and current case law instead of providing encapsulation of the term 'abuse' and would therefore be limited in this regard.

16 The analysis strives to give concretisation to the term 'abuse', allowing assumptions to be formed concerning applications for blocking patents under Article 102 TFEU. Using further analysis of case law, this book will address abuse in competition law with a fundamental interpretation based on traditional legal methods (Part V). In principle, the interpretation of EU law follows the same rules and is based on the same elements as national and international law.[25] References to all elements of interpretation – grammatical, systematic, historical and teleological – thus appear in decisions of the courts.[26] When weighing the elements, however, the Court of Justice follows its own path tailored to suit the peculiarities of EU law.

17 In general, the courts tend to conduct analysis of primary law without reference to the historical perspective.[27] This is partly not only due to the fact that documentation about the drafting of the treaties and the founding contracts were inaccessible for years[28] but also because a historical interpretation would mean binding today's legal interpretation on potentially outdated political influences. EU law is a construct of political decisions and compromises; applying a historical perspective could result in an emphasis on interests that no longer exist.[29] Nevertheless, in this book, a historical perspective will be applied to introduce Article 102 TFEU and its position within the founding of the EU as well as the influence of US antitrust law (Part V, Chapter 14, section I). This is due to the fact that the historical background will enable the formulation of a hypothesis that reflects the inherent principle of the abuse of a dominant position, despite the low importance attached to the historical perspective in EU primary law in general.

18 Unlike the historical perspective, the syntactical aspect is of central importance in the EU and the 'starting point and simultaneous limitation of the interpretation'.[30] The interpretation of EU law requires determining the meaning and scope of EU terms independently of national characterisation.[31] The first step in each interpretation of the wording is therefore to identify existing determination of the term in EU law, resulting from other provisions of primary and secondary law, or from previous case law.[32] A linguistic interpretation is only conducted in a second step if an EU-autonomous use cannot be established. Owing to the requirement to treat all language versions as equally binding, a comprehensive interpretation of the wording would essentially

25. Dederichs, 11; Wegener, in: Calliess/Ruffert, EUV/AEUV, Article 19, para. 13.
26. For example, in: GC, *AC-Treuhand AG v. Commission*, 2008, para. 114.
27. Pechstein/Drechsler, in: Riesenhuber, Europäische Methodenlehre.
28. *See* i.a. the vote of the Commission in the *Continental Can* case: ECJ, *Continental Can v. Commission*, C-6/72, 226.
29. Wegener, in: Calliess/Ruffert, EUV/AEUV, Article 19, para. 14.
30. Buck, 137; Wegener, in: Calliess/Ruffert, EUV/AEUV, Article 19, para. 13.
31. Wegener, in: Calliess/Ruffert, EUV/AEUV, Article 19, para. 13, fn. 40, with various references to the practice of the ECJ.
32. For example, in: ECJ, *Industrial Diamond Supplies v. Riva*, Case 43/77, paras 15 ff.

require a comparison of all versions, which would not be practicable today.[33] On occasions when the EU courts consider the general linguistic usage and etymologic origin of the wording as well, they generally limit comparison to a selected number of the twenty-four[34] versions of the legal text. Most often – as will be done in this book – only the English, French and German versions of the text will be analysed (Part V, Chapter 14, section II).[35]

19 The dynamic integrative character of EU law means that the methodical focus will lie in teleological interpretation (Part V, Chapter 14, section IV),[36] concerning the intent and purpose of the law. This allows for an understanding of statutory law contrary to its wording, where the wording does not comply with the purpose of the law and the intent of the current legislator.[37] As regards the contribution of EU law in general, and specifically competition law, to the goals of the Union, a teleological interpretation will focus on how a provision can contribute to these goals.

20 In primary law, a teleological interpretation generally tries to elicit the contribution of a specific provision to the general goals set out in a particular chapter of a treaty as well as the general aim of the Union as laid down in Articles 2 and 3 TEU. Owing to the vagueness of the two provisions, which further reference subsequent provisions of the treaty to concretise their meaning, little can be derived from these in individual cases.[38] Unlike in secondary law, where recitals of the preamble are often consulted to ascertain the intent of the legislator, in primary law, the preamble is of lower importance. The benchmark for teleological interpretation is the *'effet utile'*. When conflicts with other interests of the Union occur, the legislative goals have to be interpreted narrowly, although the specific goals protected by the provision under scrutiny take priority over conflicting interests.[39] Owing to the connection of the teleological interpretation with the goals of the Union, the systematic and teleological interpretations are closely related. Consequently, the result of the teleological interpretation has to fit within the systematics of EU law (Part V, Chapter 14, section III).[40] This requires compliance with outranking provisions as well as consistency within the provision itself.

21 Other than in practice, where the question of whether an objective justification can be invoked by the dominant undertaking is regularly discussed, an evaluation of potential objective justifications will not be part of this book. However, the idea that an abuse can only be found in cases where a conduct lacks justification is reflected in the proposed abuse principle in as much as the legitimacy of the interests of the dominant

33. *See* i.a. PECHSTEIN/DRECHSLER, in: RIESENHUBER, Europäische Methodenlehre, paras 17 ff.; WEILER, ZEuP 2010, 867.
34. *See* Article 55 TEU; *see infra* at para. 409.
35. PECHSTEIN/DRECHSLER, in: RIESENHUBER, Europäische Methodenlehre, para. 21.
36. *See* i.a. the decision of the Commission in the *Continental Can* case: ECJ, *Continental Can v. Commission*, C-6/72, 226 f.
37. ECJ, *Sodiaal International*, C-383/14, paras 20 and 26.
38. PIEPER, in: DAUSES/LUDWIGS, Handbuch des EU-Wirtschaftsrechts, paras 40 ff.
39. WEGENER, in: CALLIESS/RUFFERT, EUV/AEUV, Article 19, para. 16.
40. RIESENHUBER, in: RIESENHUBER, Europäische Methodenlehre, paras 53 ff.

undertaking is an important factor in the analysis of each potentially abusive conduct.[41]

IV REFERENCE TO THE PHARMACEUTICAL INDUSTRY

22 To illustrate the mechanisms of blocking patenting and related strategies, this book will use examples from the pharmaceutical industry. The reason for this is not that blocking patents can only occur in the context of pharmaceutical patents, but that surveys have identified 'blocking' to be an important motive in applying for patents in the pharmaceutical industry.[42] Additionally, patenting in the pharmaceutical industry, as in the chemical and biotechnology sector, has been and continues to be of great importance. This is because the chemical structure of compounds can easily be broken down and imitated while simultaneously revealing patent infringement; thus, enforcing a patent is relatively easy. Furthermore, in the pharmaceutical sector, owing to strict regulations and high security standards, research and development (R&D) costs up to marketability are substantial, while the manufacturing costs are considerably lower.[43] A survey conducted by the Commission on the pharmaceutical market documented a great variety of strategical usages of the patent system, which are becoming more and more widespread in the industry.[44]

23 The effect of a patent on the market is dependent on numerous factors including the protected technology itself, the scope of the patent, the structure of the relevant market and the industry. When considering the question of how a patent influences competition and innovation, general findings applicable to any industry and situation are hard, if not impossible, to gain. The role of patents is different in every sector.[45] The legislator has therefore provided exceptions for different industries (e.g., Article 53 European Patent Convention (EPC)). Specific needs in different industries are also reflected in the motivations to rely on the protection of the patent system and show themselves in the fact that certain ways of coping with an invention may be common in one industry, but not others.[46]

24 Legal analysis has to apply the law in given situations. In the field of competition law, it relies on predictions and general assumptions drawn by economists. Understandings presented by economists are part of the toolbox available to answer the legal question. It must therefore be kept in mind that the limitations of experimental set-ups and the parameters examined render robust findings and predictions difficult. Furthermore, the questions raised are economic and not legal, and therefore research set-ups are not tailored to serve the demands of legal practice. Despite its focus on the pharmaceutical industry, it is not the goal of this book to answer questions solely

41. *See infra* at para. 575 as well as at Part VI, Chapter 17, sections II and III.
42. Blind/Cremers/Müller, Research Policy, 434; EC, *Sector Inquiry, Final Report,* paras 1122 ff.
43. Grubb et al., para. 21.01.
44. EC, *Sector Inquiry, Final Report.*
45. *See infra* at fns 286 f.
46. Blind et al., Research Policy, 663 ff.

relating to the mechanism of competition in the pharmaceutical industry. Rather, the results presented by scholars and expert insights of the industry will be used as a basis for the analysis within competition law.

25 In the absence of patent protection, companies conducting pharmaceutical research would take on a heavy risk and financial burden only to risk finding competitors breaking down the chemical structure and cheaply reproducing a marketable drug. This book therefore reduces its scope to an analysis of patents for drugs. Drugs are thereby understood as the sum of all substances prepared and administered to cure illnesses and indispositions.[47] Pharmaceuticals are those substances used as medicine in drugs, but which do not differ from other chemicals by parameters. Unsurprisingly, pharmaceuticals often also have non-pharmaceutical usages.[48] Even though patents in the pharmaceutical industry can be applied for technical devices as well, these patent claims differ. Unlike patents for compounds, compositions and use, product patents for technical devices do not cover new chemical entities (NCEs) or compositions but the technical teachings to build the specific tool or machine. The introductory part thus contains a paragraph on the fundamentals of the pharmaceutical industry (Part I, Chapter 5) and on patenting within the pharmaceutical industry (Part I, Chapter 5, section IV). The motives to patent (Part II, Chapter 6) and patenting strategies (Part II, Chapter 7) will be focused on in Part II of the book.

V APPLICABLE AND COMPARATIVE LAW

26 This book analyses Article 102 TFEU, which has two results. First, an effect on the trade between Member States is a prerequisite for the application of the said provision. In practice, the criterion has been interpreted broadly.[49] Not only with patents issued under the EPC but also with patents granted for one Member State only, a segmentation of markets occurs and trade between Member States is easily affected. This book therefore will omit analysis of the effects on trade between Member States.

27 Second, the findings resulting from the analysis of Article 102 TFEU are not transferable to the law of the Member States or other national jurisdictions one-to-one. The interpretation conducted during this book is an independent interpretation of the law of the Union. Recourses to comparative law are rare in case law, but occur in the literature. Often US antitrust law is named as an important source for the first European competition law provisions in the European Coal and Steel Community (ECSC). However, there are fundamental differences in the systems of law established in the USA and the EU.[50] Comparisons with US antitrust law therefore have to reflect these institutional differences and cannot be transferred to EU law one-to-one.

47. Similarly: RICHTER, para. 92.
48. TAYLOR, in: HESTER/HARRISON, Pharmaceuticals in the environment, 5.
49. For basic information on the effect on trade criteria, *see*: O'DONOGHUE/PADILLA, 861 ff.
50. *See infra* at paras 576 ff.

28 Besides US antitrust law, German law is also often consulted when interpreting Article 102 TFEU. In contrast to the EU competition law, which the courts developed against the background of the overarching goal the law has to fulfil in the context of the Union, in German law, the development of the principle of abuse of a dominant position was detached from such a reference. From the beginning, German legal scholars searched for another basis to approach the term 'abuse' and found it in defining case groups. Misconduct falling within the scope of the prohibition of the abuse of a dominant position was divided into exploitative and exclusionary as well as market structure abuses.[51] German scholars greatly influenced the forming of EU competition law, which is why certain opinions under German law apply to EU law as well.[52] German references will therefore be consulted during this evaluation.[53]

29 With regard to patent law, this book addresses the problem that relevant blocking patents might be issued based on national patent laws of the Member States or the EPC with effectiveness in several Member States. An analysis of a blocking patent application therefore always requires being mindful of the peculiarities of the relevant underlying patent law. For reasons of clarity, this book will only refer to fundamentals laid down in the EPC, which may result in certain limitations of the findings. Yet, the fundamentals used for the argumentation are long-term precepts which also largely apply to other patent law regimes.

VI INTERNATIONAL ASPECTS

30 In order to analyse established minimal guarantees for patent protection,[54] this book turns to the Paris Convention and the Agreement on the Trade-Related Aspects of Intellectual Property Rights (TRIPS). While the TRIPS Agreement has set new standards, it has not superseded the Paris Convention. Both conventions coexist and are important foundations for intellectual property law.

31 The Paris Convention was already adopted in 1883. It addresses different intellectual property rights including patents. The most important principles introduced with the Paris Convention were the principle of national treatment and the right of priority. The principle of national treatment holds that each Member State 'must grant the same protection to nationals of other Contracting States that it grants to its own nationals'[55]. The right of priority allows the applicant who submits its application for a patent,

51. *See* i.a.: BUSCHE, in: BUSCHE/RÖHLING, Kölner Kommentar GWB, § 19, Chapter 4.
52. *See* i.a.: JUNG, in: GRABITZ ET AL., EUV/AEUV, Article 102, Chapter E. IV.
53. It is due to the German history in this field that comprehensive legal commentaries on EU law exist. Many of these commentaries will be referenced during the course of this book.
54. The TRIPS Agreement sets high standards for patent law in Articles 27-34. While patents shall be available for any inventions, whether products or processes, in all fields of technology (Article 27), patentability may only be excluded in rare cases, and exceptions to the right conferred may only be made after a careful weighing of the interest of the patent owner and third parties (Article 30). BUSCHE, in: BUSCHE ET AL., TRIPS Kommentar, Einleitung 2, paras 36 ff.; RIDDER, 21.
55. On the Paris Convention, *see* the summary provided by the WIPO: https://www.wipo.int/treaties/en/ip/paris/summary_paris.html, accessed on 27 August 2021.

trademark or design right in one Member State to also apply for protection in the other Member States within a certain time period.[56]

32 The TRIPS Agreement has its origin in the efforts of the members of the General Agreement on Tariffs and Trade (GATT) to advance free global trade. In the beginning, the GATT members negotiated the dismantling of tariff barriers to trade. Only after non-tariff barriers became part of the discussion, also the harmonisation of intellectual property protection appeared on the agenda. This was due to an initiative of the USA and their desire to curb piracy. Negotiations in the so-called Uruguay Round were broadened and addressed concerns that different levels of protection of intellectual property rights in the Member States resulted in barriers to international trade. Yet, agreeing on a minimal level of intellectual property protection on a global scale was rather difficult and in the end required concessions from both developing and industrialised countries. The end of the Uruguay Round in 1995 resulted in the founding of the World Trade Organization (WTO), which superseded the GATT. The TRIPS Agreement is a multilateral trade agreement; the TRIPS Agreement together with the GATT of 1994 and General Agreement on Trade in Services forms the three pillars of the WTO. These three agreements are binding for all WTO Member States.[57] In its Articles 8 paragraph 2[58], 31[59] and 40, the TRIPS Agreement addresses issues that fall within the scope of competition law[60].[61] The TRIPS Agreement does not only set minimal standard for intellectual property protection, it is also the contract with the most provisions concerning competition law on an international level. Until today, initiatives to harmonise competition law on an international level have mostly remained unsuccessful.[62]

33 Besides Article 40 TRIPS, in which the agreement sets minimal standards for the control of anticompetitive practices in licensing contracts, there is a broad global consensus on how anticompetitive effects of licensing contracts should be approached. This is reflected in the background note of the Organisation for Economic Co-operation and Development (OECD) on the roundtable regarding the licensing of intellectual property rights and competition law.[63] With regard to compulsory licences, which are addressed in Article 31 TRIPS, there is no such global convergence, however.[64] The same holds true for anticompetitive effects in connection with standard essential patents.[65]

---

56. On the Paris Convention, *see* the summary provided by the WIPO: https://www.wipo.int/treaties/en/ip/paris/summary_paris.html, accessed on 27 August 2021.
57. On the whole, *see* among others: Stoll, in: Busche et al., TRIPS Kommentar, Einleitung 1, paras 29 ff.; Ridder, 14 ff; Heinemann, Immaterialgüterschutz in der Wettbewerbsordnung, 574.
58. Article 8 TRIPS will be addressed in more detail *infra* at paras 664 ff.
59. Article 31 TRIPS will be addressed in more detail *infra* at paras 260 and 748 ff.
60. *See infra* at para. 75.
61. Heinemann, Immaterialgüterschutz in der Wettbewerbsordnung, 581.
62. Heinemann, Immaterialgüterschutz in der Wettbewerbsordnung, 594 ff.
63. OECD, Licensing of IP Rights and Competition Law, Background Note, para. 98.
64. OECD, Licensing of IP Rights and Competition Law, Background Note, paras 87 ff.
65. OECD, Licensing of IP Rights and Competition Law, Background Note, paras 72 ff.

34 Other than this report explaining the existing controversy with regard to standard essential patents, there is no indication that anticompetitive effects of patenting strategies have been addressed on a global level. Therefore, indications regarding globally accepted minimal standards in addressing anticompetitive effects of patenting strategies are missing, with the exception of what can be derived from the TRIPS Agreement.

PART I An Introduction to Competition

CHAPTER 3
Competition: An Approximation

I INTRODUCTION

35 Although there has always been an understanding of 'competition'[66] - the Latin noun *competitior* is translated as rival - there is a lack of scientific information regarding the perfect design of competition in economics and also the regulating laws. Since law is a societal construct dedicated to a societal aim, the question that needs to be answered in the context of competition law is about the protected object as well as the function of competition in and for society.[67] This fundamental premise had already shaped competition policy when competition was not yet seen as an organisational principle of society, but as a natural process.[68] From a legal perspective, the goal of competition law has always been the protection of the mechanism of 'competition'. Yet, the process of competition is only protected by law up to the point where it can fulfil its functions in society. The supported functions of competition in a society consequently equal the goals of the particular competition law.[69]

---

66. The UK Office of Fair Trading has described competition as the process of 'rivalry between firms seeking to win customers' business over time by offering them a better deal'. UK COMPETITION COMMISSION/OFFICE OF FAIR TRADING, para. 4.1.2. According to the ECONOMIC ENCYCLOPAEDIA OF GABLER, competition is understood as the process of at least two suppliers or demanders that strive to outrival one another through the strategic use of action parameters on a market: http://wirtschaftslexikon.gabler.de/Definition/wettbewerb.html, accessed on 3 February 2020; similarly also: COX/HÜBENER, in: COX/JENS/MARKERT, Handbuch des Wettbewerbs, 4; *see* further examples of the understanding of competition in: BORK, 58 ff.
67. CLAPHAM, in: COX/JENS/MARKERT, Handbuch des Wettbewerbs, 131; MOTTA, 17 ff. FIKENTSCHER/HACKER/PODSZUN held: 'The main task of every economy is to enable humans to meet their needs. An economy is to satisfy hunger, not to create it; to quench thirst, not to make thirsty.' FIKENTSCHER/HACKER/PODSZUN, 1.
68. BÖHM, Wettbewerb und Monopolkampf, 117.
69. A synonymous use of the functions of competition and the goals of competition policy can also be found in: KNIEPS, 4. It is the task of competition policy to decide which reference system is chosen. EUCKEN, 245 f.

36 This first chapter will start by briefly introducing the importance of competition and competition policy within the EU (section II). Next, the different concepts of competition that shaped competition policy during previous decades will be explained (section III). The introduction of competition as a concept will be complemented by a short insight on the welfare standard of competition policy within the EU (section IV).

II THE ECONOMIC CONSTITUTION OF THE EUROPEAN UNION

37 Before World War I, the political stance in Europe was hostile towards any form of legal restriction on competition.[70] Post-war inflation in the 1920s, however, demanded a general rethinking, as enterprises used their power or agreements with other market participants to raise prices. States in Europe started to develop a more critical view towards the competitive activities of private entities. During post–World War I inflation, many countries took measures against price increases resulting from cartels and powerful undertakings. Despite the countries coming up with different ideas to fight price increases, most of the adapted measures were quite limited in their effectiveness.[71] It is hardly surprising, then, that the still fragile structures of behavioural control in competition vanished again during the Great Depression and World War II. In the following period, cartels even tended to be encouraged. It was only when political leaders set about healing Europe's injuries in the aftermath of the World Wars and Winston Churchill in 1946 put forward the idea of a united Europe that protection through measures against forms of anticompetitive behaviour reappeared on the political agenda. Churchill's proposition of a united Europe was motivated not only by the people's longing for peace but also by an awareness that the economy was severely weakened and that great national economies were waiting to compete on the world market.[72]

38 The first step in the European integration was the creation of the ECSC.[73] The efforts to promote European integration then culminated in the foundation of the

70. In Swiss Law, the term 'economic constitution' is used to describe all those provisions of the constitution which are bound to provide for the coordination of economic activity and the prevention of endangerments thereof. Vallender/Hettich/Lehne, § 2, paras 35 ff.; similarly also in EU competition law: Mestmäcker/Schweitzer, § 34, paras 37 f.
71. Gerber outlines how the differences in political climate and economic situation in the European states influenced the measures taken against restrictions to competition. Whereas in Scandinavia it was believed that publicity would be enough to stop distorting conduct, in Germany undertakings abusing their economic power could be brought before a newly formed cartel court. Gerber, Tulane Law Review 1987, 63 ff.
72. On the occasion of his speech to the academic youth on the 19 September 1946 in Zurich, Winston Churchill raised the idea of a united Europe based on the model of the United States of America. He closed the speech with the often quoted sentence: 'Therefore I say to you, let Europe arise.' The speech can be downloaded and heard from: https://churchill-in-zurich.ch/de/churchill/churchills-zurcher-rede/, accessed on 3 February 2019.
73. The founding of the European Coal and Steel Community in the wake of the World Wars was led by the idea of controlling the essential production factors for war materials under a supranational organisation. Through the implication of control mechanisms of the coal and steel

European Economic Community with the Treaty of Rome (Treaty establishing the European Community, TEEC). The European Economic Community (EEC) was brought to life to foster economic strength by joining forces in an economic union through the reduction of barriers to trade, securing free movement of goods, persons and capital and through a common economic policy. Despite that the provisions in the Treaty of Paris establishing the ECSC with Article 65 and Article 66(7) contained the first competition law provisions,[74] it was not until the drafting of the TEEC that the first legislation establishing a competition law system in the EU was drafted.[75] Recognising from the past that open markets and a free economy cannot be achieved when there is no mechanism against private restraints on competition,[76] it became clear that provisions against private barriers to trade were needed. In Article 3(1)(f), the TEEC established 'the institution of a system ensuring that competition in the common market is not distorted' as a goal of the Union. Today, Articles 85 and 86 of the TEEC continue to exist as Article 101 TFEU against agreements and concerted practices and Article 102 TFEU prohibiting the abuse of a dominant position.

39 In the continued pursuit of creating an internal market, the Treaty of Maastricht was signed in February 1992 and therewith the EU was founded. In 2007, the Treaty of Lisbon amended the Treaty of Maastricht (Treaty on the European Union, TEU) and the TEEC (since called TFEU).[77] With the TFEU coming into force in 2009, the EU acquired legal personality (Article 46a TFEU). The political agenda of the EU includes the building of an internal market and a highly competitive social market economy aimed at full employment, social progress and a high level of protection and improvement of the quality of the environment (Article 3(3) TEU). To achieve these fundamental aims, the economic policy of the Union and the Member States has to be conducted in accordance with the principle of an open market economy with free competition (Article 119(1) and (2) as well as Article 120 TFEU).

40 Today, Protocol No 27 and Article 3(1)(b) TFEU which give the Union competences to establish 'competition rules necessary for the functioning of the internal market' provide the basis for the interpretation of EU competition law. Even though undistorted competition, since the enactment of the TFEU, is no longer explicitly listed as a goal of

---

industry, the community could monitor and regulate the one branch that was, in those days, relevant for war. *See* the Preamble of the Treaty of Paris.

74. *See infra* at para. 405.
75. PACE/SEIDEL, in: PATEL/SCHWEITZER, The historical foundations of EU competition law, 58; SAMKALDEN/DRUKER, Common Market Law Review 1966, 162.
76. The Member States at the time of the drafting of the Treaty of Rome were flooded with cartels, and all European countries except Italy had enacted laws against them. The concept of the abuse of a dominant position was not widespread, however. Many Member States only included the prohibition of the abuse of a dominant position in their national law during the course of European integration. *See*: GERBER, Tulane Law Review 1987, 82 ff.
77. *See*: HELLMANN, 1 ff. and 12; OESCH, para. 51.

the EU in Article 3,[78] the principle is still part of EU constitutional law[79] and decisive for the application of competition law. Its legal content is far from specific, however.

III COMPETITION AS AN OBJECT OF POLICYMAKING AND LAW

41 Market-based economies choose competition as a mechanism 'to promote economic progress and welfare'.[80] Thus, competition as an object of policy cannot be regarded as an end in itself but is dedicated to a specific purpose.[81]

42 Fundamentally, competition in a market economy has to fulfil the task of solving the problem of allocating resources optimally.[82] Welfare economics understands competition as a process that allows the creation of maximal social welfare through the simultaneous maximisation of static and dynamic efficiencies.[83] Static efficiency[84] is reached if resources are allocated in a way that does not allow one player to be better off without simultaneously leaving another worse off (so-called Pareto-optimal), and when it is only possible to produce more of one good while simultaneously producing less of another.[85] Dynamic efficiencies concern the future prospect of static efficiencies. A market is dynamically efficient if it allows for innovation. Since innovation is a costly process for which market participants have to allocate resources, dynamic efficiency is reached when competitors continuously innovate to guarantee static efficiencies in the long run as cost-effectively as possible.[86]

43 Problematic are conflicting goals that occur between the pursuit of dynamic and static efficiencies. Dynamic efficiency is important to allow competition to foster innovation. In a Pareto-efficient market, an accumulation of resources and thus investment is impossible, however, since stored resources are statically inefficient.[87] It is therefore the task of competition policy to balance static as well as dynamic efficiencies and allow competition to foster the right amount of innovation.

78. Probably due to an intervention by France, *see* the references in: Behrens, EuZW 2008, 193; Ruffert, in: Calliess/Ruffert, EUV/AEUV, Article 3, para. 26.
79. Some authors, however, see a critical degrading of competition in this act, i.a.: Basedow, EuZW 2008, 225; Behrens, EuZW 2008, 193.
80. Motta, 14.
81. In EU law, this understanding is reflected in Article 2 TEEC and Article 2 TEU. *See*: EC, *Report on Competition Policy 1996*, paras 2 ff.; Motta, 14; Goyder/Goyder/Albors-Llorens, 10.
82. Cox/Hübener, in: Cox/Jens/Markert, Handbuch des Wettbewerbs, 3.
83. Goyder/Goyder/Albors-Llorens, 10.
84. Static efficiency or Pareto efficiency refers to the most efficient state. It is the situation where producers are offering the exact amount of goods that consumers are willing to buy and for the price they want to pay. Static efficiency includes both distributive and allocative efficiency. For a deeper analysis, *see*: Motta, 40 ff.
85. *See*: Motta, 40 ff.
86. A market is dynamically efficient if it produces a maximum of new products or processes. Dynamic efficiency thus represents the optimal grade of innovation. Motta, 55.
87. All concepts of competition besides perfect competition include dynamic efficiencies and thus accept limited inefficiencies. Nowadays, even more weight is ascribed to securing dynamic efficiencies. *See*: Kartte, 45.

44 Besides the optimal allocation of resources and fostering innovation and technical progress (economic functions), traditionally, two other policy goals have been identified that can be fulfilled by competition:[88] economic freedom and distributive justice (social functions).[89] There is a consensus among free-market economists that competition is expected to contribute to the achievement of the basic social values, freedom, prosperity and justice.[90] Freedom and justice have a double function when it comes to competition. Not only does competition contribute to the realisation of freedom, understood as absence of constraints by third parties and justice in a society, but freedom is a fundamental prerequisite for competition.[91]

45 It is thus not surprising that over the last few centuries different concepts have been proposed to resolve this conflict of objectives and strive for the right balance between competitive freedom, non-economic societal goals and the minimisation of inefficiencies.[92] The competition concepts are described in the following subsection in chronological order.

1 Perfect Competition

46 Perfect competition is a theoretic condition that occurs in a well-defined market of a homogenous product where supply equals demand, where there are no barriers to entry and knowledge can be fully accessed by all participants.[93] Such a theoretic construct does not occur in real markets. Following the static model of perfect competition, competition does not allow for the creation of the accruals required to invest in innovation.[94] Despite being a theoretic model only, perfect competition was the guiding principle of competition law enforcement for some time.[95] It was only with CLARK that a turning away from perfect competition as a regulatory object for competition law occurred.[96]

---

88. Note, however, that the functions of competition can be categorised in many ways. In this sense *see*: ZÄCH, para. 20.
89. HERDZINA, 32; KNIEPS, 4 f.; EMMERICH/LANGE, § 1, paras 5 ff.
90. HERDZINA, 31 ff.
91. BÖHM, Wettbewerb und Monopolkampf, 114 ff.; HERDZINA, 33 f.; ZÄCH/HEIZMANN, para. 573. In the EU, as has been seen, competition contributes to the achievement of the internal market. *See supra* at paras 39 f.
92. *See* hereinafter as well as the discourse in: SCHMIDT/HAUCAP, 15 ff.
93. KHEMANI/SHAPIRO, para. 150.
94. CLAPHAM, in: COX/JENS/MARKERT, Handbuch des Wettbewerbs, 131.
95. For an example of influencing the idea of perfect competition *see* the controversies that occurred during the drafting of the GWB in 1957: HOPPMANN, Jahrbuch für Nationalökonomie und Statistik 1966, 287.
96. CLARK, The American Economic Review 1940, 241 f.; BOWMAN, 5. Later also: KHEMANI/SHAPIRO, para. 205.

2 Workable and Effective Competition

47 CLARK promoted the protection of competition as a workable process. The concept of workable competition assumes that market structure, behaviour and performance influence the process of competition in a circular manner.[97] Competition is not an end in itself, but serves specific purposes.[98] With the workable competition concept, CLARK tried to identify scenarios within which competition deviating from the theoretic ideal of perfect competition also resulted in preferable outcomes. Those preferable outcomes he scaled to the optimal of perfect competition. CLARK thus initially remained in the tradition of a static understanding of competition.

48 It was only in his later publications that CLARK overcame this last remnant of the perfect competition model.[99] In his concept described as 'effective competition', deviations from a static optimum were no longer seen as imperfections but as necessary elements of progress.[100] CLARK understood effective competition as a dynamic process characterised by two stages. In the first stage, market participants draw innovation-based profits, which are neutralised in a second stage.[101] In best-case scenarios, neutralisation only goes as far as innovators are still encouraged to enter stage one again (circular process). Monopoly positions are understood as necessary to ensure innovation and economic growth. As monopolies result in the reduction of competitive freedom on the market, freedom of competition of weaker players has to retrogress behind the more important aim of fostering innovation.[102]

49 Characteristic of CLARK's work is an understanding of imperfections.[103] According to CLARK, it can be positive for the economy to implement additional imperfections instead of erasing all impediments in certain circumstances. Other scholars also adopted this approach.[104] In what later became known as the Harvard School of Antitrust Analysis, the central notion of CLARK's theory prevailed that market imperfections are accepted as long as they are conducive to competition (theory of second best).

50 The boom years of the Harvard School were characterised by a rather hostile approach of competition authorities towards dominance.[105] The Harvard School was

97. Workable competition is sometimes used as a synonym for effective competition. ECONOMIC ENCYCLOPAEDIA OF GABLER: https://wirtschaftslexikon.gabler.de/definition/wirksamer-wettbewerb-51067, accessed on 4 February 2020.
98. CLARK, The American Economic Review 1940, 243.
99. *See* hereinafter at fn. 100. A significant contribution to the developments for a dynamic approach to competition is also attributed to SCHUMPETER: SCHUMPETER, 81 ff.
100. CLARK, 88.
101. SCHUMPETER, 342 ff.
102. CLARK, 68 ff.
103. CLARK notes that it has not been proved whether powerful undertakings in general do more research than many smaller undertakings together. CLARK, 80 ff. *See also*: SCHWALBE, in: OBERENDER, Effizienz und Wettbewerb, 80.
104. LIPSEY/LANCASTER, The Review of Economic Studies 1956, 11 f.; in the German literature, *see*: SCHMIDTCHEN, in: OBERENDER, Effizienz und Wettbewerb, 21.
105. SCHMIDT/HAUCAP, 15 ff.

based on the structure-conduct-performance paradigm, which anticipates that structure, conduct and performance mutually depend on one another.[106] To influence the performance of a market, scholars of the Harvard School focused on the market structure. As their predecessors, the Harvard scholars had failed to provide a tool to distinguish between 'bad inefficiencies' and 'good inefficiencies' that foster innovation.[107] Other scientific movements thus challenged the widely used concept of workable competition.[108]

51 Workable competition and effective competition[109] are frequently used as synonyms.[110] However, the concepts included in these terms nowadays differ from CLARK's first critique on common, perfect competition standards. Yet, CLARK's reformatory approach is still a common feature of all workable competition concepts. These concepts aim to provide guidelines that can serve as a basis for competition law policymaking[111] and as a valid reference point in competition law analysis. All workability concepts thus contain a deviation from the unrealistic assumptions on which perfect competition is based.[112]

3 Free Competition

52 Competition policy in post–World War II Germany was under the influence of the occupying powers. In Western Germany, policymakers therefore mainly followed the US doctrine.[113] In this political environment, the influence of a German-based school of thought on competition policy rose.[114] The so-called *Freiburger Schule* was inspired by liberalism and a rejection of both the totalitarianism of the old Nazi regime and the socialism of the Soviets.[115] Ordoliberalism, as the body of thought of the *Freiburger Schule* is called, is characterised by a hostile attitude towards private power. Unrestricted power in the hands of private parties endangers not only the process of

106. The premise of the paradigm is that the environment influences market structure, which then influences conduct on the market which in turn influences performance. BAIN, 462 ff.
107. SCHMIDT/HAUCAP, 14.
108. For an example, *see infra* at paras 56 ff.
109. Effective competition is the term used by the European Commission on its webpage: http://ec.europa.eu/competition/antitrust/overview_en.html, accessed on 4 February 2020.
110. *See*, for example, ECONOMIC ENCYCLOPAEDIA OF GABLER: https://wirtschaftslexikon.gabler.de/definition/wirksamer-wettbewerb-51067, accessed on 4 February 2020.
111. *See*: THOUVENIN, 18 ff.
112. *See* i.a.: Ruffner, 25; SCHMIDT/HAUCAP, 10 and 12 ff.; THOUVENIN, 18.
113. WURMNEST, 57 ff.
114. Note that the leaders of the Freiburg Schule had already started working together in the 1930s. *See*: HEINEMANN, Freiburger Schule, 8 ff. After the war the scholars were able to leave their isolation and take leading roles in the forming of German economic policy. *See*: GERBER, The American Journal of Comparative Law 1994b, 31 ff.; HEINEMANN, Freiburger Schule, 17.
115. It was the search for a system different from what Germany knew during the war and the Weimarer Republik that motivated the economists. GERBER, The American Journal of Comparative Law 1994a, 25 and 32 ff.; HEINEMANN, Freiburger Schule, 18 ff.

competition but also the independence of public authorities.[116] Unrestricted competition neutralises power.[117]

53 Ordoliberalism focuses on the freedom of competition.[118] In the eyes of ordoliberalists, it is the responsibility of the legislator to provide a system that restricts the creation and misuse of private power.[119] Freedom to compete should be granted only on the condition that it does not restrict the same rights of others. Competition law therefore has to fulfil the task of limiting selfish motives of market participants when interests of competition are opposed.[120] Acting against the interests of third parties should, however, be allowed when the conduct is based on better performance of the undertaking (competition on the merits).[121] Competition on the merits was seen as having two components:[122] a structural and functional one which was detached from morality, and a moral one that watched over social morality in competition.[123]

54 Free competition is still a key concern of competition. Yet, the term has experienced constant changes in meaning. The wording has played an important role in each competition concept. It is thus hardly surprising that current policy concepts also consider free competition.[124]

55 While followers of workability concepts who assume that structure, conduct and performance on a market influence one another,[125] followers of free competition concepts (liberalists) deny a correlation between market structure, market behaviour and the market result. According to liberalists, scholars have failed to prove such a

116. It can be seen that competition as understood by scholars of the Freiburg Schule had the political dimension of supporting democracy. *See*: Böhm, in: Institut für ausländisches und internationales Wirtschaftsrecht, Kartelle und Monopole im modernen Recht, 17 ff.; Wurmnest, 56.
117. Böhm, Wirtschaftsordnung und Staatsverfassung, 49 ff. On free competition, *see* the article: Ohne Wettbewerb kein freier Markt, Die Zeit, 24 July 1952.
118. Heinemann, Freiburger Schule, 18. Competition can only exist if market participants are free in their decisions and actions. *See*: Eucken, 250. The exclusion of freedom as a goal of competition raised Hoppmann's criticism. *See*: Schmidt/Haucap, 17. His concept of free competition is thus characterised by the idea that freedom is not only a fundamental prerequisite for competition but also simultaneously its function and goal. Hoppmann, Jahrbuch für Nationalökonomie und Statistik 1966, 289.
119. Böhm, in: Wolff/Würtenberger, Aus der Geschichte der Rechts- und Staatswissenschaften zu Freiburg im Breisgau, 99. In post–World War II Germany, cartels were among other factors held responsible for the rise of the Nazi regime.
120. Mestmäcker, ZHR 1973, 104 ff.
121. Böhm adopted the term '*Leistungswettbewerb*' (hereinafter 'competition on the merits'), which was introduced by Nipperdey. Böhm, Wettbewerb und Monopolkampf, 207 f.; Nipperdey.
122. This is contrary to the understanding of Böhm who used competition on the merits and fair competition as synonyms. Böhm, Wettbewerb and Monopolkampf, 92 f.
123. Baumbach/Hefermehl, in: Köhler/Bornkamm, UWG Kommentar 2001, Einleitung, para. 104 (note that the current authors of the commentary, Köhler/Bornkamm/Feddersen, are more critical of the competition on the merits concept: Köhler, in: Köhler/Bornkamm, UWG Kommentar 2020, Einleitung, para. 44).
124. *See i.a.* the critics against the concept of free competition, who still adhere to freedom in competition: Schmidt/Haucap, 21 ff.
125. Knieps, 45 ff.; *see supra* at para. 50.

correlation.[126] Liberalists follow the understanding that market structures are not determined, but develop in the course of the competitive process.[127]

4 The Chicago and Post-Chicago School

56 In the heyday of the *Freiburg Schule*, a new understanding of competition and thus a new concept of competition policy developed in the USA as well. With the emergence of the Chicago School of Antitrust Analysis, the understanding of 'the proper scope of antitrust policy'[128] changed. The Chicago School adopted the critique of ordoliberalists towards the workability concepts and rejected the assumption of a causal nexus between the structure of a market and its outcome.[129] Yet, unlike the scholars of the Freiburg Schule who were influenced by the German history of the twentieth century, their US colleagues saw the only justification for economic policy as fostering the efficiency of competition. According to followers of the Chicago School, the main function of competition was to secure welfare gains, which could be achieved through an increased efficiency of processes that allowed for price reductions.[130]

57 Fundamental to the efficiency doctrine of the Chicago School was an instrumental understanding of competition. It understood competition as a process with a certain purpose and introduced consideration of different aspects of behaviour. Because of the growing influence of the Chicago School doctrine on jurisprudence, the list of acknowledged offences per se was gradually reduced. Gradually, the Rule of Reason,[131] which had already been relatively well developed by the Supreme Court in 1911,[132] became the dominant assessment tool.[133] The influence of the Chicago School led to a less interventionistic antitrust policy.[134] The greatest weakness of the Rule of Reason approach, however, is that there are no robust findings regarding which parameters influence efficiency.[135]

58 These limitations led to the development of Post-Chicago Economics in the 1990s, under which criticism of the Chicago School was bundled. The biggest differences

126. HERDZINA, 53 ff.; HOPPMANN, Jahrbuch für Nationalökonomie und Statistik 1966, 310.
127. HOPPMANN, Jahrbuch für Nationalökonomie und Statistik 1966, 306.
128. POSNER, University of Pennsylvania Law Review 1979, 926.
129. The conceptual basis of the Chicago School was that it understood competition as a dynamic process, but took perfect competition and the monopoly as reference points. KÜNZLER, 49 ff.; SCHMIDT/RITTALER, 33 ff.; THOUVENIN, 36.
130. SCHMIDT/RITTALER, 37 ff.
131. The Rule of Reason is a doctrine in US antitrust law by which the positive and negative effects of restrictive business practice can be analysed and counterbalanced.
132. UNITED STATES SUPREME COURT, *Standard Oil v. USA*, 221 US 1, 66 ff.
133. *See i.a.*: UNITED STATES SUPREME COURT, *Continental T.V. v. GTE Sylvania*, 433 US 36, 45 and 49, which overruled the prohibition of vertical territorial restrictions proclaimed in: UNITED STATES SUPREME COURT, *USA v. Arnold, Schwinn and Co.*, 388 US 365.
134. KÜNZLER, 50 f.
135. In this respect, the Chicago School and the workability concepts which rely on the unproved correlation between market structure, behaviour on the market and the market result are similarly limited in their functionality.

between the Post-Chicago doctrine and the Chicago School resulted from their theoretical foundations.[136] Despite still relying on microeconomic theories, Post-Chicago doctrine draws its theoretical principles from industrial economics. This is because the approaches of industrial economics, mainly through the inclusion of game theory, provide more detailed insights on the functioning of markets than traditional microeconomics. At the normative level, Post-Chicago economics left behind the dispute between the Harvard and Chicago Schools regarding the function of competition.[137] Post-Chicago scholars accepted the orientation of competition towards static welfare maximisation proclaimed by followers of the Chicago School, but in contrast to the limitation to static efficiencies of the Chicago School, Post-Chicago economics integrated dynamic efficiencies into the evaluation of competition.[138] However, there is disagreement among Post-Chicago economists regarding the question of which welfare standard should apply.[139]

59 The ideology considered the assessment of each case based only on efficiency considerations. During the Clinton administration, the Post-Chicago School became increasingly criticised. Critical analysis of the established practice culminated in the 1995 Antitrust Guidelines for the licensing of intellectual property.[140] The idea of the Guidelines, issued by the US Federal Trade Commission (FTC), though not legally binding, was to provide more legal certainty by explaining the authority's general policy (§ 1 of the Guidelines).

5 Development of the *More Economic Approach* in the EU

60 The efficiency doctrine of Post-Chicago economics influenced competition policy in the EU. At the end of the millennium, the Commission was confronted with a rapidly growing Union. The commissioners feared that the increasing number of new Member States would bring the current enforcement system to its limits. In 1999, as part of the Lisbon strategy to promote a competitive and dynamic economy, the Commission published a White Paper aimed at overhauling the standards in both interpreting and applying competition law.[141] The goal of the reorientation was to eliminate uncertainties resulting from inconsistencies in the application of the law and to implement a more simplified administrative procedure.[142]

136. *See*: KÜNZLER, 51.
137. HEINEMANN, Immaterialgüterschutz in der Wettbewerbsordnung, 76 ff.
138. HEINEMANN, Immaterialgüterschutz in der Wettbewerbsordnung, 77.
139. *See infra* at paras 65 ff.
140. US DEPARTMENT OF JUSTICE/FEDERAL TRADE COMMISSION, *Antitrust Guidelines for the Licensing of Intellectual Property*.
141. EC, *White Paper*, paras 5 ff.
142. EC, *White Paper*, paras 41 f. *See also* statements of the Commissioner at that time, MARIO MONTI: MONTI, 3 f.

61 The White Paper contained information from the Commission to strengthen the role of economics in competition law enforcement with respect to cartel agreements.[143] The core demand of integrating economic insights in the analysis of potentially anticompetitive market behaviour was a departure from a form-based analysis.[144] Under the slogan of a *more economic approach*,[145] the Commission promoted an approach[146] which, like the Chicago School and Post-Chicago economics, analysed potentially anticompetitive conduct on the basis of efficiency considerations.[147] Inefficiencies that occurred as a result of anticompetitive behaviour were contrasted with efficiency gains resulting from the same behaviour. If certain conduct, despite causing some inefficiency, resulted in welfare gains overall, it was not criminalised by law.[148] Following the *more economic approach* also involved a departure from freedom of competition, as the protective object of competition law promoted by the *Freiburg Schule*.[149] Irrespective of other goals, competition policy should only focus on welfare maximisation or more precisely consumer welfare maximisation.[150] Behaviour resulting in imperfections within the process of competition or changes in the market structure should not be penalised by law if no consumer welfare losses result.

62 During the next ten years, ideas for introducing a case-by-case analysis were presented on the grounds that this would, despite undeniable difficulties for the authorities, produce fewer decision errors[151].[152] The Discussion Paper of the Commission on the application of Article 82 of the Treaty to exclusionary abuses published in 2005 stated its intention to 'adopt an approach which is based on the likely effects on

143. EC, *White Paper*, paras 56 ff. The *more economic approach* was the basis for the application of Article 101 TFEU as well as the EU merger control. Its importance with respect to Article 102 TFEU remained a highly discussed topic. *See infra* at para. 63.
144. Form-based analysis is characterised by the fact that certain types of behaviour are criminalised based on normative considerations without taking their effects into account.
145. EC, *White Paper*, para. 78. The term 'more economic approach' first appeared in the Communication from the Commission on the application of the Community competition rules to vertical restraints (follow-up to the Green Paper on Vertical Restraints). EC, *Communication on Vertical Restraints – Follow-up*, para. 2.
146. The *more economic approach* is not understood as new concept of competition policy. *See*, for example, HEINEMANN, GRUR 2008, 949; IMMENGA, ZWeR 2006, 348; SOSNITZA, in: HEERMANN/SCHLINGLOFF, Münchener Kommentar Lauterkeitsrecht, Grundlagen, para. 11; MESTMÄCKER/SCHWEITZER, § 3, para. 45.
147. *See*, for example, FUCHS/MÖSCHEL, in: IMMENGA/MESTMÄCKER 2018, Article 102, para. 9; MESTMÄCKER/SCHWEITZER, § 3, para. 43; SOSNITZA, in: HEERMANN/SCHLINGLOFF, Münchener Kommentar Lauterkeitsrecht, Grundlage, paras 10 f. *See also* the speech delivered by the former Hearing Officer for Competition Cases, MICHAEL ALBERS: ALBERS M, Kartellrechtssymposium.
148. SCHMIDTCHEN, in: OBERENDER, Effizienz und Wettbewerb, 12.
149. *See* in this respect: LOVDAHL GORMESEN, European Competition Journal 2007, 329; FUCHS/MÖSCHEL, in: IMMENGA/MESTMÄCKER 2019, Article 102, para. 9.
150. Note that the term 'more economic approach' is also used to describe the consumer welfare approach adopted in EU competition law. On the different elements of *the more economic approach*, *see*: SCHWEITZER/PATEL, in: PATEL/SCHWEITZER, The historical foundations of EU competition law, 220. The *more economic approach* therefore follows a functional understanding of competition, despite the fact that the process is named as a protective target of Article 102 TFEU. EC, *DG Competition discussion paper*, paras 54 ff.
151. Decision errors in abuse control are either the allowance of anticompetitive behaviour (false negatives) or the prohibition of pro-competitive behaviour (false positives).
152. MESTMÄCKER, 33 ff.

the market'.[153] Yet, the Discussion Paper did not fully depart from form-based analysis, but rather implemented a form-based case-by-case approach.[154] In 2009, the Commission spoke again on the matter and released the 'Guidance Paper on the Commission's enforcement priorities in applying Article 82' (hereinafter 'Guidance Paper'). The goal of the Commission's Guidance Paper was 'to provide greater clarity and predictability regards the general framework of analysis [...] to help undertakings better assess whether certain behaviour is likely to result in intervention by the Commission'.[155]

63 Critics of the *more economic approach* claim that its application does not contribute to the predictability of whether conduct is in accordance with the law.[156] Reliance on case-by-case analysis means not only that the outcome of the evaluation is unclear and the scope and effect of the law are less foreseeable to individuals but also that a complicated evaluation process is required. Moreover, the prerequisite for conducting such an evaluation is that the effects of conduct on competition can be anticipated beforehand or identified in hindsight. Critics thus doubt whether the *more economic approach* can add to the application of competition law.[157] Doubts have also been raised as to whether applying the *more economic approach* may result in a reduced application of EU competition law due to the difficulties in predicting future efficiency gains.[158] Additionally, an analysis of future effects on the economy is dependent on a myriad of largely inaccessible data[159] and therefore difficult for authorities to conduct. The same is true for market participants themselves when deciding on whether to adopt certain behaviour.[160]

IV WELFARE STANDARD

64 Objections were also raised about the permissibility of applying a consumer welfare standard under current laws. Articles 119(1) and 120 TFEU determine that EU competition policy should be conducted in accordance with the principle of an open market economy with free competition. Likewise, Articles 101 and 102 TFEU aim at removing barriers to competition.

65 Welfare economics provides two welfare concepts for analysing the effects of conduct on competition. The possible standards are social welfare (also total welfare)

153. EC, *DG Competition discussion paper*, para. 4.
154. EC, *DG Competition discussion paper*, paras 59 f.; MEIER, in: MATHIS/TOR, 56 f. Up until today both the form- and the effect-based approaches are present in the analysis. *See infra* at paras 383, 455 and 486 ff. Owing to practicability reasons, this will probably not change, as KÜNZLER showed: KÜNZLER, 457 f. Several voices in literature support a mixture of both approaches. *See*, for example, HEINEMANN, in: WALDBURGER ET AL., FS Nobel, Recht, Ökonomie und Realität, 39 f.; HEINEMANN, in: MATHIS, 232 ff.; MEIER, in: MATHIS/TOR, 61 ff.; WURMNEST, 255 f.
155. EC, *Guidance Paper*, para. 2.
156. SCHMIDTCHEN, in: OBERENDER, Effizienz und Wettbewerb, 174.
157. Recently: BLOCKX, World Competition 2019, 475 ff.
158. *See*: ZÄCH/KÜNZLER, in: ZÄCH/HEINEMANN/KELLERHALS, The development of competition law, 73.
159. On the limitations of economics in law: BLOCKX, World Competition 2019, 483 ff. and 491 ff.
160. SCHMIDT/VOIGT, WUW 2006, 1098; KÜNZLER, 106 ff.

or consumer welfare.[161] Social welfare focuses on both consumer and producer surplus and tries to maximise both. The main goal of competition in trying to maximise social welfare is the highest possible total of consumer and producer returns. The individual quantity is unimportant, as social welfare is understood as the sum of the two addends. If competition is bound to maximising consumer welfare only, it solely focuses on consumer surplus.[162] A trade-off between producer and consumer surplus with an overall view is not possible.

66 The decision on whether competition should be obliged to social or consumer welfare is also a decision about who should be profiting from efficiency gains.[163] Although legal rules are not designed to directly create welfare, they help in maintaining structures which allow for the creation of welfare or at least do not result in welfare losses. Despite the fact that economists in general favour an overall welfare standard (social welfare),[164] scholars arguing in favour of the *more economic approach* have chosen to apply the consumer welfare standard.[165] The consequence is that in cases which result in an overall societal welfare loss, competition law would not intervene if consumer welfare increases. Social welfare standards generally risk promoting unproductive investments.[166]

67 The goal that competition law should serve has been hotly debated in the EU[167].[168] The Commission in its Guidelines states that its task is 'to ensure that dominant undertakings do not impair effective competition by foreclosing their competitors in an anti-competitive way, thus having an adverse [direct or indirect][169] impact on consumer welfare'.[170] Yet, in the *British Airways* case, the Court of Justice held that the Commission is not allowed to unilaterally determine the goals of the competition policy.[171] Nevertheless, the court stressed the importance of consumer welfare considerations in the course of assessing economic justifications. 'It has to be determined

---

161. *See i.a.*: Bishop/Walker, para. 2-017; Künzler, 109; Lamping, fn. 90; Martenet/Heinemann, 32 ff.
162. Consumer welfare was introduced by Bork and was the relevant welfare standard for representatives of the Chicago School. By referring to consumer welfare, Bork, however, addressed a total welfare concept, including consumer as well as producer surplus. Wurmnest, 45. On welfare standards and the Chicago School, *see also*: Ruffner, 91 ff. and 107. This shows that caution is required with respect to the terms 'consumer' and 'total welfare' since the understanding among scholars varies.
163. Wurmnest, 126 f.
164. Monti, in: Zäch/Heinemann/Kellerhals, The development of competition law, 6; Motta, 20 ff.
165. *See i.a.*: Motta, 17 ff.; O'Donoghue/Padilla, 6; von Weiszäcker, WUW 2007, 1078 ff.
166. On the advantages and disadvantages of the welfare standards *see*: Künzler, 108 ff.; Monti, in: Zäch/Heinemann/Kellerhals, The development of competition law, 6 ff.
167. The relevant welfare standard seems to be an issue in the legal discourse in the USA as well. *See*: Wurmnest, 46 ff.
168. Exemplarily, *see* the analysis by Wurmnest: Wurmnest, 126 ff. or the debate between Basedow and von Weiszäcker in their 2007 WUW articles. *See*: Basedow, WUW 2007, 712 ff.; von Weiszäcker, WUW 2007, 1078 ff.; *see infra* at para. 471.
169. EC, *DG Competition discussion paper*, para. 55.
170. EC, *Guidance Paper*, para. 19.
171. ECJ, *British Airways plc v. Commission*, C-95/04, paras 106 ff.; AG Kokott, *in: British Airways v. Commission*, C-95/04, para. 28. Körber understands this statement as disacknowledgement of the consumer welfare standard by the ECJ. Körber, in: Immenga/Mestmäcker, Fusion, Article 2, para. 14.

whether the exclusionary effect arising from such a system, which is disadvantageous for competition, may be counterbalanced, or outweighed, by advantages in terms of efficiency which also benefit the consumer.'[172]

68 In *Post Danmark A/S v. Konkurrencerådet*, the court issued a statement that interference in the process of competition generally harms consumers' interests.[173] At least for Article 102 TFEU cases, it thus indicated an integrated understanding of the detriment of competition and consumer welfare. The Commission previously implied this notion in its Discussion Paper on the application of Article 82. Regarding the object of Article 102 TFEU, it held that its goal is 'the protection of competition on the market as a means of enhancing consumer welfare and of ensuring an efficient allocation of resources'.[174] The process of competition is thus understood in a classical economic manner, as a mechanism ensuring consumer welfare and an efficient allocation of resources.[175] Because the ECJ in *Post Danmark A/S v. Konkurrencerådet* apparently acknowledged a consumer welfare standard, it seems fair to conclude that the 'effect, to the detriment of competition and, thereby, of consumers' interests'[176] has prevailed as the standard for the analysis of Article 102 TFEU.[177] Owing to these clear statements, an in-depth analysis of the advantages and disadvantages of the consumer welfare standard will not be undertaken in this book.

69 Therefore, the finding of an abuse of the dominant position is inseparable from an 'adverse impact on consumer welfare'[178].[179] When the acquisition of patents is under scrutiny, this is a straightforward process. A prerequisite for establishing an abuse in these cases, as will be argued below, is that the acquisition prevents a product or a technology from entering the market for which there is a potential demand.[180] Unmet demands for which actual solutions exist are always to the detriment of consumers.[181]

V IMPLICATIONS

70 Competition is a dynamic process, which can be instrumental in achieving macroeconomic objectives. Competition does not exist for its own sake, however. Viewed in isolation, the process of competition and the freedom of contestants are not susceptible to protection. The laws to protect competition must therefore only secure competition

172. ECJ, *TeliaSonera Sverige*, C-52/09, para. 76. Confirmed various times, *see i.a.*: ECJ, *Post Danmark*, C-209/10, para. 69; ECJ, *Sot. Lélos kai Sia*, Joined Cases C-468/06-C-478/06, para. 68.
173. ECJ, *Post Danmark*, C-209/10, para. 44; *see infra* at fn. 1318.
174. EC, *DG Competition discussion paper*, para. 4.
175. Fox, World Competition 2003, 155 f.
176. ECJ, *Post Danmark*, C-209/10, para. 44.
177. *See in this regard*: Kroes; Fuchs/Möschel, in: Immenga/Mestmäcker 2018, Article 102, para. 12. Strongly dissenting: Körber, in: Immenga/Mestmäcker, Fusion, Article 2, para. 14.
178. EC, *Guidance Paper*, para. 19.
179. On the difficulties with regard to anticompetitive effects, *see infra* at paras 345 and 486 ff.
180. *See infra* at para. 702.
181. In this regard: Zech, ZWeR 2011, 330.

in order to obtain the desired effects. This means that competition is workable as long as its aims are still reached, despite inefficiencies.[182] Owing to their programmatic character, models of workable competition are widely used as guidelines by authorities.[183] According to EU constitutional law, competition policy should promote free markets and protect the freedom of competition. Competition law therefore implies restrictions on the freedom of competition in order to guarantee open markets and thus in return protect the freedom of competition.

71 It is the fundamental aim of competition policy to provide measures that protect the mechanism of competition and thus provide conditions in which competition can develop its full potential, irrespective of the underlying welfare standard. At the beginning of competition law in liberal regimes stood the recognition that an endurable system of competition cannot be granted by simply guaranteeing economic freedom. The fierce rivalry of unregulated competition puts the participants on the path of self-destruction.[184] This was recognised in many countries. Competition laws were enacted to provide the balance between the efficiency of free markets while setting barriers to undertakings.

72 The problem for competition law policy is that choosing a reference model of competition requires a causally determined correlation between market structure, behaviour on the market and the market result. As, under natural conditions, competition will vary sector-wise,[185] a judgment on whether conduct is interfering with the workability of competition requires detailed knowledge of both the sector and the conduct itself and is therefore difficult to establish. Research therefore tries to deliver evidence for correlations between the market structure, the market result and the conduct of undertakings on the market, but such efforts have not yet resulted in robust findings. Therefore, the law has had to adapt to changing concepts of reference systems developed by scholars studying industrial organisation.

182. In the EU this has been confirmed by the ECJ in *Metro v. Commission*: ECJ, *Metro v. Commission*, C-26/76, para. 20. *See also*: BISHOP/WALKER, para. 2-001; THOUVENIN, 18 ff.
183. KHEMANI/SHAPIRO, para. 205; also, economic scholars favour the flexibility of these concepts as they allow the best harmonisation of static and dynamic efficiencies. SCHWALBE/ZIMMER, 65.
184. BAUDENBACHER C., in: BAUDENBACHER, UWG Kommentar, Article 1, paras 2 ff.
185. *See* the statement in: ECJ, *Metro v. Commission*, C-26/76, para. 20.

CHAPTER 4

Introduction to the System of Competition Law

I THE DISCIPLINES OF COMPETITION LAW

73 As noted above, competition law is the field of law created to protect competition.[186] The form of competition that a national economy aspires to is determined by the reference system.[187] All provisions of competition law within a legal system follow the same ideal and are dedicated to protecting competition as set out in the economic constitution.[188] Competition policy therefore sets the boundaries within which the law has to develop.[189] The choice of reference system also sets the boundaries within which the provisions enacted to protect competition (competition law) have to be analysed.[190]

74 The provisions of competition law generally address different system inefficiencies. Despite the design of the provisions being dependent on the reference system, in many legislations, three regulatory areas can be identified: antitrust law, the law against unfair competition, and intellectual property law.

1 Antitrust Law/Competition Law in the Narrow Sense

75 Antitrust law seeks to eliminate restrictions to the process of competition. It is the task of antitrust law to identify and sanction restrictions of competition, which endanger its functionality[191] through limiting the freedom of manoeuvre of other

186. *See supra* at paras 38 ff.
187. *See*: BAUDENBACHER C., in: BAUDENBACHER, UWG Kommentar, Article 1, para. 19.
188. BAUDENBACHER C., in: BAUDENBACHER, UWG Kommentar, Article 1, para. 35; THOUVENIN, 507.
189. *See*: FIKENTSCHER, GRUR Ausl 1966, 181; MESTMÄCKER/SCHWEITZER, § 3, para. 72.
190. Similarly: HILTY, in: BSK KG, Article 3 Abs. 2, para. 15.
191. MESTMÄCKER/SCHWEITZER, § 3, para. 72.

market participants.[192] Restrictions falling within the scope of antitrust law are agreements between undertakings, decisions by associations of undertakings and concerted practices, which have as their object or effect the prevention, restriction or distortion of competition (Article 101 TFEU) as well as restrictions of competition resulting from the conduct of dominant undertakings. Dominant undertakings can restrict competition not only through unilateral conduct (Article 102 TFEU) but also through mergers.[193] In EU law other than in US doctrine, the term 'antitrust law' is not commonly used. This book will follow EU practice in using the term 'competition law' to address what German writers call *Kartellrecht* and US writers call antitrust law.[194]

2 Law Against Unfair Competition

2.1 Object

76 Unfair competition law is a set of rules targeted at neutralising the harmful behaviour of market participants who make use of intransparency and information deficits.[195] Unfair competition law is a general market behaviour law, a control mechanism for behaviour objectively directed at influencing competitive conditions.[196] This does not, however, mean that unfair competition law is dedicated to implementing a moral standard in the process of competition, as its name would imply. Rather, the object of unfair competition law is to provide a competitive environment in which 'necessary trust and confidence for people to take the risks of disappointment and betrayal incurred in every market transaction'[197] prevails. Rather than safeguarding general moral standards, unfair competition law is dedicated to creating an even playing field for all market participants to make sure that they can engage in open and transparent transactions.[198] Before the creation of a special field of law, the conduct of unfair competition was understood as a tort against competitors.

77 Apart from this general function of unfair competition law, statements about the aim of the law and approximations or even definitions of the term 'unfair' are rare. The literature and case law, rather than providing a definition of unfair competition, have focused on building case groups.[199]

192. *See i.a.*: AKMAN, 52; BELLAMY/CHILD, para. 1.008; EMMERICH/LANGE, § 3, paras 2 f.
193. ZÄCH, paras 92 ff.
194. On the terminology: GLÖCKNER, 4. The term 'antitrust law' is used in the USA but not in the EU where the term 'competition law' is common. *See the explanation in* para. 75.
195. *See*: SCHÜNEMANN, in: HILTY/HENNING-BODEWIG, Lauterkeitsrecht und Acquis Communautaire, 103.
196. For Switzerland, *see* SCHLUEP, in: DUTOIT, Un Droit européen de la concurrence déloyale en formation?, 69 and 81; BGE 120 II 76, para. 3.(a).
197. COLLINS, in: COLLINS, The forthcoming EC directive on unfair commercial practices, 2.
198. *See i.a.*: WEBER, sic! 2012, 232; WEBER, sic! 1998, 158.
199. BAUDENBACHER C., in: BAUDENBACHER, UWG Kommentar, Article 2, paras 5 f. For competition law, *see*: EVANS, World Competition 2005, 93 ff.

78 In certain cases, the scope of competition and unfair competition law overlap.[200] One example is spreading misleading information to consumers, which traditionally is a violation of unfair competition law,[201] as consumers are influenced in their decision-making process and cannot decide in full knowledge of all the facts.[202] Yet, such information asymmetry is also an obstacle to trade, which can have an influence on market structure and distort competition. Undertakings spreading misleading information create a competitive advantage over competitors that is not based on a better offering. They therefore win customers from those competitors who are refraining from using misleading information.[203] Consequently, this conduct has the potential to discriminate substitutes and substantially weaken, if not eliminate, competitors. Markets where demanders rely on the information of the suppliers because of significant advantages in knowledge, for example, in the pharmaceutical market, are especially jeopardised.[204]

79 At EU level, the law against unfair competition has not yet been widely harmonised. It will therefore not be analysed further within this book. Yet, unfair competition law is relevant insofar as fairness considerations in competition law first emerged within unfair competition law as well as the general principle of the abuse of rights.

2.2 Further Relevance of the Law Against Unfair Competition in This Book

80 Since the *AKZO* decision of the Court of Justice, fairness considerations are no longer limited to the general principle of the abuse of rights and unfair competition law, but have become important in the legal doctrine of competition law as well.[205] 'Any unfair commercial practices on the part of a dominant undertaking intended to eliminate, discipline or deter smaller competitors would thus fall within the scope of the prohibition of article 86 [...].'[206] Following Ulmer, early attempts at defining the scope of abuse – with recourse to the principle of competition on the merits – were based on the content of unfair competition law in Germany.[207]

200. An example is the delivery of misleading information as in the recent case of *Hoffmann-La Roche II*: ECJ, *Hoffmann-La Roche II,* C-179/16, para. 92.
201. For further conduct which can fall under the scrutiny of both unfair competition and competition law, *see*: Osti, in: Pitruzzella/Muscolo, Competition and patent law in the pharmaceutical sector, 102 f.
202. European Parliament/European Council, *Directive concerning unfair b2c commercial practices,* para. 13. *See also* the early case practice: ECJ, *GB-INNO-BM,* C-362/88, para. 17.
203. Straetmans, EuCML 2016, 199 f.
204. As example, *see*: ECJ, *Hoffmann-La Roche II,* C-179/16, para. 92.
205. EC, *ECS v. AKZO,* IV/30.698, paras 74 f.; Gerber, Fairness in Competition Law: European and US Experience, 12; fair dealing in trade secrets was of concern as early as ancient Babylon. *See* references to the Hammurabi code of law in: Pires de Carvalho, in: de Werra, Défis du droit de la concurrence déloyale, 2.
206. EC, *ECS v. AKZO,* IV/30.698, para. 74.
207. Ulmer, GRUR 1977, 656 ff.; *see infra* at paras 472 ff.

81 That the concept of fairness is important for the whole field of competition law[208] was made clear by the former Commissioner ALMUNIA when he held that rules against unilateral conduct 'help in pursuing three goals: keeping markets open and fair, promoting innovation, and making sure that no harm is done to consumers'.[209] Fair and open markets are therefore part of the same goal of removing obstacles to trade.

82 The influence of fairness considerations in EU competition law is closely linked with market integration.[210] Thus, unlike in the US where fairness seems to have vanished from competition law,[211] fairness in the EU continues to play an important role in the assessment of anticompetitive practices.[212] As the Union holds, its 'rules on competition are designed to ensure fair and equal conditions for businesses, while leaving space for innovation, unified standards, and the development of small businesses'.[213] The relevance of the notion of fairness in EU competition law is also expressed in the preamble of the TFEU in which the Member States express their intention to remove obstacles to trade 'in order to guarantee steady expansion, balanced trade and fair competition'.[214] The freedom of undertakings to compete in the Union's market is thus restricted to the requirements of fairness and good manners.[215]

83 In the context of the abuse of dominance, fairness considerations can most clearly be seen in Article 102(a) TFEU, which lists the use of unfair conditions in trade as possible abuse of dominance. Nevertheless, legal practice also includes fairness considerations in the context of the evaluation of exclusionary practices.[216] These examples show how the goals of unfair competition and competition law sometimes interlock.[217] While the law against unfair competition protects fairness within the competitive process, competition law protects players in the upstream markets and at the same market level from unfair conduct of dominant undertakings, which present a

---

208. That both unfair competition and antitrust law are based on fairness considerations, even though fair competition is the primary goal of unfair competition law only, was also argued by the US Supreme Court in 1931: UNITED STATES SUPREME COURT, *FTC v. Raladam Co.*, 283 US 643, 647 ff.; for newer practice of the United States Supreme Court, *see*: UNITED STATES SUPREME COURT, *FTC v. Actavis,* 570 US 136.
209. ALMUNIA, 3.
210. GERBER, Fairness in Competition Law: European and US Experience, 9.
211. Although fairness considerations seem to have played an important role at the time of the enactment of the Sherman Act. GERBER, Fairness in Competition Law: European and US Experience, 3.
212. *See*: GERBER, Fairness in Competition Law: European and US Experience, 6; with respect to fines: ZHENG, para. 1008; *see infra* at paras 434 and 475 ff.
213. *See*: http://europa.eu/pol/comp/index_en.htm, accessed on 5 February 2020.
214. On the interpretation of competition rules in the light of the Preamble, *see*: ECJ, *Italian Republic v. Council and Commission,* C-32/65, 405.
215. LAMPING, 31.
216. *See* the examples in: JUNG, in: GRABITZ ET AL., EUV/AEUV, Article 102, para. 214, fn. 6.
217. PIRES DE CARVALHO, in: DE WERRA, Défis du droit de la concurrence déloyale, 25 f. The importance of fairness in restricting power can also be seen in the context of standard-setting. A technology is only accepted as a standard when the owner agrees to license the technology on fair, reasonable and non-discriminatory conditions. *See infra* at para. 229.

particular obstacle to competition.[218] The close relationship between unfair competition and competition law has even led to the hypothesis that 'the act of unfair competition becomes a competition law violation when it is practiced by a competitor with a dominant position'.[219]

84 Article 102 TFEU stipulates that a dominant undertaking is only allowed to compete based on the merits of its offerings. The use of information asymmetry in order to reduce the demand for a substitute product or service, as, for example, in a misleading advertisement, results in an advantage over competitors which is unlikely to be performance related. Conduct that would qualify as a violation of unfair competition law could therefore also amount to a violation of Article 102 TFEU.

85 Yet, under Article 102 TFEU, the assessment must be conducted according to the aim of competition law. The finding of an act of unfair behaviour does not in itself amount to abuse of a dominant position as PIRES DE CARVALHO indicates,[220,221] and vice versa. Even though the concept of competition on the merits originates from the law of unfair competition,[222] non-meritocratic competition does not necessarily have to include unfair methods.[223] The delicate balance between overlapping and complementary aims of competition law and the law against unfair competition in general, and within Article 102 TFEU in particular, would therefore require an in-depth analysis which is not the subject of this book.

3 Intellectual Property Law

86 Within the system of competition law, intellectual property [224] laws contribute to solving the problem of the optimal allocation of resources for intangible assets by providing property protection.[225] Guaranteeing rights of disposal[226] is a fundamental precondition for conveyance and as such for competition itself (Article 4(1) and (2) TFEU).[227] If there were no rights of disposal, competition with the good could not exist.

218. GERBER, Tulane Law Review 1987, 101 f.; KÖHLER, in: KÖHLER/BORNKAMM, UWG Kommentar 2020, Einleitung, para. 6.18; AMSTUTZ, sic! 2011, 536.
219. PIRES DE CARVALHO, in: DE WERRA, Défis du droit de la concurrence déloyale, 25.
220. PIRES DE CARVALHO, in: DE WERRA, Défis du droit de la concurrence déloyale, 25.
221. KÖHLER, in: KÖHLER/BORNKAMM, UWG Kommentar 2020, Einleitung, para. 6.18.
222. On competition on the merits, *see infra* at paras 472 ff.
223. IMMENGA, in: IMMENGA/MESTMÄCKER, GWB Kommentar, § 24, paras 71 ff.
224. The term 'intellectual property' is often used as synonym for 'intangible goods' in the English language, irrespective of whether the good has indeed been transformed into property. *See*: LANDES/POSNER, 1.
225. *See*: GORDON who describes the considerations of the US congress concerning the establishment of intellectual property laws. GORDON, in: VON OTT/SCHÄFER, Ökonomische Analyse der rechtlichen Organisation von Innovationen, 330 ff. Note, however, that in some cases, especially in certain fields of research, even propertisation cannot establish marketability. *See*: BROCKHOFF, 119 ff. Sometimes propertisation is not the optimal option for intangibles due to societal needs. *See* the example of copyright in court decisions: LANDES/POSNER, 15.
226. *See*: ENGEL, in: VON DANWITZ/DEPENHEUER/ENGEL, Bericht zur Lage des Eigentums, 48.
227. *See i.a.* ENGEL, in: VON DANWITZ/DEPENHEUER/ENGEL, Bericht zur Lage des Eigentums, 47 ff.; KIEFER/STEININGER, 343 ff.; specifically related to the transfer of technology: SCHEUER, 17.

Economic theory predicts that in such situations, due to a lack of profitability, no one would be willing to provide resources to protect the good.[228]

87 An intangible asset[229] results from an intellectual achievement.[230] They are ubiquitous[231] and lack physical appearance. The existence of intangibles is limited to the mind of their creator.[232] To become perceptible and usable outside the mind of their creator, intangible assets need to appear as tangible, physical manifestations.[233] A physical manifestation does not diminish the intangible core in its substance. A story can be told and printed several times without fading, and a technical instruction can be used repeatedly without losing functionality.[234] What is true for perception is equally true for consumption; enjoying an intangible asset leaves other parties unaffected. Simultaneous use is possible, but does not discount the value of the asset either. Without propertisation, intangible assets, owing to their non-rivalry[235] and non-excludability, are what economists call public goods.[236] The most important characteristic of an intangible asset when it comes to justifying intellectual property law is its non-excludability.[237] Once an idea has become perceptible, whoever notices it can use it unrestrictedly.

88 The problem of public goods is that market mechanisms fail to ensure their optimal allocation. This is mainly due to their non-excludability.[238] Rational consumers are not willing to pay for a good unless they can be hindered from consuming it when they do

228. Note that there are still intellectual products, which are not protectable with IP rights, as, for example, ideas. Additionally, there are products that would be eligible for protection but are not, as, for example, certain trade secrets.
229. A 'body of ideas and expressions': LANDES/POSNER, 13.
230. THOUVENIN describes intangibles as having a limited existence restricted to the mind. THOUVENIN, 265.
231. Ubiquitous means that the assets are without limitation in time or space.
232. As intangibles do not exist physically, it is difficult to conceptualise them. This is essential to allow propertisation, however. On propertisation, particularly conferring rights on information *see*: KNIEPS, 247 f.; LANDES/POSNER, 1. The prevailing opinion interprets intangible goods as 'information'.
233. Even if intangible assets manifest themselves in tangible bodies, their 'intellectual nature' prevails independently. TROLLER, 17.
234. Similarly: GORDON, in: VON OTT/SCHÄFER, Ökonomische Analyse der rechtlichen Organisation von Innovationen, 329.
235. Public goods are non-rivalrous. Non-rivalry in economics means that an additional demander can enjoy the good without causing further costs. In other words, the marginal cost of an additional user is zero. BROCKHOFF, 116 ff.; SAMUELSON, The Review of Economics and Statistics, 387.
236. *See*: KRUGMAN/WELLS, 521; LANDES/POSNER, 329 ff. Public goods, such as fresh air, are opposed to private goods which are excludable as well as rivals in consumption. Both features allow efficient exploitation on the market. KRUGMAN/WELLS, 521 f. The term is misleading in connection with intellectual assets as they are not provided by the government for everyone, unlike a waste water system or national defence. *See*: LANDES/POSNER, 14.
237. *See*: LANDES/POSNER, 13.
238. It has been acknowledged that non-rivalry leads to inefficiencies as well. The marginal cost of additional consumers is zero. Prices above the marginal costs lead to low consumption. Non-rivalry in itself, however, does not lead to the failure of a good on the market. For additional references, *see*: NEVER, 130.

not pay.[239] Consequently, public goods either lack marketability or the market cannot provide the asset efficiently.[240] The legislator thus established an intellectual property law regime to allow for the marketability of certain public goods. There is, however, only a *numerus clausus* of intellectual property rights and the privileges conferred[241] and the requirements to be rewarded with them are exclusive (*see* Article 52(1) EPC).[242] This is because interference in competition such as the propertisation of certain goods has to be economically justified.[243]

89 The central focus of this book is patents, but their role within competition is not straightforward and has been interpreted differently over time. To understand the notion behind establishing intellectual property laws in general, and patents in particular, as well as understanding how legal scholars and policymakers solve the apparently conflicting goals of patent and competition law is the aim of the following analysis.

II PATENTS IN COMPETITION

1 Justification of Patent Law

90 Following the example of Great Britain, which was long seen as the motherland of patent law,[244] many countries enacted patent law codes at the close of the eighteenth century.[245] The legitimations for these legislative measures were diverse, however.

---

239. KRUGMAN/WELLS, 521 f.
240. GRUBER/KLEBER, 135.
241. The most important privilege the law provides is an exclusive right. Exclusive rights allow their holder to exclude third parties from using and enjoying the asset. Most of the time, however, usage cannot be blocked per se. In patent law, exclusion is limited to commercial usage. THOUVENIN, 277 ff.
242. TROLLER, 20 ff.
243. For example, balancing contradictory interests of private investors, proprietors and society *See*: BENTLY ET AL., 4 f. For a historical view on the struggles of legislators in justifying a patent system: MACHLUP, GRUR Int. 1961, 376.
244. KURZ, 375. The first codified patent law, however, dates from 1474 and was issued in Venice. This codification did not get as much attention as the British Statute of Monopolies, but most likely rang in the new era of patent law codifications. KURZ, 44 ff.; LANDES/POSNER, 1.
245. The French patent code dates from 1792, and its foundation in the USA was laid with section 8 clause 8 of the US Constitution in 1787. The Netherlands was the last European country to adopt a patent act (1910). Written histories describe privileges given to chefs in the colony of Sybaris (AD 720). Whenever a new outstanding dish was invented, the creator was given the sole right to prepare the dish for the period of one year (*see*: KURZ, 12 ff.) With the downfall of the ancient cultures, the tender signs of inventor protection vanished. It was only during the predatory capitalism of the Renaissance that the economic value of inventions was (re-)recognised. The idea of supporting inventors to secure social well-being through technical development was born. Patents had not yet been introduced, but inventors received financial support or other benefits from the authorities. These precursors of today's patents, though not patents as codified today, were known as privileges (*see*: KURZ, 20 ff.). An important distinguishing fact is the characteristic of patents as codified legal claims as opposed to the privileges that were construed as acts of mercy. The same was true for British monopolies. *See*: FOX, Monopolies and Patents, 192.

1.1 *Classical Theories*

91 The classical approaches for justifying patent law regimes can be divided into two categories: libertarian theories based on moral considerations and utilitarian theories resting on economic justifications.[246] These two theories do not stand alone but complement each other.

92 Supporters of the libertarian theories apply natural law and endorse patents based on moral and ethical arguments.[247] Following this understanding, acknowledging property rights for innovation is a natural obligation. As inventions are the 'fruit of mental labour',[248] they naturally belong to the inventor and are the result of their mental efforts.[249] The inventor's property right is an emanation of their human rights.[250] The special bond between inventor and invention will always remain, although propertisation allows the invention to gain a certain independence.[251] Based on natural law theory, it is a moral obligation to reward an inventor for their mental labour.[252] The reward is granted by providing the inventor with what is rightfully theirs: ownership of their mental product.

93 Utilitarian theorists justify patents economically, starting with the assumption that the protection of inventions should serve one goal above all, which is to foster innovation and technical progress.[253] Economic theories do not acknowledge intellectual property as a natural obligation.[254] Granting patents is rather the contractual service of society in a contract with the inventor, who in return engages in R&D and displays his or her findings. Through the privileges of the patent, which include the expectation of gaining temporary monopoly rents, the investment in research becomes less risky.[255] The prospect of receiving a patent grant works as an incentive to innovate (incentive theory).[256] Additionally, through the fact that the inventor has to disclose the invention in return for the privileges of the patent, knowledge can spread and boost further development (disclosing theory/contract theory).[257] Even if the obligation to

246. The same distinction can be found in various publications. On patents specifically: BENTLY ET AL., 397 ff.; GODT, 515; on intellectual property in general: BENTLY ET AL., 3 ff.
247. *See also*: MACHLUP/PENROSE, The Journal of Economic History 1950, 11 ff.
248. FOX, Monopolies and Patents, 193.
249. This theory originates from the time of the French Revolution. Its foundation is JOHN LOCKE's labour theory of property. *See*: KURZ, 238 ff.; MACHLUP, GRUR Int. 1961, 377; *see also the analysis in*: STIERLE, 191 ff.
250. FOX, Monopolies and Patents, 193.
251. This is still visible in copyright law today, where the originator even after disposing of all their exploitation rights keeps the moral rights, for example, the right to claim authorship.
252. Libertarian theories assume that tangible property and ideas should be treated equally.
253. *See*, for example, the legislation assignments in the US Constitution that gave Congress the power to enact IP legislation: US Constitution, Article 1, § 8, cl. 8.
254. THUMM, in: HERREN/MÜNCH/WEINMANN, Schweizer IP-Handbuch, § 2, para. 1.
255. THUMM, in: HERREN/MÜNCH/WEINMANN, Schweizer IP-Handbuch, § 2, para. 18.
256. EC, *Communication Enhancing the Patent System in Europe*, 2; *see also*: BGE 126 III 129, para. 8.a.
257. For in-depth consideration of patents and their function of disclosing information: BEIER, GRUR 1977, 284 ff.

disclose might prevent undertakings from patenting,[258] authors agree that disclosing information through patents is valuable for the economy and society below the bottom line.[259] This is due to the fact that within the information published in patent claims lies enormous potential for research. Disclosed inventions can spur further research, resulting in new inventions for the benefit of society.[260]

1.2 Modern Approach

94 While libertarian theories have mostly, albeit not completely,[261] vanished, utilitarian theories are still, despite critique,[262] present in modern-day patent law.[263] Yet, theoretical reasoning has shifted away from unilateral, inventor-centred justifications to a more comprehensive approach. This is not least due to the upswing of more economic approaches in analysing the effects of competition law. Modern justifications comprise an overall cost–benefit consideration including social costs.[264] The position of the inventor is no longer the centre of considerations. Interests of consumers and other market participants have become important as well. The prevailing opinion nowadays holds that, in order to be justified, a patent should enhance social welfare in some way.[265] This is the case when propertisation leads to a more efficient allocation of resources than leaving the intangible asset unprotected.[266] The goal of the legislator is to design the law in a manner that guarantees the most efficient allocation.[267] Consequently, scholars nowadays focus on the optimal design of the patent system[268] rather than on its justification.[269]

95 The principal aim of the patent is not only to provide the possibility for competition through propertisation or to reward an inventor but also to spur innovation and

258. *See infra* at para. 200.
259. *See i.a.*: GRANSTRAND, 83 ff.; LAMPING, 101 ff with further references.
260. HÄUSSER, in: OPPENLÄNDER, Patentwesen technischer Fortschritt und Wettbewerb, 140.
261. The most famous remnant of the libertarian theories is the granting of moral rights to copyright holders. *See infra* at paras 216 and 688.
262. *See infra* at paras 96 ff.
263. *See i.a.*: EUROPEAN PARLIAMENT/EUROPEAN COUNCIL, *Directive 2004/48/EC*, para. 2; KRASSER/ANN, §3, paras 6 ff.; OSTERRIETH, paras 6 ff.
264. *See* the considerations on social costs in: HEINEMANN, Immaterialgüterschutz in der Wettbewerbsordnung, 17.
265. All these observations can be understood in view of the wording of Article 7 TRIPS on the objectives of the protection of intellectual property: '[...] intellectual property rights should contribute [...] to the mutual advantage of producers and users of technological knowledge and in a manner conducive to social and economic welfare, and to a balance of rights and obligations'.
266. GORDON, in: VON OTT/SCHÄFER, Ökonomische Analyse der rechtlichen Organisation von Innovationen, 328.
267. Private property, together with freedom of competition, is a constituent of a free economy. As seen above, only propertisation can create incentives to administer goods. Many constitutions therefore grant a fundamental right to property that includes both tangible and intangible assets. *See supra* at fn. 227.
268. *See i.a.*: BURK/LEMLEY, 131 ff.; SCOTCHMER, 97 ff.
269. In this regard *see also*: LAMPING, 109, and *infra* at paras 99 and 264.

technical progress. The need to propertise intangible assets and reward the inventor would hardly justify the establishment of a patent system, as this could be achieved using simpler methods.[270] The patent system is primarily designed to foster innovation rather than compensate the inventor.

1.3 Critique of Patents

96 The theory that patents are perfect incentives for innovation by granting timely limited exclusivity while simultaneously ensuring disclosure and the optimal diffusion of knowledge[271] has been doubted by various scholars. The critique of patents consists of two main arguments. The first argument concerns doubts on whether patents are the optimal vehicle to foster innovation. Many scholars argue that competitive pressure itself provides sufficient incentives to innovate and those patents, at least in some fields, are not contributing to raise competitive pressure.[272] The second argument is that the influence of patents on the market structure is still unclear.[273]

97 Developments in recent years seem to support the critics. Over the last four decades, there has been a huge increase in the amount of patent applications being registered in many parts of the world,[274] from the mid-1980s to the present day. The boom is noteworthy in relation to the functioning of the patent system as it is shown not only in the absolute numbers of patent applications but also in relation to R&D spending. In both the USA and Europe, the number of patent applications and R&D dollars spent did not grow equally.[275] Data from patent applications of German origin with the EPO or PCT (Patent Cooperation Treaty)-application process doubled from 1990 to 2000 (yearly growth rate of 8 per cent), while the R&D spending only increased by about 25 per cent.[276]

---

270. LAMPING, 85 f., 96 f. and 101 ff. with further references.
271. LEVIN ET AL., Brookings Papers on Economic Activity, 783 ff.; concerning the paradoxes the patent system is built on: JEWKES/SAWERS/STILLERMAN, 188.
272. For various arguments as to why patents do not solely foster innovation: MACHLUP, GRUR Int. 1961, 378 f.; more recently: BOLDRIN/LEVINE, Journal of Economic Perspectives 2013, 18 ff.; with respect to the problem of free riders, *see*: PRETNAR, GRUR Int. 2004, 780 ff.
273. *See infra* at para. 99.
274. The WIPO (World Intellectual Property Organization) collects data on patent applications and registrations from its members on a yearly basis and refers to its statistics as covering worldwide data. However, worldwide in this sense only means data from countries that are members of the PCT treaty, the Madrid System (Madrid System for the International Registration of Marks, legal basis: Madrid Agreement Concerning the International Registration of Marks of 1891) or the Hague System (Hague System for the International Registration of Industrial Design, legal basis: Hague Agreement Concerning the International Deposit of Industrial Design of 1925). www.wipo.int/ipstats/en/, accessed on 7 February 2020. *See also*: HARHOFF DIETMAR ET AL., accessed on 14 February 2020; a rise in patent applications has also been verified by HALL in US data from 1980 to 1989. HALL, Journal of Technology Transfer, 37 ff.
275. BLIND ET AL., Research Policy, 655.
276. BLIND ET AL., 2003, 1.

98 Explanations for this range from more efficient R&D processes[277] and booming key industries[278] to the so-called friendly court hypothesis[279] and the assumption that the rise in patent applications is connected to the growing importance of using patents strategically. In other words, it is due to a change or shift in the motives to apply for a patent.[280] Taken separately, none of these explanations can fully illuminate the surge in patenting. With the above-mentioned friendly court hypothesis[281] or the rise of new sectors relying heavily on patenting, such as the biotechnology industry, different positive explanations for the surge in patenting exist. Yet, the disproportional surge in patenting has been taken as proof of inefficiencies of patents to spur innovation.[282]

99 The influence of patents on the market has long been the object of heated discourse. Since the nineteenth century, the existence of the patent system itself has no longer been questioned.[283] The debate has continued based on finding separate, sector-specific patent designs.[284] It is commonly accepted and reflected in legislation[285] that patents have neither the same significance in[286] nor the same impact on every industry.[287] It has therefore been argued that the patent system should be adapted to the needs of specific sectors.[288] Today this demand is reflected in the supplementary protection certificate available for pharmaceutical patents.

100 The relationship with intellectual property rights and the other fields of competition law has occupied scholars since the first competition law regulations and

277. HALL/ZIEDONIS, RAND Journal of Economics, 122; KORTUM/LERNER, Research Policy 1999, 21.
278. The surge in patenting is explained by the rise of new sectors such as the computer, technology and biotechnology industry. HILTY/GEIGER, IIC 2005, 636 ff.; critical results are shown by KORTUM/LERNER: KORTUM/LERNER, Research Policy 1999, 14 ff.
279. The friendly court hypothesis suggests that more patent-friendly legal environments such as supportive precedents provide an incentive to apply for patents as one expects a greater remedy. In the US, the biggest change in the patent system took place in 1982 when with the Court of Appeals for the Federal Circuit (Fed. Cir.) a specialised court for patent litigation cases was formed. Also changes in the scope of patent law are suspected to have had an impact on patenting. *See* the so-called Texas Instrument effect as well as the reactions to the *Polaroid* decision of the US District Court of Massachusetts in 1976: DISS. MASS., *Polaroid Corp. v. Eastman Kodak Co.*, 641 F. Supp. 828, 108 ff.; COHEN/NELSON/WALSH, NBER Working Paper Series, 27 ff.
280. HARHOFF DIETMAR ET AL., accessed on 14 February 2020; HALL/ZIEDONIS, RAND Journal of Economics, 122 ff.; HILTY/GEIGER, IIC 2005, 638; BLIND ET AL., Research Policy, 655 ff.
281. *See supra* at fn. 279.
282. THUMM, in: HERREN/MÜNCH/WEINMANN, Schweizer IP-Handbuch, § 2, para. 33.
283. MACHLUP, GRUR Int. 1961, 375.
284. This was requested by JEWKES/SAWERS/STILLERMAN, who concluded that, despite their imperfections, patents are still the best alternatives to protect innovation, but scholars should concentrate on finding a more accurate design for the system. JEWKES/SAWERS/STILLERMAN, 188 ff.
285. *See* Article 53 EPC on the exceptions to patentability.
286. *See*, for example, the results of several studies on the relevance of patents for undertakings in different industries. COHEN/NELSON/WALSH, NBER Working Paper Series, 16 ff.; MANSFIELD, Management Science 1986, 175; EC, *Sector Inquiry, Final Report*, para. 253.
287. Economic research has revealed patents to be rather inefficient in certain circumstances at guaranteeing an appropriate return on investment for many products as well as processes. HALL/ZNTIEDONIS named this the patent paradox. HALL/ZIEDONIS, RAND Journal of Economics, 102.
288. *See supra* at fn. 268.

intellectual property laws emerged. The reason for this is the nature of property rights which is to curtail the scope of action of others with respect to specifically assigned assets. As the source of conflict is rooted in the nature of both property rights and the process of competition, ever since the enactment of the first competition law regulation, the dispute has been an inherent part of legal practice. Over the process of legal discourse, the influence of each legal field has changed alternately.[289]

2 The Relationship Between Patent and Competition Law

101 Since the core of ownership is governing the rights of disposal immanent in each property right, strong property rights can convey a position of supremacy for the proprietor. If this position results in monopolies, it endangers competition. Competition law protects the process of competition, and among the means of competition, the law to secure competition controls monopolies. Property rights thus strike a delicate balance. On the one hand, they must not be strong enough so that resulting monopolies do not limit competitive activities too much. On the other hand, they have to provide strong enough protection to encourage competition.

102 In the context of patent law, the supremacy immanent in the rights of disposal has been interpreted differently over time, leading to a handful of principles that have influenced the complex relationship between monopoly-phobic competition and power-conveying intellectual property law. These different principles will be outlined in this section. The first area of focus will be the development in the USA. The birth of competition enforcement is seen in the enactment of the US Sherman Act in 1890.[290] The second subsection focuses on the development in the EU. The subsections are structured chronologically.

2.1 Development of the Underlying Principles Based on the Example of the USA

a Conflict Thesis

103 In the early days of antitrust enforcement, intellectual property rights and the linked privileges were recognised as exceptions to the general principles of a free market and were beyond the scope of antitrust law. The then widespread conflict thesis[291] understood intellectual property rights and antitrust law as two diametrically

289. FRÜH compares the shift in power to a rocking pendulum. FRÜH, 5.
290. Note that the Canadian parliament in 1889 passed the first competition law statute in the Western world. The Canadian Act for the Prevention and Suppression of Combinations formed in restraint of Trade of 1889 therefore predates the US Sherman Act of 1890. The Canadian legislation had several deficiencies, however. Among the most noteworthy are limitations with respect to enforcement possibilities. *See*, for example, HALLADAY, Canadian Competition Law Review 2012, 157 ff.; ROSS, Review of Industrial Organization 1998, 3 ff.
291. The wording originates from the German doctrine where it is known as *Konfliktthese*.

conflicting antagonists. While intellectual property rights can on the one hand establish a legal monopoly,[292] the goal of competition law is to protect the process of competition by fighting actual monopolies.[293] Right holders could execute the property right almost without limitation.[294] In 1902, the US Supreme Court in the case of *E. Bement & Sons v. National Harrow Co.* protected a distorting price-fixing agreement with the argument that rights obtained under patent law could generally be used or sold without restriction. Antitrust scrutiny in this case would - following the court - violate the principle of freedom of contract that belongs to every intellectual property holder.[295]

104 The conflict thesis was widely criticised for its strict view of understanding right holders as monopolists per se. This static view fails to recognise the innovation-enhancing effect of intellectual property right regimes. Thus, in the USA in the early twenties, the pendulum swung towards a less strict understanding of the boundaries of the two fields of law. Ten years after *Bement & Sons*, the Supreme Court in 1912 in its famous *Bathtub Decision* denied the antitrust immunity of intellectual property laws and declared that conduct involving intellectual property rights was subject to scrutiny under the Sherman Act.[296] The US Supreme Court decisions of 1912 and 1917 meant that noticeable tensions arose, as the frontiers between the two bodies of law had yet to be defined.[297]

b Compatibility (Harmony) Thesis

105 As a result of the tensions, proposals and ideas for new principles to resolve the conflict between antitrust and intellectual property laws flourished.[298] The starting point for doctrine and jurisprudence was the deadlocked view remaining from the conflict thesis which, on the one hand, saw intellectual property rights as monopoly positions[299] and, on the other hand, the ideal of perfect competition as a regulatory purpose. To combine the legally guaranteed monopolies with the monopoly-hostile antitrust rules, courts turned to the essence of the intellectual property right and adopted a long-term focus. This development led to the birth of a new understanding

292. Legal or statutory monopolies are undertakings which move independently owing to the privileges conceded by law.
293. FUCHS/MÖSCHEL, in: IMMENGA/MESTMÄCKER 2018, Article 102, paras 1 ff.; ULLRICH, in: IMMENGA/MESTMÄCKER, Gewerblicher Rechtsschutz und Urheberrecht im Binnenmarkt, 2018, para. 2.
294. TOM/NEWBERG, Antitrust Journal 1997, 168 ff.
295. UNITED STATES SUPREME COURT, *Bement v. National Harrow Co.*, 186 US 70, 91.
296. UNITED STATES SUPREME COURT, *Standard Sanitary Mfg. Co. v. USA*, 226 US 20, 49. The renunciation of the *Bement* judgment was later confirmed in 1917. *See*: UNITED STATES SUPREME COURT, *Motion Pictures Patents Co. v. Universal Film Mfg. Co.*, 243 US 502, 502 ff.
297. *See i.a.*: HEINEMANN, Immaterialgüterschutz in der Wettbewerbsordnung, 42 ff.; TOM/NEWBERG, Antitrust Journal 1997, 173.
298. TOM/NEWBERG, Antitrust Journal 1997, 170 ff. Note that there are scholars who connect the renunciation of the 'immunity doctrine' with the development of the Rule of Reason. *See*: BODEWIG, GRUR Int. 1997, 958.
299. *See i.a.*: UNITED STATES SUPREME COURT, *Motion Pictures Patents Co. v. Universal Film Mfg. Co.*, 243 US 502, 516; UNITED STATES SUPREME COURT, *Crown Die & Tool v. Nye Tool*, 261 US 24, 37.

of intellectual property rights. As intellectual property rights are granted in order to spur innovation and development, at their core they share the same goal with antitrust law and are thus compatible (*compatibility thesis*). Still stuck in the tradition of a strictly formalistic approach, two spheres were distinguished and a priority rule proclaimed. Within the scope of the law, intellectual property rights were seen as legally approved monopolies. The holder operating within the scope of the intellectual property law did not have to fear antitrust scrutiny.[300] Conduct that was not covered by the scope of intellectual property law was open to the scope of antitrust scrutiny. Such conduct was automatically seen as an abuse of antitrust regulation and repressive measures were the general consequence.[301] Crucial to the approach, widely known as *inherency doctrine* (in German 'Inhaltstheorie'), was defining which conduct crossed the line determined by the intellectual property law.

106 In the meantime, the importance of antitrust law rose, and practice became less favourable towards intellectual property laws.[302] The newly adopted tone was visible with respect to licensing agreements. Only restraints necessary for the exploitation of the property right that could not be replaced with competition-enhancing restraints were considered lawful (so-called necessary and ancillary restraints). As a result of the still formalistic approach, the new environment, which was friendly towards antitrust scrutiny, led to the declaration of the 'Nine No No's'.[303] In 1970, a speech of the Antitrust Division of the US Department of Justice (DOJ) introduced a catalogue containing nine licensing clauses previously recognised as antitrust violations.[304]

107 The catalogue, however, never found its way into court practice. The fixed idea of intellectual property and antitrust law having diametrically opposed goals that cannot be harmonised other than by assigning each to its reserved sphere was becoming more and more subject to critique. The main reason was that the strongly formalistic approach did not consider the factual circumstances of the behaviour in question. With a clear distinction between intellectual property-protected, legitimate and intellectual property extrinsic, generally antitrust-violating conduct failed to recognise certain competition-threatening conduct. intellectual property rights undeniably provided their holder with a beneficial position that could endanger competition. The rules of

300. The US Supreme Court expressed this view in 1940 as follows: 'The patent law confers a limited monopoly.' United States Supreme Court, *Ethyl Gasoline Corp. v. United States*, 309 US 436, 456.
301. Critical: Heinemann, Immaterialgüterschutz in der Wettbewerbsordnung, 46; Ullrich, GRUR Int. 1996, 557. One of the most famous cases where the court strictly followed the inherency doctrine was *International Salt Company v. United States of America*. Monopoly power in the said case was, according to the court, limited to the machine and not also the product (salt). United States Supreme Court, *International Salt Co. v. USA*, 332 US 392, 395 ff.
302. Bodewig, GRUR Int. 1997, 958.
303. *See* the descriptions of this development in: Kleissl, 61 f.; Ullrich, GRUR Int. 1996, 557.
304. Wilson, Patent and Know-How License Agreements: Field of Use, Territorial, Price and Quantity Restrictions, Address Before the Fourth New England Antitrust Conference, 6 November 1970, cit. after: Hovenkamp, Alabama Law Review 2008-2009, 114, fn. 50. Even though it remained unclear whether the Nine No-No's were violations per se of antitrust law, all nine types of conduct had been held as abusive in previous court rulings. *See*: Tom/Newberg, Antitrust Journal 1997, 179 ff.

antitrust law therefore needed to apply to intellectual property rights as well. The assumption of complete harmony through the two spheres fails to satisfy the needs of competition policy.[305]

c Complementary Thesis

108 In the 1970s, a number of scholars with an economic background therefore started to challenge the common standards. In 1973, BOWMAN published the first noticeable work that explicitly challenged the assumed conflict of interest between the two bodies of law.[306] By mixing the strength of the two theories of compatible goals and conflicting means, BOWMAN managed to present the most convincing approach. He understood that both fields compatibly aimed at increasing welfare through promoting innovation and competition. BOWMAN concluded that the optimal pursuit of the same goal required the collaboration of both fields of law.[307] Following BOWMAN, intellectual property and antitrust law were thus compatible. Intellectual property rights, on the one hand, assign property, which is a fundamental prerequisite for competition. Antitrust law, on the other hand, regulates the use of property rights in competition to ensure welfare increases.[308] Antitrust law is bound to secure that those short-term losses in efficiency caused by the granting of property rights are compensated in the long term through effective competition.[309] This new awareness had the consequence that the use of privileges granted with the intellectual property right could at the same time be held inadmissible under antitrust law.[310]

109 Since then, the complementarity of the two fields has been widely acknowledged. Nowadays, scholars[311] as well as legal practice[312] have gone so far as to declare the 'neutrality' of the two bodies of law.[313] The starting point of this acknowledgement was the publication of the 1995 Antitrust Guidelines for Licensing of Intellectual Property by the FTC. The idea of the Guidelines, though not legally binding, was to provide more legal certainty. The FTC, in the Guidelines, proclaimed three fundamental standards that are still relevant today. The FTC first declared that antitrust law should treat intellectual property rights as it would treat any other assets. Section 2.2. states: '[...]

305. *See*: KLEISSL, 50.
306. *See* hereinafter at fn. 307.
307. BOWMAN, 1 ff.; later also i.a. DREXL, GRUR Int. 2004, 720 f.; HEINEMANN, Immaterialgüterschutz in der Wettbewerbsordnung, 619 f.
308. LAMPING, 147.
309. SULLIVAN/GRIMES/SAGERS, § 12.1, 681; DREXL, GRUR Int. 2004, 721.
310. For example, the accumulation of patents to make market entry impossible or the refusal to license patents. HOVENKAMP, Federal Antitrust Policy, para. 7.11.
311. *See i.a.*: SULLIVAN/GRIMES/SAGERS, § 12.1; TOM/NEWBERG, Antitrust Journal 1997, 173 f.
312. *See*: FED. CIR., *Atari/Tengen v. Nintendo*, 975 F.2d 832.
313. A similar development in the EU has been pursued by the ECJ. *See*: ECJ, *Spain v. EU Council*, C-350/92, 1995, para. 21; ECJ, *Thetford v. Fiamma*, C-35/87, para. 16. Reservations against the immunity of intellectual property, however, did not result in a neutral understanding of the relationship between the two fields but was supportive for the development of the doctrine of separation between existence and exercise.

Nor does such market power impose on the intellectual property owner an obligation to license the use of that property to others. As in other antitrust contexts, however, market power [...] would be relevant to the ability of an intellectual property owner to harm competition through unreasonable conduct in connection with such property.' Second, it held that intellectual property rights do not automatically induce dominance. Third, it concluded that licensing is generally pro-competitive.[314]

2.2 *Development in the EU*

a Existence and Exercise

110 In the EU, the legal doctrine of 'separation between existence and exercise' has been predominant for a long time.[315] This theory has been used to limit the application of community law to the property regimes of the Member States. Since the founding of the EU, the level of national sovereignty has been constantly debated. From the beginning, the EU Member States were hesitant to assign power to the Union. Limiting the influence of the EU legislator was fundamental to getting the states committed to the Union and therefore crucial for building a community in the first place. This was the reason for the introduction of Article 345 TFEU which will be introduced later.[316]

111 The doctrine states that the existence of an intellectual property right cannot be challenged with competition law. Apart from the existence, however, the exercise of the right is subject to competition law scrutiny. Any exercise of an intellectual property right thus has to be compatible with competition law. Union law cannot be used to proceed against an intellectual property right itself, but it can undermine the execution of the right. Since the decisions of the Court of Justice in *Consten/Grundig*[317] and *Parke Davis*[318], the theory of the separation between existence and exercise has also been used as the basis for the application of competition law on the exercise of intellectual property rights.[319] The court decided that even though effects on the market might exist, the use of the trademark in competition could not be subject to the scrutiny of

314. US DEPARTMENT OF JUSTICE/FEDERAL TRADE COMMISSION, *Antitrust Guidelines for the Licensing of Intellectual Property*, section 2.0.
315. For a brief explanation, *see*: FRÜH, 9 f.
316. *See infra* at paras 640 f.
317. In this case, the court had to analyse exclusive distributorship. ECJ, *Consten/Grundig*, Joined Cases C-56/64 and 58/64, 306.
318. ECJ, *Parke, Davis and Co. v. Probel and Others*, C-24/67, 71 f.
319. The doctrine was used not only to evaluate the relationship between intellectual property law and Article 102 TFEU but also with regard to Article 101 TFEU and the free movement of goods. *See i.a.*: ECJ, *Parke, Davis and Co. v. Probel and Others*, C-24/67; ECJ, *Deutsche Grammophon v. Metro*, C-78/70, paras 7 ff. In the context of the Union's fundamental freedoms, the distinction did not function as a pattern to exclude the specific exercise of intellectual property rights from the scrutiny of competition law, but to narrow the foreclosing effect of intellectual property rights. ULLRICH, in: IMMENGA/MESTMÄCKER 2018, Gewerblicher Rechtsschutz und Urheberrecht im Binnenmarkt, para. 51.

competition law. Only contracts concerning the use of a trademark can violate the Union's competition law.[320]

112 These arguments and the court decisions were widely criticised,[321] and in the 1990s the courts started to abandon the practice.[322] The main reason for the criticism was that a separation between existence and exercise fails to recognise the essence of property rights. When asked about the core of the patent right, economists usually cite the protection from imitation;[323] lawyers more generally mention the right to forbearance.[324] HEINEMANN concludes: 'the existence of a [intellectual property] right includes the sum of all executive powers'.[325] A consequence of this is that the bundle of privileges obtained through a patent is considered to be the core of the patent right. Following the critics, a clear separation between the existence and exercise of a property right is almost impossible. Many scholars have therefore held the doctrine incapable of offering a suitable instrument to determine the application range of EU competition law.[326] Even though continual criticism led to the factual abolishment of the doctrine,[327] the courts have not explicitly abandoned it so far,[328] although the practice is nevertheless widely recognised as outdated and factually abandoned in the context of intellectual property rights.

b *The Specific Subject Matter*

113 The principle of the specific subject matter is related to the separation between existence and exercise.[329] Some authors even use the terms synonymously in the context of competition law.[330] In terms of their conceptual background, both doctrines clearly follow the tradition of the inherency doctrine (formalistic, content-related

320. ECJ, *Consten/Grundig*, Joined Cases C-56/64 and 58/64, 345.
321. *See i.a.*: HEINEMANN, Immaterialgüterschutz in der Wettbewerbsordnung, 196 ff.; HARACOGLOU, 105.
322. Since 1990, no court decision has explicitly contained the doctrine as the basis for argumentation at least not in an IP case. The Commission explicitly declared the doctrine as inexistent in its *AstraZeneca* decision. Indeed, the result of the *AstraZeneca* case, namely, that the application for a supplementary certificate can be abusive, does not comply with the separation between existence and exercise. EC, *AstraZeneca*, COMP/A.37.507/F3, para. 741.
323. *See*: BUNDESRAT, *Bericht Parallelimporte und Patentrecht*, section 3.2., 12.
324. *See*: GODT, 552.
325. Translation by the author from: HEINEMANN, Immaterialgüterschutz in der Wettbewerbsordnung, 197.
326. This statement is supported by the fact that the ECJ has so far only once declared an exercise of intellectual property rights as belonging to the 'existence'. This was in 1988 in the judgment of *Erauw-Jacquery v. La Hesbignonne*. Additionally, the court declared the first placing of an IP-protected good on the market as belonging to the 'existence' sphere as well. ECJ, *Erauw-Jacquery v. La Hesbignonne*, C-27/87, para. 9.
327. The ECJ referenced the doctrine in 1990 for the last time: ECJ, *HAG II*, C-10/89, para. 16.
328. SACK, wrp 1999, 594.
329. ECJ, *Deutsche Grammophon v. Metro*, C-78/70, para. 11; ECJ, *HAG II*, C-10/89, para. 12.
330. GASTER, Computer und Recht 2005, 249.

approach[331]). Therefore, the specific subject matter is a further development of the separation doctrine rather than a doctrine which has superseded it.

114 The specific subject matter was introduced as a formalistic priority rule deduced from the separation between existence and exercise. It is understood as a bundle of privileges that comes with the intellectual property right.[332] These privileges represent the core of the right. As such, they cannot be subject to the scrutiny of competition law. An inherency doctrine-analogous understanding of the relationship between intellectual property and competition law thus remains the underlying concept. The approach, however, considers the critique addressed above that the existence of an intellectual property is hard to separate from the privileges it provides in the form of executive power. To overcome this hurdle, the specific subject matter defines certain executive powers as being immanent to the property right. Examples are the right to oppose patent infringements and the execution of the patent.[333]

115 A closer look at the court practice in the EU reveals that intellectual property rights are left untouched by competition law as long as they do not exceed the specific subject matter.[334] At the same time, the Court of Justice has not automatically assumed the anticompetitiveness of conduct that exceeds the specific subject matter, but rather applies a case-by-case analysis.[335] Contrary to the separation between existence and exercise, the doctrine was not used to form competition law-immune intellectual property law zones. Therefore, it has been concluded in the literature that the concept was used to justify the application of the Union's competition law on property rights rather than restrict them.[336] It is argued that the application of competition law has to be additionally justified by exceptional circumstances whenever conduct is considered to belong to the specific subject matter of the intellectual property right. For conduct outside the specific subject matter, extra justification is not required.[337] In *Volvo v. Veng*, the Court of Justice argued that defending one's right can amount to an abuse of the dominant position, even if only the substance of the right is at stake.[338]

116 In addition, the principle of the specific subject matter does not fully overcome the issues of formalistic approaches and the artificial separation element. Unsurprisingly, the specific subject matter is thus frequently criticised and is not seen as a useful

331. *See supra* at fn. 225.
332. Definition according to: HEINEMANN, Immaterialgüterschutz in der Wettbewerbsordnung, 303.
333. ECJ, *Allen & Hanburys v. Generics*, C-434/85, para. 11.
334. EILMANSBERGER earlier identified the function of intellectual property rights as an independent factor for determining whether the conduct falls within the scope of competition law. EILMANSBERGER, EuZW 1992, 633. HARACOGLOU even goes as far as to understand the specific subject matter as an attempt to harmonise the two fields of law. HARACOGLOU, 104.
335. ECJ, *Windsurfing International v. Commission*, C-193/83, para. 72.
336. HEINEMANN, MR-Int. 2014, 6, with reference to the analysis in: HEINEMANN, Immaterialgüterschutz in der Wettbewerbsordnung, 305 ff.; dissenting: GASTER, Computer und Recht 2005, 249.
337. *See* the analysis in: EBENROTH/BOHNE, EWS 1995, 401 ff.
338. ECJ, *Volvo v. Veng*, C-238/87, paras 8 ff.; ECJ, *CICRA v. Renault*, C-53/87, paras 15 ff.

evaluation tool in competition law cases.[339] In practice, the importance of assigning conduct to the specific subject matter of the intellectual property right seems to have faded. In 1981, the Commission declared that the registration of a trademark used by a competitor could qualify as an abuse of the dominant position. The Commission therewith opened the use of intellectual property rights to the scrutiny of competition law. In 1990, this view gained ground when the General Court in the *Tetra Pak I* case overruled the Court of Justice practice dating from the *CICRA v. Renault* case according to which the mere 'securing [of] benefits of an exclusive right granted by law'[340] cannot qualify as an abuse of dominance.[341] For the first time, the court examined the compatibility of a secondary patent acquisition with Article 102 TFEU.[342] Later, in its *AstraZeneca* decision, the Commission more generally held that the use of public procedures leading to the acquisition of a patent is open to competition law.[343]

c The Modern Approach

117 Constant criticism of the formalistic approach in the tradition of the inherency doctrines led the courts and the Commission to adopt a more economic view gradually including the circumstances of the case in the decision finding.[344] The Commission's *AstraZeneca* decision can be interpreted not only as following the tradition of a wide application of competition law on intellectual property rights but also as a departure from the specific subject matter.[345] According to the argumentation, 'conduct ha[ving] anti-competitive objects and effects may give rise to liability under competition law', irrespective of whether other laws provide remedies as well.[346] This statement not only allows for the simultaneous sanctioning of conduct under competition law as well as intellectual property law[347] but also conveys the idea that the Commission applies the rules of competition law to all situations where the conduct of private parties leads to a restriction of competition, irrespective of whether intellectual property rights are

339. EBENROTH/BOHNE, EWS 1995, 400 f. Note that the principle is primarily held impracticable in competition law cases, but not necessarily with regard to the free movement of goods. HEINEMANN, Immaterialgüterschutz in der Wettbewerbsordnung, 322; KÄLLER, 272.
340. ECJ, *CICRA v. Renault*, C-53/87, para. 15.
341. GC, *Tetra Pak I*, T-51/89, para. 23; JUNG, in: GRABITZ ET AL., EUV/AEUV, Article 102, para. 228 with reference to: MESTMÄCKER, in: SCHMIDT/SCHWARK, FS Raisch, Zum Begriff des Missbrauchs in Article 86 des Vertrages über die Europäische Gemeinschaft, 448.
342. *See* for details, *infra* at paras 407 ff.
343. EC, *AstraZeneca*, COMP/A.37.507/F3, paras 741 ff.; GC, *ITT Promedia v. Commission*, T-111/96, para. 139.
344. DE BRONETT, EWS 2013, 2 f.
345. The specific subject matter is still present in EU practice and is heavily criticised by HEINEMANN: HEINEMANN, MR-Int. 2014, 6.
346. EC, *AstraZeneca*, COMP/A.37.507/F3, paras 74 ff.; supportive of equal treatment of intellectual property and other forms of property: HARACOGLOU, 113 ff. For Switzerland: HILTY, in: BSK KG, Article 3 Abs. 2, para. 25.
347. In Germany confirmed by the BGH in the decision *Standard-Spundfass*: BGH, *Standard-Spundfass*, KZR 40/02, paras 26 ff.

involved.[348] The literature understands this development as a departure from the formalistic approach in favour of an approach considering the specific circumstances.[349]

118 The fundamental idea put forward in the literature is the realisation that short-term losses in efficiency have to be outweighed by long-term efficiency gains to justify intellectual property rights. To grant a positive outcome on the overall assessment, it is thus advisable to apply competition law to intellectual property rights irrespective of whether the core of the right is affected.[350] This is convincing, as it is the task of competition law to protect competition. Innovation and property rights in general are no exception.[351] The modern approaches suggest that there is no specific subject matter untouchable by competition law.[352] According to modern understandings, it is important that both fields of law can perform their functions.[353] In practice, the peculiarities of specific property rights thus have to be considered.

119 Similarly to the development in the USA, the practice in the EU seems to have arrived at the stage of accepting the scrutiny of competition law on intellectual property rights in any case where the property rights are instrumentalised in an anticompetitive manner.[354] Therefore, the core of intellectual property rights can be used in an anticompetitive manner.[355]

120 Competition law and intellectual property laws are nowadays seen as external barriers to one another.[356] While competition law should be allowed to intervene whenever the privileges granted through intellectual property laws result in an unintended restriction on competition, competition law cannot apply in situations where the restriction to competition is covered by the aim of the intellectual property right in question.[357] Therefore, in order to apply competition law on conduct involving

348. With the same result also: HEINEMANN, Immaterialgüterschutz in der Wettbewerbsordnung, 461; KÄLLER, 150 ff.; dissenting: FAULL/NIKPAY, para. 10.228.
349. HEINEMANN, Immaterialgüterschutz in der Wettbewerbsordnung, 319 ff.
350. MERDZO, ZEuS 2005, 146.
351. SEDEF, in: WIEBE, Wettbewerbs- und Immaterialgüterrecht, 523 ff.; ULLRICH, GRUR Int. 1996, 556.
352. KÄLLER, 152 ff.
353. The ECJ has frequently stressed the function of property in society and thus applied a functional understanding when confronted with restrictions of the right. *See i.a.:* ECJ, *Schräder v. Hauptzollamt Gronau*, C-265/87, para. 15; ECJ, *Germany v. Council*, C-280/93, para. 78; ECJ, *Kadi and Al Barakaat International Foundation v. Council and Commission*, Joined Cases C-402/05 P and C-415/05 P, para. 355; this case was recently referred to by AG WAHL in: AG WAHL, *in: Kotnik and Others*, C-526/14, para. 87.
354. LAMPING, 148 ff.; MERDZO, ZEuS 2005, 173. *See also* GOVAERE who in 1996 argued in favour of a neutral understanding of intellectual property rights in competition law cases: GOVAERE, para. 10.12.
355. HEINEMANN, GRUR 2006, 706.
356. Note that intellectual property rights may not be able to perform their function in the absence of competition law scrutiny. *See*: HILTY, in: BSK KG, Article 3 Abs. 2, para. 23.
357. Similarly: HEINEMANN, in: HEIZMANN/LOACKER, UWG Kommentar, Lauterkeitsrecht und Immaterialgüterrecht, paras 9 and 16. There is therefore little point in applying the 'Swiss view' according to which certain effects of intellectual property rights are excluded from the scrutiny of competition law from the outset. *See infra* at fn. 1772.

intellectual property rights, a functional approach is required.[358] This requirement cannot be satisfied with a rigid formalistic distinction, but rather demands a comprehensive case-by-case analysis.[359]

3 Restriction of Property Rights for the Goals of the Union

121 It becomes clear from the above that holders of intellectual property rights have to accept constraints to their rights in order to counter threats to the essential purpose of the Union as laid down in the EU treaties. Conflicts in this context usually occur in connection with provisions securing the free movement of goods (Articles 34-36 TFEU), cartels and restrictive agreements (Article 101 TFEU) or the abuse of a dominant position (Article 102 TFEU).

122 intellectual property rights only exist within the scope intended by the legislator in the relevant jurisdiction. Their territorial limitation therefore conditions the limitation of intellectual property rights in both their existence and the privileges they convey. The fact that intellectual property rights and the inherent privileges end at jurisdictional borders results in a situation where, for the same asset, mutual intellectual property rights in different Member States might exist, where they can only be violated or invoked in the specific jurisdiction. For the Union's internal market, this endangers the free movement of goods.[360] It leads to the question of whether the holder of an intellectual property right in Member State A can invoke their sole right of distribution against imports to Member State A from Member State B or whether this right is exhausted after the launch of the product in Member State B.

123 In the case of *Deutsche Grammaphon v. Metro*, the question was first raised and concerned copyrights. The Deutsche Grammophon Gesellschaft sold records in the EU either directly or via subsidiaries. In Germany, the Deutsche Grammophon Gesellschaft fixed resale prices at 19 DM. In other Member States, for example, in France, the records were sold at a lower price. It was therefore possible for Metro, which refused to sign a price-fixing agreement with Deutsche Grammophon Gesellschaft to buy reimported records from France and sell them at a lower price in Germany. Before German courts, Deutsche Grammophon invoked its sole right of distribution and obtained an injunction, which prohibited Metro from selling the records in Germany.[361] German law therefore allowed Deutsche Grammophon to rely upon the copyright for the sole purpose of preventing the distribution of products which were launched with

358. A functional understanding led to the formulation of the essential facility doctrine. HEINEMANN, Immaterialgüterschutz in der Wettbewerbsordnung, 507 ff. Similarly: KEMPEL, fn. 48. In Switzerland: HILTY, in: BSK KG, Article 3 Abs. 2, para. 22.
359. With respect to Switzerland, but nevertheless of general validity: HILTY, in: BSK KG, Article 3 Abs. 2, para. 30.
360. *See the argument in*: ECJ, *Sirena v. Eda*, C-40/70, para. 7.
361. ECJ, *Deutsche Grammophon v. Metro*, C-78/70, 489 f.

its own consent in France and Germany. In the eyes of the Court of Justice, however, in allowing this invocation, German law would authorise isolating national markets. The verdict of the German court therefore contradicted the provisions imposing the free movement of goods.[362]

124 The Court of Justice with this decision defined the principle of EU-wide exhaustion (regional exhaustion) for copyrights. Once a product protected by a copyright was sold with the consent of or by the right holder in a Member State, this product could be resold within the EU without the possibility for the right holder to block the sale by invoking their copyright. Consequently, the privileges immanent in the copyright were limited to where they contradicted the purpose of the Union. Since the decision in *Deutsche Grammaphon v. Metro*, the principle of regional exhaustion for copyrights has been included in Article 4(2) of both Directive 2001/29/EC and Directive 2009/24/EC.[363]

125 For patent law, the principle of exhaustion has not found its way into a Directive. The Court of Justice is clear in its decisions, however. In the 1974 case of *Centrafarm*, the Court of Justice argued that patented holders could not invoke their sole right to use an invention against imports of products from Member States where they have been launched by them or with their consent. A different conclusion would provide the patent holder with the power to separate markets and therewith restrict trade between Member States.[364] With the establishment of the European Economic Area (EEA) in 1992 and Article 2 of Protocol 28 of the EEA Agreement, the region was expanded for all intellectual property rights for which the courts have applied regional EU-wide exhaustion. Also, in the case of patents, exhaustion has since applied whenever a product was wilfully launched by the patent holder in a Member State of the EEA.

126 From the principle of exhaustion in connection with the free movement of goods, we learn that the holder of an intellectual property right has to accept limitations to rights and privileges where invoking them would lead to results contrary to the goals of the EU. Over the years, intellectual property rights have been involved in several cases concerning potential abuse of a dominant position, prohibited agreements or concerted practices. The relevant case law for this book will be the subject of deeper analysis in Part IV. At this stage of the analysis, the awareness that intellectual property rights have since been restricted when contradicting the goals of the Union or being

362. ECJ, *Deutsche Grammophon v. Metro*, C-78/70, paras 11 ff.
363. The ECJ recently in a preliminary ruling decided that the principle of exhaustion based on Directive 2001/29/EC (Information Society Directive) does not apply when digital copies of books (e-books) were distributed. *See*: ECJ, *Nederlands Uitgeversverbond and Groep Algemene Uitgevers*, C-263/18, paras 43 ff. Different was the decision concerning used software based on Directive 2009/24/EC (Computer Programs Directive). The legislator in the Computer Programs Directive, according to the ECJ, wanted to treat physical and digital copies equally. ECJ, *UsedSoft v. Oracle*, C-128/11, paras 58 ff.
364. ECJ, *Centrafarm*, C-15/74, paras 9 ff.; confirmed in: ECJ, *Merck v. Stephar*, C-187/80, para. 14.

involved in a practice distorting competition as sanctioned in Articles 101 and 102 TFEU will suffice.

III IMPLICATIONS

127 It can be seen that competition, unfair competition and intellectual property law have not developed simultaneously. Still, competition law in the narrow sense (also called antitrust law) and unfair competition law traditionally form a union referred to as competition law. Both prevent market failure, which would arise in the absence of regulation. intellectual property laws contribute to the functioning of competition by allowing an optimal allocation of resources.[365] All disciplines of competition law in a jurisdiction share the same reference system and thus strive for the same desired form of competition.[366]

128 In both examined jurisdictions, the first attempt to regulate the relationship between intellectual property law and competition law was characterised by a formal demarcation between the two fields but then shifted to describe the relationship as 'neutral' or 'compatible'. Both terms stand for an approach referred to as functional understanding of the fields of law, which has already been described as 'divergent convergence'.[367] In order to ensure that the fields of law can perform their function, each has to be applied cautiously with respect to the peculiarities of the other. Intellectual property rights, which are granted in order to allow competition with otherwise public goods, can only be justified as long as the functioning of competition is ensured.[368] A compartmentalised understanding of intellectual property and competition law does not contribute to their mutual goal.[369] Regarding blocking patents, this means that not only does the use of the exclusionary right granted with the property fall under the scope of competition law but also the acquisition of the right itself might contradict the goal of maintaining and protecting a system of undistorted competition.[370] An abuse of a dominant position is conceivable in cases where the acquisition of an intellectual property right raises high market entry barriers and therefore leads to a compartmentalisation or division of the market without predominant beneficial effects in the end.[371] Furthermore, since the abuse of a dominant position is aimed at protecting competitors from exclusionary and exploitative conducts,[372] an abuse of a

365. *See supra* at paras 86 f.
366. HILTY, in: HILTY/HENNING-BODEWIG, Law against unfair competition, 3.
367. HEINEMANN, MR-Int. 2014, 10.
368. LEMLEY, Texas Law Review 1057.
369. SCHMIDT understands competition law as 'second tier regulator of the IP rights' to reach more socio-economic goals: SCHMIDT, World Competition 2019, 454.
370. JUNG, in: GRABITZ ET AL., EUV/AEUV, Article 102, para. 229.
371. *See*: GC, *Tetra Pak I*, T-51/89, paras 23 ff.; BELLAMY/CHILD, para. 9-064. That the execution of a patent right is not protected where it leads to the compartmentalisation of the market has already been decided in *Hoffmann-La Roche*: ECJ, *Hoffmann-La Roche v. Commission*, C-85/76, paras 100 ff.; with respect to blocking patents: JUNG, in: GRABITZ ET AL., EUV/AEUV, Article 102, para. 231.
372. *See supra* at para. 75 as well as *infra* at paras 429 ff.

dominant position is also possible in cases where the acquisition of an intellectual property right is used to either exclude competitors to an unwarranted degree or implement exploitative conditions in licensing contracts.[373]

373. For an overview, *see*: HILTY/FRÜH, 157 ff.

CHAPTER 5

Introduction to Competition in the Pharmaceutical Market

I INTRODUCTION

129 When analysing competition, one always has to understand the peculiarities of a specific sector. This chapter therefore provides an introduction to the competitive environment in the pharmaceutical sector, which will be at the centre of this analysis.

130 Owing to the density of regulation,[374] it has been doubted whether competition in the pharmaceutical market in fact exists. However, the pharmaceutical market is also characterised by a process of innovation, adaption and selection whose results are not predictable. Market players in the pharmaceutical market, as in other markets, use different parameters to improve their situation in the market. In economics, the market is broadly defined as the place where supplier and demanders meet to exchange a certain product. The main market players on both the supply and the demand side and the relevant types of products (types of drugs) will be introduced in section II.

131 As certain parameters such as prices to varying degrees are regulated, others such as product innovation, product development (reduction of side effects, increased efficiency, etc.) and product diffusion (e.g., marketing[375]) become more important.[376] Success in R&D is thus fundamental to survival in the market. The R&D process forms the focus of section III.

---

374. Regulations in the pharmaceutical market consist of legal and administrative measures applied in order to secure quality and safety standards. For example, *see* the description of the regulated process of drug research, *supra* at Chapter 3, section III.
375. As direct marketing to consumers is forbidden in the EU (Directive 2001/83/EC), marketing activities concentrate on presentations to physicians, information in journals, and the founding of conferences. Most notably, budgets for marketing at both the global and European level exceed R&D expenses. *See*: EC, *Sector Inquiry, Final Report,* paras 73 ff.; RAASCH, 55 ff.
376. EMMERICH, in: HEIDUK/EMMERICH, Arzneimittelmarkt und europäisches Wettbewerbsrecht, 179.

132 Based on the insights gained from the R&D process, it becomes possible to understand the importance of patents within the pharmaceutical industry. Section IV presents an overview of the different pharmaceutical patents. Knowledge about patenting in the pharmaceutical market, then, allows potential reference points for patenting strategies to be worked out. Patenting strategies will be the focus of Part II.

II THE SITUATION IN THE MARKET

1 Supply Side

133 Two kinds of suppliers compete on the supply side of markets for pharmaceutical products: originators and generic companies.

134 Originator companies focus on research and strive to find NCEs as well as providing incremental improvements to already known substances or new indications, new routes of administration, etc. According to the Commission's sector inquiry, the majority of originators reported primarily striving to provide solutions for unmet medical needs. Traditionally, originators were characterised by a global presence and a vertically integrated structure. Originators conducted a wide range of activities in-house from fundamental research to marketing and life-cycle strategies. Mostly fuelled by the growing influence of bio-pharmacy, such as for example gene and cell therapy,[377] within the pharmaceutical sectors, small- and medium-sized Enterprise (SMEs) specialising in R&D for niche fields emerged in recent years.[378] These SMEs aimed at licensing or selling molecules to larger pharmaceutical companies, which then conducted all the necessary clinical trials and obtained marketing approval.[379]

135 Competition between originators occurs on two levels. Visible on the surface is the competition between two or more, to some degree, substitutable products, whereby substitutability concerns the use of a drug to meet a specific medical need. Relevant factors in this competition are the efficiency, mode of action, potential side effects, breadth of potential patient groups, and galenic forms.[380] Competition on price is of less relevance. Its importance is dependent on the national price regulation for pharmaceuticals.[381] Originators strive for pharmaceutical products with limited substitutability. They conduct research to find new or highly improved medication. To reach this goal, originators compete through innovation.[382] It is the race for innovation where the decision on who will lead the market is made.[383]

---

377. Gene and cell therapies are the current booms in the industry. *See*, for example, https://www.nature.com/articles/d41573-019-00154-0, accessed on 28 July 2020.
378. Cockburn, Innovation Policy and the Economy 2006, 26.
379. EC, *Sector Inquiry, Final Report,* para. 55.
380. Galenics concerns the different application forms of an active molecule such as with injections, pills, and ointments.
381. EC, *Sector Inquiry, Final Report,* para. 58.
382. EC, *Sector Inquiry, Final Report,* para. 59.
383. Dreher, ZWeR 2009, 152.

136 Generic companies, in contrast to originators, focus on producing mostly generic drugs rather than developing new molecules. Generic companies provide generic products,[384] that is, products with an equivalent dosage and delivery form to the originator product (bioequivalent[385]), after patent protection expires.[386] Generic companies also engage in the further development of original compounds with new dosage or galenic forms. Within these activities, generic companies engage in patenting as well. With lower R&D risks as well as reduced requirements to obtain market authorisation for generics and further develop medical products with known active substances (only reduced clinical tests required), generic companies are able to offer pharmaceuticals at a much lower price than originator companies.[387]

137 Competition between originator and generic companies therefore mainly focuses on the factor price. When generic companies engage in further development, originators and generic companies compete through innovation as well.[388] In the competition between originators and generic companies, blocking patents are used not just to hamper competition regarding innovation but also to delay generic entry.[389]

2 Demand Side

138 On the demand side of the pharmaceutical sector, at least for prescription drugs, the consumer (patient), the decision-maker (physician) and the bearer of the costs (health insurance or social security system)[390] are three different players. The end consumers of pharmaceutical products are patients, but their consumption decision is greatly influenced if not pre-empted by the physician. When suffering from more complex conditions, patients do not have enough knowledge (information asymmetry) and, in the case of prescription drugs, the authorisation to make a consumption decision. The decision taken by physicians is also limited by their knowledge of treatment possibilities for the diagnosed disease. Physicians in general have a 'prescription repertoire' of a limited number of pharmaceutical drugs.[391] In gaining their

384. Generics and biosimilars are often mentioned in the same breath. Generics are chemically produced and contain the same active substance as the original drug. Biologically produced active substances cannot be copied by another generic company, however. Biosimilars are imitations of biologically produced original drugs with similarity in terms of activity, tolerability, safety and efficacy. On the difference between original, biosimilar and generic products, *see*: https://www.vfa.de/de/patienten/artikel-patienten/originale-generika-biosimilars.html, accessed on 9 February 2020.
385. On bioequivalence, *see infra* at fn. 395.
386. FISCHER/BREITENBACH, 37.
387. On generic companies, *see*: EC, *Sector Inquiry, Final Report,* paras 88 ff. and 99 ff.
388. For reference to the R&D activity of generic companies, *see*: FELDMANN, 257 f., especially fn. 178.
389. *See*: EC, *Servier,* AT.39612, para. 2770.
390. Additionally, with regulatory authorities which approve of drugs and also set the prices for certain drugs the state also interferes in competition on the drug market. *See supra* at para. 135.
391. *See*: RAASCH, 57 f. with further references.

information, physicians are to a great part dependent on the pharmaceutical companies.[392] There is therefore a risk of physicians being biased by pharmaceutical advertising efforts.

139 Patients, in most social security systems, contribute to social security either via taxes or insurance premiums irrespective of their demand for medical services and drugs. Although it is generally the physician who takes the consumer decision, especially for prescription drugs, systems with consumer incentives tend towards an exaggerated demand (moral hazard). Even if most systems know about individual cost-sharing models to cushion this effect, the situation is comparable to subsidised products, and results in welfare losses.[393]

140 The demand side in the drug market is further characterised by high product loyalty. This is accredited to the prescribing physicians and the patients alike. Patients naturally have reservations about the efficiency and potential side effects of different drugs. The importance of branding in pharmaceutical companies has even shown a habituation to brands and specifics of the drug such as its colour and form, etc.[394] Furthermore, physicians, who are primarily responsible for curing the patient, build trust in effective and well-tolerated drugs. Paired with insensitivity towards prices, it has been noted that physicians can be hesitant to prescribe generic products.[395]

3 Products (Types of Drugs)[396]

3.1 New Medical Entities

141 Certain originator drugs consist of new medical entities (NMEs).[397] NMEs are active substances which have not yet been approved within the specific jurisdiction.

---

392. RAASCH, 55 f.
393. DRABINSKI/ESCHWEILER/SCHMIDT, 8 ff.
394. *See* the remarks by RAASCH and FACKELMANN with respect to Viagra®: RAASCH, 40; FACKELMANN, 40.
395. GRABOWSKI/VERNON, The Journal of Law & Economics 1992, 332 f. This is also due to the fact that generic and original drugs are not identical but only bioequivalent. Bioequivalence means that there is no significant difference between the generic and the original drug with regard to the bioavailability (extent and rate to which an active ingredient reaches the systemic circulation). The acceptance interval is between 80 per cent and 125 per cent. *See*: EMA, Guidelines for the Investigation of Bioequivalence, 15; PERGER/FATTINGER, Schweiz Med Forum 2012, 237: https://www.deutschesapothekenportal.de/rezept-retax/dap-lexikon/bioaequivalenz/, accessed on 28 July 2020. Therefore, a switch to a generic drug is not generally supported by all patients, and physicians have to be cautious when prescribing generics depending on the therapy. *See*: PERGER/FATTINGER, Schweiz Med Forum 2012, 237 ff.
396. Note that the overview provided here focuses on variations of the API and thus leaves out reformulations, i.e., drugs with the same API but a different formulation and sometimes also different mode of administration. Anadin® Extra for example exists as soluble tablet and swallowable tablet with different formulations.
397. The Federal Drug Administration (FDA) distinguishes between NMEs as defined above and NCEs (new chemical entities). NMEs contain at least one new active substance, while with NCEs none of the substances used within the compound have previously been approved. *See* section 505(b) of the Federal Food, Drug and Cosmetic Act.

3.2 *Me-too Drugs*

142 Follow-on or me-too drugs are active substances with slightly different chemical structures from the first drugs and only small differences with regard to their pharmacokinetics.[398] Me-too drugs are therefore used for the same indications.

143 Me-too drugs are small-scale innovations which are responsible for most technological advances.[399] Me-too drugs as substitutes foster competition and provide a wider choice of products for patients and physicians (e.g., different tolerances).[400] They can also show new indications, as, for example, the antidepressant imipramine does. Imipramine has since the nineteenth century been used in chemistry, first within the dyeing industry and then as an antihistamine. Chlorpromazine, a compound structurally related to imipramine, was the first antipsychotic of the class. When testing imipramine for its antipsychotic activity, it surprisingly demonstrated anti-depressive effects.[401]

144 There are, however, also critical voices raised against me-too drugs. Arguments against me-too drugs include their use in life-cycle strategies (to keep the price high), their potential lack of patentability requirements due to the relatively low level of development risks and costs, and concerns that money is directed to the development of me-too drugs rather than 'actual inventions'.[402]

3.3 *Second-Generation Products*

145 Second-generation products are essentially based on the original products but are further developed. They have a similar pharmacodynamic (mode of action) and pharmacokinetics[403] to the existing products.[404] Second-generation products contain small changes in the chemical structure of the active substance. They may appear in new crystalline or saline forms, new formulations, new combinations or metabolites.[405] They may also provide enhanced compliance, efficiency, selectivity or facilitated administration.

398. CRISAND, 117 f.; WILD/PUIG, Gesundheitswesen 2004, 717 f. An example of me-too drugs is non-ionic X-ray contrast mediums.
399. WERTHEIMER/LEVY/O'CONNOR, in: FARQUHAR/SUMMERS/SORKIN, Investing in health, 78 f.
400. WERTHEIMER/LEVY/O'CONNOR, in: FARQUHAR/SUMMERS/SORKIN, Investing in health, 86 ff.
401. WERMUTH ET AL., 129.
402. WILD/PUIG, Gesundheitswesen 2004, 718.
403. For an explanation, *see infra* at fn. 453.
404. EC, *Sector Inquiry, Final Report,* para. 990.
405. *See infra* at paras 176 ff.

3.4 Generics

146 Generics are copies of known drugs (reference medicine). Generics therefore contain the same active substance, the same dosage, the same galenic form and are used to treat the same condition. As the form, colour and name of the original drugs might be protected by other laws or property rights, such as trademark laws, generics often have a different appearance from the reference medicine.[406] Generics might contain different inactive substances from the reference drugs, but these inactive ingredients do not change the efficiency of the generic drugs. A drug will only be approved as a generic drug when the applicant can 'demonstrate essentially the same rate and extent of biological availability of the active substance in the body when administered in the same dose',[407] that is, when it is bioequivalent.

III DRUG RESEARCH

1 Drug Research and Development

1.1 Costs and Duration

147 The drug development process is characterised by low success rates and high uncertainties.[408] Despite current advances in R&D, still only one in several thousand tested compounds receives market approval. On average, the development of a drug from discovery to approval by the European Medicines Agency (EMA) takes ten to twelve years.[409] Switzerland and the USA report broadly the same figures.[410]

148 The absolute costs for developing a new drug vary greatly and are hard to estimate. Calculations are based on different variables, for example, 'the estimated average length of development, the average size and cost of clinical trials and the probability of success that products will finally make it to market'.[411] The numbers in different studies about the cost of drug development, conducted between 2001 and 2011, show considerable variation[412] and recent studies provide greatly differing figures of between 0.648[413] and 1.8 billion[414] dollars. Currently, the results of a study

---

406. *See* the definition in: https://www.medicinesforeurope.com/generic-medicines/did-you-know/, accessed on 9 February 2020.
407. https://www.medicinesforeurope.com/generic-medicines/did-you-know/#section-4, accessed on 9 February 2020.
408. Petrova, in: Ding/Eliashberg/Stremersch, Innovation and marketing in the pharmaceutical industry, 24 f.; Fischer/Breitenbach, 41.
409. Fischer/Breitenbach, 42; *see also*: Grubb et al., para. 21.03; Raasch, 16.
410. Dickson/Gagnon, Discovery Medicine 2009; Interpharma, 60.
411. WHO, *Promoting access to medical technologies and innovation*, 108.
412. Morgan et al., Health Policy 2011, 7 and 9.
413. Prasad/Mailankody, JAMA Internal Medicine 2017, 1572 f.
414. DiMasi/Grabowski/Hansen, Journal of Health Economics 2016, 31.

by DiMasi et al. are frequently cited.[415] These authors suggest that the average out-of-pocket R&D costs[416] for the development of a drug including post-approval expenditure are around USD 1.8 billion.[417] The biggest part of development costs – approximately 45 per cent on average – is spent during the clinical trial phase.[418] Unsurprisingly, therefore, the tendency is for costs to differ depending on whether the drug consists of an NCE or a substance where a modification has been used before in a compound, such as in second-generation or me-too drugs. Yet, this also falls short as an explanation, as R&D costs for drugs containing NCEs also vary greatly.[419] With these high figures, it comes as no surprise that in the pharmaceutical industry, a relatively high percentage of profits are reinvested into R&D. In its final report on the pharmaceutical sector inquiry conducted in 2008, the European Commission found that originator companies globally invested 18 per cent of their annual turnover into R&D.[420] These figures are even more remarkable against the background of studies suggesting that only 30 per cent of all newly introduced drugs achieve a positive net present value, while others do not cover the R&D expenses with their revenues.[421]

149 It can therefore be concluded that engaging in the development of new drugs is costly and provides a high risk to the undertaking conducting the research.[422] As a relatively high percentage of the turnover gets reinvested, undertakings depend on continuous research success.[423] But, as will be shown below, the development process of a new drug is lengthy and has a low success rate.[424]

1.2 Pharmaceutical Product Life Cycle

150 The demand for products and the diffusion of technologies are cyclical in nature and typically run in the same pattern.[425] The product life cycle describes the time from the first appearance on the market until its market exit. The most popular models have four to five distinct phases: introduction, growth, maturity, saturation and decline.[426] The introduction, growth and maturity phases are characterised by increasing sales figures, whereas during saturation and decline, the sales figures diminish until the final

415. *See i.a.*: Dickson/Gagnon, Discovery Medicine 2009; Petrova, in: Ding/Eliashberg/Stremersch, Innovation and marketing in the pharmaceutical industry, 25.
416. Out-of-pocket costs are those costs that have to be paid directly, but do not include the time value of the money invested.
417. DiMasi/Grabowski/Hansen, Journal of Health Economics 2016, 31.
418. On the different phases of drug development, *see infra* at Part I, Chapter 5, section III.2.
419. WHO, *Promoting access to medical technologies and innovation*, 107.
420. EC, *Sector Inquiry, Final Report*, paras 77 f.
421. Bauer/Fischer, International Business Review 2000, 721.
422. *See also*: Raasch, 17.
423. Jacob, in: Pitruzzella/Muscolo, Competition and patent law in the pharmaceutical sector, 87.
424. *See infra* at Part I, Chapter 5, section III.2.
425. *See* the overview of the different empirical studies on the product life cycle: Bauer/Fischer, International Business Review 2000, 704 f.
426. Raasch, 13 f.

market exits. Owing to high investments for market cultivation during the introduction phase, products generally start to be profitable during the growth phase.[427]

151 After the market launch, pharmaceuticals follow a similar life cycle.[428] The duration of the phases is, however, dependent on the relevant product. Research suggests that pioneer and early-following drugs reach their maximum turnover on average within eight years after the market launch, while late-followers reach this point after three years on average.[429] A study conducted by BAUER/FISCHER also revealed the importance of the order of market entry. Late entrants have a significantly shorter life cycle, and the second supplier on the market has to accept a 40 per cent lower market share than the pioneer.[430] Market exclusivity is therefore crucial.

152 Patent expiry is another important factor during a drug's life cycle. Patents in pharmaceutical innovation are normally applied for at an early stage, and research continues for an average of twelve years until the market launch after the application.[431] This is due to the fact that the undertaking needs to secure its research successes, as it is normally under pressure from competitors conducting research on the same illnesses and receptors.

153 The product life cycle of pharmaceuticals does not start at market entry therefore, but with the discovery period and consists of an 'off-market' as well as an 'on-market' period. The R&D or 'off-market' phase is thereby characterised by time pressures: first to apply for patents, then to keep the following R&D phases as short as possible in order to secure as much market exclusivity for the drug as possible. The longer the patent validity, the longer products will generate an increase in turnover.[432] Strategies which lengthen the patent protection of the original product or aim at marketing a second-generation product are therefore a vital part in the management of product life cycles in the pharmaceutical industries.[433]

2 Systematics of Drug Development

154 The R&D process of drugs is both cost-intensive and time-intensive and is a risky endeavour.[434] The height of the financial burden taken by undertakings engaging in pharmaceutical research becomes apparent when looking at the development procedure of a new pharmaceutical product. The following section gives a brief descriptive overview of drug development.

427. RAASCH, 25 f.
428. *See*: FISCHER/BREITENBACH, 261; RAASCH, 15 with further references.
429. BAUER/FISCHER, International Business Review 2000, 714.
430. BAUER/FISCHER, International Business Review 2000, 714 f. with further references.
431. *See supra* at para. 147.
432. To react to the needs of the pharmaceutical industry, many countries as well as the EU have introduced the SPC to enlarge the period of exclusivity granted through the patent. *See infra* at fn. 939.
433. FISCHER/BREITENBACH, 261 f.; *see infra* at Part II.
434. *See supra* at paras 147 f.; RAASCH, 17.

2.1 *A Brief Historical Perspective*

155 Before the eighteenth century, pharmaceutical research did not exist. Healing effects on the human body were discovered randomly after consumption. Why substances had healing effects remained unknown.[435] It was only with the development of chemistry in the course of the nineteenth century that the foundation for pharmaceutical research was laid.[436] A key factor was the discovery of methods to isolate individual substances and conduct organic synthesis.[437] At first, there was only little detailed knowledge of the effects of substances, and serendipity continued to play an important role.[438] Early research in the pharmaceutical industry was therefore characterised by random screenings of natural or chemical compounds in rather small laboratories and with small quantities produced during research.[439] Despite these inefficiencies, many important developments in pharmacology[440] date from the twentieth century, such as the antibiotics penicillin and streptomycin, and the antihistamine pyrilamine or cimetidine, which inhibits the production of stomach acid.[441]

156 In the 1980s, the process of pharmaceutical R&D became more systematic. The development of new high-throughput and in vitro screening methods and in-depth knowledge of the stages of diseases and their mode of action within a human body, and thus the possibility to define molecular targets allowed comprehensive and targeted research. Nowadays, not only can targets be defined on a molecular basis but also the active ingredients can be designed according to the required interaction with the target.[442] However, despite advances in R&D drug discovery, the chances of a compound receiving marketing approval are less than 1 per cent.

2.2 *Drug Discovery Today*

157 Today the process of drug discovery follows a general pattern with different periods following one another. The different periods will be introduced hereinafter.[443]

435. DREWS, 43. TAYLOR, in: HESTER/HARRISON, Pharmaceuticals in the environment, 2.
436. DREWS, 38 ff.; TAYLOR, in: HESTER/HARRISON, Pharmaceuticals in the environment, 3.
437. BÜCHI, 20 ff.
438. LOMBARDINO/LOWE, Nature Reviews Drug Discovery 2004, 855.
439. LOMBARDINO/LOWE, Nature Reviews Drug Discovery 2004, 855; PETROVA, in: DING/ELIASHBERG/STREMERSCH, Innovation and marketing in the pharmaceutical industry, 25.
440. Pharmacology investigates the interaction of substances on an organism. TAYLOR, in: HESTER/HARRISON, Pharmaceuticals in the environment, 2 f.; DREWS, 41.
441. LI, 2 ff.; STONE GEORGE, https://www.acs.org/content/acs/en/education/whatischemistry/landmarks/penicillin.html, accessed on 12 February 2020.
442. LOMBARDINO/LOWE, Nature Reviews Drug Discovery 2004, 855 ff.
443. A brief overview of the development process is also given in: GRUBB ET AL., para. 21.03.

a Discovery Period (Basic Research)

158 In the discovery period, basic research is conducted. The pharmaceutical company develops a fundamental understanding of the disease (its states, causes and pathway) as well as the biochemical processes running within the human body during the different stages of the disease.[444] Based on these findings, it then chooses a target molecule. These target molecules (proteins) tend to be receptors or enzymes which the drug will either block, modulate or enhance.[445] After choosing the target molecule, a lead compound must be found which can act on the target molecule. With the help of high-throughput screenings (HTS) and other technologies,[446] pharmaceutical companies test thousands of compounds from chemical libraries for a potential reaction with the target molecule.[447] The researchers then identify the compounds which are effective, do not bind other molecules and can therefore potentially be used as active ingredients in the drug (lead identification).[448] At this stage of the development process, many pharmaceutical undertakings apply for compound patents for the leads.[449]

159 The leads identified in the screening have to be further analysed with respect to their 'drug-ability', namely their suitability to be modulated into a consumable form while still being able to interact with the target, and capable of being further modified to increase efficiency and reduce potential side effects. The result is the selection of a handful of suitable candidates for active compounds.[450] At this stage, the compounds are normally registered for patent approval.[451]

b Preclinical Trials

160 The transition from the discovery period to preclinical trials is smooth. The identified leads have to undergo further tests and modifications, which may not be clearly assigned to one or another phase. The focus in particular is on developing a preliminary delivery form and receiving answers about the toxicity[452] and

444. BAYER, *Vom Molekül zum Medikament,* 4; FREISSMUTH/OFFERMANNS/BÖHM, 69.
445. BAYER, *Vom Molekül zum Medikament,* 4.
446. For an overview and analysis of the different identification methods, *see*: KESERU/MAKARA, Drug Discovery Today 2006, 741 ff.
447. On HTS in detail, *see*: SZYMAŃSKI/MARKOWICZ/MIKICIUK-OLASIK, International Journal of Molecular Sciences 2012.
448. TAYLOR, in: HESTER/HARRISON, Pharmaceuticals in the environment, 11.
449. FELDMANN, 311; EUROPEAN FEDERATION OF PHARMACEUTICAL INDUSTRIES AND ASSOCIATIONS, *The Pharmaceutical Industry in Figures,* 6.
450. BAYER, *Vom Molekül zum Medikament,* 4 ff.
451. RAASCH, fn. 122; TAYLOR, in: HESTER/HARRISON, Pharmaceuticals in the environment, 11.
452. Toxicity testing provides important information as regards dosage. Pharmacologists have to understand not only which amounts of the compound lead to poisoning symptoms but also at what dosage therapeutic effects show. During toxicity testing, the effect of the compound is

pharmacokinetics[453] of the compound.[454] After the preclinical trials, the compounds have to meet safety requirements to be approved for clinical trials, where they are first tested on humans.

c *Clinical Trials*

161 After a successful preclinical phase and the granting of authorisation,[455] the clinical trials start. The clinical phase is the most regulated and cost-intensive phase of pharmaceutical development. It is the period in which the remaining active substances are first tested on humans. Clinical trials are divided into three phases. In phase I, the compounds are tested on a number of healthy volunteers. The goal of this phase is to gain knowledge of the side effects and the path of the substances through the body, thus, to get a more profound understanding of the safety of the compound.

162 About 30 per cent of all compounds which have clinical trial applications do not enter phase II.[456] It is only in phase II that the active substance is first tested with patients. The test provides results about the efficacy and tolerability of the active substance. With insights from phase I, researchers try to evaluate the optimal dosage.[457] Phase II trials only involve a handful of patients. Even at this stage, only 50 per cent of the compounds entering phase II will proceed to phase III.[458]

163 In phase III the drug is tested with a wider population of several hundred patients. Phase III marks the first 'reality check' of the compound. The test group should therefore represent the target group of the drug and be as heterogeneous as possible. Phase III delivers a risk–benefit assessment of the drug as a new compound compared to other therapies with similar active substances which are already on the market.[459]

---

tested at different dosages and over different time frames. The focus is on the effect of the compounds on fertility, potential teratogenic and mutagenic effects as well as postnatal development. DREWS, 158 ff.

453. Pharmacokinetics gives answers about the absorption, distribution, metabolism and excretion of the drug. Researchers in so-called Absorption, Distribution, Metabolism and Excretion (ADME) studies collect information about the journey of the compound within a living organism. While many of these tests can be conducted in vitro, animal testing is indispensable, as successful in vivo trials are legally required for clinical trial approvals. According to figures provided by Roche, at least 70 per cent of all serious side effects can be discovered while conducting animal testing.
454. DREWS, 156 ff.
455. Numbers from the USA, which are also cited for Germany, show that of five thousand-ten thousand compounds identified, an average of only nine receive authorisation for clinical trials. VERBAND DER FORSCHENDEN ARZNEIMITTELHERSTELLER, 8 f.; PETROVA, in: DING/ELIASHBERG/STREMERSCH, Innovation and marketing in the pharmaceutical industry, 25.
456. FELDMANN, 312.
457. DREWS, 161 f.
458. FELDMANN, 313.
459. DREWS, 165 f.; FELDMANN, 313 f.

d Marketing Approval and Monitoring

164 After successful clinical trials, market authorisation can be obtained. Data suggest that around 90 per cent of all compounds successfully passing phase III of the clinical trials finally reach the market.[460] In the EU a centralised approval path as well as national, decentralised and mutual recognition paths are available. Certain medical products such as medicines derived from biotechnology, or advanced therapy medicines, have to be submitted via the centralised approval path (Regulation (EC) No 726/2004, Appendix). The centralised path results in market approval for all EU Member States as well as the Member States of the EEA and requires a single application to the EMA. In the decentralised and mutual recognition approval procedures, an in-depth evaluation of the submitted data is only conducted in one Member State. In the other Member States, the application can be received based on approval in the first state (mutual recognition approval) or simultaneously based on the evaluation of the reference Member State (decentralised approval).

165 After the marketing approval, the clinical trials continue. In a last and fourth phase of clinical trials, the drug is further monitored. The focus here is on rare side effects, long-term effects and effectiveness. In the event of discovery of unexpected serious side effects and limited effectiveness, market approvals can be revoked, as in the case of drugs containing flordipine where severe liver damage was found to occur.[461]

IV THE IMPORTANCE OF PATENTS FOR THE PHARMACEUTICAL SECTOR

166 Inherent to chemical compounds is the fact that numerous methods exist with which their structure can be broken down. At the same time, (re-) production costs are comparably low compared with research expenditure. Once a drug is on the market, competitors can therefore easily market bioequivalent drugs shortly after market entry and significantly underprice the inventor while still operating a profitable business. Without patent protection, undertakings engaging in pharmaceutical research would run into danger of being driven out of the market, and research activity would remain low.

167 Patents in the pharmaceutical industry are not just theoretically important or mainly for bargaining power as in many technology-based industries.[462] Easy detectability of chemical structures brings the advantage that it is relatively easy to identify infringements and to prove them in court. Pharmaceutical undertakings therefore give

460. Feldmann, 314 f.
461. EMA, *Withdrawal of pain medicine.*
462. *See also supra* at paras 22 ff.

special attention to patenting and life-cycle strategies aimed at granting maximal patent protection.[463]

1 Types of Pharmaceutical Patents

168 In the literature, pharmaceutical patents are categorised into product patents, process patents and use patents (*see* Article 64(3) EPC), depending on the patented subject matter. Patent claims concerning drugs can cover active ingredients, excipients, formulations (product patents), processes for the manufacturing of the drug (process patents) or its ingredients as well as the application or dosage (use patents). The next section outlines the patent categories covering drugs, formulation or application methods. Patents covering technical devices or manufacturing methods are not the subject of this book and will therefore not be further commented on.

1.1 Product Patents

169 In the pharmaceutical industry, product patents cover chemical substances (molecules).[464] Active ingredients as well as excipients and formulations can be patented. The patented subject matter is the molecule defined by the technical teaching which is used for the isolation, synthetisation or production of the molecule or the formulation.[465] Natural and synthesised substances can both act as active ingredients in drugs. The understanding that the patent is granted as a reward for providing a substance leads to the scope of product patents. Product patents are the broadest possible in the sense that they grant absolute protection for all usage forms and production methods, even those unknown at the time of filing the patent application.

170 Patent law requires patents covering products to be clearly identifiable. In pharmacology, patent claims for product patents include structural (Markush claim[466]) or molecular formulae, as product-by-process claims[467] or a definition of the product by its parameters.[468] An example of a product patent is EP 0916675 B1 which protected Sildenafil, the active compound in the potency pill Viagra®, until 2013. Product-by-

463. *See supra* at para. 153.
464. Product patents can cover either end or intermediate products. Intermediate products in chemistry result during a chemical process and can be further transformed into end products. These intermediate chemical products, owing to difficulties in proving infringing acts, offer only limited possibility to block competitors. *See*: FACKELMANN, 79 f. Therefore, intermediate patents will not influence further discourse here.
465. MELULLIS, in: BENKARD ET AL., EPÜ, § 52, para. 149.
466. AHN, 40 f.; DOMEIJ, 68.
467. Product-by-process claims define the product via the method applied in manufacturing it ('product X obtainable by process Y'). EPO, *Guidelines for Examination*, F. IV. 4.12.; TESCHEMACHER, in: SINGER ET AL., EPC 2019, Article 84, paras 29 f.
468. EPO, *Guidelines for Examination*, F. IV. 4.11. Definitions of products by parameters (by determination of the basic materials' nature and quantity) are only accepted when the product cannot be defined by its structural or molecular formula as in the case of mixtures and solutions.

process claims are not to be confused with process patents, as product-by-process patents are claims for the product as such and not the process.[469]

171 Galenic (such as capsules, pills, vaccines) and dosage forms can also be subject to patent claims.[470] An example can be given from Sildenafil. The summary of patent WO 2013/085904 which claims 'oral spray formulations and methods for administration of sildenafil' reads as follows:

> An oral spray formulation for delivery of sildenafil to treat diseases such as pulmonary arterial hypertension and/or SSRI-induced sexual dysfunction. [...] In one aspect, the oral spray formulation may comprise sildenafil or a pharmaceutically acceptable salt thereof. In another aspect, the oral spray formulation may comprise sildenafil citrate.
>
> In yet another aspect, the oral spray formulation comprising sildenafil or a pharmaceutically acceptable salt thereof may have a pH of about 1.5 to less than 3.0. In some embodiments, the pH of the formulation is about 2.2 ± 0.5. In a certain embodiment, the pH of the formulation is about 2.2.[471]

1.2 Process Patents

172 Process patent claims cover the methods used to manufacture the compound.[472] The patent provides its owner with the sole right to manufacture the said compound with the claimed process. The scope of process patents includes the compound gained with the patented method (Article 64(2) EPC), but not bioequivalents gained by other processes.[473] Unlike product patents, process patents therefore do not protect the product 'compound X' in general, but only the 'compound X gained by process Y', that is, only those compounds gained by the patented process. Before absolute product protection was introduced, process patents were the only method of gaining (indirect) product protection.[474]

1.3 Use Patents

173 The EPC in Article 52(4) denies patentability to human or veterinarian medical treatment methods, as methods are seen as lacking industrial application. Yet drugs and their manufacture are not excluded by Article 52(4) EPC. Therefore, patents covering the therapeutic use of new compounds or compounds which are not known to have medical indications can be applied for, even if the treatment they are used in is

469. BoA, *Amorphous TPM v. ENICHEM*, T 0020/94, para. 4.4.; EPO, *Guidelines for Examination*, F. IV. 4.12.
470. Lindner, in: Singer et al., EPC 2019, Article 54, paras 149 ff.
471. WO 2013/085904.
472. On process patents *see i.a.*: Müller, 67 ff.; Fischer/Breitenbach, 232; Grubb et al., para. 4.59.
473. Fischer/Breitenbach, 232.
474. Melullis, in: Benkard et al., EPÜ, § 52, para. 149; *see the case*: BGH, *Imidazoline*, X ZB 2/71.

not patentable in itself.[475] It is also possible to patent the new therapeutic or diagnostic use of a known compound with known medical indications (second medical use, Article 54(5) EPC).[476]

174 Pharmaceuticals can have different therapeutic indications.[477] Sildenafil, for example, was originally developed to cure high blood pressure and angina pectoris.[478] However, during clinical trials, its impact on erectile dysfunction was discovered. Subsequently, Sildenafil received marketing approval for the treatment of erectile dysfunction as well as pulmonary hypertension. Currently, it is also under scrutiny as to whether Sildenafil in low dosages could be applied alongside chemotherapy to help cure prostate cancer.[479] In 2016, the Chinese Guangzhou Downlight Biotech Company applied for a patent covering the use of low dosage of Sildenafil as antitumour drug.[480]

175 In Europe, claims for second medical use patents previously took the form of so-called Swiss type claims, which read as follows: 'use of substance X in the manufacture of a medicament for the treatment of condition Y'. Since 2010 and a decision by the Enlarged Board of Appeal of the EPO (BoA), however, use patents under the EPC take the form of purpose-limited product protection claims ('Use of substance or composition X for the treatment of disease Y.').[481]

2 Different Pharmaceutical Products

176 The different categories of product, process and use patents open a field of opportunities not only for product development but also for strategic patenting and life-cycle strategies. Within product patents, there is great potential for secondary patents and the marketing of second-generation products, as active ingredients exist in variations with different characteristics and thus slightly different biological activities and pharmacological effects.

475. SINGER/STAUDER, in: SINGER ET AL., EPC 2003, Article 52, paras 61 ff. and 83 (the chapters on the patentability of pharmaceuticals can no longer be found in the new edition).
476. FISCHER/BREITENBACH, 232 f.; MÜLLER, 73 ff.; SINGER/STAUDER, in: SINGER ET AL., EPC 2003, Article 52, paras 84 f.
477. Different therapeutic indications also lead to the off-label use of drugs. An off-label use is the use of a drug to cure a condition for which it was not approved. The ECJ in its recent case *Hofmann-La Roche II* had to evaluate the strategy of Roche in trying to limit the off-label use of its drug Avastin. *See*: ECJ, *Hofmann-La Roche II*, C-179/16.
478. With further examples, *see*: AHN, 51.
479. ALBERS, Focus Magazin 24 May 2015; TETENS.
480. Patent No CN106389437A (registered in the EPO as WO2018064851 (A1)).
481. MÜLLER, 79 f.

2.1 *Structurally Similar Active Substances*

a *Isomers*

177 Isomers[482] are molecules with identical molecular formulae and weight but a different arrangement of the molecules (stereoisomers) or linkage of the atoms (constitutional isomers). Enantiomers are either left- or right-handed mirror images of each other. In pharmacology, enantiomers are of great importance as they are characterised by different physical properties and can show differences in biological activity.

178 In some drugs, an equal amount of both enantiomers is present as an active substance (racemic mixture), although in most cases, either the left- or right-handed molecule shows the desired effect or is more suitable for the intended purpose. Pharmaceutical undertakings can therefore try to patent a compound based on the more effective molecule or the racemic mixture as a further development. Enantiomer patents have a higher likelihood of being challenged.[483]

b *Crystalline Forms*

179 Solid materials in crystalline form have the potential to be polymorphs, which means they possess the ability to occur in different forms without changing their chemical composition. As these crystalline forms have different characteristics, such as solubility, stability, filterability, and melting behaviour, for pharmaceutical undertakings, crystalline forms therefore provide important potential for developing a compound.[484]

c *Derivates, such as Salts, Esters or Ethers*

180 Active ingredients are generally acids or bases. As with other structurally similar active ingredients, derivatives such as salts[485], esters[486] or ethers[487] have different chemical characteristics. In general, these characteristics, such as superior solubility or higher stability, provide important sources for the improvement of drugs.[488] Esters, for example, often have better tolerance and efficiency than the basic molecule.[489]

482. On isomers *see*: AHN, 43 ff.; ELLERY/HANSEN, 160 f.; FACKELMANN, 86 ff.
483. AGRANAT/WAINSCHTEIN, Drug Discovery Today 2010, 163.
484. On crystalline forms *see*: ELLERY/HANSEN, 161 f.; FACKELMANN, 81 ff.
485. Salts are combinations of acids and bases.
486. Esters are the result of a chemical reaction of an acid with an alcohol or phenol.
487. Ethers are organic compounds containing an oxygen atom bound to either two alkyl or aryl groups. For the definition, *see*: https://www.thoughtco.com/definition-of-ether-605107, accessed on 29 October 2018.
488. ELLERY/HANSEN, 162 f.; FACKELMANN, 84 ff.
489. BERTHOLD, 110 for further reference.

2.2 *Metabolites and Prodrugs*

181 Metabolites are intermediate substances that occur during the metabolic process within the body. Metabolites can have pharmacological effects and are therefore used in compounds when producible outside of the body.[490]

182 Prodrugs contain inactive substances which, when administered, are transformed into metabolites. In these cases, it is the metabolite which has the wanted pharmacological effect and not the inactive substance included in the compound. Prodrugs are important in cases where the administration of the metabolite itself is less favourable due to, for example, poor absorption, distribution, or toxicity[491].[492]

2.3 *Combinations of Ingredients*

183 New compounds can also consist of a combination of active ingredients of approved drugs. In combination, the active ingredients interact and can enhance known healing effects or develop new ones. Sometimes healing effects can also be derived from the combination of two inactive substances.[493]

3 Reference Points for Patenting Strategies

184 On the supply side of pharmaceutical markets, originators compete with other originators by striving for new improved drugs as well as providing different therapy alternatives for the same treatment (substitutes). With generic companies, originators compete after losing exclusivity. Generic companies engage in this battle by providing cheaper equivalents of the products of the originator. Room for the originator to engage in patenting strategies exists in all these situations.

185 Second-generation products are an important source of competition for originator companies and are therefore also an important focus of patenting strategies for the originator marketing the first-generation product. At the same time, launching second-generation products is an important goal for the originator, as incremental innovations on a successful product are also important to compete with generics of the first-generation product. Unsurprisingly, the pharmaceutical sector inquiry conducted by the Commission revealed that second-generation products are often launched promptly before patent expiration of the first-generation product.[494]

490. Fackelmann, 100 ff.
491. The use of prodrugs is therefore popular in chemotherapy, where the pharmacological effect should be limited to cancer cells. *See*: Ellery/Hansen, 163.
492. On prodrugs and metabolites, *see i.a.*: Ellery/Hansen, 163 f.; Fackelmann, 105 f.; Richter, paras 93 ff.
493. On combinations, *see i.a.*: Ahn, 50; Fackelmann, 108 ff.; Müller, 69 f.
494. EC, *Sector Inquiry, Final Report,* para. 989.

V IMPLICATIONS

186 The pharmaceutical industry is not only highly regulated, but competitors on the market also engage in large, cost-intensive and high-risk R&D projects and rely heavily on patents. On the supply side, originators compete with each other as well as with generic companies. Originators compete with one another on the basis of product-specific factors, while price is the relevant factor in competition with generic companies.

187 Patents are key for both forms of competition. First, as a matter of competitive pressure from other originator companies in research races, inventions in the pharmaceutical industry are patented at an early stage of the drug discovery process. The insights gained in the R&D process allow an understanding of the crucial role of patents in the pharmaceutical industry.

188 Second, generic companies are only allowed to enter the market when the patent on the drug provided by the originator has expired. As prices will drastically fall after generic entry, it is in the interests of the originator companies to maintain patent protection for a maximal period. As outlined above with respect to the price levels after patent expiration, it comes as no surprise that originator companies will be creative when it comes to patenting, and will regularly attempt to apply for patents strategically.

Part II Strategic Patenting

CHAPTER 6
Why Firms Patent

189 From the insight into the pharmaceutical industry gained in Part I Chapter 5, we learn that patents can be crucial to securing survival in the market for many reasons, such as protecting their innovation to secure leeway for further R&D projects. This chapter addresses possible underlying motives for applying for patents (section II).[495] The focus of this book will be on the phenomenon of blocking patents (section III).[496] Chapter 6 starts with a brief outline of patentability requirements (section I).

I PATENTABILITY REQUIREMENTS

190 Patents can be granted for inventions that are new, involve an inventive step and are susceptible to industrial application (Article 52(1) EPC as well as Article 27(1) TRIPS). While these requirements impose different challenges in different sectors, patentability of chemicals and therefore pharmaceuticals has long been disputed.[497] There was a fear that it could lead to an increase in the price of medication,[498] and there was also a question over the technical nature of chemical compounds.[499] The following chapter gives a short insight into the challenges for pharmaceuticals in meeting the patentability requirements.

495. Motives to patent reflect the possible benefits expected from the specific functions of the patent system. In the literature, these mechanisms are often explained as functions of the patent and examined from the perspective of the patent system itself. As this book focuses on the compatibility of specific patent strategies with competition law, it is more helpful to elaborate on the peculiarities of the patent system from the perspective of strategic management. For an overview of the significance of patents, *see infra* at paras 196 ff. and also: BERTHOLD, 88 ff.
496. *See supra* at paras 1 ff.
497. *See*: MÜLLER, 26 ff.
498. MÜLLER, 27 ff.
499. MÜLLER, 37 ff.

1 Inventions

191 Inventions require the inventor to provide a technical teaching. The problem with natural substances as regards patentability is that mere discoveries lack an inventive step and thus patentability. Natural substances are excluded from patentability when they are known and can be obtained in pure form. Synthesis in these cases provides a known substance rather than a new one. Patentability in chemistry and biotechnology therefore requires the inventor to provide a method for isolating the natural substance or synthetically producing it.[500] In the pharmaceutical industry, providing a method to isolate, synthesise or manufacture a substance is considered a patentable invention, but the simple identification of laws of nature or molecules is considered a discovery and lacks patentability.

2 Novelty

192 Only those inventions which include at least one technical feature that is not considered prior art are classed as new. Prior art is defined as the bundle of knowledge available to the skilled person. The EPC thereby applies the concept of absolute novelty. According to the principle of absolute novelty, all knowledge made public[501] by means of a written or oral description, by use, or in any other way,[502] before the date of filing of the European patent application anywhere in the world is considered prior art (Article 54(2) EPC). Prior art also includes the content of filed but not yet published patent applications pending at the EPO (Article 54(3) EPC). Whether the applicant did in fact know of the prior art publication is not relevant (objective novelty).[503]

193 When deciding on novelty as well as the inventive step, a person skilled in the art is taken as the reference.[504] The person skilled in the art has to virtually compare the invention with state-of-the-art knowledge. An invention lacks novelty if it only contains a mixture of state-of-the-art knowledge.[505] In the pharmaceutical industry, the novelty requirement does not exclude patentability of novel indications of known substances. With respect to pharmaceuticals, the novelty requirement has been discussed concerning the patentability of metabolites. Even though they are generally considered to be patentable, because the mere fact that an active ingredient metabolises within the body does not imply common knowledge.[506] It is not possible to block

500. Bacher, in: Benkard/Asendorf, Münchener Kommentar PatG, § 1, paras 92 f.; Melullis, in: Benkard et al., EPÜ, § 53, para. 48; Teschemacher, in: Singer et al., EPC 2019, Article 83, para. 18.
501. Confidential information is not publicly available in this sense. *See*: BoA, *Macor v. Kvaerner*, T 830/90, para. 3.2.2.
502. Note that under the EPC, information made public to only one person is considered to be state of the art. *See*: BoA, *Telemechanique v. Siemens Nixdorf*, T 482/89, para. 3.
503. Melullis, in: Benkard et al., EPÜ, § 3, para. 77.
504. Lindner, in: Singer et al., EPC 2019, Article 54, paras 58 ff.
505. Domeij, fn. 276; BoA, *Copolymere/Du Pont*, T 124/87, paras 3.4. f.
506. Vossius/Vossius/Vossius, GRUR 1994, 475.

generic entry based on a secondary patent covering a metabolite according to precedence from Germany (*Terfenadine case*) and the USA.[507]

3 The Inventive Step and Non-obviousness

194 In order to be patentable, an invention also has to involve an inventive step. This requirement goes further than novelty. It involves an objective,[508] qualitative assessment of all prior art references. The starting point of the assessment is the closest state of the art. The relevant benchmark is the 'teaching a skilled person draws from these documents'.[509] The invention should not be obvious. This means that the differences between the invention claimed and the closest state of the art must be assessed with regard to whether a skilled person would have proposed the same technical solution. Therefore, inventions are considered obvious if a skilled person would have proposed the same solution based on the state of the art without using skills or abilities beyond those expected of a skilled person.

4 Applicability

195 Inventions can only be patented when they are commercially applicable. For inventions concerning drugs, this requirement has not proved to be an issue. Pharmaceutical product, process and usage patents are always commercially applicable within the commercial activity of a pharmaceutical undertaking in manufacturing and selling drugs.

II MOTIVES TO PATENT

196 The property right offers an intense source of power for patent holders, as they are put in a position where they can interfere with a rival's business just by not granting licences or appropriate licensing terms.[510] If a competitor cannot receive a licence on fair conditions, they either need to develop other methods that do not interfere with the already patented technology (inventing around), withdraw from further efforts in the market, or agree on the proposed unfair licensing terms. All these alternatives impose an extra financial burden on the competitor with the risk of hampering competition. The drawback of the power embodied in the property right is that the patent holder can take advantage of it to block competitors.

507. OLG München, *Terfenadin*, 6 U 5155/92; S.D.N.Y, *In Re Buspirone Patent Litigation*, 185 F. Supp. 2d 340, 363.
508. Kroher, in: Singer et al., EPC 2019, Article 56, paras 4 ff.
509. Kroher, in: Singer et al., EPC 2019, Article 56, para. 16.
510. *See* the case law described *infra* at paras 416 ff. *See also* the overview over abusive practices involving patents in: Hilty/Früh, 157 ff.

197 Although the acquisition of patent rights can be motivated by the expectation of acquiring a tool to hamper competitors,[511] the prospects of receiving protection from imitations and returns on R&D are considered the most important reasons for an undertaking to engage in patenting[512] in most industries.[513] The following provides a closer examination of the motivations for applying for a patent. In the literature, patenting motives are often divided into three groups: *traditional motives*[514], *strategic motives*[515] (including blocking motives which are also sometimes referred to as strategic motives in a narrower sense) and *exchange* or *economic asset motives*.[516] This section will focus on these three groups and the functions of patents that underlie the different motives. Regardless of the surge in the strategic use of patents, traditional motives are the most important to engage in patenting. Yet data from the USA and Japan show that blocking competitors also ranks highly as a motive to patent. In the samples evaluated by COHEN ET AL., 80 per cent of the patent holders in the USA reported that they had applied for product patents to block competitors.[517]

1 Traditional Motives

198 Due to being at the same time 'non-excludable' and a 'good of non-rivalry'[518] technical inventions could, once the idea had become perceptible, be used unrestrictedly by everyone.[519] Patent protection allows the patent holder to restrict the use of the patented technology and thus provides a mechanism for financial exploitation of the invention. Patents therefore function as *exclusion and protection mechanisms* against

511. That blocking motives are not a theoretical problem is shown in the literature on patent management. The authors note undertakings that have applied for broad patents, patent clusters and blocking patents and list examples of successful entities that have relied on such strategies. *See*: GASSMANN/BADER, 25 and 44.
512. It is interesting that not using intellectual property and relying on lead time advantages was identified as the most favoured way of securing innovation. BLIND ET AL., Research Policy, 657 and 662; BLIND ET AL. 2003, 57 f.
513. For product technology, the protection mechanism seems to be the primary reason for patenting. When it comes to process technologies, protection is slightly less important and usually does not rank highest. BLIND ET AL., Research Policy, XII; GRANSTRAND, 210 f.
514. The functions of patenting reflecting the traditional motives are referred to as primary functions in the literature. BURR ET AL., Chapter 4.2.1.; RAHN also uses the term 'primary function' but only lists the granting of monopoly rights as a function. RAHN, GRUR Int., 378; EC, *Sector Inquiry, Final Report,* paras 251 ff.
515. In the literature, the functions of patenting reflecting strategic motives are referred to as secondary functions. BURR ET AL., Chapter 4.2.2; for the pharmaceutical sector, these functions are described in: EC, *Sector Inquiry, Final Report,* paras 257 and 468.
516. This categorisation is close to the one provided by: WURZER/MÜLLER, NZZ 20 June 2007. A similar categorisation of the motives to patent can also be found in: BLIND/CREMERS/MÜLLER, Research Policy, 429; COHEN/NELSON/WALSH, NBER Working Paper Series, 25 ff.
517. COHEN ET AL., Research Policy 2002, 1358.
518. Non-rivalry and non-excludability are the two characteristics of public goods. *See i.a.*: KRUGMAN/WELLS, 524 ff.; FRITSCH, 77; GORDON, in: V. OTT/SCHÄFER, Ökonomische Analyse der rechtlichen Organisation von Innovationen, 329 ff.; public goods are opposite to private goods which are excludable as well as rivals in consumption. KRUGMAN/WELLS, 520 ff.; *see supra* at para. 87.
519. *See supra* at paras 86 f.

rivals.[520] The patent right gives its owner the sole power to dispose of the innovation. Consequently, the law declares as unlawful every use of the patented invention without permission of the right holder which is not private.

199 This protects the market position of the patent holder and allows for financial exploitation.[521] Through the sole right to use the patented technology, the patent holders can exploit their innovation either indirectly through charging higher market prices or directly through charging licence fees.[522] The right of disposal therefore raises the expected return and reduces the risk posed to investments in R&D.[523] Patents in this traditional sense work as incentives to innovate ('incentive function', 'financing function').

200 In exchange for the monopoly power, patent holders have a legal obligation to disclose the patented information (*information function*[524]). The technical writing would, in the absence of a patent system, potentially remain hidden.[525] The patented technology becomes accessible and public owing to the obligation to disclose.[526] Consequently, patents allow society to participate in the gain and further the development of knowledge. The informative content of patents also helps to steer research[527] and business strategy, as it allows assessment of rivals' positions.[528] Despite being an obligation and generally not responded to positively by inventors,[529] disclosing information can be useful for the patent applicant. Spreading the information propagates the technology and can attract investors or licensees (*signalling function*).[530]

2 Strategic Motives

2.1 Blocking Motive

201 The side effects of rendering innovation into a tradeable commodity are the increased costs for competitors entering the market,[531] either directly imposed through higher R&D expenses required to invent around or having to pay licence fees or

520. BURR ET AL., Chapter 4.2.1.2.
521. BERTHOLD, 93.
522. EC, *Sector Inquiry, Final Report,* para. 252.
523. *See*: BURR ET AL., Chapter 4.2.1.1.
524. Among others: BURR ET AL., Chapter 4.2.1.3.
525. THUMM, in: HERREN/MÜNCH/WEINMANN, Schweizer IP-Handbuch, § 2, paras 16 ff.; BEIER, GRUR 1977, 284.
526. A vivid description is provided by: HÄUSSER, in: OPPENLÄNDER, Patentwesen technischer Fortschritt und Wettbewerb, 138 f.; EC, *Sector Inquiry, Final Report,* para. 1093.
527. BURR ET AL., Chapter 4.2.1.3; HÄUSSER, in: OPPENLÄNDER, Patentwesen technischer Fortschritt und Wettbewerb, 140. Economists have argued that the information disclosed through patents increases social welfare as it prevents the waste of funds.
528. The obligation to disclose information might also prevent undertakings from applying for a patent, because they may fear assessment of their own position.
529. *See*: DUGUET/KABLA, Économie et Économétrie de l'innovation 1998, 304 and 318.
530. BURR ET AL., 40 ff.; GRANSTRAND, 212 f.
531. BERTHOLD, 93.

indirectly imposed through delayed market entry as well as lower expected and actual gains.[532] If a patent applicant applies for a patent to exploit these hampering effects, blocking is no longer a side effect, but becomes a motive.[533]

202 Patents applied for out of blocking motives have the purpose of preventing competitors from using and patenting similar technologies. Methods include applications for broad patents as well as patents which are not intended to be used in business (blocking patents).[534] Additionally, blocking motives include strategies aimed at systematically suing competitors for infringements. Right holders actively pursuing blocking strategies generally enforce and exercise their rights aggressively.[535]

203 The blocking motive cannot easily be isolated from other motives for applying for a patent. The reason is that the transition between patents used to prevent competitors from copying, and patents used to block competitors, is fuzzy. Patents almost automatically convey a blocking potential. Therefore, it is not usually possible to identify a blocking patent without inside information on the patent strategy, unless the patent holder has already made attempts to enforce the patent.

204 In an early study of patents registered at the German patent office, OPPENLÄNDER identified about 11 per cent of the patents in its sample to have remained unused.[536] Around 7 per cent were categorised as stock and only 4 per cent as blocking patents.[537] The blocking intention may not exist when filing the patent but may develop when a patent holder realises that blocking is the worthiest exploitation of the patent.[538] In other cases, patents may just remain unused for circumstantial reasons. In the pharmaceutical industry, unused patents could be patents covering active substances of drugs which failed testing[539]. These patents cannot be considered as blocking. Stock or sleeping patents cover marketable technologies which remain unused due to financial or other considerations. Sleeping patents carry the risk that blocking intentions will eventually come up.[540] There was an example from England where the reason to leave a patent stocked evolved over time. In 1945, a steelworks installed a hot rolling mill with the intention of operating it for about twenty years. However, in 1949, the same steelworks developed and patented a cold rolling process that would allow much more productive efficiency. To avoid damaging the investment made in constructing the hot rolling mill, the steelworks postponed the construction of the cold

532. BURR ET AL., 38 f.; GRANSTRAND, 214.
533. GLAZIER, 11.
534. *See infra* at paras 209 f.; LANDES/POSNER discuss patent suppression: LANDES/POSNER, 320 f.
535. GASSMANN/BADER, 36 ff.
536. The sample contained 53.3 per cent of all patents still valid in 1970. The patents belonged to twelve of eighty-nine possible patent classes. OPPENLÄNDER, in: OPPENLÄNDER, Patentwesen technischer Fortschritt und Wettbewerb, 49. Unfortunately, we cannot draw on more recent studies and estimations.
537. OPPENLÄNDER, in: OPPENLÄNDER, Patentwesen technischer Fortschritt und Wettbewerb, 66.
538. For example, the situation described by SCHECHTER/THOMAS where an improvement cannot or will not be marketed because of its dependency on the basic patent. SCHECHTER/THOMAS, 462.
539. On the high risks of drugs failing the trials, *see supra* at paras 162 ff.
540. LANDES/POSNER, 321.

rolling mill and did not use this technology until a competitor claimed for the grant of a compulsory licence.[541]

2.2 *Other Strategic Motives*

205 Rather than blocking competitors, the power of patents can also be used to strengthen the position of the patent holder across business transactions.[542] Patents can be used as sham patents, as bargaining chips either in cross-licence negotiations[543] or patent pools[544] and to prevent lawsuits or, as the example of Texas Instruments in the semiconductor industry shows, to secure its holder's freedom to operate.[545]

206 Sham patents are applied for to frustrate competitors concerning the actual line of R&D of the undertaking. These patents are characterised by the fact that the patent holder stops paying the required fees soon after the application.[546] Sham patents are therefore unlikely to be blocking.

207 Patents function like assets in trade. They are most helpful in building a solid bargaining position in cross-licence negotiations. In complex product industries especially,[547] where a commercialised product is based on many interdependent patents,[548] applying for patents to improve their own bargaining position is a common motivation.[549] When competitors are mutually dependent, patents can also hinder lawsuits. Patenting is said to be the best strategy to avoid litigation.[550] In cumulative technologies, it is likely that the harmed patent owner will likewise violate the patents of the infringer.[551]

208 As patents entail a restriction on competitors to patent and commercialise their own innovations, blocking and securing one's own room for manoeuvre are closely linked and can influence competition equally.[552] It therefore becomes clear that the motivations of the patent holder do not necessarily anticipate the effect of the patent on

541. Greif, GRUR Int 1981, 735, fn. 30.
542. Macdonald, Information Economics and Policy 2004, 144.
543. Grindley/Teece, California Management Review 1997, 9.
544. 'Patent pools can be defined as an agreement between two or more patent owners to license one or more of their patents to one another or to third parties.' WIPO, *Patent Pools and Antitrust*, para. 1. *See also infra* at paras 623 f.
545. *See*, for example, on the development of the radio, *infra* at para. 230.
546. Gassmann/Bader, 37.
547. Complex technologies are the opposite of discrete technologies. In discrete technologies, inventions, and therefore patents, are not usually connected and stand solidly in the sense that often one patent builds the sole foundation of a product. Sectors dominated by discrete technologies are the pharmaceutical or chemical industries. For discrete technology, *see*: Cohen/Nelson/Walsh, NBER Working Paper Series, 19.
548. Burr et al., 42 f.
549. Cohen/Nelson/Walsh, NBER Working Paper Series, 25 f.
550. Cohen/Nelson/Walsh, NBER Working Paper Series, 26.
551. Rivette/Kline list Dell as an undertaking that has pursued this strategy. *See*: Rivette/Kline, Harvard Business Review 2000, 57; on patents as bargaining chips: Granstrand, 210 ff.; Organisation for Economic Co-Operation and Development, *Patents and Innovation*, 25.
552. Similarly: Blind et al., Research Policy, 663.

competition and innovation. Furthermore, patents as 'currency of a knowledge-based economy'[553] send signals to potential investors, influence stock market value and potentially the reputation of an undertaking.[554] This can attract customers as well as potential, highly qualified, employees.[555] Internally undertakings sometimes even use patents to motivate employees.[556]

III BLOCKING PATENTS

1 The Phenomenon

209 The term 'blocking patents'[557] includes all those patents that serve a strategic purpose but protect an invention which is not intended to be commercialised, licensed or further developed.[558] Blocking patents are therefore only motivated by the prospect of obstructing competitors and not traditional motives. Even though all patents, in their nature as property rights, hold blocking power, the potential to hold up technological development immanent in a blocking patent is – compared with other patents – more concrete. The reason is that the technology protected with a blocking patent cannot be licensed but must be invented around to 'get by'.

210 As blocking patents render inventing around more difficult, they are used within shielding, fencing and clustering strategies and address the concerns of the dominant undertaking that competitors will succeed in providing a substitute to satisfy demand.[559] The existence of a blocking patent per se therefore reduces the possibility for rivals to improve their own technology or launch a related marketable product. Blocking patents consequently forestall the possibility of entering the market or improving a product. The technology protected by a blocking patent is thus *per definitionem* deprived of competition. It is therefore evident that these patents are sensitive in the light of competition law.[560]

2 'Blocking Trademarks'

211 A conceptually equivalent phenomenon of applying for blocking patents is known in trademark law. Companies learning from the plans of competitors try to register the trademark to block or complicate the market entry of the actual creator of the sign.

553. ARUNDEL/PATEL, European Trend Chart on Innovation 2003, 3.
554. BURR ET AL., 40 ff.; GRANSTRAND, 213; REISS, 50.
555. So far this *signalling motive* has not been identified as important: BLIND ET AL., Research Policy, 657.
556. BLIND ET AL., Research Policy, 663 and 665.
557. A careful approach to the term 'blocking patent' can be found in: ZECH, ZWeR 2011, 314.
558. BERTHOLD, 95; BOUCHARD, 123; GILBERT/NEWBERY, The American Economic Review 1982, 514 and 517 f.; LAMPING, 138.
559. LAMPING, 138 f.
560. *See*, for example, FTC, *Report: To Promote Innovation*, 5 ff.

Unlike in patent law where bad faith is not decisive, in trademark law bad faith at the time of the trademark registration leads to its nullity. In a preliminary ruling, the Court of Justice had to decide on the validity of the trademark on golden chocolate Easter bunnies. These products identified through the trademark in question had already been produced for decades, before the trademark was applied for. Both the Swiss chocolate manufacturer Lindt & Sprüngli and its German competitor Franz Hauswirth GmbH had been selling golden chocolate Easter bunnies in a similar shape for a long time. However, in 2000, Lindt & Sprüngli, after taking legal proceedings against competitors producing similar bunnies, registered its golden bunny as a trademark. Franz Hauswirth GmbH challenged the registration, and the Court of Justice in a preliminary ruling decided that bad faith is apparent not only when an 'applicant applied for registration of a sign as a Community trade mark without intending to use it, his sole objective being to prevent a third party from entering the market'[561] but also when the sole intent of a registrant is to compete unfairly with already existing competitors using the same or a similar sign.[562]

3 Appearance

212 Blocking patents do not only appear in the form of patents meeting the patentability requirements. Applications for blocking patents can also cover technologies that are obviously not meeting patentability requirements but are still filed.[563] Blocking patent strategies can therefore include the registration of obviously invalid patents.[564] From the perspective of the patent applicant, the worst-case scenario is that the patent examiner rejects the grant. In this case, the undertakings will lose the fees paid for the patent application process.[565] In a best-case scenario the patent will be granted.

213 When a patent is granted that does not meet the patentability requirements, society provides an exclusive right without being rewarded through the disclosure of new technology that would spur innovation. Patent holders thus enjoy a property right they are technically not entitled to. The problem with theoretically invalid patents is that they are still formally valid until their validity is challenged and the invalidity is determined by a court. It can be rational for an undertaking to apply for a patent, even if the technology obviously lacks patentability. Within the evaluation of strategic patent applications in the light of competition law, it will thus be important to

561. ECJ, *Schokoladenfabrik Lindt & Sprüngli*, C-529/07, para. 44.
562. ECJ, *Schokoladenfabrik Lindt & Sprüngli*, C-529/07, paras 46 ff. OG THURGAU, *Limmi I*, Z1.2002.2, paras 2.a.aa. ff.; confirmed on appeal in: BGer 4C.169/2004.
563. *See*: EC, *Servier*, AT.39612, para. 5.
564. This type of patent made a first noteworthy appearance in the famous *Walker Process*: UNITED STATES SUPREME COURT, *Walker Process Equipment Inc v. Food Machinery & Chemical Corp*, 382 US 172, 1965.
565. Note that a scenario where the patent is granted at first but then challenged in court could end as a worst-case scenario, as the costs of the litigation may not be offset by the benefits of the previous exclusivity.

distinguish between patent applications that are probably valid and the applications for patent claims that are probably or obviously invalid.[566]

214 Grants of obviously invalid patents are the result of system inefficiencies.[567] Two typical sources are the design of the patent law itself, as in Switzerland,[568] or the organisation of the acquisition process, as research from the USA indicates.[569] The reasons for tolerating or even implementing imperfections in the revision process of patent applications are efficiency considerations with respect to time and money. Data from the United States Patent and Trademark Office (USPTO) suggest that the resources available during the revision process influence the quality of granted patents. At the USPTO, it is the sole responsibility of one patent examiner to grant a patent or, in its negative sense, to find grounds for rejecting the application. Due to the limited time available for each examination, patents will be granted if, within the time available for the revision, no grounds for refusal can be found. Data provided by FRAKES/WASSERMAN suggest that the same patent examiner will grant more patents and provide fewer objections concerning obviousness when confronted with restrictions on the available time for the revision.[570]

IV IMPLICATIONS

215 This chapter has shown that there are numerous motives for applying for patents. Although traditional motives such as the protection of their own innovation are undoubtedly important, the use of patents for strategic causes is also common. From this brief introduction, it can already be seen that many motives can influence the application for a patent. The motives are not relevant when applying for the patent, however, since the patentability requirements do not involve usage intentions.[571] What

566. *See infra* Part VI, Chapter 18, sections II and III.
567. Critiques of the patent system therefore concentrate not only on the scope of and reasoning for patent protection but also on the fact that patent offices can fail to recognise patent applications that do not meet the patentability requirements. Such patents impose market entry barriers and serve as bargaining power without being justifiable as fostering innovation.
568. The Swiss Federal Institute of Intellectual Property – unlike the USPTO and the EPC – is, under Article 59(4) PatA, only obliged to carry out a limited examination of the formal patentability requirements set out in Article 1 PatA. Substantive examination only includes commercial applicability (including reference to traditional knowledge and generic resources), consistency and clarity of the claim, the relevant application date as well as a characterisation of the technology as a technical teaching. The Institute does not examine other requirements such as novelty, non-obviousness and usefulness.
569. FRAKES/WASSERMAN, The Review of Economics and Statistics 2017, 562.
570. FRAKES/WASSERMAN, The Review of Economics and Statistics 2017, 562; with respect to the limited budget and therefore increased pressure on examiners: JAFFE/LERNER, 131 f. There is also the possibility that the applications were not motivated by blocking intentions. While applicants that wilfully apply for an obviously invalid patent with the additional intention of using it as a blocking patent make use of both possibilities provided in the design of the patent system (type 1), others only use one (types 2 and 3) or none (type 4).
571. *See supra* at Part II, Chapter 6, section I.

the focus on blocking patents has further shown is that patents applied for from the same motive (blocking) can appear in different forms. This diversity in both motives and appearance provides patent holders with a wide array of options in using patents to reach their goal of developing and applying patenting strategies.

CHAPTER 7

Patenting Strategies

I DEVELOPMENT OF PATENTING STRATEGIES

216 Patents are granted to inventors for a contribution beyond the current state of the art. The patent is thus rewarded for an achievement based on outstanding performance in a specific field or, one could also say, to reward an inventor for merits of innovation.[572] Since the mere knowledge immanent in an invention is not tradeable, the patent allows the inventor to compete on the market with their achievements. Without property protection, only objectified items of the invented concept would be tradeable. Once traded, everyone could copy the object and start their own business.[573] At worst, the inventor to whom society owes the benefit of the technology would only be paid once for a single object, i.e., the machine or drug containing the innovative idea. The value of the reward given through patent law is not straightforward; it is

572. *See supra* at Part II, Chapter 6, section I.
573. A famous historical example where even cross-country copying occurred is the textile manufacturing industry at the end of the eighteenth century. At that time the USA was cultivating most of the world's cotton but could not process it due to a lack of technology. The British, on the other hand, could not cultivate cotton but had a well-developed textile industry. One advantage the British textile industry had at that time was Richard Arkwright's water spinning frame, a spinning machine driven by water (horses at first) instead of manpower (patented in 1769). The water spinning frame also automatically drew out the fibres it processed. The machine enabled the industrial production of textiles. The British authorities feared an exchange of knowledge with the USA. But instead of profiting from the technological advantage by selling access to the technology, the British government imposed a travel ban to the USA on British textile workers in order to block the technology from the Americans. Despite that law, in 1789 Samuel Slater, a former apprentice to a leading English cotton mill, travelled to the USA where he spread the knowledge and rebuilt Arkwright's machine. The transfer of knowledge resulted in the industrial revolution in the USA and huge losses for the British industry. Interesting also is the fact that the water spinning frame made its way to continental Europe in a similar way, where the technology also fired the starting pistol for the industrial revolution. POOLEY JAMES: https://www.ipwatchdog.com/2017/07/05/americas-industrial-revolution-based-trade-secret-theft/id=85377/, accessed on 15 January 2020.

dependent on the circumstances of the market in which the patented technology is applied as well as the strategies of the patent holder. Through the patent right, the law does not provide the inventor with a value that equals their investment, but with a means to compete with the invention.[574] The value of the patent is dependent on its performance, and the revenue on the patent portfolio's merits.[575]

217 Since the mid-1980s, the number of patent applications has increased in many parts of the world.[576] This surge, however, was not matched by an equal rise in R&D spending and therefore caused discussion about a possible disturbance of the functioning of the patent system. As other explanatory approaches could not fully explain the surge in patent applications, it was assumed that there may have been a change or shift in the motives to apply for a patent.[577] Assumptions were made that undertakings might have found ways to profit from patents by using them strategically. Thus, the allegation resonates that applicants applying for patents are not only motivated by the prospect of receiving property protection and the possibility of receiving a return on their R&D investments.[578] This theory is supported by famous patent litigation cases which show that patents are sometimes critical to securing an undertaking's existence and that mismanagement can cost millions.[579]

218 The most famous of these cases was *Polaroid Corp. v. Eastman Kodak Co.* In 1976, Polaroid Corp. sued Eastman Kodak Co. for infringing twelve of Polaroid's patents on instant colour photography.[580] Since 1950 Kodak had been an important supplier of negative material for Polaroid, and the two companies had even held numerous meetings to discuss possible business cooperation or licensing deals. The meetings were never fertile, however. In 1969, Kodak ended negotiations and started developing its own instant colour camera. Despite enormous efforts and the raising of considerable funds, Kodak only realised a breakthrough after buying and probably examining large quantities of Polaroid's SX-70 cameras.[581]

219 What followed the lawsuit of 1976 was one of the longest and most spectacular legal battles in the history of patent law. Only after over a decade was the case finally settled in 1990. In its ruling in 1985, the US District Court of Massachusetts found

574. LEMLEY/SHAPIRO, Journal of Economic Perspectives 2005, 76 ff.
575. *See* the similar wording used in the assessment of Servier's strategy by the EC: EC, *Servier*, AT.39612, para. 2793.
576. *See supra* at para. 97.
577. *See supra* at fn. 280.
578. COHEN/NELSON/WALSH, NBER Working Paper Series, 4 and 17; similarly: ARUNDEL/PATEL, European Trend Chart on Innovation 2003, 2.
579. Although *Polaroid v. Kodak* is the most frequently mentioned case, previous conflicts, such as challenges to Bell's 'telephone patent' No 174 465 from 1876, which survived over six hundred trials, and Marconi's attempts to uphold the validity of his 'Four sevens' (No 7777) patent, showed the importance of successful IP management. KURZ, 433 ff. and 445 ff.
580. Final decision, after various appeals, by the Federal District Judge A. D. Mazzone: DISS. MASS., *Polaroid Corp. v. Eastman Kodak Co.*, 641 F. Supp. 828.
581. *See*: WARSHOFSKY, 85. Note that Kodak did not agree with this understanding of Judge Rya Zobel. *See*: WARSHOFSKY, 80 ff.

Kodak guilty of having infringed seven of ten argued patents.[582] In consequence, Kodak was forced by an injunction to stop the production and sales of instant cameras.

220 A later appeal to the Supreme Court was denied and Kodak finally paid a total of USD 909 million in damages. Furthermore, as well as paying the enormous damages, Kodak was compelled to close a factory, dismiss workers and buy back the cameras that were still on the market.[583] They became worthless as no further Kodak film was allowed to be sold after the injunction came into force.[584] Consequently, Kodak completely lost the market after the verdict.[585]

221 This case shows the brutal consequences a patent strategy can have for an undertaking and highlights the growing importance of patenting for management.[586] Most undertakings nowadays debate basic questions about patenting at management level.[587] The reasons for applying for patents have become more diverse than originally intended by the legislator when creating the patent system.[588]

II OFFENSIVE VERSUS DEFENSIVE PATENTING

222 Patenting strategies can either be motivated by the intention to protect one's own inventions and the idea of creating a safety zone to secure room for manoeuvre, or for the purpose of intervening in a competitor's R&D process by either hampering further development or making the market launch of a product impossible. Depending on their aim, patent strategies are often categorised as either offensive or defensive strategies.[589] This distinction first occurred in a paper by ARUNDEL/PATEL in 2003[590] and has since been adopted by many authors.[591]

223 There is no consensus on the distinctive features, however. Some categorisations distinguish between strategies where the application of patents is motivated by the intention to protect the company's inventions (offensive patenting) and others motivated by the intention to react to existing patents of competitors (defensive patenting). Following this differentiation, the aim of offensive patenting is to maximise and strengthen the holder's position in a technical field and to protect the company's own

582. One patent was not considered infringed and the other two were held invalid. For a critical analysis of the case, *see also*: WARSHOFSKY, 77 ff.
583. RIVETTE/KLINE, 96.
584. Brief introductions to the case also in: WARSHOFSKY, Chapter 3; RIVETTE/KLINE, 95 ff.
585. GLAZIER, 158; WARSHOFSKY, 87 ff.
586. In the literature, the importance of successful patent management has since been an important matter to address. *See i.a.*: ERNST, in: HOMMEL/KNECHT, Wertorientiertes Start-up-Management, 313 ff.; RIVETTE/KLINE, 44 ff. and 57 ff.
587. *See*: BENNET, Business in North Carolina, 64; GRANSTRAND, 225 f.
588. *See supra* at paras 86 ff.
589. *See*: BURR ET AL., 94 ff.; as well as hereinafter at fn. 590.
590. ARUNDEL/PATEL, European Trend Chart on Innovation 2003, 3; in the German literature, GREFERMANN/RÖTHLINGSHÖFER in 1974 grouped strategies as 'active' and 'passive' patenting. GREFERMANN, 31 ff.
591. As i.a.: BLIND/CREMERS/MÜLLER, Research Policy, 429; GRANSTRAND, 214.

scope of action. Defensive patents are targeted at minimising the impact of patent strategies of rivals on their own portfolio[592] or even intervening in the competitor's strategy. One example of such a defensive strategy is 'pre-emptive' patenting which will be presented in more detail below.[593]

224 Other categorisations base the distinction on the intention to monetise the asset. The term 'offensive patent' then refers to patents monetised by licensing or litigation.[594] Defensive patents, in this context, are accumulated to be used as bargaining power. A frequent reason to file for a defensive patent is an intended improvement of the holder's position in cross-licence negotiations or as retaliation power to prevent others from challenging patent validity.[595]

225 However, other authors categorise strategies as offensive if they are targeted at rivals and focused on limiting their actual or future scope of action.[596] With the instrument of filing lawsuits against possible patent infringers or directed at invalidating third-party patents, patent holders offensively deter rivals from being too active in the relevant market.[597] Hence offensive patents can also refer to those which are actively enforced.[598] Defensive patents, according to this categorisation, arm the patent holder for potential lawsuits, hold reputational functions and therefore ensure freedom of manoeuvre.[599]

226 The distinction between offensive and defensive patenting is relevant for the chapters that follow as it comes down to balancing the interests of patent and competition law. Strategies targeted at protecting the companies' own inventions more often tend to be in line with the aim of the patent law and are thus less problematic with respect to competition law concerns.[600] Owing to the lack of consensus in the literature, this book will not distinguish between offensive and defensive patenting. Rather, the analysis will be based on the interests involved and the nature of the conduct.

III PATENTING STRATEGIES AND THEIR BLOCKING IMPACT ON COMPETITION AND INNOVATION

227 The impact of patents on competition and innovation has been the subject of many, primarily economic, publications. When analysing the findings, unfortunately, one cannot escape the conclusion drawn by THOUVENIN that even though certain effects can be identified which are typically caused by patents, it is almost impossible to make

592. GASSMANN/BADER, 37 f.
593. *See infra* at paras 256 ff.
594. HARHOFF DIETMAR ET AL., accessed on 14 February 2020.
595. GRANSTRAND, 214 f.
596. Also 'reactive patenting': FAIX, WiSt 2001, 518.
597. This category is similar to the first attempts referenced in fn. 590; for further references *see*: BURR ET AL., 94 ff.; GASSMANN/BADER, 36 f.
598. FAIX, WiSt 2001, 518.
599. GRANSTRAND, 214.
600. *See infra* at paras 499 ff.

general valid statements on the impact of patents on competition. This is because the actual impact of patents on competition is dependent on factors such as the design of the law, the scope of the patent claim, the situation in the market and the strategy[601] of the patent holder.[602] Against this background, the following section tries to collate the effects generally attributed to the different types of patent strategies introduced above and to draw general conclusions for blocking patents within the strategies addressed. The focus is therefore on the influence of the strategy on innovation, as promoting innovation is not only the aim of the patent system but also integral to competition law.

1 Basic Patent

1.1 Definition

228 Basic patents[603] are those patents which are first granted for an invention.[604] They therefore often cover the core of a technology or product.[605] In the pharmaceutical industry, basic patents, for example, cover the active ingredient of a drug (Article 1 EEC No 1768/92).[606] Basic patents contrast with secondary patents which are related to the basic patent but cover an improvement or variation.[607] In the pharmaceutical industry, secondary patents can, for example, cover new salt or crystalline forms, optical isomers, new usage or dosage forms, a new form of delivery or new processes to manufacture it.[608] Secondary patents are of great importance in pharmaceutical life-cycle management and thus in strategic patenting within the industry.[609]

1.2 Blocking Potential of Basic Patents

229 Basic patents tend to have high potential to block competitors[610] in cases where they have a broad scope and widely cover parts of a product,[611] as it is genuinely hard

601. An introduction to the different patenting strategies can also be found in: BERTHOLD, 102 ff.
602. THOUVENIN, 279.
603. The term 'basic patent' is clarified in Article 1 para. c of Regulation (EC) No 469/2009. A basic patent is one which 'protects a product as such, a process to obtain a product or an application of a product'.
604. SILVERMAN, JOM 1995, 50; RAHN, GRUR Int., 378; in the context of SPCs, the basic patent is the patent that should be extended with an SPC. The term thus differs. On basic patents and SPCs *see*: STIEF/BÜHLER, in: HAEDICKE/TIMMANN, Patent law, paras 35 ff.
605. *See*: BERTHOLD, 102; LANGE, Anspruchspolitik im Rahmen der Patentanmeldung, 14.
606. *See supra* at Part II, Chapter 7, section III.1; EC, *Sector Inquiry, Final Report,* para. 138.
607. *See* on secondary patents: AHN, 28 ff.; KAPCZYNSKI/PARK/SAMPAT, PloS one 2012; SAMPAT/SHADLEN, SCID 2015, 229.
608. *See* the listing provided by: EC, *Sector Inquiry, Final Report,* para. 138.
609. On second-generation products in the pharmaceutical industry: ELLERY/HANSEN, 159 ff.
610. Note that any patent, including secondary patents, can theoretically hinder the development or launch of a product. The less important the technology, however, the less severe the blocking power. Thus, both basic patents and secondary patent strategies are listed as mainly blocking.
611. This strategy is suggested to patent managers as a fruitful tool in a life-cycle strategy. GASSMANN/BADER, 99.

to invent around them.[612] The literature indicates that competitors can be prevented from driving their own developments further through the mere presence of a strong basic patent.[613] The blocking power of a basic patent increases when it becomes part of an industry standard.[614] Standards can either be technologies that have proved themselves in the market (such as Windows Operating System) and have thus become de facto standards or they can be set by standard-setting organisations (SSO[615]) to simplify the application and usage of technology.[616] Once it has become a standard, a technology is difficult to get round. Every successful competitor in the particular field has to include the standard in their own products and thus license the technology. To avoid blocking in cases of standard-setting, so-called FRAND commitments have been developed. The owner of the standard technology has to agree to license the technology on FRAND terms to prevent hold-ups.[617]

230 A similar effect can occur in industries based on incremental innovation.[618] In such industries, a product is protected by a myriad of patents. On the one hand, a patent holder in such a situation has the power to forestall the launch of an entire technology.[619] On the other hand, in this case, the patent holder has no possibility to exploit their (part of the) invention, which reduces the risk of deadlock. Yet, deadlocks can still occur, as the development of the radio shows.[620] The technical features and principles needed to build a radio were all discovered or developed by different, independent researchers such as Hertz and Edison.[621,622] In the USA, various researchers therefore held patents on basic technologies which were all needed to build a radio.[623] Due to these interdependencies, no patent holder could have produced a radio with personally owned patents only. As inventing around the given technologies was not an option, cooperation would have been necessary for each party involved to earn a return on their R&D expenses and for the public to be endowed with a new

612. Inventing around is difficult per se, as the unfolding of new ideas is unenforceable. GLAZIER, 32 ff.
613. *See infra* at paras 618 ff.
614. BARTON, Antitrust Law Journal 2001, 872.
615. SSOs are industry groups with the task of setting common standards in various, significant areas. *See*: LEMLEY, SSRN Journal 2003, 1892.
616. A common example for a regionally set standard is sockets. Without standardisation, it could not be guaranteed that all electronic devices bought could be plugged in at home.
617. On competition law concerns that might still be raised, *see*: BABEY/RIZVI, WUW 2012, 810 ff.
618. *See supra* at fn. 547.
619. SHAPIRO, in: JAFFE/LERNER/STERN, Innovation policy and the economy, 120.
620. On the development of the radio *see*: GRINDLEY/TEECE, California Management Review 1997, 10 f.
621. It comes as no surprise that for the inventor of the radio, or more precisely of a technique to transport data wirelessly, many names are included. In 1943, the UNITED STATES SUPREME COURT in the ruling *Marconi Wireless Tel. Co. v. United States* held that Marconi's Patent No 763,772 was invalid as it did not contain an additional invention to the state of the art. Indirectly, the court therewith named Tesla as the inventor of the radio. *See*: UNITED STATES SUPREME COURT, *Marconi Wireless Tel. Co. v. United States,* 320 US 1.
622. It was noted that there were 'hundreds of individual pieces': STURMEY, 15.
623. Note that in Great Britain, where Marconi started to make his idea public, The Marconi Wireless Telegraph and Signal Company Ltd. collected and held all the relevant patents needed to develop the radio. HAGEN, 58.

technology. However, the companies could not agree on licensing their technology.[624] The block was finally resolved by the forming of a corporation – the Radio Corporation of America, RCA – that assimilated all the relevant patents. The patent holders, now shareholders of the corporation, were eventually willing to cross-license and attempts to further develop the technique started.

231 It becomes clear that the economic environment influences the impact of a patent strategy on the market. Therefore, general predictions on the effect of a patent strategy are generally hard to make and an evaluation of the competitive environment is indispensable. As blocking patents are used to prevent competitors from providing a substitute to a given demand, in the pharmaceutical industry blocking with basic patents is possible when a dominant undertaking has developed an active substance which could be used in a me-too drug but is withheld from the market to avoid it competing with their own drug. The use of blocking patents in shielding, fencing and clustering strategies, that is, patents covering further developments of basic patents, will become more likely.

232 From a strategic point of view, the application of a basic blocking patent needs to be distinguished from ad hoc blocking. Ad hoc blocking is a strategy where only a few patents are used to protect a technology. Such forms normally occur in the case of random inventions, ad hoc efforts, small resources or negligence of portfolio management on the part of the applicant. The power of ad hoc blocking is limited, as inventing around is relatively simple,[625] and it will not be focused on in this book.

1.3 Effects of Blocking Basic Patents on the Market

233 It is widely acknowledged that patents do not automatically create a monopoly or a dominant position on the market, as the relevant market is generally determined by all substitutable or substantially interchangeable products,[626] not only the patented product itself. Products using a patent-protected technology can therefore compete with similar products. The exceptions are pioneering patents which offer the only solution to satisfy a specific, existing or emerging need. The development of other solutions in these cases is not believed to be successful or is deemed impossible.[627]

234 In other cases, inventing around a basic patent might be considered an economic disaster, for example, when consumers are locked in (barriers to innovation) or when inventing around would add little value to the basic patent.[628] The effect of a basic patent on competition is thus, as has generally been concluded, heavily dependent on

624. Although the refusal to license was probably not the idea while applying for the patent, the situation on the market created an equally delicate situation.
625. On ad hoc blocking: GRANSTRAND, 219.
626. *See infra* at paras 281 f.
627. KRASSER/ANN, § 3, para. 47; on this paragraph: THOUVENIN, 279 f.
628. FTC, *Report: To Promote Innovation*, Chapter 2, 21 f.

its economic uniqueness or the uniqueness of the patented technology to satisfy a need or demand.[629]

235 The impact of basic patents and follow-on innovation has been investigated for patents covering the technology of research tools. Evidence found by WALSH ET AL. suggests that a restriction on access to research tools which are key to follow-on innovation can delay further development. This effect can be lower, depending on the availability of different lines of innovation to solve the problem or the availability of shortcuts not using the technology of the basic patent. Since the availability of potential shortcuts or alternatives can be the result of further research and may not be known when applying for the basic patent, it is difficult to estimate the effect that barely accessible or, in the case of blocking patents, inaccessible basic technologies might have on follow-on research and innovation.[630]

236 The most robust but also rather obvious finding from the economic literature which applies to broad patent clusters as well as broad basic patents is that the broader the patented claim, the harder it is to invent around or develop follow-on innovation and the higher the probability that follow-on innovation will infringe the primary patent.[631] The protection a patent provides is limited by the likelihood of someone inventing around.[632] Therefore, a basic patent will be more likely to prevent follow-on innovation if the scope is broad.[633] An example of a situation where it is likely that blocking basic patents will impede innovation in pharmaceutical technology is when researchers patent a receptor with a specific therapeutic approach.[634] Receptors respond to certain information from outside a cell in a specific, determined way and are therefore not interchangeable. Yet, the crux for competition regulators is that low-cost access to key innovation can result in reduced research activities overall due to lower incentives for the initial innovator.

237 Although there is little evidence of cases where a basic patent has impeded further development,[635] there are indications that small firms especially refrain from innovating when confronted with a broad patent held by a dominant undertaking, due to the imminent litigation costs.[636] One example, discussed in the literature,[637] is the case of *Rochester v. Pfizer et al.* Pfizer in this case challenged the validity of a patent held by the

629. Listing more factors in the context of the effect of licensing agreements on competition: ULLRICH/HEINEMANN, in: IMMENGA/MESTMÄCKER 2018, Teil GRUR B, para. 41.
630. WALSH/ARORA/COHEN, in: MERRILL/COHEN, Patents in the knowledge-based economy.
631. As already indicated above: THOUVENIN, 279 f.
632. GILBERT/NEWBERY, The American Economic Review 1982, 519.
633. On the difficulties of implementing a patent regime providing incentives for both the innovator of the basic technology and the innovator of follow-on inventions, *see*: SCOTCHMER, 116 ff.
634. The revelation of the receptor/point of attack often results in a highly competitive race for developments and modifications. *See*: UNGER, Medizinische Klinik 2006, 259; and further *infra* at para. 710.
635. WALSH/ARORA/COHEN, in: MERRILL/COHEN, Patents in the knowledge-based economy, 331 ff.
636. COHEN/NELSON/WALSH, NBER Working Paper Series, 25.
637. WALSH/ARORA/COHEN, in: MERRILL/COHEN, Patents in the knowledge-based economy, 297.

University of Rochester which covered broadly all COX-2 inhibitors.[638] COX-2 inhibitors are anti-inflammatory drugs and an essential component of many conventional analgesics. Raising obstacles to the use of COX-2 inhibitors could thus have had an immense impact on the market and the development of analgesics.

238 However, within life-cycle strategies in the pharmaceutical industry, basic patents are mainly applied for in the case of NMEs which cure a disease for which the applicant has already marketed a drug.[639] For originators, the application of basic patents for NMEs is thus a viable tool to strengthen their position. Despite generally yielding benefits comparable to the first cure, these patents cover a new active ingredient and can therefore not be understood as secondary patents. Yet, the final drug is a substitute for the available cure. NMEs have to undergo the same phases of development as the first cure for a specific disease and the development period is likely to be comparable in length. Thus, patent expiry is a threat to NMEs as well. These patents are mainly covering important breakthroughs in medicine and are not likely to be used as blocking patents. However, this does not mean that patents on NMEs always result in new medication.

239 Developing a marketable drug is a high-risk venture, as has been shown. In situations where the already marketed drug is still patent protected, the launch of the drug covering the NME may erode profits of the established drug. The patent holder may therefore delay the market entry of the new drug. Yet, because of the threat of patent expiry for the NME, such a delay is potentially not durable and is probably based on operational justifications.

2 Fencing and Flooding

2.1 Definition

240 Fencing[640] and flooding are common patenting strategies which both include the aggregation of several patents (such aggregations are called clusters or thickets)[641] linked to a basic patent in order to limit the possibilities to invent around. An example of a product protected by a cluster consisting of twenty-two interlocking patents was Gillette's shaver with two independently moving blades. The reason for establishing the patent cluster, according to Gillette, was to ensure that 'no one could duplicate that

638. FED. CIR., *University of Rochester v. GD Seale & Co./Pfizer*, 358 F.3d 916.
639. ELLERY/HANSEN, 159.
640. Sometimes the terms 'shielding', 'surrounding' or 'building patent walls' appear as synonyms to describe this form of patent aggregation.
641. *See also*: EC, *Sector Inquiry, Final Report*, paras 484 ff.; SCHNELLE, GRUR-Prax 2010, 169.

product'.[642] Blocking patents are frequently a part of fencing and flooding strategies,[643] but patents in patent aggregations are not necessarily blocking patents.[644]

241 Fencing is a strategy which normally only targets certain specific development streams. When applying a fencing strategy, a patent holder decides to limit only a few 'lines or directions of R&D'.[645] Visually the picture of a circle or fence best describes this situation. One can imagine the basic patent standing in the centre surrounded by the aggregated patents serving as protective barriers and supporting the main patent's blocking power[646] by blocking development streams. With these patent aggregations, patent holders make up for basic patents failing to prevent imitation, substitution and protect further developments.[647]

242 In the above-mentioned case of *Polaroid v. Kodak*, Kodak accused Polaroid of having used the fencing strategy to shield their key inventions.[648] Unfortunately in the verdict this was not taken into consideration. On the contrary, each patent was inspected carefully and judged individually. The court's reasoning therefore did not create a precedent for the analysis of patent strategies involving patent aggregations. A patent cluster was also formed by Servier to protect the blockbuster perindopril. After the expiration of the primary patent protecting the process to gain perindopril, it was still protected with three patents.[649] Apparently, Servier was not satisfied with this protection and decided to pursue a strategy including filing for 'blocking patents' to create 'a cluster of process patents around the molecule'.[650] Servier in fact applied for a number of perindopril-related patents which were internally described as 'blocking' or 'lacking inventive step[s]' and covered, for example, a crystalline form and another saline form of perindopril. Unlike earlier case law, the focus of the courts has now shifted towards the 'overall' strategy.[651]

243 The issue with patent aggregations is that the infringement of a 'guarding patent' will most likely also infringe the core patent. A fencing patent's goal is to hinder competitors from circumventing the centred patent. Patents belonging to such a

642. BUSH, Gillette's former VP of corporate R&D, cited after RIVETTE/KLINE, Harvard Business Review 2000, 58. For another example *see* the cases of *Tetra Pak II, infra* at para. 327, or Servier, *infra* at para. 362.
643. LAMPING, 138 f.; EC, *Servier,* AT.39612, paras 114 ff.
644. *See*: LAMPING, 140 ff. *See also:* BURR ET AL. who locate blocking patents within defensive patenting strategies but not offensive patenting strategies. Offensive patenting strategies according to their terminology provide the basis for the development of the company. BURR ET AL., 94 and 98.
645. GRANSTRAND, 221.
646. On fencing in connection with blocking patents, *see*: LAMPING, 138 f.
647. RAHN, GRUR Int., 378; patenting fences might also be a strategy by competitors to limit the patent holder's scope of action (picket fence strategy or bracketing). GLAZIER, 34; RAHN, GRUR Int., 378 f.; RIVETTE/KLINE, Harvard Business Review 2000, 58.
648. *See supra* at paras 218 ff.
649. EC, *Servier,* AT.39612, para. 114.
650. EMPLOYEE OF SERVIER, cited after the EC in: EC, *Servier,* AT.39612, para. 115.
651. EC, *Servier,* AT.39612, paras 115 ff. and 182; *see infra* at paras 360 ff.

cluster[652] protect not only the core technology but also variations thereof or related technology. Fencing is a popular way of blocking other possible technical solutions that can achieve the same result.[653] As a consequence, patent fences limit the possibilities to invent around by covering alternatives.[654] Attempts to invent around, besides becoming costlier and more time-consuming, also carry a lower chance of success, which results in fewer attempts to circumvent and thus fewer subsequent innovations. The effect of the blocking power is enhanced when combined with a refusal to license; this is more to do with the effort needed to develop and produce a final product than the effect of reducing the possibilities.

244 Flooding is a less targeted strategy than fencing. It refers to a strategy in which various, generally weak patents related to the basic patent are accumulated. Flooding can be used as a strategy in cases where the R&D direction is not yet clear and a fence is thus not appropriate.[655] Flooding patents usually contain variations of the primary patented technology and are targeted at hindering its commercial exploitation or further development. By flooding, a company increases its bargaining power in licence negotiations as well as simultaneously reduces the possibility for rivals to invent around.

245 Fencing and flooding strategies can be used both to hedge one's own technology and to interfere with a rival.[656] In the case of flooding, rivals may flood primary patents by applying for various other generally weak patents. When the prior patent holder finds itself opposed to a flooding strategy, it becomes almost impossible to use their invention without infringing at least one surrounding rivalling patent. This situation results in a gridlock where neither of the patent holders can exploit their technology. Such mutual blockades often force patent holders into cross-licensing.[657] Cross-licensing is lucrative for the flooders as their contributions to the technology are normally minor compared with those of the holder of the primary patent.[658] Many known cases where firms have engaged in flooding strategies have come from Japan.[659] One famous case is the litigation between Fusion Systems and Mitsubishi Electric about patents covering high-power microwave lamps.[660]

246 A company owning many flooding patents can obviously hinder market entrance. Even though flooding patents tend to be rather weak, it is almost impossible to succeed in declaring all patents of a flood invalid. Therefore, a great number of patents held by

---

652. Most often the term 'cluster' is used to describe patent families built after the above given example. *See*: RIVETTE/KLINE, Harvard Business Review 2000, 58.
653. GRANSTRAND, 221.
654. LAMPING, 138 f.
655. GRANSTRAND, 221.
656. For fencing, *see* the reference *supra* at fn. 647.
657. SANKARAN, The Journal of Law and Technology 2000, 394; *see infra* at para. 249.
658. WOLFSON, George Washington Journal of International Law and Economics 1993, 533.
659. SANKARAN, The Journal of Law and Technology 2000, 395; WOLFSON, George Washington Journal of International Law and Economics 1993, 532.
660. *See*: 'Fusion System's efforts to compete in Japan', available at: http://digitalcollections.library.cmu.edu/awweb/awarchive?type=file&item=485463, accessed on 17 February 2020.

just one company can intimidate and deter rivals from challenging the validity of these patents. Applying for that many patents might nevertheless not be a suitable strategy for every undertaking as the costs of litigation and patenting have to be borne in mind. Flooding is thus not generally economical.[661]

2.2 Effects of Blocking Patents on the Market in Fencing and Flooding Strategies

247 Patenting strategies, such as shielding, fencing or flooding, where many patents cover parts of a technology or where a basic patent is accompanied by related patents, such as process patents, can raise rivals' costs. The rise in costs is even higher when blocking patents are used within the strategy. Patent clusters not only force (potential) competitors to make greater efforts to invent around but competitors also run a higher risk of infringing patents. A multitude of patents also makes it more difficult for competitors to determine which parts of a technology are already protected by patents and which are not.[662] Patent strategies resulting in a vast number of patent applications therefore risk impeding innovation.[663] The effects of patent clusters with numerous patents covering parts of the technology are comparable to those of broad basic patents, as inventing around the thicket is generally more difficult.

a Different Patent Holders Holding Patents of a Patent Cluster

248 When patents are distributed among different patent holders, a situation can result where no one dares to launch a product, either out of fear of infringing a patent or because of mutual blocking, when no patent holder is willing to license its patent to competitors.[664] In this situation, as none of the patent holders can exploit their patent and secure returns on R&D – which reduces incentives to innovate – research has identified a tendency to engage in cross-licence negotiations when many patent holders hold the patents needed for a product.[665] MERGES/NELSON argue that rivalrous structures, despite certain obvious inefficiencies, generally result in faster technical progress and are preferable to situations where only a few hold patents.[666] Apart from when there are a number of different patent holders involved, cross-licensing is also likely when patents comprise narrower and fewer claims.[667]

661. GRANSTRAND, 221.
662. 'Mapping out the patent landscape' was, for example, named the first challenge in developing Gillette's sensor shaver by BUSH, Gillette's former VP of corporate R&D. Cited after RIVETTE/KLINE, Harvard Business Review 2000, 58.
663. HAEDICKE, in: HAEDICKE/TIMMANN, Patent law, para. 8; JUNG, ZWeR 2004, 392 f.
664. HELLER/EISENBERG, Science 1998, 699.
665. COHEN ET AL., Research Policy 2002, 1356 f.
666. MERGES/NELSON, Columbia Law Review 1990, 908.
667. COHEN ET AL., Research Policy 2002, 1365.

249 Cross-licensing is a typical remedy to overcome the threat of gridlocks when a number of patent holders own parts of a technology. Yet, engaging in cross-licensing negotiations and investment in research to circumvent competitors' patents can constitute a waste of resources for society.[668] The exact amount of wasted resources accounted for by the strategic use of patenting is hard to determine. Additionally, when cross-licensing agreements or patent pools concern patents covering a substitute technology, such agreements can lead to collusion in oligopolies and a situation where some market participants jointly hold a blocking patent position which blocks market entry.[669] This raises the probability of (tacit) collusive pricing, which thwarts the initial positive effects of collaboration.

b One Patent Holder Holds the Patent Cluster

250 When one patent holder assembles a huge patent portfolio, they can suppress the technology that society would potentially benefit from, which means such patents are not of much value to society. Although they are technically one step ahead of prior art and therefore patentable, they only contribute substitutable technology to the public and do not result in competition as they are held by the same entity. Despite the high likelihood that these unused technologies would not be economically superior to their marketed equivalent, the suppressed technologies could have been profitably marketed by a competitor, thus leading to competition in the market. Additionally, 'patent fences may not only preclude innovations that substitute for some core innovation but also inventions that may improve upon the original invention'.[670] This is particularly likely in cumulative technology industries.

251 Besides withholding useful technology from society, large patent portfolios in the possession of a single holder can also impede the market entry of rivals by raising the costs of market entry, either by requiring higher sums to invent around or by requiring higher costs associated with licensing or challenging the validity of the patents. They have the potential to 'foster[ing] broader monopolies than anticipated by patent policy'[671] and thus consequently wall off areas of technology.[672]

252 A side effect of large patent portfolios is seen in a mechanism described as the 'snowball effect'. Patent holders who have accumulated a massive patent portfolio in one field are also more likely to buy related patents held by individual inventors or entities. From the perspective of competition law, this form of patent accumulation is of greater concern than patenting based on one's own research efforts. This is because the negative effects attributed to huge patent portfolios apply while, at the same time, a potential rival is eliminated and the company holding numerous patents cannot

668. Walsh/Arora/Cohen, in: Merrill/Cohen, Patents in the knowledge-based economy, 332.
669. Harhoff/Engel/Möschel 2007, 14 f.; Scherer/Ross, 625.
670. Cohen/Nelson/Walsh, NBER Working Paper Series, 28.
671. Cohen/Nelson/Walsh, NBER Working Paper Series, 28.
672. Arora, Research Policy 1997, 401.

justify the property rights by having contributed technology to society. Consequently, acquisitions of technology with exclusive licences or acquisitions of whole portfolios strengthen the dominant position by preventing competing products.[673]

253 The effect of patent-conglomerates on potential market entrants has been documented in the pharmaceutical industry for generic producers as well as originators. In the case of generic producers, their ability to enter the market can be affected as the entry of a generic producer is only possible after the expiration of all patents covering the originator's compound. Owing to the considerably lower prices of generic products compared with the original medicines, hindering the market entrance of generic products can cause deadweight losses.[674] For such an effect to take hold, it is not required that all alternatives for substances, dosage and galenic forms or production are blocked, as a high number of patents increases the difficulty of evaluating potential infringements of secondary patents through generic entry.[675] The effect of secondary patents on competition is therefore the highest at the end of the exclusivity period of the basic patent and grows with the density of the patent cluster.[676]

254 An originator who opposes secondary patents faces potentially higher costs of expansion and further development. They also need to decide whether to challenge the validity of the patents. Owing to the vast number of patents and therefore an incapacity to challenge them all, uncertainty would be likely to remain.[677] When the claims of originators overlap with R&D programmes or even patents held by another originator company, research activity can be blocked. The detrimental effect of such blocking is evident, especially in cases where the two originators involved cannot agree on a licence to resolve the hold-up.[678]

3 Evergreening

255 Evergreening[679] refers to a practice that is especially popular in the pharmaceutical industry. The basic idea underlying the strategy is the patenting of slight improvements to the main drug. Each of them is rewarded the full patent term, which consequently leads to an extension of the active substance's patent term. Either generic entrance in these cases is not possible or the generic drugs lose attractiveness for consumers, as the originator still owns the newest (best) form of the compound.[680] Although the strategies of evergreening and applying for blocking patents can both be used within an overall patenting strategy, the strategies differ conceptually. Both

673. GC, *Tetra Pak I*, T-51/89, para. 23.
674. EC, *Sector Inquiry, Final Report*, 94.
675. AHN, 229 and 233; EC, *Sector Inquiry, Final Report*, paras 525 ff.; ULLRICH, in: DREXL/LEE, Pharmaceutical innovation, competition and patent law, 246; VESALA, in: BALLARDINI/BRUUN/NORRGÅRD, Transitions in European patent law, 273.
676. AHN, 228; EC, *Sector Inquiry, Final Report*, paras 523 ff.
677. VESALA, in: BALLARDINI/BRUUN/NORRGÅRD, Transitions in European patent law, 273.
678. EC, *Sector Inquiry, Final Report*, 412.
679. A well-founded examination of evergreening strategies can be found in: BERTHOLD.
680. On the whole, *see*: BERTHOLD, 18 ff.

strategies raise competition law concerns, however. Therefore, evergreening is briefly addressed within this book.[681] Owing to the conceptual difference, a detailed analysis will not be provided, however.

4 Pre-empted Patent Application

256 Blocking strategies do not always aim at receiving patent grants. Pre-emptive patenting makes use of the mechanism that even technologies covered by rejected patent applications become prior art and therewith non-patentable.[682]

257 The same effect achieved using pre-empted patent applications can also be achieved by disclosures in defensive publications in journals or through presenting current research and breakthroughs in presentations. However, defensive publications are not as effective as patent filings and may not be recognised by the patent officer when examining patent applications and therefore may not prevent the grant of patents. Such a failure could only be corrected through expensive litigation.[683] In practice, innovators publishing defensively to foil a rival's intention try to minimise this risk through targeting publications that are most likely to be read by the patent office.[684]

258 Disclosed or pre-emptively patented technology becomes state of the art and thus unpatentable. This might render innovation in this field less prosperous, but it does not hamper innovation or the launch of the marketable product itself. The strategy of pre-empted patent application has therefore not been at the forefront in legal writing and is only included here for comprehensive coverage in this book.

IV PATENT LAW REMEDIES TO COUNTER BLOCKING PATENTS

259 Above, with reference to the principle of exhaustion, it has been seen that in certain situations limitations to intellectual property rights have to be implemented in order to guarantee the functioning of competition and the goals pursued by the laws of the Union.[685] While it has been stated that competition law provides a limitation to the strategic use of intellectual property rights when they interfere with the goals of competition law,[686] the question of whether also intellectual property rights provide remedies for behaviour interfering with the aim of the law has so far been omitted.

260 A short insight has been given with respect to a lack of remedies to tackle motives of using the patent beyond the aim of the patent law or to distort competition when

681. *See infra* at paras 652 f.
682. GUELLEC/MARTINEZ/ZUNIGA, Economics of Innovation and New Technology 2012, 3.
683. ARUNDEL/PATEL, European Trend Chart on Innovation 2003, 3.
684. On the paragraph: BAKER/MEZZETTI, Journal of Law and Economics 2005.
685. *See supra* at para. 126.
686. *See supra* at paras 117 ff. and 126.

applying for the patent. Intentions to use the patent do not have to be shown when filing the patent application.[687] The non-usage of a patent prima facie has no consequences from a patent law perspective. Unlike in trademark law, where the failure to use the trademark can result in the loss of the right,[688] failure to use the patent results neither in the loss of the claim nor in an obligation to use the technology. However, the latter can inasmuch be enforced as the TRIPS Agreement in Article 31 requires its Member States to provide a mechanism to grant compulsory licences. Many European countries have therefore implemented compulsory licensing regimes within their patent laws, though with differences in their design.[689]

261 The different compulsory licensing regimes have in common that the insufficient exploitation of the patent against public interests[690] (as, e.g., in Austria, the Czech Republic or Germany[691]) or for a certain period of time (as, e.g., in Austria, the Czech Republic, France or Switzerland) demand the grant of a licence.[692] Many patent laws therefore provide a remedy for competitors who are hindered by an unused patent.[693]

262 Despite the different designs within national legislations, one can say that compulsory licences in patent law are granted in order to counteract the exclusive rights of the patent holder in situations where they exercise them in a manner that does not contribute to the aim of patent law[694] and is opposed to the public interest.[695] Critical is that society enjoys unfettered access to innovative products. Even though competition law considerations might be included in the weighting of interests when arguing compulsory licence cases,[696] the functioning of competition, which belongs to the scope of competition law, is not protected through the compulsory licences granted in patent law.[697]

263 Overall, one can say that cases might occur where both the threshold of a competition law intervention and the preconditions for obtaining a compulsory licence under patent laws are met. Additionally, patent laws theoretically allow for the

687. *See supra* at para. 215; *see also*: VESALA, in: BALLARDINI/BRUUN/NORRGÅRD, Transitions in european patent law, 275. In trademark law this is different, however. *See supra* at para. 211 and *infra* at paras 672 ff.; for recent case law, *see*: ECJ, *Sky and Others*, C-371/18, paras 72 ff.
688. *See infra* at para. 672 ff.
689. On compulsory licensing in European countries, *see*: EPO, *Compulsory licensing in Europe*. The EPC does not contain rules with respect to compulsory licences, however.
690. That is, for example, when society is not sufficiently supplied with a certain good.
691. On compulsory licences in Germany, *see*: HEINEMANN, Immaterialgüterschutz in der Wettbewerbsordnung, 180 ff.
692. *See*: EPO, *Compulsory licensing in Europe*.
693. Note that the permission to demand compulsory licences has remained a rarely used possibility in several countries. Switzerland reports zero cases of compulsory licences granted for insufficient exploitation. *See*: HEINRICH, Article 37, para. 3; Germany had only few cases. *See*: JUNG, ZWeR 2004, fn. 160; WOLFF, 23 f. Apparently, compulsory licences do not play a major role in India as well. *See*: HÖHNE, in: BUSCHE ET AL., TRIPS Kommentar, Article 31, fn. 10.
694. According to HEINRICH, the aim of patent law is not reached, when valuable patents get stored away. *See*: HEINRICH, Article 37, para. 1.
695. *See i.a.*: HEINRICH, Article 37, para. 1; WOLFF, 20 f.
696. This is disputed, however, as the analysis of HEINEMANN shows: HEINEMANN, Immaterialgüterschutz in der Wettbewerbsordnung, 185 f.
697. HEINEMANN, ZWeR 2005, 201.

inclusion of competition law concerns within the public interest consideration.[698] Yet, patent law does not provide (sufficient) remedies to counteract threats to the functioning of competition that result from patenting strategies or the use of the patent in competition.[699] Patent law and competition law remedies therefore complement each other, just like competition law and intellectual property laws function as external barriers to one another.[700]

V SUMMARY OF THE PRECEDING EVALUATION

264 It is often difficult to draw a line between motives that are in accordance with the aim of the patent system and those which are not. In most cases, the boundaries are blurred. Strategic patenting can be classified among this grey area.[701] From a patent law perspective, using a patent strategically does not necessarily mean 'unlawful'. Patent law itself is relatively ill-equipped when it comes to providing remedies to eradicate inefficiencies. Under the EPC, the intentions of the patent holder to use the patent in accordance with the aim of the patent system are neither relevant when applying for the patent nor during its period of validity.[702] Furthermore, the refusal to license a technology as well as inefficient exploitation of the patent only rarely result in the grant of compulsory licences based on national patent laws.

265 Yet, strategic patents necessarily raise the costs for rivals to invent around or to do business in the relevant sector[703] and therefore might need stricter competition law scrutiny. It is evident that certain patent strategies have increased negative economic effects while at the same time failing to provide a pro-competitive potential compared with what could be expected from patents in terms of incentives to innovate.[704] Finding the right balance between competition and patent law is difficult, as failure carries the risk of harming innovation.[705] Low standards for patentability or inefficient remedies for abusively executed patent rights can hamper competition and innovation in the same way as patentability requirements that are set too high or have too strict practice concerning the use of the patent system.

---

698. HEINEMANN, Immaterialgüterschutz in der Wettbewerbsordnung, 185 f.; JUNG, ZWeR 2004, 406 ff. JUNG, however, applies a narrow understanding and argues that competition law concerns can only be included within the limits of patent law. Dissenting: RAUDA, GRUR 2007, 1023.
699. HEINEMANN, ZWeR 2005, 205; JUNG, ZWeR 2004, 404 ff. This has, for example, been seen in the case of *Hilti*, where the licence fee demanded itself constituted an abuse of the dominant position, because the General Court found that asking the large fee 'was needlessly protracting the proceedings for the grant of licenses of right'. GC, *Hilti v. Commission*, T-30/89, para. 99. The grant of a compulsory licence would not make up for the protracting of the proceedings.
700. *See supra* at para. 120; JUNG, ZWeR 2004, 407.
701. *See i.a.*: BLIND ET AL., Research Policy, 656 ff.
702. On the failure of patent law to provide a remedy for patents obtained after having provided misleading information to the patent office, *see*: VESALA, in: BALLARDINI/BRUUN/NORRGÅRD, Transitions in european patent law, 275.
703. GRANSTRAND, 221.
704. Similarly, also: VESALA, in: BALLARDINI/BRUUN/NORRGÅRD, Transitions in European patent law, 274; EC, *Sector Inquiry, Final Report*, 201.
705. FTC, *Report: To Promote Innovation*, Ex. Summary, 3.

266 To complicate the situation even more, competition is not automatically distorted after driving out a competitor.[706] Likewise, the strategic use of the patent system does not automatically have a negative influence on innovation. Patents, though not generally insurmountable, act as market entry barriers.[707] The use of blocking patents within patenting strategies further aggravates the market-barring effect, as they cannot be licensed but need to be invented around or challenged as invalid. The presence of blocking patents thus strengthens the market position of the patent holder. When blocking patents are used within a patenting strategy, the chance of a negative influence on innovation is therefore higher or more likely than with other patents.

267 The above examples make clear that patents can be used strategically in many ways and that patent strategies can have a serious impact on the functioning of competition. Owing to the design of patent systems, it is relatively easy to use patents strategically. Patent systems often also lack control mechanisms at the patent office, through either low patentability requirements or little evaluation effort on the part of the authority.[708]

268 While blocking strategies are, in trademark law, sanctioned with nullity by the intellectual property right, there is no such remedy in patent law.[709] The question to be answered in this book is whether, in certain cases, competition law can provide a remedy. Alongside different questions that will be raised and answered during this analysis, one question will resonate. Can interventions of competition law be justified when the intellectual property law itself is silent on the matter? This question will be answered at the end of the book in Part VI, Chapter 18. Initially, the analysis will focus on the abuse of a dominant position. This analysis starts hereinafter with a focus on the definition of the dominant position (Part III).

706. ECJ, *TeliaSonera Sverige*, C-52/09, para. 94.
707. *See infra* at paras 312 f.
708. An additional reason why it is relatively easy to use patents strategically is that patent laws lack effective remedies to provide protection against the abusive use of the patent. This second factor will be addressed further *infra*. *See* paras 661 ff.
709. *See supra* at paras 211 and 260.

PART III Defining Markets and Establishing Dominance

CHAPTER 8

Market Power Versus Dominance: Introduction and Definition

269 The question raised by this book is whether an application for blocking patents, that is, the application for a specific patenting strategy, is an abuse of the dominant position under Article 102 TFEU.

270 In 1978, the Court of Justice was first asked to define dominance as an element of Article 102 TFEU. In the case of *United Brands*, it adopted a definition previously presented by the Commission in its *Continental Can* decision[710] according to which a dominant position is:

> [...] a position of economic strength enjoyed by an undertaking which enables it to prevent effective competition being maintained on the relevant market by giving it the power to behave to an appreciable extent independently of its competitors, customers and ultimately of its consumers [...].[711]

271 An exact year later, the court confirmed this definition in the case of *Hoffmann-La Roche*.[712] Since then, the definition has been used in several other judgments without undergoing any revision.[713] The understanding of the dominant position in the context of Article 102 TFEU did not change even with the transformation from the Treaty

710. In the *Continental Can* case, the Commission paraphrased dominance as warranting 'global freedom of action', that is a state which allows an undertaking to operate without paying attention to other participants in the relevant market. EC, *Continental Can*, IV/26.811, II. B. para. 3. Unfortunately in the judgment following the appeal, the ECJ focused on the abuse of a dominant position and omitted an examination of the dominance term. *See*: ECJ, *Continental Can v. Commission*, C-6/72, paras 18 ff.
711. ECJ, *United Brands*, C-27/76, para. 65; *see also*: EC, *Guidance Paper*, para. 10 with further references.
712. ECJ, *Hoffmann-La Roche v. Commission*, C-85/76, para. 38.
713. *See*: EC, *Guidance Paper*, para. 10. Some authors expect that in the course of the integration of the *more economic approach* and changes in the understanding of what abuse is, the practice related to the dominance term will also change. FUCHS/MÖSCHEL, in: IMMENGA/MESTMÄCKER 2018, Article 102, para. 79.

establishing the European Community (TEC) into the current TFEU in 2009.[714] Remarkable in this context is the wording in the judgment of *Michelin I.* After its release, it sparked a debate over the relationship between the two components of a dominant position: the *ability to prevent effective competition* and the *power to behave independently*. The definition in *United Brands* connected these two elements with 'by' which led to the conclusion that both elements were features describing the same powerful position. In *Michelin I*, however, the court changed the wording slightly and linked the elements with 'and',[715] apparently implying a cumulative relationship. Even though the Court of Justice never clarified this confusion, it cited both cases as references when defining a dominant position[716] and did not apply Article 102 TFEU any differently. It is thus widely agreed that both characteristics describe the same state of 'global freedom of action'[717].[718] With this definition, the Court of Justice built a bridge between the economic concept of market power and the sociological understanding of power as shaped by MAX WEBER. Power, according to WEBER, is the ability to have one's will against all odds.[719]

272 The concept of dominance as used within competition law has its foundation in the economic concept of market power. In economic terms, market power is defined as 'the ability of a firm (or group of firms) to raise and maintain a price above the level that would prevail under competition'[720] - in simple terms, pricing power. Substantial market power can be equated with dominance.[721]

273 As significant market power is not a global position of strength, but only one in relation to the specific competitive environment,[722] in competition law, dominance is assessed in relation to actual as well as possible competitive constraints.[723] Competitive constraints can be imposed by actual and potential competitors as well as the bargaining strength of the undertaking's customers.[724] In order to 'identify [...] the competitive constraints faced by an undertaking'[725], one has to know the relevant market.

714. *See*: FUCHS/MÖSCHEL, in: IMMENGA/MESTMÄCKER 2018, Article 102, para. 73.
715. ECJ, *Michelin I*, C-322/81, para. 37.
716. For a *Michelin I* citation *see*: GC, *BBC v. Commission*, T-70/89, para. 51; for a *United Brands* citation *see*: GC, *British Airways plc v. Commission*, T-219/99, para. 189.
717. EC, *Continental Can*, IV/26.811, II. B. para. 3.
718. WEISS, in: CALLIESS/RUFFERT, EUV/AEUV, Article 102, para. 8; GRILL, in: LENZ ET AL., EUV - AEUV - GRCh, Article 102 AEUV, para. 12; BRINKER, in: SCHWARZE ET AL., EU-Kommentar, Article 102, para. 11.
719. HEIZMANN starts evaluation of the Swiss practice of establishing a dominant position with reference to WEBER's sociological concept of power as presented in § 16 of his basic work entitled 'Wirtschaft und Gesellschaft'. HEIZMANN, para. 296.
720. It is not known when this definition first occurred, but it has been accepted in the literature and economic theory as well as on an international political level for decades. BISHOP/WALKER, para. 3-002; HEIZMANN, para. 296; LANDES/POSNER, Harvard Law Review 1980, 937; MOTTA, 40 f.
721. *See i.a.*: COSCELLI/EDWARDS, in: LIANOS/GERADIN, Handbook on European competition law, 352; JONES/SUFRIN, 331; WHISH/BAILEY, 25.
722. *See*: EC, *Guidance Paper*, para. 10.
723. EC, *Guidance Paper*, para. 10.
724. EC, *Guidance Paper*, para. 12.
725. EC, *DG Competition discussion paper*, para. 12.

274 Thus, dominance is assessed in two stages: the definition of the relevant market and the assessment of whether an undertaking holds a dominant position in it. The definition of the relevant market in which the undertaking acts as a competitor is the starting point for any analysis of an Article 102 TFEU case. Before attention shifts to the concept of abuse in Article 102 TFEU, this Part will give a brief introduction to the mechanisms of defining the relevant market (Chapter 9) as well as establishing the dominant position of an undertaking therein (Chapter 10). While elaborating on the general concepts and methods applied in practice, the focus will be on the influence of patents on both the definition of the relevant market and the establishment of a dominant position.

275 This Part will close with a summary of the relevance of the definition in the market and the establishment of a dominant position for Article 102 TFEU cases involving patents (Chapter 11). This Part is mainly introductory, broadly describing the relevant mechanisms. It is not the intention here to expound on theories, criticism and case law in detail.

CHAPTER 9

Market Definition

I THE RELEVANT MARKET: A DEFINITION

276 The relevant market is the area with respect to a traded good (product, service, information, etc.[726]),[727] time and place where 'there can be effective competition between the products which form part of it'.[728] Defining the relevant market[729] is the starting point for all analysis of the effects of competitive constraints and therefore of all competition law analysis.[730] Owing to the lack of appropriate methods to determine the position of an undertaking in a market directly, a dominant position can only be determined indirectly via defining the relevant market as a first step.[731] The aim of defining the relevant market is thus to 'identify in a systemic way the competitive constraints that the undertakings involved face'.[732]

277 Undertakings generally face three forms of competitive constraints which have to be considered: 'demand substitutability, supply substitutability and potential competition'.[733] Competition between products requires a certain level of interchangeability between them. When defining the relevant market, one seeks to identify close substitutes; therefore, demand- and supply-side substitution are the only relevant

726. For an analysis of the market definition for information markets, *see*: MURER/ZURMUEHLE, in: EPINEY/HEHEMANN/KERN, Schweizerisches Jahrbuch für Europarecht 2014/2015, 464 ff.
727. A cohesive analysis of the book that relevant markets in the sense of competition law are not limited to products and services can be found in: FRÜH, 152 ff.
728. ECJ, *Hoffmann-La Roche v. Commission*, C-85/76, para. 28.
729. The relevant market, as understood in competition law, differs from the understanding of markets in economics as well as in common language. *See* the introduction given by CANAPA: CANAPA, 101 ff. with further references. For an analysis of the different understandings of markets, *see also*: FRÜH, 140 f.
730. EC, *Commission Notice on the definition of relevant market*, paras 2 ff.
731. *See i.a.*: JONES/SUFRIN/DUNNE, 61; ECJ, *Continental Can v. Commission*, C-6/72, para. 32.
732. EC, *Commission Notice on the definition of relevant market*, para. 2; *see supra* at fn. 725.
733. EC, *Commission Notice on the definition of relevant market*, para. 13.

factors that need to be considered.[734] Potential competition is only relevant when analysing an undertaking's position in the market.[735] Markets in competition law are traditionally established considering the relevant products or services as well as their temporal and geographic dimensions according to the demand-side-oriented market concept. This means that substitutability of the relevant products is mainly analysed from the perspective of customers and their willingness to switch to a different product (substitute product), rather than from the suppliers' point of view and their ability to switch production.[736] The influence of supply-side substitution has proved to be difficult to distinguish from potential competition. Supply-side substitutability is therefore, according to the Commission Notice on the definition of the relevant market, only analysed if the supplier can switch immediately.[737]

II PATENTS AND THE DEFINITION OF THE RELEVANT MARKET

278 The conflict between patents and competition is resolved, and the rules of competition law apply to patents while considering their peculiarities.[738] Consequently, with respect to the definition of the relevant market, it follows that the general criteria apply when patent-protected products[739] are involved.[740] This means that substitutability has to be analysed following the demand-side-oriented market concept.[741] It is therefore not admissible to deduce the relevant market from the scope of protection of the intellectual property right, namely to equate the two, but the substitutability of the relevant product has to be analysed. Unlike legal monopolies where the state exclusively delegates a task to an undertaking,[742] intellectual property rights do not monopolise a market.[743] Although situations can result where there are no substitutes for the demand side, these are an exception and not the general rule.[744]

279 When patent rights appear to be relevant in a market definition, certain differences occur, the most important of which is the fact that patents cause vertically related markets,[745] since patents generate a demand not only for products based on patent-protected technology but also the technology itself. The US DOJ and the FTC with their Antitrust Guidelines for the Licensing of Intellectual Property (hereinafter 'IP Licensing

734. EC, *Guidelines on market analysis 2018,* paras 35 ff.
735. EC, *Guidelines on market analysis 2018,* paras 27 and 54; BELLAMY/CHILD, para. 4.020.
736. The demand-side-oriented market concept is limited to certain markets such as two-sided or innovation markets. *See*: DREHER, ZWeR 2009, 156.
737. EC, *Commission Notice on the definition of relevant market,* para. 20.
738. *See supra* at paras 70 ff.
739. On the influence of patents on the definition of the relevant market, *see*: ALBERT, 94 ff.
740. HEINEMANN, in: DREXL, Research handbook on intellectual property and competition law, 61; ULLRICH/HEINEMANN, in: IMMENGA/MESTMÄCKER 2018, Teil GRUR B, para. 45.
741. *See supra* at para. 277.
742. KEMPEL, 44.
743. ALBERT, 100 ff.; ULLRICH/HEINEMANN, in: IMMENGA/MESTMÄCKER 2018, Teil GRUR B, para. 42; US DEPARTMENT OF JUSTICE/FEDERAL TRADE COMMISSION, *Antitrust Guidelines for the Licensing of Intellectual Property,* Chapter 2.2.
744. ALBERT, 101 ff.; KEMPEL, 44.
745. *See* the fundamental analysis of ALBERT: ALBERT, 94 ff.

Guidelines') set the foundation for defining markets when intellectual property rights are involved. This defined and distinguished first the product markets[746] which contain the products based on a technology, second, the technology market[747] and, third, the innovation markets which consist of the technology itself and the R&D[748] and are upstream to the product markets. Practice in the EU followed this example and defines vertically separated markets as well.[749]

280 The different markets rely on each other in that the input from one market (upstream market) is required to produce a product on the other market (downstream market). As part of a product, the protected technology becomes an integral part of the product market.[750] In upstream technology or licensing markets, the technology can be traded independently from the final product. As a purchasing market, the technology market is, despite the close linkage to the product market, independent of it. Patented technologies are the result of R&D activities and products of R&D processes. To ensure access to R&D and thus technology markets, it has therefore been discussed to assign competitive relationships that exist at the stage of research activity to a market. Most doctrines share the conviction that certain competitive effects 'cannot [in any case] be adequately addressed through the analysis of goods or technology markets'[751] only.[752] Yet, the existence of such innovation markets is highly controversial.[753]

III PRODUCT MARKET

1 General Considerations

281 The relevant product market[754] includes all substitutable or sufficiently interchangeable products with respect to the product in question (Article 1 paragraph 1(j) (ii) of Regulation (EC) No 772/2004). Products are substitutable with respect to their characteristics (intended use[755]) if they 'are particularly suitable for satisfying constant needs and are only to a limited extent interchangeable with other products'.[756] Additionally, they have to be functionally interchangeable and customers would

746. *See* hereinafter at Part III, Chapter 9, section III.
747. *See* hereinafter at Part III, Chapter 9, section IV.
748. *See* hereinafter at Part III, Chapter 9, section V.
749. With reference to the practice: ALBERT, 94 ff.; LAMPING, 156 ff.; ULLRICH/HEINEMANN, in: IMMENGA/MESTMÄCKER 2018, Teil GRUR B, para. 45.
750. ULLRICH/HEINEMANN, in: IMMENGA/MESTMÄCKER 2018, Teil GRUR B, para. 39.
751. US DEPARTMENT OF JUSTICE/FEDERAL TRADE COMMISSION, *Antitrust Guidelines for the Licensing of Intellectual Property*, Chapter 3.2.3.
752. *See*: DREXL, Journal of Competition Law and Economics 2012, 515 ff.
753. *See infra* at paras 301 f.
754. In German legal language, the term 'product market' was introduced to distinguish the traditional market concept from innovation and technology markets. In English legal language, the term 'product market' has traditionally been used to differentiate the product dimension of a market (substitutability) from the geographical dimension. For further reference, *see*: FRÜH, fn. 875.
755. EC, *Commission Notice on the definition of relevant market*, para. 36.
756. ECJ, *Michelin I*, C-322/81, para. 37.

switch between the producers in case of relative price changes.[757] Substitutability is also dependent on the conditions of competition as well as the supply and demand in the market.[758] Substitutability with respect to products can be assessed from the perspective of either the demand or the supply side. Demand-substitutability enables the identification of those products 'which consumers could easily switch to in the case of a relative price increase', while supply-substitutability seeks to identify the extent to which suppliers would switch to produce or offer the relevant product following a relative price increase.[759] Examples of corresponding non-price changes are reductions in product quality or service.[760] Substitutability is not only dependent on the product itself but also defined with respect to a certain territory and time. However, the dimension of time is, compared with the other two components, of lesser importance and is only relevant for seasonal products.[761]

282 In terms of the definition of the relevant product market, quantitative and qualitative approaches can be adopted. Quantitative assessments require sufficient and reliable data. Where data cannot be provided, qualitative approaches are taken. Limits on the availability of data also lead to situations where the results of quantitative assessments are supplemented by qualitative evidence. Accordingly, the Commission in *Wanadoo Interactive* conducted a quantitative assessment through the SSNIP-test (Small but Significant Non-transitory Increase in Price test)[762] based on survey data, but later supplemented the results with qualitative evidence such as technical features, performance, differences in use and prices.[763] The authorities thereby do not follow a strict pattern but adopt an open approach using all the evidence available.

2 Quantitative Approaches

283 A quantitative approach to determining demand-substitutability is via the cross-price elasticity of demand. As proposed by the Commission in its Notice on the definition of the relevant market, cross-price elasticity is generally evaluated by

757. FAULL/NIKPAY, 1.139.
758. GC, *Tiercé Ladbroke SA v. Commission*, T-504/93, para. 81.
759. EC, *Guidelines on market analysis 2018*, para. 38; JONES/SUFRIN/DUNNE, 104.
760. FAULL/NIKPAY, 1.139.
761. *See i.a.*: FUCHS/MÖSCHEL, in: IMMENGA/MESTMÄCKER 2018, Article 102, paras 68 ff. Examples where the temporal dimension of the market played a role were the cases of *ABG/Oil Companies* and *United Brands*: EC, *ABG/Oil Companies*, IV/28.84, 9; ECJ, *United Brands*, C-27/76, paras 14 ff.
762. *See* hereinafter at paras 283 f.
763. EC, *Wanadoo Interactive*, COMP/38.233, paras 193 ff.; the same approach is also proposed by the EC in the 2002 Guidelines on the assessment of significant market power. EC, *Commission guidelines on market analysis 2002*, para. 48 (the revised Guidelines from 2018 do not contain this clear instruction, but list the SSNIP-test as well as qualitative evidence as relevant factors: EC, *Guidelines on market analysis 2018*, paras 24 ff).

applying the SSNIP-test.[764] This test (sometimes also called the hypothetical monopolist test[765]) evaluates the price-elasticity of demand. It seeks to answer the question of whether 'customers would switch to readily available substitutes or to suppliers in response to a hypothetical small (in the range of 5 to 10 per cent) but permanent relative price increase in the products and areas being considered'.[766] If consumers would not switch in cases of a price increase, the good and its potential substitute are considered to be in separate markets. If they would switch, the product is considered as providing close competitive constraints.[767]

284 Though providing valuable results when good data are available, the feasibility of the SSNIP-test is limited in bad data situations.[768] Its applicability is also limited in cases where price is not the decisive factor for the consumer decision[769] or when prices are not exposed to market forces, which are both the case for pharmaceuticals.[770] Additionally, special caution is required in non-merger cases, where current market prices are already monopoly or quasi-monopoly prices. The SSNIP-test in such situations calls for an erroneously wide market definition.[771] This mistake was made by the US Supreme Court in the case of *United States v. El du Pont de Nemour and Co.*[772] which has since become known as the 'Cellophane Fallacy'[773] as the case concerned the packaging material cellophane.[774]

3 Qualitative Approaches

285 Despite the tendency for predominantly applying qualitative approaches in the past, they cannot be considered exclusively.[775] Since the issuing of the Commission's Notice on the definition of the relevant market, it is clear that the Commission and courts have applied a plurality of approaches.[776] To ensure that the definition of the relevant market is as accurate as possible, the Commission and courts try to consider

764. EC, *Guidelines on market analysis 2018*, para. 29.
765. *See*: WHISH/BAILEY, 26.
766. EC, *Commission Notice on the definition of the relevant market*, para. 17.
767. On the SSNIP-test, *see i.a.*: KLEIN, WUW, 171 ff.; MOTTA, 102 ff.; SCHWALBE/ZIMMER, 70 f.; WHISH/BAILEY, 26 f.
768. *See i.a.*: ECJ, *AstraZeneca v. Commission*, C-457/10 P, paras 28 and 59.
769. This issue has been addressed by scholars evaluating potential market definitions for social media. WEBER WALLER, North Carolina Law Review 2012, 1785; THÉPOT, World Competition Law and Economics Review 2012, 208. On the difficulties in defining markets for data based products, *see*: MURER/ZURMUEHLE, in: EPINEY/HEHEMANN/KERN, Schweizerisches Jahrbuch für Europarecht 2014/2015, 464 ff.
770. COSCELLI/OVERD, European Competition Law Review 2007, 294 ff.
771. MOTTA, 105.
772. UNITED STATES SUPREME COURT, *USA v. E. I. du Pont de Nemours & Co.*, 351 US 377, 1956, 395 ff.
773. EC, *DG Competition discussion paper*, 13.
774. SCHWALBE/ZIMMER, 84 f.
775. WURMNEST rightly notes that the described deficiencies make the consideration of other factors necessary, and identifies precedence for qualitative factors. WURMNEST, 313 and 321 f.
776. *See*: WURMNEST, 314.

all available factors as indications of interchangeability.[777] Therefore factors immanent in the product or the market are also considered relevant, such as a product's characteristics or its application possibilities.[778] The Commission did not allow limited substitutability in terms of functionality to suffice as a stand-alone criterion.[779] In the case of *Perrier/Nestlé*, it therefore decided, on the basis of other factors, such as the motivation of consumers, the composition of the product and pricing, that both companies' bottled source water and soft drinks were in distinct markets, despite both having the function of quenching thirst.[780] Additionally, the competitive conditions as well as the structure of the markets were used to provide information on the substitutability of products.[781] In the case of *Time Warner/EMI*,[782] these factors allowed for the conclusion that two different markets for music exist, as the same product was available on two different sales channels, online and in stores on CD.[783] In the case of *United Brands*, the fact that the price of bananas only faced competition at certain periods of the year allowed the Court of Justice to define a separate market for bananas.[784]

4 Pharmaceutical Product Markets

286 Central to the analysis, when defining the pharmaceutical product market,[785] is demand-side substitutability[786].[787] Usually, supply-side substitution is not considered. The industry's particularities on the supply side, consisting of, for example, long and high-cost R&D expenses, patent protection and regulatory requirements result in high market entry barriers and generally render a fast switch in production impossible.[788]

287 On the demand side, consumer decisions are significantly dependent on the prescribing physician. Therefore, when defining the relevant market, this calls for an

777. EC, *Commission Notice on the definition of relevant market*, para. 25. The pluralism of approaches was important in the case of *Hilti* where the GC, with reference to the competitive conditions, relativised quantitative evidence offered by Hilti. GC, *Hilti v. Commission*, T-30/89, para. 18.
778. *See*: Früh, 192 ff.
779. EC, *Nestlé/Perrier*, IV/M.190, para. 9; EC, *Wanadoo Interactive*, COMP/38.233, paras 193 ff.; GC, *Tetra Pak II*, T-83/91, para. 64; GC, *Hilti v. Commission*, T-30/89, paras 64 ff.
780. EC, *Nestlé/Perrier*, IV/M.190, paras 10 ff.
781. EC, *Commission Notice on the definition of relevant market*, para. 36; ECJ, *Michelin I*, C-322/81, para. 37; GC, *CEAHR v. Commission*, T-712/14, para. 67.
782. The merger notification was withdrawn by the parties after the Commission informed them of its preliminary position. EC, *Press Release, EMI/Time Warner*, IP/00/1122.
783. *See*: Mestmäcker, ZUM 2001, 187. The documents of the case, EC, *Time Warner/EMI*, COMP/M.1852, are no longer available from the Commission (last checked 19 February 2020).
784. ECJ, *United Brands*, C-27/76, paras 23 and 33.
785. On defining pharmaceutical product markets, *see also* the analysis by Athanasiadou: Athanasiadou, 280 ff.
786. The ECJ in its latest case on defining pharmaceutical markets, *Hoffmann-La Roche II*, decided that if the conditions for lawful off-label sales are met, the drug using off-label belongs to the same market as other substitutable products. ECJ, *Hofmann-La Roche II*, C-179/16, paras 59 ff.
787. Also in recent case law, *see infra* at paras 368 ff.
788. Siebert/Pries, PharmaR 2007, 148; *see supra* at paras 147 ff.

analysis of the characteristics of not only the drug and its indication but also medical formulary practice.[789] The price is not relevant in defining substitutability, as patients and doctors are less price sensitive,[790] and the price is less influential in consumer decision-making than in other industries.[791] Determining the relevant product markets for pharmaceuticals therefore starts with identifying the drug's indications, contraindications and side effects.[792] In a second step, the drug's mode of action and application has to be considered. Oral dispensation forms, injections or ointments are usually considered to be in different product markets,[793] and different modes of action can justify a narrower market definition. The effect of proton pump inhibitors (PPIs), for example, is to block gastric acid. The same effect can also be achieved with H2-receptor antagonists (H2-blockers). Indications of PPIs and H2-blockers therefore broadly overlap, with PPIs generally being favoured for more severe conditions and H2-blockers for milder ones.[794] Yet, in the case of PPIs and H2-blockers, the General Court and Commission defined two separate product markets after an overall assessment, including prescribing practice (differentiated therapeutic use and asymmetrical substitution) and efficiency.[795]

288 The World Health Organization (WHO) and the European Pharmaceutical Market Research Association (EphMRA) maintain widely harmonised Anatomical Therapeutic Chemical classification systems (ATC) which classify active substances according to their indications. The system categorises active substances on five levels. The first level differentiates active substances according to the organ or system they act on (e.g., blood circulation), the second and third levels classify therapeutic indications and the fourth and fifth consider chemical classification. It has become established practice of the Commission to take the ATC classification as the starting point when defining the relevant product market in merger cases.[796] The starting point for the analysis is the third level of the ATC system.[797] In the case of *Servier*, the ATC classification was considered as well, but did not serve as the starting point.[798] In non-merger cases, the ATC classification can be an important reference as it marks a commonly agreed classification based on the indication of active substances.[799]

789. SIEBERT/PRIES, PharmaR 2007, 148; *see supra* at paras 138 ff.
790. An exception might be when the differences in price are exorbitant, as in the case of aspirin when compared to Ticlopidine which was twenty-four times more expensive. EC, *Sanofi/Synthelabo*, COMP/M.1397, para. 31.
791. On the whole paragraph, *see*: EC, *Servier*, AT.39612, paras 2135 f.; *supra* at paras 138 ff.
792. *See*: EC, *Servier*, AT.39612, paras 2144 ff.
793. *See*: EC, *AstraZeneca*, COMP/A.37.507/F3, para. 18 with respect to Losec where the decision only concerned orally dispensed Losec.
794. ECJ, *AstraZeneca v. Commission*, C-457/10 P, para. 41.
795. Upheld on appeal: ECJ, *AstraZeneca v. Commission*, C-457/10 P, paras 27 ff.
796. *See*: SIEBERT/PRIES, PharmaR 2007, 148 with reference to the Commission's practice in merger cases.
797. GC, *Servier v. Commission*, T-691/14, para. 1427; GC, *AstraZeneca v. Commission*, T-321/05, para. 154.
798. EC, *Servier*, AT.39612, paras 2165 ff.
799. *See also*: GC, *Servier v. Commission*, T-691/14, para. 1426.

289 The next step in defining the relevant product market is an analysis of the prescription practice of the physicians[800] and the consumption habits of patients, namely their willingness to substitute a known drug. Important factors influencing the prescription habits are product differentiation and marketing efforts by pharmaceutical companies, as physicians have a limited range of medication they prescribe.[801] Furthermore, both patients and physicians are often hesitant to switch to another drug, especially in long-term therapies, when the first drug has proved to be effective and suits the patient. However, lock-in effects can also influence the willingness to switch. Such lock-in effects might present themselves as health risks occurring from even short periods of suboptimal dosage.[802] Being the first therapy on the market is therefore important with respect to the loyalty of prescribers as well as the acceptance of patients. In general, these effects increase with the duration of the therapy where the drug is used or with difficulties in finding the optimal dosage.

IV TECHNOLOGY OR LICENSING MARKETS

1 General Considerations

290 Technology markets consist of a licensed technology[803] (Article 1(1)(b) TT-GVO) as well as the substitutes of the technology.[804] The definition of the technology market already implies that it is not sufficient to base the definition on the scope of the patent itself. Scopes of patents other than of government monopolies do not themselves establish a relevant market.[805] The scope of the technology market is determined analogous to the scope of the product market by recourse to the demand-side-oriented market concept (Article 1(1)(k) TT-GVO).[806] This is justified in that patented technologies can be understood as the product of upstream research efforts. Following the demand-side-oriented market concept therefore, technologies which are interchangeable with respect to their characteristics in as much as the demander would switch to them in the case of a small but permanent increase in relative price are understood as being close substitutes.[807]

291 EU case law has imposed low requirements on the existence of a licensing market. The Court of Justice held it sufficient that a hypothetical market for licences could be

800. Within these considerations, off-label uses of drugs can also influence the definition of the relevant market. *See*: SIEBERT/PRIES, PharmaR 2007, 151.
801. *See supra* at paras 138 ff.
802. The switch from perindopril to other ACE inhibitors has shown the risk of a loss of optimal blood pressure. EC, *Servier*, AT.39612, para. 2379.
803. Technology is thereby widely understood as generally including the fruits of R&D efforts. *See*: KËLLEZI, sic! 2005, 554.
804. EC, *Technology Transfer Guidelines*, paras 21 ff.; US DEPARTMENT OF JUSTICE/FEDERAL TRADE COMMISSION, *Antitrust Guidelines for the Licensing of Intellectual Property*, para. 3.2.2.
805. KEMPEL, 44.
806. ULLRICH/HEINEMANN, in: IMMENGA/MESTMÄCKER 2018, Teil GRUR B, paras 46 f.; EC, *Servier*, AT.39612, para. 2623.
807. JONES/SUFRIN/DUNNE, 105 ff.

identified.[808] The fact that no licence has or will be sold is not obstructive. The reason for accepting a hypothetical market is that the presence of a licensing market cannot be dependent on the conduct of the undertaking under scrutiny, namely the willingness to sell licences. Determinative, however, is the identification of two stages of production which 'are interconnected inasmuch as the upstream product is indispensable for the supply of the downstream product'.[809] The identification of vertically integrated product and technology markets is thus the norm when patents are involved.[810]

292 As with product markets,[811] defining the relevant technology market starts with identifying substitute technologies to the technology covered by the patent.[812] In order to be valuable substitutes, technologies have to be economic (sufficiently efficient and meeting potential regulatory requirements, sunk costs[813]) as well as functionally substitutable (solution to the same demand) alternatives.

2 Pharmaceutical Technology Markets

293 From the insight gained in the development process of pharmaceuticals as well as regarding pharmaceutical patents, we know that the technologies required to produce a final drug are manifold. It requires, for example, knowledge about the effects of a given active substance (basic patent) or its improvements, the know-how and technology to isolate or manufacture a specific molecule or the final formulation and their scale-up for mass production as well as knowledge about dosage and galenic forms.[814] The production of a drug is normally staged in two distinct steps: first, the production of the active ingredient and second, the production of the drug itself which includes the mixture of the active ingredient with excipients as well as the production of the galenic forms.[815] As with complex products, the final drug can therefore be dependent on several technologies which in theory together with their substitutes can all constitute an independent technology market.[816] In pharmaceutical technology markets, such an understanding would result in the definition of different technology markets such as the market for the technologies needed to manufacture the active compound or the market for the technologies required to mix active ingredients with excipients.

808. ECJ, *IMS Health*, C-418/01, para. 44.
809. ECJ, *IMS Health*, C-418/01, para. 45.
810. HEINEMANN, in: DREXL, Technology and competition, 607.
811. The Commission in the hearing before the GC in the *Servier* case stressed that the definition of the relevant technology market is a separate analysis. *See*: GC, *Servier v. Commission*, T-691/14, para. 1614.
812. EC, *Servier*, AT.39612, para. 2623.
813. With respect to sunk costs and the difficulty of the SSNIP-test to identify those, *see*: KËLLEZI, sic! 2005, 554.
814. EC, *Servier*, AT.39612, paras 2616 and 2624.
815. SIEBERT/PRIES, PharmaR 2007, 150.
816. Generally, with respect to specialisation along the value chain, *see*: FRÜH, 467; with respect to SEPs: EC, *Google/Motorola Mobility*, COMP/M.6381, para. 61.

294 A dominant position with respect to a necessary technological step in the production of drugs can result in the foreclosure of rivals, as it is necessary to comply with the technology owing to a lack of substitutes.[817] This situation is comparable to standard essential patents, where the holder of such a patent can block access to the final product market.

295 From the perspective of originator and generic companies, it must be doubted whether demand for acquiring technologies independent of the aim to market a final product or to deprive competitors of an alternative indeed exists.[818] The ultimate reason for owning and thus acquiring technology is rather to secure access to the product market.[819] Originator and generic companies make use of derived demands in vertically integrated markets. In these markets, demand in the product market influences demand in the technology market and, conversely, supply in the technology market influences supply in the product market.[820] Accordingly, changes in the 'patent landscape', through either newly applied patents or exclusive licensing agreements of all the technologies required to produce the final drug, influence competition in the product market.[821] The Commission in the case of *Servier* held:

> The technology is not simply geared towards producing the API, but towards meeting the requirements for obtaining marketing authorisation for the final formulation based on the API[822]. [...] The API technology may form a bundle of proprietary rights including patent rights, know-how and other proprietary information, which are necessary to produce and successfully commercialise an API, as well as final products based thereupon.[823]

296 In the pharmaceutical industry, technologies for manufacturing the active substance (Active Pharmaceutical Ingredient (API)) of a given drug often lack a substitute. Practice acknowledges the importance of APIs for the production of drugs. In merger cases, APIs are thus considered a separate, vertically integrated product market to the

817. *See* the same considerations in: EC, *Google/Motorola Mobility*, COMP/M.6381, paras 54 and 61.
818. When undertakings which only engage in R&D are under scrutiny, the conclusion may be different, as the commercial activity of such undertakings is not focused on the final product market, but on selling licences. It might therefore be worth distinguishing a 'licensing market'. For the distinction between licensing and technology markets, *see*: THEUNE, GRUR Int. 1977, 67 f. Note that, as THEUNE points out, the aim of a licensor may be directed towards the product markets depending on the licensing contract and whether the fee is dependent on final sales.
819. THEUNE, GRUR Int. 1977, 68.
820. In practice, the relationship of supply and demand in technology and product markets is influential rather than determinant, at least in cases where a given technology can be used in more than one final product and therefore belongs to more than one upstream product market. FRÜH, 236.
821. On licensing agreements, *see*: THEUNE, GRUR Int. 1977, 67.
822. On the definition of API, *see* hereinafter at para. 296.
823. EC, *Servier*, AT.39612, para. 2618.

market of the final drug (procurement market[824]).[825] All technologies for manufacturing APIs therefore form the technology market downstream to the product market for APIs, which is upstream to the product market of the final drug.[826] Technologies within the API technology market may consist of technology for the production process and bioequivalent forms of the API (substitutes).[827] The technology market for the API was analysed in the *Servier* case,[828] where the acquisition of an API technology was under scrutiny. The investigation of the Commission showed that the perindopril API could not be produced by using the technology to gain APIs of other molecules, for example, other angiotensin-converting enzyme (ACE) blockers. Furthermore, it was found that an easy switch either from companies producing other APIs to produce perindopril API or away from producing perindopril API in the case of a price increase of 5 per cent-10 per cent was not possible. The demand was therefore inelastic and the relevant market was defined as consisting of the API technology.[829]

297 The definition of the relevant technology market can therefore be limited to defining the market of the technology of the acquired patent and its actual and potential substitutes. This approach considers the fact that limited access to one technology alongside the development cycle - for example, of the API - can hamper access to the final product market, irrespective of whether substitutable technologies exist for other stages of the process. Vertical integration is further relevant when assessing market power and the effects on competition. As regards market power, in the technology as well as the product market, it should be considered that an undertaking which successfully receives market authorisation for a drug must have access, via its own patents, licences or material suppliers, to the technology for all necessary steps within the development cycle, irrespective of whether competitors own different corresponding technologies. Consequently, its ability to behave independently in both markets is obviously greater the more patents it owns compared with what it has licensed.[830] Regarding the effects on competition, the vertical integration has to be borne in mind in as much as the patent may hinder not only innovation in the technology market and the competition on downstream product markets but also innovation in the upstream and downstream technology or innovation markets.

V INNOVATION MARKET

298 'An innovation market consists of the research and development directed to particular new or improved goods or processes, and the close substitutes for that

824. Procurement or purchasing markets are upstream to the product market and consist of markets for raw or operating materials.
825. EC, *Teva/Ratiopharm*, COMP/M.5865, paras 393 ff.; EC, *Mylan/Perrigo*, COMP/M.7645, para. 125.
826. On vertically integrated technology markets in general, *see*: ARORA/FOSFURI/GAMBARDELLA.
827. EC, *Servier*, AT.39612, para. 2618.
828. For a detailed analysis of the case, *see infra* at paras 360 ff.
829. EC, *Servier*, AT.39612, para. 2664.
830. *See infra* at paras 312 f.

research and development. The close substitutes are research and development efforts,[831] technologies, and goods that significantly constrain the exercise of market power with respect to the relevant research and development, for example by limiting the ability and incentive of a hypothetical monopolist to retard the pace of research and development.'[832]

299 The idea of defining a separate innovation market originates from the IP Licensing Guidelines. In US antitrust law, innovation markets are defined in order to analyse the effect of research cooperation or mergers, as, for example, in the case of *Ciba-Geigy and Sandoz* when forming Novartis.[833] Mergers of research facilities can reduce R&D activity or incentives to engage in R&D, for example, when the merging firms are the only ones engaging in R&D. When defining innovation markets, practice thus acknowledges that competition needs to be protected at the level of innovation.[834] Especially with research for next-generation products, it is often unclear what the future product (market) will be. Competition law could not be applied, therefore, without the defining of innovation markets. However, a deferred intervention might come too late.[835]

300 Starting with the Commission's Guidelines on the applicability of Article 101, the concept of innovation markets[836] appeared in EU law as well:

> In the first scenario, which is, for instance, present in the pharmaceutical industry, the process of innovation is structured in such a way that it is possible at an early stage to identify competing R&D poles. Competing R&D poles are R&D efforts directed towards a certain new product or technology, and the substitutes for that R&D, that is to say, R&D aimed at developing substitutable products or technology for those developed by the co-operation and having similar timing. In this case, it can be analysed whether after the agreement there will be a sufficient number of remaining R&D poles.[837]

Owing to the example given in the Guidelines, two R&D poles additional to the relevant one are considered sufficient.[838]

301 The usefulness of innovation markets is highly disputed.[839] Supporters claim that innovation markets are characterised by rivalry which shows itself in coordination

831. The EU Guidelines on the applicability of Article 101 define substitutes as 'R&D aimed at developing substitutable products or technology for those developed by the co-operation and having similar timing': EC, *Guidelines on the applicability of Article 101*, para. 120.
832. US Department of Justice/Federal Trade Commission, *Antitrust Guidelines for the Licensing of Intellectual Property*, para. 3.2.3; also i.a.: Schwalbe/Zimmer, 83.
833. *See*: Bodewig, GRUR Int. 1997, 964; Stirnimann, 108 f.; both with further reference to the literature and US practice; FTC, *Press Release Ciba-Geigy/Sandoz.*
834. Bishop/Walker, para. 4-043; on the importance of competition in innovation also: Tom/Newberg, Antitrust Journal 1997, 222 ff.
835. Bishop/Walker, para. 4-043.
836. While the issue of competition in innovation is broadly elaborated (*see hereinafter*), the Guidelines use the term 'innovation market' only *en passant* when providing examples. *See*: EC, *Guidelines on the applicability of Article 101*, para. 147.
837. EC, *Guidelines on the applicability of Article 101*, para. 120.
838. EC, *Guidelines on the applicability of Article 101*, para. 140.
839. For an in-depth analysis of pros and cons: Barth, 61 ff.; Früh, 274 ff.

with respect to the planning of R&D as well as the race to achieve breakthroughs. Undertakings do not plan their own R&D on a blank sheet, but rather consider the activities of competitors and react to changes in the R&D landscape.[840] Accordingly, innovators, fuelled by the prospect of obtaining patent protection ('the-winner-takes-it-all') or profiting from first-mover advantages, seek to be the first to achieve breakthroughs.[841] Furthermore, innovation can be demanded independently, as, for example, in research cooperation or where interface information is required.[842] As a counterargument, it has been advanced that the success of R&D efforts is not foreseeable, with respect to either technologies or products.[843] R&D other than the product in product markets is the input rather than the output of the market.[844] General statements on the optimal level of R&D activity and how this could be reached are therefore not really possible.[845] These difficulties led FUCHS to conclude that the innovation market is but a mental figure.[846]

302 When analysing the application of a blocking patent within the pharmaceutical industry, competition in innovation markets, other than in the form of potential competition, is of limited importance. In Article 102 contrarily to merger cases, the analysis occurs *ex ante*. An in-depth analysis of future effects which would require defining an innovation market is therefore not needed. Furthermore, the behaviour under scrutiny occurs on the technology and thus a downstream market. This means that all conduct occurring during research, for example, in research cooperation, does not fall within the scope of Article 102 TFEU when it concerns NMEs where there is, as yet, no technology or product market. Additionally, in order to establish dominance in the technology market, it will be important to consider potential competition, which at the level of technology markets can only stream from innovation. The finding of a dominant position will therefore include the finding that innovation is not likely to yield a substitute product within a reasonable time. Also, the finding of an abuse that has the 'effect of hindering the maintenance of degree of competition still existing in the market or the growth of that competition'[847] includes considerations with respect to innovation, as growth in technology and thus product markets can only stream from innovation. A more in-depth analysis of innovation markets as independent markets will therefore not be provided within this book.

840. ULLRICH, Kooperative Forschung und Kartellrecht, 151 f.
841. BARTH, 62; *see also* the analysis by FRÜH: FRÜH, 238 ff.
842. *See i.a.*: ARORA/FOSFURI/GAMBARDELLA, 20 ff.; GC, *Microsoft*, T-201/04, para. 662; ULLRICH, in: ZÄCH/CORREA, Towards WTO competition rules, 271.
843. *See i.a.*: BÜHLER/LEHMANN, AJP 1997, 659; FUCHS, in: IMMENGA/MESTMÄCKER 2018, Einl. FuE-GVO, para. 47.
844. BARTH, 72 ff.; FRÜH, 275.
845. For a critical analysis of SCHUMPETER's thesis according to which the growing size of an undertaking positively influences R&D, *see*: BARTH, 68 ff.
846. FUCHS, in: IMMENGA/MESTMÄCKER 2018, Einl. FuE-GVO, para. 47.
847. ECJ, *Hoffmann-La Roche v. Commission*, C-85/76, para. 91; *see infra* at paras 453 and 476.

CHAPTER 10

Establishing a Dominant Position

I GENERAL CONSIDERATIONS

303 Dominance, or in economic terms, substantial market power,[848] is understood as the state where an undertaking can act independently because of a lack of competitive constraints.[849] When assessing whether an entity is holding a dominant position, one evaluates its degree of independence (*power to behave independently*). However, conceptualising independence in a market is easier said than done. This is mainly because full independence is not even given in a monopoly. If you want to sell something, you simply need a buyer willing to buy your product the way you offer it. Even dominant undertakings therefore cannot act fully independently of their (potential) buyers.

304 In economics, market power is understood as a position of strength that allows the undertaking to profitably rise prices and maintain this over a certain period of time.[850] Various shades of pricing from slightly above the marginal cost price, to pricing close to the monopoly price, occur. Market power, following the economic understanding, can thus be assessed from two sides, as difference from the monopoly price or as difference from the marginal cost price. Economic assessments of market power can therefore result in various graded outcomes from 'inexistent'[851] to 'significant' or 'substantial'.[852] Dominance as an element of Article 102 TFEU is a precondition for the application of the provision and is consequently not differentiable in grades. Once the threshold of substantial market power is reached, an undertaking is dominant.

848. *See supra* at fn. 721.
849. *See supra* at paras 269 ff.
850. *See supra* at para. 272.
851. Note that inexistent market power is not realistic in real markets. These concepts only exist in theoretical models (Bertrand Model). MOTTA, 115 f.
852. MOTTA, 40 ff.; LANDES/POSNER, Harvard Law Review 1980, 939; WHISH/BAILEY, 25.

305 The relationship between market power and dominance shows best in merger control. Article 2(3) EC Merger Regulation forbids mergers leading to the significant impediment of effective competition particularly as a result of the creation or strengthening of a dominant position.[853] Cumulating market powers can therefore result in a dominant position.[854] In other words, if an undertaking has so much market power that it can act independently and prevent effective competition in the above-stated way in the relevant market, it is dominant, according to competition law.[855] In order to agree on the existence of a dominant position, it is therefore necessary to evaluate market power. A direct assessment of the dominant position in the judicial understanding is impossible.[856]

II RELEVANT FACTORS IN ASSESSING MARKET POWER

306 In order to determine whether an undertaking is holding substantial market power in the defined relevant market, literature and practice list three (often only two) main domains to be assessed: first, the situation in the relevant market including actual and potential competition as well as countervailing buyer power,[857] second, the structure of the undertaking under scrutiny, and, third, the undertaking's behaviour in the market.[858]

307 As regards the situation in the market, indications of market power are absolute and relative market shares. Absolute market shares of over 70 per cent raise a strong presumption of dominance, while shares between 50 per cent-70 per cent carry a weaker presumption. Market shares between 40 per cent and 50 per cent do not raise a presumption of dominance, but require close examination of the facts.[859] Shares below 40 per cent are only capable of supporting the finding of a dominant position in exceptional cases.[860] Relative market shares focus on the cumulative market shares of competitors and the gap between the largest (dominant) firm and its next largest competitor. The relative position of an undertaking compared with its competitors is of

853. With this article, the Merger Regulation introduced the significant impediment to effective competition test (SIEC test) with which the effect of mergers on competition is analysed. For a broader analysis of the SIEC test, *see i.a.*: CANAPA, 96 ff.; KÖRBER, in: IMMENGA/MESTMÄCKER 2012, Article 2 EC Merger Regulation, paras 183 ff.
854. On the relationship between market power and the dominant position: KÖRBER, in: IMMENGA/MESTMÄCKER 2012, Article 2 EC Merger Regulation, para. 411. *See also* the Swiss doctrine, which understands market power as a position between a general insignificant influence on the market and a dominant position. ZÄCH, para. 573.
855. In this manner also: GRILL, in: LENZ ET AL., EUV - AEUV - GRCh, Article 102 AEUV, para. 10.
856. BISHOP/WALKER, paras 3-010 and 3-053; WURMNEST, 261 ff.
857. *See i.a.*: EC, *Guidance Paper*, para. 12; BISHOP/WALKER, paras 3-013 ff.
858. *See i.a.*: FUCHS/MÖSCHEL, in: IMMENGA/MESTMÄCKER 2018, Article 102, para. 86; JUNG, in: GRABITZ ET AL., EUV/AEUV, Article 102, para. 88.
859. *See also*: ECJ, *AKZO*, C-62/86, paras 59 f.; EC, *Guidance Paper*, paras 13 f.
860. O'DONOGHUE/PADILLA, 147.

great importance for an undertaking's ability to behave independently. This is considered to be high if relative market shares remain stable over a period of time.[861]

308 With absolute market shares of over 70 per cent, courts usually do not conduct a further in-depth analysis of other factors.[862] This practice has been widely criticised, however.[863] Beneath market shares, therefore, great importance is attributed to potential competition. The higher the chance of new market entrants, the higher the competitive pressure on incumbent firms. Market entry barriers[864] are of great importance in the assessment of potential competition.[865] Notable factors for determining the openness of the market are required initial investments, long-expected pay-off periods of the investments, network effects, the importance of distribution networks, required marketing activities, economies of scale, switching costs of consumers[866] as well as administrative or legal and technological barriers[867] in the form of patents, etc.[868] In economics, the degree of contestability (contestable markets) of a market provides information on how easily new entrants can enter the market (degree of potential competition).[869]

309 Countervailing buyer power is another factor used to determine the dynamics of a market. Countervailing buyer power is the competitive pressure emanating from buyers. That is their power to bargain with suppliers based on their economic weight (size, commercial significance) as well as the alternatives available (other suppliers, possible vertical integration or the possibility to sponsor new entrants or expansions).[870]

310 As regards the characteristics of the undertaking itself, financial and economic strength including profitability, global presence, distribution networks, the capacity to increase output and so on, as well as vertical integration, brand recognition, access to key innovation and knowledge (including patents) are considered to be relevant.[871]

---

861. BELLAMY/CHILD, para. 10.026; KÖRBER, in: IMMENGA/MESTMÄCKER 2012, Article 2 EC Merger Regulation, para. 240; GC, *General Electric v. Commission,* T-210/01, para. 150.
862. ECJ, *Hoffmann-La Roche v. Commission,* C-85/76, para. 41.
863. *See i.a.*: FUCHS/MÖSCHEL, in: IMMENGA/MESTMÄCKER 2018, Article 102, para. 96; JUNG, in: GRABITZ ET AL., EUV/AEUV, Article 102, para. 96; *see also* with further references to Swiss literature: HAGER/MURER, recht: Zeitschrift für juristische Weiterbildung und Praxis 2015, 201.
864. For an analysis of different existing definitions of barriers to entry, *see*: O'DONOGHUE/PADILLA, 152 ff.
865. *See i.a.*: BISHOP/WALKER, paras 3-020 ff.; FUCHS/MÖSCHEL, in: IMMENGA/MESTMÄCKER 2018, Article 102, para. 98; DAVIS/ST QUINTIN/TRITTON, para. 12-092.
866. *See*: O'DONOGHUE/PADILLA, 157 ff.
867. *See*: O'DONOGHUE/PADILLA, 155 f.
868. *See i.a.*: DAVIS/ST QUINTIN/TRITTON, 12-093 ff.; FUCHS/MÖSCHEL, in: IMMENGA/MESTMÄCKER 2018, Article 102, para. 98; GAUSS, 103 ff.
869. *See* the introduction to contestable markets in: HEINEMANN, in: DREXL, Research handbook on intellectual property and competition law, 54 f.; *see also* BISHOP/WALKER, paras 3-021 f.
870. *See i.a.*: EC, *Guidelines on the assessment of horizontal mergers,* para. 64; EC, *Guidance Paper,* para. 18; BISHOP/WALKER, paras 3-031 f. The idea of countervailing buyer power has already been addressed above with the notion that a supplier without a buyer willing to purchase is not going to last. *See supra* at para. 303.
871. FUCHS/MÖSCHEL, in: IMMENGA/MESTMÄCKER 2018, Article 102, paras 103 ff.; O'DONOGHUE/PADILLA, 160 ff.

The clearer the result of the evaluation of the market structure, the less important the characteristics of the undertaking.[872]

311 This notion also applies to the third relevant evaluation criterion, the conduct of the undertaking itself.[873] Analysing market conduct at this stage comes with difficulties and the risk of circular arguments. Conduct is ambivalent in as much as it is difficult to distinguish whether the conduct is adopted as a result of the 'room for manoeuvre', insufficient competitive pressure or as a reaction to competitive pressure. Price reductions are not clear conduct, therefore. Worthy of note are strategies such as the 'creation of psychological market entry barriers through aggressive strategies'[874] against potential entrants or independent pricing strategies.[875]

III MARKET POWER AND PATENTS

312 As market entry barriers, intellectual property rights[876] and therefore patents are of fundamental importance in the evaluation of a dominant position.[877] Even though the intellectual property right itself does not 'confer [a dominant] position',[878] the privileges granted therewith can allow the patent holder to prevent effective competition.[879] Intellectual property rights influence both the structure of the market - as market entry barriers[880] - and the characteristics of the undertaking, as access to knowledge.[881]

313 Patents prevent competition by imitation and therefore also market entry with an imitating product. They represent a technological lead that a competitor not only has to match but also has to outperform in order to realise market entry or expansion. Rather than preventing entry, patents restrict it.[882] Whether a patent acts as a market entry barrier has to be decided based on the actual and potential substitutability of the patented technology. Where competition by substitution does not exist or only to a limited degree and where potential entry in the form of a substituting technology not infringing the patent is unlikely, the patent functions as a barrier to entry.[883] As a consequence, an evaluation of the effects of the patent on competition by substitution

872. Fuchs/Möschel, in: Immenga/Mestmäcker 2018, Article 102, para. 102.
873. Fuchs/Möschel, in: Immenga/Mestmäcker 2018, Article 102, para. 111.
874. Fuchs/Möschel, in: Immenga/Mestmäcker 2018, Article 102, para. 114 (translation by the author), *see also*: Bellamy/Child, para. 10.041.
875. *See* the decision of the Commission in: EC, *ECS v. AKZO,* IV/30.698, para. 69.
876. For brands, *see*: Canapa, 20 ff.
877. *See*: Ullrich/Heinemann, in: Immenga/Mestmäcker 2018, Teil GRUR B, para. 49; GC, *Tetra Pak II,* T-83/91, para. 110; critical: von Weiszäcker, in: Oberender, Effizienz und Wettbewerb, 48 f.
878. GC, *AstraZeneca v. Commission,* T-321/05, para. 270.
879. GC, *AstraZeneca v. Commission,* T-321/05, para. 270.
880. *See supra* at para. 308.
881. *See supra* at para. 310.
882. Langinier, Journal of Economics and Business 2004, 359.
883. Overall: Lamping, 161.

has to be made.[884] The clearest are cases where the patented technology itself forms the relevant product market or where the patented technology is indispensable for entering the market[885] as in the case of de facto standards.[886] The foreclosing effects originating from patents are therefore higher for pioneering innovations and broad patents.

884. In this sense also: ALBERT, 83 ff.; HEINEMANN, in: DREXL, Research handbook on intellectual property and competition law, 63; ULLRICH/HEINEMANN, in: IMMENGA/MESTMÄCKER 2018, Teil GRUR B, para. 49.

885. *See i.a.*: ECJ, *IMS Health*, C-418/01, paras 48 f.; GC, *Microsoft*, T-201/04, paras 31 ff.

886. EC, *Microsoft*, COMP/C-3/37.792, para. 472.

CHAPTER 11
Consequences for the Evaluation of Conduct Involving Patents

314 An application of Article 102 TFEU requires the undertaking to be dominant in the relevant market at the moment when it engages in potentially incriminating conduct. With applications for blocking patents, this means that the undertaking is required to be dominant in the relevant market at the moment when it acquires the patent. The market definition in theory allows vertically integrated markets to be defined: the product and the technology as well as the innovation market.[887] The conduct of acquiring a patent directly influences the competitive situation with regard to technology, that is, the 'middle level' of market integration (technology market). A patent acquisition thus has the power to influence the final product market as well as the innovation market with regard to future innovations.

315 The finding of an abuse of a dominant position requires the vertically integrated markets to be defined as well as conducting an isolated analysis of the effects of the technology acquisition on each of the markets. In the USA, the acquisition of a patent can be unlawful, 'for example, [if] the dominant competitor in a market acquires a patent covering a substantial share of the same market that he knows when added to his existing share will afford him monopoly power'.[888] The court does not allow antitrust scrutiny of the patent acquisition prior to the existence of a relevant product market,[889] however. Likewise, in EU case law, as has recently been shown in the *Servier* decision by the General Court,[890] there is still a focus on the product market. A separate assessment of the effects on the different market levels is missing in practice.

887. *See supra* at Part III, Chapter 10.
888. 2ND CIR., *SCM Corp. v. Xerox Corp. v. Monitowoc Co.*, 645 F.2d 1195, para. 50.
889. 2ND CIR., *SCM Corp. v. Xerox Corp. v. Monitowoc Co.*, 645 F.2d 1195, para. 51.
890. *See infra* at paras 368 ff.

316 As regards the establishment of the dominant position, a closer look at the potentially abusive strategies is required. Patents generally contribute to the independence of an undertaking, as it can rely on certain technical teachings and prevent others from using the same. Patents are therefore a factor which, when considered with others, might result in finding an undertaking dominant in a specific market. The significance of a patent in this regard is dependent on the breadth of the definition of the relevant market.[891]

317 Owing to the fact that a dominant position must exist at the time of the relevant conduct, it becomes evident that relevant patent applications which could open the scope of Article 102 TFEU will most likely not be for basic primary patents. Basic patents are generally the ones protecting new solutions to existing demands or at least new substitutable technology.[892] A dominant position existing at the time of the acquisition of the patent is more likely when an undertaking applies for or acquires a patent covering a new substitutable technology to a technology it already owns.[893] This was the case in the example of the English steelworks mentioned above. The cold rolling process, which was developed only four years after the introduction of the hot rolling mill, was a substitute, but was kept unused until a competitor sought to license the technology.[894] Acquisitions opening the scope of Article 102 TFEU are most likely to involve secondary patent applications or patent acquisitions (secondary acquisitions as opposed to applications for patents).[895] First, it is more likely that the undertaking conducting such a strategy is already dominant in the market, and, second, strategies which involve more than one secondary patent are more likely to result in barriers to entry because of the breadth of the patents when combined.[896]

891. *See in this regard also*: HEINEMANN, in: DREXL, Research handbook on intellectual property and competition law, 63.
892. *See supra* at para. 228.
893. On the exclusionary effect of patent accumulations, *see*: ALBERT, 87 ff.
894. *See supra* at para. 204.
895. *See* the decision of the United States Court of Appeal of the Second Circuit: 2ND CIR., *SCM Corp. v. Xerox Corp. v. Monitowoc Co.*, 645 F.2d 1195, para. 50.
896. On the breadth of patents and their effect on competition, *see supra* at paras 236 and 251.

Part IV Implications from Case Law and the Patent Misuse Doctrine for Blocking Patent Applications under EU Competition Law

CHAPTER 12

Case Law on the Abuse of a Dominant Position and Patents

I INTRODUCTION

318 The task of identifying illegitimate conduct in order to draw a line between legitimate and illegitimate conduct is difficult, especially when the foundation is a vague provision such as Article 102 TFEU. As the Court of Justice, as supervisor of the application and supreme authority in interpreting EU law, delivers authoritative interpretations of the treaty,[897] the starting point for the evaluation of whether the application of blocking patents could amount to an abuse of a dominant position is to look at the case law. The following analysis will thus present and comment on cases concerning the alleged abuse of a dominant position by acquiring intellectual property rights. The analysis therefore includes decisions by not only the Court of Justice but also the Commission and the General Court. The decisions by the General Court and the Commission are mainly considered where the case has not (yet) been presented to the Court of Justice.

II *CICRA AND OTHERS V. RENAULT*

319 Against the background of the legal framework dominated by the doctrines outlined above[898], it comes as no surprise that the Court of Justice was hesitant to accept the scrutiny by competition law of the registration process of intellectual property rights. The question of whether the mere acquisition of an intellectual

897. *See supra* at para. 14.
898. *See supra* at Part I, Chapter 3, section III.

property right through application can be classified as abusive was first raised in the EU in 1988 in the case of *CICRA and Others v. Renault* (hereinafter '*CICRA v. Renault*').

320 The legal dispute was adjudicated during a time when voices in Italy were increasingly challenging the patentability of car spare parts. The national court in Italy submitted the opinion that the protection of separate bodywork components was unjustified[899] because the holder of an exclusive right on the entire bodywork (design right) was already enjoying enough exclusivity to guarantee a return on their R&D.[900] The national court thus asked the Court of Justice whether the registration of property rights on spare parts, where independent manufacturers of these parts were excluded, could be classified as an abuse of the dominant position under Article 102 TFEU.[901]

321 The Court of Justice in Luxembourg disagreed with the national case. It held that 'the mere fact of securing the benefit of an exclusive right granted by law, [...], cannot be regarded as an abusive method of eliminating competition'.[902] It argued that the exercise of the right might be prohibited,[903] but 'the mere fact of obtaining protective rights [...] does not constitute an abuse of a dominant position within the meaning of Article 86 of the Treaty'.[904] Therewith the court concluded that the national legislator decides which intangible assets are worth protecting with an intellectual property right.

322 From the wording of the judgment, it can be deduced that, with this statement, the Court of Justice created an exemption from competition law scrutiny for the mere primary acquisition of intellectual property rights. However, considerations of the market structure and the effect of the conduct were not put forward for justification, which means that the decision is an example of court practice strictly applying the doctrine of separating existence and exercise. The ruling is therefore of only limited importance for current practice. The low influence of the prejudice in *CICRA v. Renault* is also evidenced by the fact that it was the only case where the Court of Justice argued on such absolute terms.

III *TETRA PAK I*

323 Only two years later the General Court modified the apparently absolute finding in the *Tetra Pak I* decision. This case was different from the *CICRA v. Renault* in that it concerned a patent acquisition and the patent acquisition was secondary (licence).

899. ECJ, *CICRA v. Renault*, C-53/87, para. 5.
900. ECJ, *CICRA v. Renault*, C-53/87, para. 5. A similar idea forms the basis of section 3 (d) of the Indian Patent Act by which the patentability of secondary pharmaceutical patents in India has been reduced. Newly discovered forms, property or usage of already known components cannot be registered as patents unless they are significantly more effective. The said condition is a patent requirement. The conflict was thus resolved by patent law itself. *See*: KANKANALA/NARASANI/RADHAKRISHNAN, 19.
901. ECJ, *CICRA v. Renault*, C-53/87, para. 7.
902. ECJ, *CICRA v. Renault*, C-53/87, para. 15.
903. ECJ, *CICRA v. Renault*, C-53/87, para. 16.
904. ECJ, *CICRA v. Renault*, C-53/87, para. 18.

Tetra Pak Rausing Advocate General obtained an exclusive patent licence on a UHT-milk packaging process through the takeover of the Liquipak Group. Tetra Pak in those days held market shares of around 90 per cent in aseptic packaging and 50 per cent in fresh milk packaging in the Union's market. At the time of the takeover, only one undertaking besides Tetra Pak Rausing could produce and sell aseptic milk-packaging machines within the EU. Moreover, the connected knowledge of the filling technique was considered essential to enter the vertically integrated market for equipment and cartons.[905] Tetra Pak Rausing was thus declared undoubtedly dominant in both markets.[906]

324 Through the takeover and the connected exclusive licence transfer, the market power of the already dominant undertaking increased. According to the Commission and the General Court, this concentration and other market characteristics led to a situation where entrance into the market was delayed or even prevented. Already before the takeover, competition in the market had been rather weak. For the additional lack of objective justifications,[907] Tetra Pak Rausing was held guilty of having abused its dominant position by acquiring the exclusive licence.

325 The court supported the argument of the Commission that the abusive nature of the acquisition was established by the presence of a supplementary element.[908] This supplementary element was seen in the context of the case. The acquisition of the licence was considered as having 'the practical effect of precluding all competition in the relevant market'.[909] The Commission even argued that the effects on the market were equivalent to a takeover.[910] With this judgment, the General Court withdrew the immunity of privileges granted by intellectual property rights from the immunity of competition law, but the court also denied per se the illegality of such conduct[911] in holding that the 'circumstances surrounding the acquisition' as well as 'in particular its effects on the structure of competition' should be considered.[912] An intellectual property right, through either the mere existence or the mere refusal to license does not, in the absence of supplementary elements, result in an absolute barrier to entry. Both the Commission and the General Court therefore reached the conclusion that the conduct constituted an abuse of dominance as long as Tetra Pak Rausing insisted on the exclusivity of the licence.[913]

905. EC, *Tetra Pak I*, IV/31.043, para. 47; GC, *Tetra Pak I*, T-51/89, para. 7.
906. EC, *Tetra Pak I*, IV/31.043, para. 44.
907. EC, *Tetra Pak I*, IV/31.043, para. 49.
908. ' [...] but also had the effect of preventing, or at the very least considerably delaying, the entry of a new competitor into a market where very little if any competition is found'. EC, *Tetra Pak I*, IV/31.043, para. 45.
909. GC, *Tetra Pak I*, T-51/89, para. 24.
910. EC, *Tetra Pak I*, IV/31.043, para. 47.
911. This argument shows the influence of the Rule of Reason long before the emergence of the discussion about a *more economic approach* in EU competition law.
912. GC, *Tetra Pak I*, T-51/89, para. 23.
913. EC, *Tetra Pak I*, IV/31.043, paras 45 ff.; GC, *Tetra Pak I*, T-51/89, paras 23 f.; JUNG, in: GRABITZ ET AL., EUV/AEUV, Article 102, para. 229.

326 This case is remarkable for two reasons. First, the General Court for the first time applied Article 102 TFEU to the acquisition of patents, in respect of an exclusive licence. Even though it held that the acquisition as such did not qualify as an abuse and thereby remained within the previous practice, it did allow scrutiny of the 'circumstances surrounding the acquisition'. Second, the additional element which gave the conduct its abusive character was the effect of the conduct on the market. No additional element was established besides the effect on the market.[914] This decision contradicts the definition of abuse given by the Court of Justice as well as the aim of the provision, which is not to deprive dominant undertakings of competing but only by 'methods different from [...] normal competition'.[915]

IV *TETRA PAK II*

327 When the Commission in 1991 examined the conduct of Tetra Pak Rausing on the markets for aseptic packaging and fresh milk packaging again, the company was still dominant in both markets and held similar market shares as in 1985.[916] To protect its aseptic brick packaging technology, Tetra Pak pursued a patent strategy that included not only the patenting of fundamental technologies for aseptic packaging processes, machines and materials developed during the 1960s but also several modifications and tweaks. Because of this extensive patent policy, at the time of the investigation of the company by the Commission, the company held over hundred patents for aseptic brick cartons as well as machines. Without further registration of patents, the protection was set to expire at the beginning of the twenty-first century.[917] The patenting strategy (flooding) was not analysed as a potential abuse of the dominant position but was considered indirectly under the strengthening of the constraints on competition implied by the system of tied sales.[918] Tetra Pak had imposed the obligation on customers of its machines to use Tetra Pak cartons and supplies (tying[919]).[920] In the end, the abuse identified in the case consisted of various types of conduct. Central was the imposition of numerous contractual clauses on customers to bind them to the company, tying sales of cartons and supplies and charging discriminatory prices for cartons and machines.[921] This was accompanied by several strategies targeted at affecting competitors and driving them out of the market, as, for example, the takeover of competing companies.[922]

914. GC, *Tetra Pak I*, T-51/89, paras 23 ff.
915. ECJ, *Hoffmann-La Roche v. Commission*, C-85/76, para. 91.
916. EC, *Tetra Pak II*, IV/31.043, paras 100 ff.
917. EC, *Tetra Pak II*, IV/31.043, para. 22.
918. EC, *Tetra Pak II*, IV/31.043, paras 162 ff.
919. On tying, *see infra* at paras 461 ff.
920. EC, *Tetra Pak II*, IV/31.043, paras 117, 119, 137 and 151; GC, *Tetra Pak II*, T-83/91, paras 137, 140 f. and 170.
921. GC, *Tetra Pak II*, T-83/91, para. 242.
922. EC, *Tetra Pak II*, IV/31.043, paras 165 ff.; GC, *Tetra Pak II*, T-83/91, paras 124 ff.

V *MAGILL, IMS HEALTH* AND *MICROSOFT*

328 In the case of *Volvo v. Veng*, which concerned the protection of car spare parts as with *CICRA v. Renault*, the question of whether and to what extent a refusal to license constitutes an abuse of a dominant position was raised.[923] An answer was only provided by the court in the later cases of *Magill* and *IMS Health* which, in contrast to the rest of the cases presented here, concerned the licensing of a copyright rather than a patent.

329 In the *Magill* case, broadcasting companies refused to deliver weekly programme previews to Magill which meant that Magill was then not able to produce complete TV magazines. The broadcasting companies justified their refusal with the existence of a copyright on the previews. The refusal to provide access to the protected information was considered abusive because it resulted in the prevention of a new product without objective justification, for which there was potential consumer demand and which the dominant undertaking did not want to market itself[924] with the foreclosure of the downstream market for programme previews.[925]

330 After the *Magill* case, it remained unclear whether the criteria of preventing a new product and the foreclosure of competition on a vertically integrated market were cumulative conditions for the finding of abuse. For refusals to license, this question was answered in the affirmative in the *IMS Health* case.[926] IMS Health supplied regional sales data on pharmaceutical products. To define sales regions, IMS Health used a specific brick structure which it developed in collaboration with members of the pharmaceutical industry and which became standard in the industry. In its *IMS Health* decision, the Court of Justice further concretised the criteria of a downstream market in that it considered it to be sufficient that a potential or hypothetical market existed. This is the case whenever two different stages of production exist and the supply of the upstream product is necessary for the production of the downstream product.[927]

331 The third case in this series is the *Microsoft* case. In 2004, the Commission held that Microsoft had abused its dominant position in the market for PC operating system by bundling the Windows operating system with the Windows Media Player[928] as well

923. ECJ, *Volvo v. Veng*, C-238/87, para. 8.
924. Confirmed in: GC, *Tiercé Ladbroke SA v. Commission*, T-504/93, para. 131; this strict rule became important in the case of *IMS Health*, where IMS wanted to launch a competing product equivalent or similar to the one of the holder of the copyright. ECJ, *IMS Health*, C-418/01, para. 49.
925. ECJ, *RTE and ITP v. Commission*, Joined Cases C-241/91 P and C-242/91 P, paras 51 ff.
926. ECJ, *IMS Health*, C-418/01, paras 44 ff. Note that the cumulation of the said criteria in the *IMS Health* decision provoked criticism in literature, mainly with respect to the requirement of preventing a new product. *See i.a.*: Conde Gallego, GRUR Int. 2006, 25 ff.; Eilmansberger, King's Law Journal 2005, 335 f.; Heinemann, IIC 2005, 71 ff.; Lamping, 249 ff. and 283 ff.; Ridyard, ECLR 2004, 669 f. Others principally argued in favour of the criteria. *See*, for example, Höppmann, GRUR Int. 2005, 459; Merdzo, ZEuS 2005, 168 ff.
927. ECJ, *IMS Health*, C-418/01, para. 44.
928. EC, *Microsoft*, COMP/C-3/37.792, paras 792 ff., esp. para. 1066.

as its dominant position in the market for workgroup server operating systems by withholding interoperability information[929].

332 According to the Commission, Microsoft had held back information on its Windows operating system without which competitors could not develop competing WGOS interoperable with the Windows system. Unlike in the *Magill* and *IMS Health* cases, before entering the market of WGOS Microsoft did provide the necessary interoperability information and therefore only refused to supply the information after participating in the market. Nevertheless, the Commission analysed the case based on the criteria elaborated in the aforementioned cases but broadened the previously criticised condition of the prevention of a new product.[930] The abuse was established based on the following cumulative conditions:

- in the first place, the refusal relates to a product or service indispensable to the exercise of a particular activity on a neighbouring market;[931]
- in the second place, the refusal is of such a kind as to exclude any effective competition on that neighbouring market;
- in the third place, the refusal prevents the appearance of a new product[932] for which there is potential consumer demand.[933]

333 An interesting point was made by the Commission with regard to the criterion of indispensability and the argument of Microsoft that competitors could have accessed the information via reverse engineering. The Commission found reverse engineering to require considerable efforts and the chance of success to be uncertain. Furthermore, interoperability has proved to be important to be a viable competitor, and interoperability, even after being successfully accessed through reverse engineering, would be dependent on the characteristics of Microsoft's Windows operating system which may change due to upgrades or similar changes. Reverse engineering was thus not considered a viable alternative for competitors.[934] Factually, indispensability was not understood as actual elimination from the market, but rather as factual elimination of competition in that the information was required to be able to compete. Also, the prevention of a new product was analysed with respect to innovation in that it was not only the limitation of products but also technical development that could result in prejudice to consumers.[935] In the case of *Microsoft*, this prejudice was manifested in a limitation of consumer choice.[936]

929. EC, *Microsoft*, COMP/C-3/37.792, paras 692 ff., esp. paras 779 ff.
930. On the difficulties, *see*: HEINEMANN, GRUR 2006, 712.
931. Note that a refusal to supply can also affect the market in which the undertaking is dominant on rather than just a vertically integrated market. *See*: EC, *British Midland v. AerLingus*, IV/33.544, para. 26. For a critical analysis of the requirement of indispensability, *see*: EILMANSBERGER, King's Law Journal 2005, 337 ff.; EILMANSBERGER, Common Market Law Review, 158 f.
932. As in the case of *IMS Health*, this criterion caused criticism. *See infra* at fn. 935.
933. GC, *Microsoft*, T-201/04, para. 332.
934. EC, *Microsoft*, COMP/C-3/37.792, paras 685 ff.
935. EC, *Microsoft*, COMP/C-3/37.792, paras 693 ff.; upheld on appeal: GC, *Microsoft*, T-201/04, paras 647 ff. This was criticised in literature: HAUSMANN, for example, criticised that the

VI *ASTRAZENECA V. COMMISSION*

1 Facts of the Case

334 In 2005, the Commission imposed a fine on AstraZeneca, a Swedish-British pharmaceutical concern, for having abused its dominant position in the market for PPIs[937]. PPIs are drugs that reduce the production of gastric acid in the stomach through the blocking of an enzyme in the gastric parietal cells.[938] To the broad public, they are known as 'stomach protection'. AstraZeneca's blockbuster Losec contains omeprazole as an active substance, which belongs to the class of PPIs.

335 In its investigation, the Commission analysed two instances of conduct by AstraZeneca. One of those debated was the strategy of AstraZeneca in relation to its application for an supplementary protection certificate[939] for Losec. The other concerned the withdrawal of a dosage form at the end of the patent's term. AstraZeneca lodged an action for the annulment of the decision. The final say in this matter belonged to the Court of Justice which delivered its judgment on 6 December 2012. The following sections will only focus on the argument of the Court of Justice regarding the acquisition of the supplementary protection certificate.

336 The prerequisites for the granting of supplementary protection certificates, as set out in Article 3 of Regulation No 469/2009 concerning the supplementary protection certificate for medicinal products, are the existence of a basic patent[940] as well as approval to sell the patented substance as a drug. An supplementary protection certificate can only be granted once. The scope of supplementary protection certificates

Commission by including the 'limiting of production, markets or technical development' extended the scope of the abuse. HAUSMANN, MMR 2008, 383 f.; RIDYARD, ECLR 2004, 673; in this respect also: THYRI, WUW 2005, 397; other authors used the *Microsoft* case to argue against the approach of the ECJ in the *IMS Health* decision. *See*: HEINEMANN, IIC 2005, 72 ff.

936. GC, *Microsoft*, T-201/04, paras 651 f.
937. PPIs were considered a separate product market, separated in retail channels (hospital and retail). EC, *AstraZeneca*, COMP/A.37.507/F3, para. 504; upheld on appeal: GC, *AstraZeneca v. Commission*, T-321/05, paras 61 ff.
938. Another drug class that also proactively reduces the production of gastric acid, though in a different way, is h2-antihistaminika (histamine h2 receptor blocker). However, the PPIs are more efficient and are preferred as they have a longer effect as a result of directly targeting the proton pump. *See*: GERALD, 414; EC, *AstraZeneca*, COMP/A.37.507/F3, paras 34 ff.
939. Since Council Regulation (EEC) No 1768/92 became effective on 2 January 1993, it has been possible to register for SPCs for medical products in the EU. Due to the peculiarities of pharmaceutical research and patenting, medical substances are only launched as drugs after a long period of research and trials. Thus, most of the exclusivity guaranteed by the patent has passed when the drug is finally launched. Patent holders consequently have only limited time left to earn a return on R&D. Through the SPC, an exclusive right sui generis, the patent holder should be rewarded with an additional period of exclusivity. Technically, even though an SPC often has the same extent of protection as the patent before it, the SPC is not an extension of the patent itself but a supplementary instrument.
940. *See supra* at paras 228 ff.

is limited to the claim of the basic patent covered by the authorisation.[941] After the launch of a product on the market, there is only a limited period within which an supplementary protection certificate application can be filed (Article 7 (EC) No 469/2009). What raised concern in this case was the fact that AstraZeneca had provided numerous patent offices with wrong information on the date of the first technical authorisation of Losec in order to obtain the supplementary protection certificate for Losec.[942] Through this wrongful information – AstraZeneca provided the date for the first approval of the price instead of the market approval and claimed deviant understanding of 'first authorisation'[943] – the undertaking was able to acquire supplementary protection certificates it was not entitled to and was thereby also able to extend duration of patent protection beyond the allowed time. The Commission and the subsequent court instances saw the submission of misleading information, which was such as to lead to the granting of an exclusive right the applicant was not entitled to, as conduct beyond competition on the merits. The behaviour of AstraZeneca in the process of registering the exclusive right was consequently declared abusive under EU competition law.[944]

2 Reasoning Concerning the Acquisition of the Supplementary Protection Certificate by Delivering Misleading Information

337 The argument of the Commission, which was confirmed by the General Court and the Court of Justice, was based on the objective nature of the conduct.[945] While 'simple inaccuracies, negligent misstatements or the expression of debatable opinions' would not qualify as an abuse of the dominant position, the behaviour of AstraZeneca did, being characterised by continuity and consistency.[946] AstraZeneca provided information without indicating that it was based on an allegedly divergent understanding of 'first authorisation'. For the patent offices and AstraZeneca's competitors, other information than that provided by the company was not accessible.[947] Even when the

941. The court practice is more liberal than the wording allows us to perceive. The ECJ decided in 1999 that the SPC does protect not only the active substance but also its derivatives such as salts or esters, if they are included in the scope of the basic patent. ECJ, *Farmitalia*, C-392/97, para. 21.
942. Due to the transitional provision in Article 19 (EC) No 469/2009, getting an SPC was only possible for drugs that had been launched after a certain date (specific for each Member State). Supported by the ECJ in: ECJ, *Hässle*, C-127/00, para. 79. Losec was, however, launched before the crucial date in many countries. The outcome of the Hässle case was of no relevance for the declaration of abusive practice in the sense of Article 102 TFEU. EC, *AstraZeneca*, COMP/A.37.507/F3, para. 666.
943. AstraZeneca justified its practice with the vague provision that the undertaking could not recognise which exact date it had to deliver to the authorities. EC, *AstraZeneca*, COMP/A.37.507/F3, paras 667 ff.
944. EC, *AstraZeneca*, COMP/A.37.507/F3, paras 628 ff.; ECJ, *AstraZeneca v. Commission*, C-457/10 P.
945. EC, *AstraZeneca*, COMP/A.37.507/F3, paras 913 ff.; GC, *AstraZeneca v. Commission*, T-321/05, para. 496; ECJ, *AstraZeneca v. Commission*, C-457/10 P, para. 154.
946. GC, *AstraZeneca v. Commission*, T-321/05, para. 338.
947. EC, *AstraZeneca*, COMP/A.37.507/F3, para. 747.

patent offices demanded clarification, AstraZeneca refrained from providing all the relevant data or clarification in most cases - though not to the patent offices of the United Kingdom and Ireland.[948] This led the Commission to conclude that AstraZeneca was neither challenging the current interpretation by providing arguments for a different understanding of Article 3(d) (EC) No 469/2009 nor negligently misunderstanding the guidelines, but was rather trying to receive supplementary protection certificates even though it had no claim. As a result of the special responsibility of dominant undertakings, AstraZeneca would have had the obligation to specify that it had provided the dates of the first price approval. Only this conduct would have allowed a suitable reaction from the authorities. The responsibility of dominant undertakings even goes as far as having an obligation to notify the authorities about potentially mistakenly granted exclusive rights, according to the General Court.[949]

338 To justify the finding of an abuse of the dominant position, the Commission adduced two arguments: the nature of the provided information and the character of the conduct. The information provided by AstraZeneca was declared as having the potential to influence the patent office in its decision to grant the intellectual property right. The circumstances in this case, namely that the patent office had only limited discretion and no obligation to review the provided information, were factors influencing the misguiding nature of the information.[950] The applicant in such circumstances can rely on the acceptance of the submitted information without expecting further questioning by the authority. The theoretical chance that the patent office would verify the information was declared unimportant as, in practice, patent offices in the case of supplementary protection certificates have limited discretion, restricted to an evaluation of formalities.[951] Anticompetitive effects resulting from the conduct of AstraZeneca cannot therefore be attributed to the conduct of the authorities, but are attributable to the undertaking itself. The use of public procedures and regulations can constitute an abuse of the dominant position if the conduct of the dominant undertaking distorts the decision-making of the authority which leads to the granting of a right which helps to create or protect market power.[952] It was therefore concluded that the submission of the information constituted an abuse, regardless of whether the authority was in fact deceived.[953]

339 According to the Commission, the abusive nature of the conduct lay in the implementation of the strategy to receive an supplementary protection certificate, even though AstraZeneca in fact did not have a claim. The Commission followed the

948. GC, *AstraZeneca v. Commission*, T-321/05, para. 495.
949. GC, *AstraZeneca v. Commission*, T-321/05, para. 358.
950. Note that more recent case law shows the difficulties in establishing an abuse of dominance based on allegedly misleading statements: ECJ, *Agria Polska v. Commission*, C-373/17 P, paras 51 ff.
951. GC, *AstraZeneca v. Commission*, T-321/05, para. 357.
952. GC, *AstraZeneca v. Commission*, T-321/05, para. 329; ECJ, *AstraZeneca v. Commission*, C-457/10 P, paras 82 ff.
953. EC, *AstraZeneca*, COMP/A.37.507/F3, paras 679 ff.; GC, *AstraZeneca v. Commission*, T-321/05, para. 361; ECJ, *AstraZeneca v. Commission*, C-457/10 P, paras 62 ff.

arguments presented by Advocate General Tizzano in the case of *General Motors* who concluded that irrespective of its success, behaviour aimed at restricting competition always falls within the scope of Article 102 TFEU.[954] Following these arguments, an abuse consists of the implementation of a strategy with the intention of restricting competition. The Commission thereby detached the finding of an abuse from the actual effects on competition. Unlawfulness of certain conduct cannot be dependent on the reaction of third parties.[955] The delivery of 'objectively misleading representations [...] which are of such a nature as to lead those offices to grant it [the applicant] supplementary protection certificates to which it is not at all or only for a shorter period entitled to, thus resulting in a restriction or elimination of competition, constituted an abuse of that position'.[956]

340 Proof of the existence of an underlying strategy going beyond competition on the merits was seen in the fact that the undertaking knowingly delivered misleading information.[957] Indications or even proof of an intention to block competition was not seen as being necessary to classify the conduct as abusive, but constituted a relevant factor in the evaluation of that conduct.[958] The critical factor in this case was the ability of the misleading information to lead the authority to grant exclusive rights not covered by the aim of the law and against the objectives of competition.[959]

341 The argument provided by AstraZeneca that conduct connected with the application for an supplementary protection certificate cannot qualify as an abuse of the dominant position because it lacks the potential to influence the competition was declined. The courts and the Commission held that supplementary protection certificates potentially influence the market structure and thus potential competition even before coming into force at the moment when the patent expires. There is no provision in legislation to extend the term of protection, for example, because it is believed that it would decrease the patent holder's motivation to innovate further, as the patent holder would be able to extend their monopoly right without investing in R&D.[960] The effects of an application for an supplementary protection certificate are therefore comparable with the acquisition of an exclusive licence.[961]

3 Analysis of the Case

342 With the judgment in the case of *AstraZeneca*, the Court of Justice for the first time accepted that the primary acquisition of an exclusionary right might constitute an

954. AG Tizzano, *in: General Motors*, C-551/03 P, paras 77 f.
955. GC, *AstraZeneca v. Commission*, T-321/05, paras 331 & 360.
956. GC, *AstraZeneca v. Commission*, T-321/05, para. 361.
957. EC, *AstraZeneca*, COMP/A.37.507/F3, paras 667 ff.; GC, *AstraZeneca v. Commission*, T-321/05, paras 358 and 493.
958. GC, *AstraZeneca v. Commission*, T-321/05, paras 356, 359 and 493 ff.
959. GC, *AstraZeneca v. Commission*, T-321/05, para. 361.
960. GC, *AstraZeneca v. Commission*, T-321/05, para. 367.
961. EC, *AstraZeneca*, COMP/A.37.507/F3, para. 767.

abuse of the dominant position.[962] The court followed the approach taken in the *Tetra Pak I* decision and argued that it would be inconsistent not to apply Article 102 TFEU to the acquisition of intellectual property rights as the provision had already been declared applicable to the acquisition of an exclusive licence.

3.1 Comment on the Concept of Abuse as Used in the AstraZeneca *Case*

a Elements of Abuses

343 At first sight, it is difficult to place the argumentation within a legal doctrine, to identify a pattern within it. On closer examination, however, a pattern emerges with structural features similar to those found in criminal law in civil law countries.

344 With the argument that the delivery of information misleading authorities to grant a property right to which the applicant is not entitled can qualify as an abuse of dominance, the finding of an abuse under Article 102 TFEU becomes dependent on the ability of the chosen conduct to distort competition.[963] The requirement of a causal link between the behaviour and the establishment of a barrier to competition in the form of an unjustified property right further underlines the importance of the nature of the conduct. Choosing methods generally suitable to influence competition is, as argued by the courts and the Commission in the *AstraZeneca* case, not sufficient for the finding of an abuse of dominance. Rather, the method chosen must be embedded in a strategy that is determined to achieve a specific anticompetitive goal. However, a direct intention to achieve an anticompetitive goal is not required. Both the Commission and the courts concluded that it is sufficient that not all objective circumstances can be fully explained otherwise than being part of a strategy aimed at reaching an anticompetitive goal. Establishing an abuse therefore first requires a 'suitable object' consisting of conduct capable of misleading authorities as well as an underlying strategy objectively designed to serve no other aim but to distort competition.

b The Relevance of Showing Anticompetitive Effects

345 Analogous to the threshold theory in criminal law, an abuse is presumed when the success of the followed strategy is only dependent on the reaction of third parties or, in other words, when the dominant undertaking has taken all the steps required for the establishment of a barrier to competition and to preserve power. An actual result in the

962. It therewith reacted to the findings of the Commission in the pharmaceutical sector inquiry. There the Commission found evidence that the strategic filing of patents can deter market entry. *See*: EC, *Sector Inquiry, Final Report*, paras 467 ff.
963. A link between the dominant position and the abuse is not required in EU law. *See*: ECJ, *Continental Can v. Commission*, C-6/72, para. 27, as well as *infra* at paras 439 ff.

form of anticompetitive effects is not required, however.[964] Following this understanding, a hazardous effect on the legal system does not start with actual damage to competition, but with attempts to distort competition.

346 This approach allows an evaluation of the conduct of the undertaking independent of the reaction of third parties. This procedure ensures that the same conduct does not lead to impunity in one case and penalisation in another because the conduct together with the reaction of authorities or competitors did or did not culminate in a distortion of competition. For actual anticompetitive effects not to be included in the argumentation of the *AstraZeneca* case, despite being in line with previous case law,[965] put a dampener on the evolving influence of the *more economic approach*,[966] where a legal intervention is only desirable and allowed when competition is in fact distorted.[967] The dispute concerns the fundamental question of whether favourable outcomes are more likely following a formalistic or a *more economic approach*.[968]

347 In this regard, cases where the right holder uses the right beyond the purpose of patent law, for example, if he or she is not entitled to the right, should be judged differently from cases where there is no violation of patent law. In the absence of a formal right, the assessment should concentrate on the fact that the property right lacks justification and yet has been acquired or maintained. As dominant undertakings have a special responsibility to compete only on the merits, an analysis which relies too heavily on actual anticompetitive effects could result in an ineffective application of competition law (type II errors) in cases involving unjustified property rights.[969] These considerations support the application of different criteria for those forms of strategic patenting.

c *Is There a 'Role' for Intent?*

348 The role of intent is controversial. Due to the fact that the abuse of a dominant position is an objective concept, 'fault' is not required to declare conduct abusive.[970] Yet, in cases where the application of a blocking patent is under scrutiny, it is the

964. GC, *AstraZeneca v. Commission*, T-321/05, paras 361 ff.
965. *See* the previous practice in: ECJ, *TeliaSonera Sverige*, C-52/09, para. 64.
966. Seitz, EuZW 2013, 380.
967. *See supra* at paras 60 ff.
968. On the Commission's Guidance Paper, *see:* Gravengaard/Kjaersgaard, European Competition Law Review 2010, 304 f.; on the strengths and weaknesses of the *more economic approach*, *see*: Heinemann, GRUR 2008, 949 ff.; on the intention of the Commission in promoting the *more economic approach*, *see*: Fuchs/Möschel, in: Immenga/Mestmäcker 2018, Article 102, para. 8.
969. This is supported by Wurmnest's conclusion that the extent to which effects on the market influence the decision of competition authorities and courts can and should vary depending on the conduct. *See*: Wurmnest, 256.
970. *See:* EC, *Deutsche Post AG*, COMP/35.141, para. 40.

strategic orientation of the conduct which contributes to the anticompetitive character.[971] It is thus not surprising that the courts based their findings mainly on the existence of the mere intent to apply measures beyond competition on the merits in the *AstraZeneca* case.[972] A strategic orientation not only can manifest itself in a direct anticompetitive intention but can also be inferred based on other considerations such as the intent to obtain a patent by devious means or with a lack of intention to foster innovation.[973] Both anticompetitive and right-exploiting intent influence the assessment of abusive behaviour in a similar way. Proof of either can contribute to an assessment and help distinguish unobjectionable from abusive conduct.

349 Due to the privileged position of a dominant undertaking, the intent to improve their market position with means outside of competition on the merits has to fall within the same category as a direct intent to drive competitors out of the market. The reliance of the court on the subjective element as an important factor in the analysis is thus supported.[974] Due to the importance of the subjective component in the cases of blocking patents, a deeper insight into the relevance of intent in the case of Article 102 TFEU will be given below.[975]

3.2 *Interim Conclusion on Cases Involving Patents Within the Abuse Concept Delivered by the Court*

350 After the *AstraZeneca* case where the Court of Justice concluded that anticompetitive effects do not need to be shown, the general question of whether favourable outcomes can best be reached by including or omitting effects on competition came back onto the table. In cases involving patents, the question of how favourable outcomes can most likely be reached is even more delicate. Legal practice not only needs to guarantee legal security, transparency and predictability but a result should also be in line with the aim of both the patent and competition law.

351 As it is in the very essence of patents to have an impact on competition,[976] the starting point for clarification is the common goal of competition and patent law:

971. *See* the comments on the Sector Inquiry by Drexl: Drexl, in: Drexl/Lee, Pharmaceutical innovation, competition and patent law, 309; on the general importance of intent as an assessment tool: Eilmansberger, Common Market Law Review 2005, 147 ff.
972. ECJ, *AstraZeneca v. Commission*, C-457/10 P, para. 197; the EC in its decision in the *Servier* case also listed the purpose of strengthening the dominant position or abusing it as a distinct feature to distinguish illegal from legal behaviour under Article 102 TFEU. *See*: EC, *Servier*, AT.39612, para. 2762.
973. *See* the comments on the Sector Inquiry by Drexl: Drexl, in: Drexl/Lee, Pharmaceutical innovation, competition and patent law, 309 f.
974. *See also*: Eilmansberger, Common Market Law Review 2005, 136.
975. *See infra* at paras 499 ff.
976. *See* the ECJ's decision in the case of *Phil Collins et al.* The court stated that exclusive rights, by their very nature, affect trade as well as competitive relationships. Thus, they fall within the scope of the TFEU. ECJ, *Collins and Patricia Im- und Export v. Imtrat and EMI Electrola*, Joined Cases C-92/92 and C-326/92, para. 22.

fostering innovation. Nowadays, fostering innovation is, as has been seen,[977] the prevailing motivation for maintaining the patent system. This aim should not be prevented by the application of competition law. If the Commission argues that it would lack consistency to not apply Article 102 to the acquisition of intellectual property rights when it has already been applied to the acquisition of an exclusive licence, the inverse conclusion must be that a restriction of the right to patents bears greater risk to innovation than the mere restriction of exclusive licences.[978]

352 Patents, through making competition by imitation impossible, foster innovation. A patent's blocking effect is, up to a certain level, intended.[979] Indeed, through providing a patent system, society offers a protection mechanism for intangibles that is widely, though not without dissenting voices,[980] recognised as encouraging innovation.[981] Thus, there is some interest for an economy to encourage patent applications, which is why the application of competition law must be limited to the cases where innovation and competition are endangered. The application of competition law should not result in a situation where successful innovators, competing with accepted means, are sanctioned, as this could be detrimental to both competition and innovation.[982] To strike the balance between fostering innovation by patent applicants while at the same time keeping the markets open for the competition, it is therefore important that other companies are not deterred unduly by the blocking effect immanent in each patent.

353 In the case of refusals to license, the trade-off between the innovation incentive of the patent holder and the harm of the refusal to license on the market is relevant for the finding of an abuse. Just like in these cases, a disproportion between the legitimate interest of the patent holder and harm to competition could be used for delineation in the case of patent acquisition as well.[983] An abuse could only be found when the pro-competitive benefits immanent in the patent are incapable of compensating anticompetitive effects. On account of the rationale of patent law, such an imbalance can only be identified where it is not intended by the legislator.[984] Therefore an abuse can only be considered when there is a potential that the patent will have effects going beyond those intended by law.[985]

977. *See supra* at paras 94 f.
978. Similarly: VESALA, in: BALLARDINI/BRUUN/NORRGÅRD, Transitions in European patent law, 284; KJØLBYE, World Competition 2009, 179.
979. This provoked voices which concluded that an applicant seeking to exclude others cannot be moving beyond the edges of legality. KJØLBYE, World Competition 2009, 182.
980. *See*: BOLDRIN/LEVINE, Journal of Economic Perspectives 2013, 9 and 20; *see also supra* at paras 96 ff.
981. On the pros and cons of the patent system and the controversial question as to whether patent systems support innovation *see supra* at paras 96 ff.
982. *See* concerns raised by: KJØLBYE, World Competition 2009, 181.
983. VESALA, in: BALLARDINI/BRUUN/NORRGÅRD, Transitions in European patent law, fn. 45.
984. Similarly: REINDL, IIC 1993, 64.
985. Similarly, for example, GC, *Magill*, T-76/89, para. 58; DREXL, in: DREXL/LEE, Pharmaceutical innovation, competition and patent law, 319; KJØLBYE, World Competition 2009, 172 and 181 ff.. ZECH held that conditions not addressed in patent laws can render the use of patents abusive form a competition law perspective. ZECH, ZWeR 2011, 318 f. For the established law practice

354 The nature of the patent conveys an exclusionary right and can have both competition-enhancing and distorting effects alike; thus, carefully weighing those effects is the only way to achieve a delicately balanced judgment of the conduct.[986] Taking another approach to patent acquisitions, namely granting immunity and conditioning the abuse on the usage of the exclusionary right in trade, would allow the patent holder to avoid sanctions when deciding not to use the patent.[987] This again would make patent protection obsolete since patents are granted to allow the exploitation of otherwise public goods. Forcing market participants not to compete should not be the result of applying competition law, and this is also the reason why it is not sufficient to leave it to other fields of law, namely the patent law itself, to prevent negative impacts of patents on the market. The same argumentation also leads to the conclusion that it is not sufficient to focus competition law scrutiny on the execution of patents, as threats to competition that result from the exclusionary right itself cannot be tackled therewith.[988]

355 Apart from these general statements, the impact of patents depends on their scope, strengths and the situation on the market and is therefore not very obvious.[989] A mere reliance on a case-by-case analysis does not foster legal security, transparency or predictability. In order to have a deterrent effect on future conduct, liability under Article 102 TFEU has to be predictable.[990]

356 Despite the attempt to tackle harmful patenting strategies at the beginning, when acquiring the property right, the problem remains that the finding of the abuse is always based on an *ex post* analysis of the conduct at a time when actual or potential harm has already occurred. Penalisation of potential harm can therefore only be desirable when the preventive effect of such an approach would help foster innovation and competition overall. One of the reasons is that competition law has to complement patent law. Patent law lacks legal remedies against patenting strategies and thus makes problematic patenting strategies attractive. The lack of remedies against problematic patenting strategies endangers the patent system's overall benefit for society.

VII *BOEHRINGER INGELHEIM*

357 In February 2007, the Commission opened proceedings against the German pharmaceutical manufacturer Boehringer Ingelheim. The company was under suspicion of having abused its dominant position in the market for chronic obstructive

that the potential of a conduct to result in anticompetitive effects is sufficient for the finding of an abuse, *see*: ECJ, *TeliaSonera Sverige*, C-52/09, para. 64.

986. On the challenge to differentiate and tackle both effects through competition law *see*: VESALA, in: BALLARDINI/BRUUN/NORRGÅRD, Transitions in european patent law, 283 ff.

987. GC, *AstraZeneca v. Commission*, T-321/05, para. 362.

988. DREXL, in: DREXL/LEE, Pharmaceutical innovation, competition and patent law, 312 f.; dissenting: O'DONOGHUE/PADILLA, 546; less strict: LAMPING, fn. 747.

989. VESALA, in: BALLARDINI/BRUUN/NORRGÅRD, Transitions in European patent law, 284; THOUVENIN, 279; *see supra* at para. 236.

990. VESALA, in: BALLARDINI/BRUUN/NORRGÅRD, Transitions in European patent law, 288.

pulmonary disease (COPD) drugs[991] by abusing patent procedure and the patent system. The practice under scrutiny was filing for patents without merit to block potential competitors.[992] Boehringer Ingelheim, which is active in R&D for new COPD medication, filed various patents on a drug combining four active ingredients for the treatment of COPD.[993] Three of these active ingredients were already known, one of which had recently been discovered by the Spanish competitor Almirall. Almirall claimed that, once granted, the patent would allow Boehringer to block not only Almirall's combination drugs but also the launch of a mono drug including only the new active ingredient discovered by Almirall.

358 The investigation of the Commission was closed when Boehringer agreed to remove the blocking position and to license the product in two Non-Member States.[994] This indicates that the blocking was in fact considered decisive for the opening of the investigation.

359 In the *AstraZeneca* case, the conduct had been declared abusive mainly because of its nature not being consistent with competition on the merits. The fact that in this case the Commission closed its investigation at the very moment when Boehringer agreed to license the product and thus remove the anticompetitive effect in the market raises doubts as to whether this ruling is consistent with the finding in the *AstraZeneca* case concerning a departure from the more economic to a more form-based approach. Judging from the limited documentation available, an abandonment of the exclusivity led to impunity in this case, irrespective of the fact that Boehringer seemed to have applied for an exclusionary right for an invention it did not make itself and with the intention of blocking Almirall. Yet, as Article 9 of Directive No 1/2003 allows for the closure of proceedings through commitments, the fact that Boehringer Ingelheim agreed to remove the blocking positions cannot be regarded as anticipation of whether the actual and likely effects on competition were necessary for categorising the conduct as abusive.

VIII *SERVIER*

1 Facts of the Case

360 The French pharmaceutical manufacturer Servier held the patent on the perindopril molecule until its expiration in 2003.[995] Perindopril is an API[996] that is used to

991. Boehringer Ingelheim owed its dominant position to its blockbuster Spiriva.
992. *See*: Straus, GRUR Int 2009, 94; EC, *Press Release, Boehringer Ingelheim v. Almirall*, IP/11/842.
993. Boehringer received a patent grant on one combination. This grant was later revoked by the UK High Court of Justice as well as the EPO due to obviousness and insufficiency. EC, *Press Release, Boehringer Ingelheim v. Almirall*, IP/11/842. Note that in the pharmaceutical industry 'new formulations of existing active ingredients' are patentable in principle. *See*: EC, *Servier*, AT.39612, para. 65.
994. On the case of Boehringer Ingelheim: EC, *Press Release, Boehringer Ingelheim v. Almirall*, IP/11/842; Faull/Nikpay, para. 16.151.
995. 'Perindopril Compound Patent', EP0049658, *see*: GC, *Servier v. Commission*, T-691/14, para. 4.

cure high blood pressure (hypertension), heart failure (cardiac insufficiency) and coronary heart diseases.[997] In drugs, perindopril is administered in saline forms.[998] As well as in mono-products, perindopril, which belongs to the group of so-called angiotensin-converting enzyme inhibitors (ACEIs)[999], can also be found in combination products.[1000]

361 In November 2008, the Commission opened an investigation against Servier and several generic drug producers. The evidence revealed details of Servier's strategy to secure the market position of its blockbuster[1001] perindopril[1002] after the expiration of the basic patent on the substance. To delay generic market entry, Servier not only acquired many processes and crystalline[1003] patents[1004] for perindopril and its production but also entered into deals with generic companies whenever they threatened to enter the market (reverse payment settlements) or circumvent the (blocking) patent cluster.

362 Documents found during the investigation also revealed that the strategically applied-for patents were internally referred to as 'blocking' or 'paper patents' that sometimes did not even require research effort.[1005] This led to the situation that between 2001 and 2009, only a limited number of technologies to generate perindopril were not owned by Servier. After a pharmaceutical manufacturer succeeded in developing a new technique to produce perindopril that did not infringe on Servier's numerous patents,[1006] Servier purchased this technology and added it to its maze of blocking patents[1007] to defend its market position.[1008] Servier thus strategically acquired patents originarily through patent application and secondarily through legal transaction. Remarkable in this case is that the portfolio of blocking patents (applied between 2000 and 2003) did not prevent the development of circumventing technologies (acquisitions by Servier started at the end of 2004). As internal documents show,

996. An API is the substance (or a combination of substances) in a drug that is responsible for the therapeutic effect of the drug. For a definition, *see*: WHO, *Definition of a pharmaceutical ingredient*, 3.
997. EC, *Servier*, AT.39612, paras 86 ff.
998. The two saline forms of perindopril (perindopril arginine and perindopril-tert-butylamine) that existed at the time of the investigation are bioequivalent. An advantage of the arginine saline is that it is more robust in warm and humid climates. *See*: http://www.pharmawiki.ch/wiki/index.php?wiki = Perindopril, accessed on 22 February 2020.
999. '[...] inhibiting the action of a body compound called angiotensin converting enzyme': EC, *Servier*, AT.39612, para. 2144.
1000. For all drugs that include perindopril and are commercially available in Switzerland, *see*: https://compendium.ch/search/all/perindopril/startwith/de, accessed on 22 February 2020.
1001. Blockbusters are drugs that create annual sales of at least USD 1 billion.
1002. On the general profitability (not net sales) of perindopril *see*: EC, *Servier*, AT.39612, paras 2369 ff.
1003. Such as EP 1 296 947 (annulled by the EPO in May 2009), *see*: EC, *Servier*, AT.39612, para. 5.
1004. On process patents and patents on crystalline forms, *see supra* at paras 168 ff.
1005. EC, *Servier*, AT.39612, paras 5 and 115.
1006. Azad, for example, developed a process resulting in new polymorphic forms of perindopril that infringed neither the process patents nor the product patents held by Servier. EC, *Servier*, AT.39612, Chapter 8.2.2.2.
1007. EC, *Servier*, AT.39612, para. 2776.
1008. EC, *Servier*, AT.39612, paras 6 and 139 ff.

the goal of buying competing technologies was simply to defend Servier's own way of generating perindopril.[1009] The secondary acquisition was thus an additional strategy because their own efforts in R&D and patenting did not seem to be enough to block others from marketing perindopril.

363 As an additional strategy, Servier launched a second-generation perindopril based on another salt (arginine instead of erbumine). The intention was to drop the first-generation after the launch of the second-generation perindopril to extend patent protection which was due to expire on the first generation ('AstraZeneca strategy'). The withdrawal of the first-generation drug makes a fast generic entry impossible, as a marketed original drug is crucial to its admission.[1010] However, what was disturbing about the second-generation drug, apart from the competition law concerns, was that the second-generation drug was a bioequivalent and thus no improvement on the first-generation perindopril.[1011] In the following summary of the argumentation, the focus will be on the patent and technology acquisition. Considerations on the appraisal of the reverse payment settlements and the implementation of new regulatory standards under competition law will be excluded.

364 In its press release, the Commission announced that it had fined Servier and five generic companies which had engaged in the reverse payment settlements. The actors in the reverse payment settlements were charged and fined under Article 101 TFEU. As Servier had pursued a strategy that combined[1012] various acts of questionable conduct, it was also under the scrutiny of Article 102 TFEU by the Commission. In 2018 the General Court reversed the Commission's decision on this point owing to a different market definition.[1013]

2 Reasoning of the Commission Concerning the Acquisition of the Azad Technology

365 To decide whether the secondary acquisition of a technology is in accordance with competition on the merits, and capable of foreclosure, the Commission focused on three elements. First, it evaluated whether the acquired technology was a serious 'source of competition'. That is, if the technology was advanced to a degree that it was 'potentially enabling' in 'overcoming barriers to entry'. Second, it analysed 'whether the purchased technology was effectively removed from the market as a potentially enabling source of competition'. This element is not met if the acquirer is willing to

1009. EC, *Servier*, AT.39612, paras 6 and 107 ff.
1010. *See i.a.*: ECJ, *AstraZeneca v. Commission*, C-457/10 P, para. 149; SEITZ, EuZW 2013, 380; also the provision § 24b (1) of the German Medicinal Product Act which is based on Directive 2001/83/EC. For a more detailed analysis of the foundations of the provision *see*: BERTHOLD, fn. 316.
1011. *See supra* fn. 998; EC, *Servier*, AT.39612, paras 8, 218 ff. and 246 ff.
1012. The wording of the decision indicates that the combination of the conduct was the critical factor leading to the scrutiny under Article 102 TFEU. EC, *Servier*, AT.39612, para. 9.
1013. *See infra* at paras 368 ff.

license the technology on attractive conditions. Third, whether the acquisition had the potential to render market entry more difficult or impossible; in other words, whether the acquisition potentially delayed market entry significantly.[1014]

366 All elements were affirmed in the case of Azad. Its technology was considered a source of competition in the relevant market, as Azad had already overcome obstacles in the form of Servier's patents and other market regulations. Ready to enter the market, even generic companies were seeking collaboration with the company. After the acquisition of Azad's technology by Servier, the generic companies claimed a lack of alternative technologies to produce perindopril. Servier neither offered licences[1015] nor allowed Azad to further use its knowledge. After Servier removed the Azad technology from the market, there were therefore no appropriate alternatives left that would have allowed competitive entry into the market since perindopril as a commodity was not obtainable. The secondary acquisition of the Azad technology blocked all legal ways to enter the market and thus delayed and hampered market entry, despite risky launches of probably infringing formulations by a handful of generic companies.[1016]

367 Despite the clearly established foreclosing potential of the Azad technology acquisition, the conduct was assessed together with five reverse payment settlements, as part of a large exclusionary strategy. The application of the numerous blocking patents as well as the strategy of strengthening the quality standards in the industry was only seen as a 'factual element helping to [...] assess[...] the anti-competitive foreclosure effect of Servier's conduct'.[1017] The final declaration of abuse of a dominant position remained reserved for the package the Commission called the overall strategy, including the Azad acquisition and reverse payment settlements.[1018] This was despite the statement that the findings concerning the acquisition of technology were 'limited to the circumstances of this case and should not be construed as a general prohibition of technology acquisitions by dominant undertakings'.[1019] Additionally, intent did not play a major role in the evaluation of the Azad technology acquisition. None of the three criteria established by the Commission to evaluate the technology acquisition made any reference to subjective criteria. Internal documents showing intention were only considered circumstantially.

3 Definition of the Relevant Market

368 Even though there is more than one active ingredient in the group of ACEI and other substances to cure high blood pressure, perindopril, because of trial results and

1014. On this paragraph: EC, *Servier*, AT.39612, para. 2800.
1015. One exception was Arrow. The company received a licence offer after it asserted compensation claims before the Swiss courts. Arrow refused the offer.
1016. EC, *Servier*, AT.39612, 8.2.2.; a summary of the analysis in para. 2881.
1017. EC, *Servier*, AT.39612, para. 2772.
1018. EC, *Servier*, AT.39612, para. 2987.
1019. EC, *Servier*, AT.39612, para. 2917.

a successful marketing strategy, was considered the leading ACEI by the Commission. Additionally, there were various supporting facts for the conclusion that other available drugs were not exact substitutes.[1020] This view was shared by other pharmaceutical manufacturers. A survey revealed that non-ACEI manufacturers did not consider their products as competing with perindopril and even competing ACEI did not have equivalent success in the retail channel.[1021] On the basis of the ATC system[1022] and after a careful examination of the market, including prescription habits, locked-in effects, the fact that high financial expenditure would have been required to invent around perindopril,[1023] etc., the Commission defined the product market[1024] and declared Servier as being dominant therein.[1025] The market, in the view of the Commission, was limited to original and generic perindopril, segmented along two distribution channels, one for hospitals and another for retail.[1026] The abuse and thus the investigation was concentrated on the retail market. Geographically every Member State where the conduct had effect was considered a separate market. Also, in the technology market which was defined as at least an EU-wide market for perindopril API technologies (technologies to generate the APIs),[1027] Servier was considered dominant.[1028]

369 The General Court, however, found the Commission's definition of the relevant market erroneous and declared that the Commission has exceeded its margin of discretion in defining the relevant market.[1029] Based on the ATC classification system, General Court found no reason to distinguish perindopril from 'other ACE inhibitors with respect to their therapeutic use',[1030] as all ACE inhibitors including perindopril have corresponding therapeutic indications and modes of action.[1031] All ACE inhibitors are therefore grouped together in the ATC system on the third and fourth levels. The Commission erred in defining the relevant market based on the fifth ATC level.[1032] The General Court furthermore disagreed with the Commission that medical studies suggested perindopril to be more efficient compared with other ACE inhibitors. With respect to efficiency, perindopril and other ACE inhibitors show similar results.[1033] According to the court, the choice of considered studies was too limited[1034] and the

1020. EC, *Servier*, AT.39612, paras 2204 ff. and 2222.
1021. EC, *Servier*, AT.39612, paras 2264 and 2269.
1022. On the practice of defining the relevant product market based on the ATC system, *see supra* at para. 288.
1023. EC, *Servier*, AT.39612, para. 140.
1024. *See supra* at paras 286 ff.
1025. EC, *Servier*, AT.39612, paras 2593 ff.
1026. EC, *Servier*, AT.39612, paras 2403, 2535 ff. and 2549.
1027. EC, *Servier*, AT.39612, paras 2603 and 2664 ff.
1028. EC, *Servier*, AT.39612, para. 2758.
1029. GC, *Servier v. Commission*, T-691/14, paras 1588 ff.
1030. GC, *Servier v. Commission*, T-691/14, para. 1429 (French original, translated by the author).
1031. This is also indicated by different available medical guidelines. *See*: GC, *Servier v. Commission*, T-691/14, paras 1431 ff.
1032. GC, *Servier v. Commission*, T-691/14, paras 1428 f.
1033. GC, *Servier v. Commission*, T-691/14, para. 1457.
1034. GC, *Servier v. Commission*, T-691/14, paras 1442 ff.

Commission was not allowed to base its argumentation on the internal documents of Servier.[1035]

370 The General Court furthermore criticised the Commission for relying on a survey of prescribers supplied by Servier which was used to prove that perindopril was the preferred ACE inhibitor, despite the fact that for reportedly eighty-one out of hundred patients an equivalent treatment existed.[1036] Furthermore, other originators such as AstraZeneca and Merck Sharp & Dohme considered their ACE inhibitors as competing with perindopril. According to the General Court, the finding of the therapeutic uniqueness of perindopril could not be upheld.[1037]

371 Besides the wrongly established therapeutic uniqueness of perindopril, according to the court, the Commission had further erred in its evaluation of the prescription practice[1038] and the patient's willingness to switch treatment.[1039] Lastly, the General Court also criticised the Commission's evaluation of the competitive situation in the market. First, it had not considered the significance of promotional activities.[1040] Second, it had focused on price changes to evaluate competitive pressure on perindopril and had thus disregarded the characteristics of the pharmaceutical market where the consumer's choice is not predominantly influenced by the price.[1041,1042]

372 As a result, the relevant product market could not be limited to perindopril. The General Court consequently also rejected the Commission's finding of a dominant position of Servier in the product market. The dominant position of Servier was mainly established by the Commission based on the market shares and the existence of relatively high economic rents. Owing to the erroneous definition of the relevant market, these calculations could not be upheld.[1043] In the market for ACE inhibitors, Servier's market shares were found to be lower than 25 per cent and perindopril was not leading in sales.[1044] Also, the calculation of the rents was based on the finding that the market consisting only of perindopril was not competitive before generic entry occurred.[1045] The Commission's decision was also repealed with respect to the finding of a dominant position in the technology market. This was due to the fact that the Commission had based its finding of a dominant position of Servier in the upstream technology market on its allegedly dominant position in the product market on derived demands. As the court held that Servier did not hold a dominant position in the

1035. GC, *Servier v. Commission*, T-691/14, paras 1466 ff.
1036. GC, *Servier v. Commission*, T-691/14, paras 1476 ff.
1037. GC, *Servier v. Commission*, T-691/14, paras 1479 f.
1038. According to the Commission, prescribers' loyalty allegedly resulted in limiting the competitive pressure on perindopril. GC, *Servier v. Commission*, T-691/14, paras 1513 and 1589.
1039. GC, *Servier v. Commission*, T-691/14, paras 1540 and 1589.
1040. GC, *Servier v. Commission*, T-691/14, paras 1565 and 1589.
1041. On the peculiarities of competition in the pharmaceutical market, *see supra* at Part I, Chapter 5.
1042. GC, *Servier v. Commission*, T-691/14, paras 1579 and 1589.
1043. GC, *Servier v. Commission*, T-691/14, para. 1600; *see in the literature*: KILLICK/JOURDAN/PÊCHEUX, Journal of European Competition Law & Practice 2019, 25 ff.
1044. GC, *Servier v. Commission*, T-691/14, paras 1604 f.
1045. GC, *Servier v. Commission*, T-691/14, para. 1606.

downstream markets, the finding of a dominant position in the technology market could also not be upheld.[1046]

4 Comment

4.1 Implications for the Primary Acquisition of Blocking Patents

373 From the Commission's decision in the *Servier* case, it is hard to derive precedence for the evaluation of primary acquisitions of blocking patents under Article 102 TFEU. Through the dichotomy between primary and secondary acquisition applied in the decision, the Commission might have introduced an evaluation scheme forming groups of different conduct varying with respect to their property rights dimension. As will be further outlined in this book,[1047] it is highly supported to take a different approach in cases where the right holder is entitled to the right compared with where it is not. However, to fully support this assumption with case law, the Commission would have had to address at least those blocking patents lacking inventiveness separately from the overall strategy. The fact that the EC did not analyse the conduct and even more so held that 'the assessment [...] will take into account the full factual setting, including other practices flowing from the strategy for which the contribution to foreclosure effects is not established in this decision',[1048] does not allow conclusions to be drawn on a precedence of the Commission towards the application of blocking patents as an independent violation of Article 102 TFEU.

374 Instead, the Commission avoided an analysis of this specific conduct. That the patent maze created by Servier consisted partly of blocking patents was only included in the analysis in order to justify the finding of Servier's dominant position and the circumstances in the case, despite clear evidence showing anticompetitive intent.[1049] Crucial for the Commission deciding on an abuse of a dominant position was the fact that Azad had been successful in circumventing the patent maze and especially the most constrictive patent but had been stopped by Servier from marketing its product.[1050] 'Servier not only attempted to enforce its patents, but attempted systematically and continuously to prevent generic entry when its patents could fail to block the generic companies' market access.'[1051] Under Article 102 TFEU Servier was eventually only charged for both the settlements and buying the technology of its competitor after

1046. GC, *Servier v. Commission*, T-691/14, paras 1615 ff.
1047. *See infra* at Part VI, Chapter 18, sections II and III.
1048. EC, *Servier*, AT.39612, para. 2766.
1049. *See supra* at para. 362.
1050. Patent EP 1 296 947 which covered the alpha form of perindopril erbumine. Patentability of the alpha form was highly contested since most of the known and patented processes generated this form of perindopril.
1051. EC, *Servier*, AT.39612, para. 2773.

the successful circumvention of Servier's own patents, but not for creating the patent maze.[1052]

375 Owing to the Commission's approach in fining Servier for the overall strategy, the General Court refrained from analysing conduct separately.[1053] The question remains how the court would have analysed the acquisition of the Azad technology had the Commission analysed the conduct separately and established a dominant position of Servier in the technology market independent of its position in the product market. It will be interesting to see whether, after the defeat in the General Court, the Commission adapts its practice and starts analysing patenting strategies as separate conduct with an infringing nature. Even though the main error identified by the General Court lay in the definition of the relevant product market, the General Court, by refraining from further analysis of the allegedly abusive conduct, also demonstrated the limits of the finding of a single continuous infringement.[1054] Following the author, a separate analysis of the patenting strategies should at least be conducted when a separate technology market is defined. This is due to the justifications for defining a separate technology market in the first place, which is a more precise capturing of the competitive landscape and securing competition at an early stage. There is little point in separately analysing competitive constraints in vertically integrated markets without also analysing the effects of potentially infringing conduct in these markets.

376 The relevance of the *Servier* decision of the Commission on the evaluation of primary acquisition of blocking patents remains unclear. Even before the launch of its overall strategy, Servier, following the Commission, held significant market power in the market for perindopril since apparently, apart from the generic version, no other antihypertensive medicine was a substitute for the drug.[1055] The applications for at least a couple of blocking patents fell during this time, when the main patent on perindopril was still valid and Servier dominant.[1056] Additionally, internal documents clearly displayed the intention of Servier behind the technology acquisition as well as the fact that certain patents obviously did not meet the patentability criteria. Judging from the precedence in *AstraZeneca*, this combination should have been enough to at least provoke an independent analysis by the Commission, especially since in *AstraZeneca*, the Court of Justice held that actual anticompetitive effects are not required once the potential of conduct to have such effects is proven.[1057] Moreover, for at least some of the blocking patents, it was established that they did not meet the patentability requirements and thus, as in the case of *AstraZeneca*, had been granted without *Servier*

1052. 'both sets of behaviour jointly constitute an abuse of dominance under article 102 of the Treaty'; EC, *Servier*, AT.39612, para. 2764.
1053. GC, *Servier v. Commission*, T-691/14, para. 1631.
1054. GC, *Servier v. Commission*, T-691/14, para. 1631.
1055. *See* statement in the EC's Press Release: EC, *Press Release, Commission fines Servier*, IP/14/799.
1056. On the relevant time for assessing an acquisition of a protective right: ECJ, *AstraZeneca v. Commission*, C-457/10 P, para. 110.
1057. ECJ, *AstraZeneca v. Commission*, C-457/10 P, para. 112.

being entitled to them. In the *AstraZeneca* case, the grant of an unjustified property right qualified the behaviour as abusive.[1058]

377 The question arises whether the Commission with its decision in *Servier* turned away from the precedence in *AstraZeneca*. Advocates of a more economic approach would support such a development based on the argument that Article 102 TFEU should only sanction conduct that effectively distorts competition.[1059] With respect to the maze of blocking patents in the *Servier* case, the Commission held that they were aimed at cementing the dominant position and blocking generic entrance, but at the same time stated on various occasions that, despite the maze, circumvention was possible. Thus in *Servier* owing to the successful circumvention by Azad, a distortion did not arise. Yet, this argument suggests that the declaration of conduct as abusive and the sanctioning of a dominant undertaking for abusive behaviour is dependent on the reaction of competitors in respect of their willingness to cope with the higher hurdles, the economic cost of inventing around and their success in doing so. A dominant undertaking could, following this line of argument, avoid sanctions if it found itself up against innovative competitors able to circumvent blocking positions no matter how statistically unlikely a circumvention was. This is not the idea of Article 102 TFEU, however, where it is immanent in its character as an absolute offence.

4.2 *Implications for the Secondary Acquisition of Blocking Patents*

378 With respect to the analysis of secondary acquisitions of a patent under Article 102 TFEU, the Commission seems to have followed the trend of the *more economic approach* and applied a rather strict standard for the assumption of anticompetitive foreclosure.[1060] When analysing the secondary acquisition of technology, the question is whether the property right should be limited with respect to the right to exclude others, similar to the cases of refusal to license. A comparison of the elaborated criteria shows the following.

The reasoning in the *Servier* and *Tetra Pak I* decisions reveals that the compliance of secondary acquisition with Article 102 TFEU is based on:

- whether the acquired technology is 'potentially enabling' in 'overcoming barriers to entry', in other words, a serious source of competition;
- 'whether the purchased technology was effectively removed from the market as a potentially enabling source of competition', in other words, whether the acquirer licenses the technology on fair conditions; and

1058. ECJ, *AstraZeneca v. Commission*, C-457/10 P, para. 108.
1059. On the *more economic approach, see supra* at paras 64 ff.
1060. Note that the EC even referred to the less strict practice according to which 'a certain degree of competition does not preclude the finding of an appreciable restriction of competition' or a conduct has to be 'capable of producing foreclosure effects on the market'; EC, *Servier*, AT.39612, paras 1227, 2763 and 2766.

- whether the acquisition has the potential to render market entry more difficult or impossible, in other words, whether the acquisition potentially delays market entry.[1061]

379 In the *Microsoft* decision, the refusal to license was found abusive when it:

- withheld information indispensable to the exercise of a particular activity in a neighbouring market;
- potentially excluded effective competition in the neighbouring market; and
- prevented the appearance of a new product or limited technical development for which there was potential consumer demand.[1062]

380 Other than in cases of a plain refusal to license, secondary acquisitions directly influence the market structure as well as the position of the acquiring undertaking; in analysing the effects, the technology being held by a competitor is different from the situation where the technology is held by the dominant undertaking. In refusal to license cases, however, the dominant undertaking is already the holder of the technology. Furthermore, in these cases, the dominant undertaking itself has developed the technology and engaged in R&D activities, whereas the acquiring undertaking does not have the same expenses. It is therefore surprising that the precondition of limiting technical development for which there is potential consumer demand did not find its way into the evaluation of secondary acquisition as well.

381 Rather, the Commission relied on the effective removal of the technology from the market. In view of the above-mentioned change in the market structure and the characteristics of the undertaking itself as well as the missing patent law justifications for the legal monopoly in the hands of the dominant undertaking, this comes as a surprise. In cases where the acquired technology is a serious source of competition, which is the first precondition for the finding of an abuse, this removal should not be justifiable by proving that fair licences are granted. Both patent and competition law reasons are missing to justify such a verdict. It should rather be analysed whether the acquisition prevents the emergence of a new product or technical development for which actual or potential demand exists, as with refusals to license which at least prima facie have less immediate effect on market structure and thus residual competition.

382 This precondition would also fit with the third, as suggested by the Commission, which is the potential to render market entry more difficult, as both criteria allow evaluation of the technological market situation. The potential to invent around and thus the limiting of technological development should be an important criterion when assessing conduct including intellectual property laws. Whether inventing around constitutes real alternatives should therefore be considered during the evaluation of the conduct. To balance the proposed criteria, it must apply that successful inventing

1061. *See supra* fn. 920 and fn. 1014 as well as *infra* at para. 445.
1062. *See supra* at para. 329.

around cannot influence the judgment on the abusive character of conduct when inventing around was previously considered unlikely.

383 Unlike the second criterion, the first and third also seem to hold when compared with the criteria defined in refusal to license cases. Even if the right to acquire an exclusive licence or an intellectual property right is protected based on the undertaking's freedom to conduct business, it is not granted limitless, in that the dominant undertaking should not be allowed to remove serious sources of competition in the already imbalanced market, thereby weakening it even more. The holder of a patent in 'plain' refusal to license cases, in contrast, protects their own assets required through superior performance and should thus be forced to grant access only in limited cases, namely where the access to the technology is crucial for competition. A slight amendment of these requirements would be supported in order to meet the aim of patent law; the hindering of technical development should qualify as a factor for the finding of an abuse.[1063]

384 Interestingly, with respect to both the Azad technology acquisition and the patent maze, the Commission did not argue based on the clearly established anticompetitive intent. Intent, despite being admitted as a highly relevant factor in evaluating the character of conduct by the Court of Justice, was only considered in order to evaluate the circumstances in the market, not the conduct under scrutiny. In this respect, it is interesting to look at the balance between form-based and effect-based criteria in the assessment of the Commission.[1064] The three criteria applied by the Commission seem to pursue the target of balancing both approaches. It first evaluated the potential of the purchased technology to enhance competition, in other words, whether there was in fact something valuable at stake for the process of competition. It then asked for the removal of the technology from competition and thus for a proven effect on competition. At the same time, under the permission that actual foreclosure effects are not necessary to prove the abusive character of conduct, the third criterion, borrowed from the Court of Justice's judgment in *TeliaSonera Sverige*,[1065] moderates the influence of actual effects on competition. The character of the conduct is considered relevant in influencing competition, irrespective of the existence thereof.[1066] It seems that with this decision the Commission tried to satisfy the call for the higher influence of economic considerations without accepting decreases in the predictability. Despite including actual effects, the evaluation is based on objective considerations. Thus, though it may seem otherwise, the *Servier* decision did not allow for the conclusion that the Commission had distanced itself from the mainly form-based approach in *AstraZeneca*.

1063. Similarly: Heinemann, GRUR 2006, 712; EC, *Guidance Paper Enforcement Priorities*, para. 87.
1064. This focus of the Commission is expressed in: EC, *Servier*, AT.39612, para. 2812.
1065. 'capable of making it more difficult, or impossible, the entry of those competitors onto the market concerned'; ECJ, *TeliaSonera Sverige*, C-52/09, para. 63.
1066. On the three criteria: EC, *Servier*, AT.39612, para. 2800.

IX CONCLUSIONS DRAWN FROM CASE LAW

385 In cases where curtailing a competitor's range of action endangers their competitiveness, according to LAMPING, the mere application for a patent should be declared as an abuse of the dominant position.[1067] While the court rulings in the EU have long followed the ideology established in *CICRA v. Renault*, namely that the acquisition of intellectual property rights cannot be subject to competition law, recent inquiries by the Commission (*Boehringer Ingelheim*[1068] and *Servier*[1069]) as well as the Court of Justice's ruling in *AstraZeneca* seem to support LAMPING's conclusion. In these recent cases, however, the Commission identified additional tort to 'just patenting' and did not conduct an isolated analysis of the acquisition. Even in the case of *Servier*, where internal documents according to the Commission undoubtedly identified certain patents as blocking patents, only the combination of patenting and reverse payments was assessed under Article 102 TFEU.[1070] If no additional tort, such as the agreements in *Servier*, can be found, the Commission has so far closed proceedings, as in *Boehringer Ingelheim/Almirall*. The limited published information on the *Boehringer* case gives reason to conclude that Boehringer Ingelheim applied for patents and then denied the competitor Almirall access to the technology. After the patent holder agreed to grant licences to the competitor, the Commission closed the proceedings.[1071]

386 The primary acquisition (application) of a property right first came under the scrutiny of Article 102 TFEU in the *AstraZeneca* case. The reasoning in this case yet remains the only comprehensive analysis of a primary acquisition, as the case of *Boehringer Ingelheim* was closed with the commitment of Boehringer to remove blocking positions, and in the *Servier* decision where the application for blocking patents was documented, the Commission did not conduct an isolated analysis of the primary acquisition under Article 102 TFEU. Other than the *AstraZeneca* decision and the few details known about the *Boehringer* case, which allow the conclusion that the conduct raising concerns was in fact applications for patents and keeping them as blocking positions, we lack precedence. Following the *Servier* case, one could conclude that the primary acquisition of patents is not considered an abuse of a dominant position unless combined with other strategies such as tying or pay-for-delay agreements.[1072] This is even more so since the *AstraZeneca* case concerned the acquisition of an supplementary protection certificate and therewith supplementary protection based on a patent and not the application for a genuine patent.

387 In the *AstraZeneca* case, the primary acquisition of the supplementary protection certificate was considered abusive because AstraZeneca provided wrong information to the patent office in a setting where allegedly it must have been known that

1067. LAMPING, 229.
1068. EC, *Press Release, Boehringer Ingelheim v. Almirall*, IP/11/842.
1069. EC, *Press Release, Commission fines Servier*, IP/14/799.
1070. EC, *Servier*, AT.39612, para. 2764.
1071. EC, *Press Release, Boehringer Ingelheim v. Almirall*, IP/11/842.
1072. In this respect: BEJRANANDA, 122.

verification of the information was unlikely and therefore the applied for property right would be granted. AstraZeneca's conduct resulted in a distortion of the decision-making process of the authority and ultimately the granting of an unjustified property right. This provided a barrier to competition owing to its missing justification through law and its effect on the market in the creation or protection of the dominant position. In the case of supplementary protection certificates, this effect is shown in the delay of generic entry.

388 The acquisition of an supplementary protection certificate, however, is fundamentally different from the application of a patent in that the patent must reveal a novel technical teaching, whereas the supplementary protection certificate is based on a patent and does not add to the technical knowledge. Furthermore, applying for an supplementary protection certificate does not require R&D investment. In this respect, the application for an supplementary protection certificate is comparable to the secondary acquisition of a patent (licence or transfer). Compared to the primary acquisition of a patent, with a secondary acquisition, the undertaking does not bear the risk of failed R&D programmes. Based on these considerations, arguments supporting the abusive nature of a secondary or supplementary protection certificate acquisition can only cautiously be applied to the evaluation of the patent application without considering the differences of the two forms of acquisition in the light of the aim of the patent system and its intended effects on competition in both the technology and product markets.[1073]

389 Differences ensue concerning the legitimate interests of the acquirer. A patent applicant submitting a patentable innovation to the patent office is entitled to be granted a patent. A licensee, however, neither has the right to receive the privileges immanent in the licence nor those of an exclusive licence. This must, of course, not distract us from realising that licensing is of high significance within the patent system. It is a mechanism which allows returns on investments to be secured while at the same time enhancing competition. Through licensing, the licensee becomes entitled to use the technology and commercialise products based therein. Consumers can then profit from the technology and even from competition in the product market if more than one licensee enters the market.

390 From the perspective of competition as well as the aim of patent law, exclusive licences result in less favourable outcomes, however. That only one player is allowed to use the technology in commerce prevents competition with the product. To fulfil their needs, consumers in these cases might only have the chance to switch to products using alternative technologies, if available. However, since a licensee does not contribute to technology, any blocking effect resulting from the acquisition of a licence is not immanent in the system and thus prima facie more difficult to justify. In applying the perspective taken in recent literature, namely that propertisation of technology is favourable if overall the benefits outweigh the costs, when applying competition law to

1073. In this respect also: AG Kirschner, *in: Tetra Pak I*, T-51/89, para. 74.

the acquisition of exclusive rights, one should therefore distinguish between the primary and the secondary acquisition of patents.

391 Another reason for this argument is the fact that the possible behaviours are limited by the scope of the legal privileges obtained. In a licence contract, the contractual parties stipulate the possible scope of action. While the patent holder is more powerful, the impact of a patent on competition is less predictable compared with that of an exclusive licence. The holder of an exclusive licence is left with only two possible options. One of these is the sole use of the licensed technology. The other, as in the case of *Tetra Pak I*, would be to license the technology exclusively but eschew using it for business. The patent holder has several options though. As well as sole use of the technology and keeping the patent as a blocking position, the patent holder is also able to spread the technology through licensing. The holder of the patent is not limited in their competences by a contract and they hold much more power compared with the licensee. Yet, the above example also shows that the purchase of an exclusive licence has a higher likelihood of being a threat to the competition compared with the acquisition of a patent. However, this statement may not be true when an additional element accompanies the acquisition of the patent, for example, when the patentability requirements are not met, as in the case of *AstraZeneca*.

392 The most important reason for a differentiated approach is thus the aim of the patent law itself. Society, as has previously been noted, provides a patent right without in turn being rewarded through the disclosure of new technology. Patent applicants in these situations exploit inefficiencies of the patent system in the application process, namely the small chance of a detailed examination by the patent office. Blocking patents covering technologies meeting the patentability requirements fulfil the functions of the patent system. They disclose innovation and reward the patent holder for their R&D efforts. Even if in certain industries or situations only limited R&D is required to provide a patentable innovation, at least in theory rewardable R&D investments accrue to yield a patentable invention. This is also true for blocking patents. Patent law does not guarantee a fixed reward, but rather one dependent on the economic situation in the market and the efforts of the patent holder with respect to licensing or marketing products. Therefore, it is part of the functioning of the patent system itself that the patent holder is to a certain degree responsible for seeking monetary reward and also for the method of doing so. The question, therefore, is whether the patent system implies an unspoken expectation that the patent holder will make their invention available to society, not only through disclosure but also de facto through products or licences, at least in those cases where there is an actual or potential demand for the product or technology.

393 Summing up, as in the *Boehringer* case especially, the blocking intentions of the patent applicant were clearly established apparently without further consequences, one could reach the conclusion that the primary acquisition of a patent does not qualify as an abuse of a dominant position, unless the applicant is not entitled to the patent, as in the *AstraZeneca* case. There is, however, no rationale for such a position. When acquiring a blocking patent, the dominant undertaking, in concrete terms, seeks to either prevent consumers from being able to select between different products or prevent competitors from entering into the market. The intentions pursued by a dominant undertaking when applying for a blocking patent therefore are aimed at achieving effects which have been identified as a violation of competition law in other case groups.[1074]

1074. 'It is apparent from the case-law of the Court that, in order to determine whether the undertaking in a dominant position has abused such a position by its pricing practices, it is necessary to consider all the circumstances and to investigate whether the practice tends to remove or restrict the buyer's freedom to choose his sources of supply, to bar competitors from access to the market, to apply dissimilar conditions to equivalent transactions with other trading parties, thereby placing them at a competitive disadvantage, or to strengthen the dominant position by distorting competition.' ECJ, *Deutsche Telekom v. Commission*, C-280/08 P, para. 175 with further references.

CHAPTER 13
Implications of the Patent Misuse Doctrine

I LIMITATIONS OF THE CONCLUSIONS DRAWN FROM CASE LAW

394 As the mere application for a patent has not been subject to independent analysis by the courts or the Commission, the analysis of case law on the abuse of a dominant position and intellectual property rights only provides limited guidance on how the application for a patent could be analysed under Article 102 TFEU. Besides the conclusion drawn above that the primary and secondary acquisitions have to be evaluated differently owing to the deviating interests involved,[1075] case law leaves it difficult to identify characteristics to differentiate between abusive and non-abusive applications for patents.

395 In order to work out the lines between abuse and rightful use of patents in EU law, authors have proposed using the US patent misuse doctrine as a guideline, which has previously been used in antitrust cases.[1076] This chapter will also follow that direction to find out whether the patent misuse doctrine provides implications for how cases involving the application of patents could be analysed under EU competition law.

396 Owing to the limitations of the patent misuse doctrine as a principle, let alone interpretative guidance for EU competition law, the chapter will remain largely introductory. However, the patent misuse doctrine is an important legal concept and has been used to analyse the legitimacy of conduct involving patents for quite a while in the USA. Thus, an analysis of Article 102 TFEU cases involving patents would not be complete without a look at its characteristics.

1075. *See supra* at paras 385 ff.
1076. Critically: HEINEMANN, Immaterialgüterschutz in der Wettbewerbsordnung, 586 f.

II PATENT MISUSE DOCTRINE

1 Definition and Scope of the Patent Misuse

397 A misuse, following the understanding of the patent misuse doctrine, consists of any conduct improperly expanding the scope of the intellectual property right.[1077] Still today, however, the courts in the USA do not agree whether the patent misuse doctrine has developed to be raised as a claim itself.[1078] The legal nature of patent misuse as an independent claim is unclear.

398 With the patent misuse doctrine, a method to limit the abuse of patents outside the scope of antitrust laws exists.[1079] The doctrine is an objection that can be raised against a patent holder claiming rights. According to the doctrine, claims of the patent holder can be dismissed if the patent has been misused, irrespective of whether the alleged infringer of the patent was affected by the misuse. A misuse of the patent therefore factually results in the loss of enforceability for the patent holder as long as the conduct continues and its effects have not been eliminated.[1080]

399 In principle, the doctrine is thus independent of antitrust law. A patent misuse does not automatically amount to a violation of section 2 Sherman Act.[1081] However, a violation of the patent misuse doctrine, that is, if the conduct exceeds the scope of the patent law, is subject to analysis under the Rule of Reason, 'where the reasonableness of the restraint on competition is determined'.[1082] Conduct not protected by the scope of patent law thus opens an investigation under antitrust law.[1083] Where it results in unreasonable restraints, the conduct is considered a violation of antitrust law.

2 Limitations of the Patent Misuse Doctrine in Identifying Abusive Behaviour

400 It has, however, been doubted whether insights defining the scope of 'abuse' in Article 102 TFEU can be gained from the doctrine.[1084] One reason is the conceptual basis of the patent misuse doctrine which was developed as a defence for potential

1077. Though the patent misuse is the most famous doctrine, the application of the principle to copyright and trademark law has been confirmed as well. For copyright law in: 4TH CIR., *Lasercomb America v. Reynolds*, 911 F.2d 970; *see also*: BAKER MCCLANAHAN, Washington and Lee Law Review 1992, 213; for trademark law in: 7TH CIR., *Helene Curtis Industries Inc. v. Church and Dwight Co. Inc.*, 560 F.2d 1325.
1078. *See* the memorandum, opinion and order by Judge Lee in the case of *Continental v. iBiquity*: N.D. ILL., *Continental Automotive GmbH et al. v. iBiquity Digital Corporation*, 14 C 1977, 13.
1079. *See i.a.*: FED. CIR., *B. Braun Med. Inc. v. Abbott Labs*, 124 F.3d 1419, 1426; FED. CIR., *Mallinckrodt Inc v. Medipart Inc*, 976 F.2d 700, 708.
1080. KOBAK, Antitrust Law Journal 1996, 355 f.
1081. KOBAK, Antitrust Law Journal 1996, 356.
1082. LIM, Michigan Telecommunications and Technology Law Review 2014, 324.
1083. *See the analysis in*: RIZIOTIS, GRUR Int 2004, 368.
1084. HEINEMANN, Immaterialgüterschutz in der Wettbewerbsordnung, 586 f.

patent infringers to oppose an infringement claim. This was because injunctions in common law were only possible within the framework of equity[1085].[1086] Since raising equity claims requires the claimant to come with 'clean hands', the objection that any misuse occurred with the property law was a possible defence against infringement claims.[1087]

401 Another reason is the fact that the patent misuse doctrine does not stand on solid principles to identify misuse conduct, either independently of antitrust law concerns or with respect to antitrust law.[1088] The application of the patent misuse doctrine led to the building of case groups[1089] as had the practice on the abuse of a dominant position in EU case law. The patent misuse doctrine therefore presents itself as conceptually independent of antitrust law and without clear understanding of misusing behaviour. This having been said, the patent misuse doctrine and antitrust law do overlap in large parts, as case law shows.

3 Implications for Further Analysis

402 The patent misuse doctrine, despite the said difficulties, allows for the assumption that, when used in antitrust law, it targets cases where competition has been affected by the property right beyond a tolerable degree normally resulting in property protection. The misuse conduct is seen in the 'impermissibl[e] broaden[ing] of the "physical or temporal scope" of the patent grant with anti-competitive effect'.[1090] This indicates that the legitimacy of the conduct might consist in factors relevant to distinguishing abusive from non-abusive behaviour. The notion that conduct which broadens the scope granted by law raises competition law concerns will remain central to this analysis.

403 Following insights from case law as well as the implications of the patent misuse doctrine, the analysis will now centre on Article 102 TFEU. In order to penetrate the concept of abuse and provide comprehensive analysis on the research question, Part V investigates Article 102 TFEU with respect to the abuse concept in EU competition law following the traditional interpretative topoi.[1091]

1085. On equity, *see infra* at para. 553.
1086. Nowadays, injunctions are part of patent law (35 USCA 283), but preliminary injunctions are still not. *See*: Riziotis, GRUR Int 2004, 368.
1087. For US case law *see i.a.*: United States Supreme Court, *Morton Salt Co. v. G.S. Suppiger Co.*, 314 US 488, 492 ff.; also, with further references: Heinemann, Immaterialgüterschutz in der Wettbewerbsordnung, fn. 59.
1088. Feldman, Hastings Law Journal 2003, 399 ff.
1089. *See* the examples given in: Riziotis, GRUR Int 2004, 368 ff.
1090. Fed. Cir., *Windsurfing Int'l Inc. v. AMF Inc.*, 782 F.2d 995, para. 39; confirmed in: Fed. Cir., *B. Braun Med. Inc. v. Abbott Labs*, 124 F.3d 1419, 1426.
1091. On this method, *see supra* at para. 16.

PART V The Concept of Abuse in EU Competition Law

CHAPTER 14

Analysis of Article 102 TFEU

I DRAFTING HISTORY OF ARTICLE 102 TFEU

404 It has already been pointed out that little is known about the drafting procedures of EU primary law and that a historical perspective does not apply when interpreting EU law.[1092] Yet, what is known of the drafting process with regard to Article 102 TFEU, in respect of Article 86 of the TEEC, provides a partial explanation for the difficulties with the interpretation of the article.

405 Before the enactment of the TEEC, the idea of preventing certain conduct of dominant undertakings was already present at a multinational level in Europe. The law of the ECSC contained a provision aimed at preventing dominant undertakings from implementing excessive prices or unreasonable terms and conditions. According to Article 66 § 7 of the Treaty establishing the European Coal and Steel Community (Treaty of Paris), a dominant undertaking is abusing its position when it uses its power contrary to the purpose of the contract.[1093] The adoption of the said competition rules was the result of a US intervention.[1094] It is said that the US government otherwise would have denied financial support to the Community.[1095] The awareness of the importance of restricting the use of private economic power lasted until the drafting of the TEEC, which built the EEC.[1096] The drafters shared a mutual understanding of the

1092. *See supra* at para. 17.
1093. The Treaty of Paris can be seen as the first supranational competition law code. At this time, all European countries, except for Italy, had enacted laws against cartels. The concept of the abuse of dominance was not that widespread, however. Many Member States included this principle in their national law in the course of European integration. *See*: GERBER, Tulane Law Review 1987, 64 f.
1094. VON DER GROEBEN, 259.
1095. PACE/SEIDEL, in: PATEL/SCHWEITZER, The historical foundations of EU competition law, 58.
1096. Under the European Economic Community, the European Atomic Energy Community was also founded in Rome in 1957.

need to establish competition law rules to prevent private parties from building barriers to trade between Member States. Competition law would therefore support the building of the common market, raise wealth and guarantee stability.[1097] The design of the law as well as the future economic order of the Union was controversial, however.

406 The final Article 86 of the TEEC did not sanction monopolisation but addressed the abuse of a dominant position,[1098] even though the drafters seemed to have had doubts regarding the practicability of the term 'abuse'[1099] and its contradiction with the US model. One might therefore ask why the drafters chose to rely on the term 'abuse' to circumscribe the sanctioned range of behaviour nonetheless. The answer seems to lie in the intended nature of the competition law provisions in the TEEC. As the documentation shows, it was not intended by the drafters to apply and enforce the competition law provisions directly. The provisions were rather categorised as general principles or guidelines,[1100] and all questions on procedural aspects were left open.[1101]

407 Against this background, it is surprising that Article 102 TFEU in its contemporary form is equivalent to Article 86 of the TEEC. Not only was the Treaty amended several times without changing the article on the abuse of a dominant position but also the provision became a directly applicable norm.[1102] The transformation from a general principle to a directly applicable norm did not show in statutory law. Conceptually Article 102 TFEU is therefore still a general principle and its regulatory content ambiguous.

408 The following sections will aim to shed light on the substance of the term 'abuse' in Article 102 TFEU to provide guidance on the fine line between abusive and non-abusive behaviour. With the insights gained from the textual (section II) and systematic (section III) environments the evaluation will embark on analysing the meaning of abuse with reference to previous court practice (Chapter 14, section IV, 2), established measurements to distinguish abusive from non-abusive behaviour (Chapter 14, section IV, 3) and the importance of showing anticompetitive effects and intent (Chapter 14, section IV, 4).

1097. Comité International créé par la Conférence de Messina, *Spaak Report*, 3.
1098. To distinguish the newly established European model, authors used to call it the 'abuse principle'. *See*: Gerber, 174. The terminology 'abuse principle' should not be confused with the term 'abuse principle' as it is understood in EU law today. *See infra* at paras 590 f.; Heinemann, ZSR 2016, 443 f.; Pace/Seidel, in: Patel/Schweitzer, The historical foundations of EU competition law, 60.
1099. Akman, Oxford Journal of Legal Studies 2009, 288.
1100. This was proposed by the German delegation, *see*: Schulze/Hoeren, 167. The German notion seems to have survived, since the Articles 85 and 86 were drafted broadly. Gerber, for example, talks of a 'constitutional' function of the articles and the Member States understood the provisions as 'programmatic statements'. Gerber, 345 f.
1101. Schweitzer, in: Ehlermann/Marquis, European competition law annual 2007, 137.
1102. 'The direct applicability of the competition rules was not foreseen [...].' Schweitzer, in: Ehlermann/Marquis, European competition law annual 2007, 137.

II TEXT-BASED APPROXIMATION

1 The Search for an EU-Autonomous Characterisation of the Term 'Abuse'

409 Text-based analysis of EU law leaves scholars with the problem that legal texts exist in twenty-four official languages which are all equally binding. To avoid confusion with the definition of judicial terms among the jurisdictions of the Member States, legal interpretation of EU law first tries to interpret vague terms autonomously.[1103] This method seeks to find an already established understanding at a Union level. In most cases, however, unless there is a consolidated usage of the term, the analysis will be limited to finding the relevant term in other treaties, directives or guidelines and identifying a common thread.

410 As in other jurisdictions, in the EU, the term 'abuse' is not only widely used but also used in different contexts. Beyond Article 102 TFEU, *abuse* does not appear as specific sanctioned conduct and thus as the core of a prohibition norm within EU law. The exception to this finding is the general prohibition of the abuse of rights. The abuse of rights and the abuse of a dominant position are conceptually different, however. Owing to the complexity of the relation between the general prohibition of the abuse of rights and the abuse of a dominant position, a detailed discussion is conducted in Chapter 15 below to closely work out the relationship.[1104]

411 Generally, the term 'abuse' is found in the context of health issues within EU law, as, for example, in substance abuse, where abuse is a synonym for harmful excessive use. *Abuse* also appears to describe (continuing) violations of physical, psychical and sexual integrity, for example, in provisions protecting children or women. *Abuse* in these contexts consists of an action intentionally hurting the other person's integrity.

412 All these forms of abuse seem to have in common that they comprise a more or less conscious use of one's own power for the disadvantage of oneself or someone else. In the case of substance abuse, the relevant power lies in the access to substances which are used for one's own consumption to a hazardous extent and thereby to the disadvantage of oneself. Physical, psychical and sexual abuses consist of the use of a powerful position to violate someone's integrity.

413 In economic law, the term 'abuse' is part of market abuse regulation. Market abuse is a general concept encompassing 'unlawful behaviour in the financial market'. In the context of market abuse regulation, it includes 'insider dealing, unlawful disclosure of inside information and market manipulation'.[1105] The relevant conduct is therefore harmful to market integrity, the safeguarding of which is the object of the

1103. *See supra* at para. 19.
1104. *See infra* at paras 528 ff.
1105. Regulation No 17/62/EEC, para. 7.

market abuse regulation.[1106] Rather than naming specific misconduct, *abuse* is used as a general term and includes all conduct prohibited by the regulation.[1107] The same is true for the use of the term in tax law. Tax abuse, which unlike market abuse has not yet been used as an 'official term' in directives and regulations, encompasses tax evasion and other illicit behaviour.[1108]

414 These findings suggest that the term 'abuse' within EU economic law constitutes a collective term for illicit behaviour. There is, however, no other provision where the term takes the form of a specific violation as in Article 102 TFEU. Judging from the above, it therefore seems fair to conclude that an isolated EU-autonomous interpretation of *abuse* as it is used in the context of Article 102 TFEU has not (yet) crystallised and therefore cannot provide a well-founded basis for interpretation. Yet, as will be seen below,[1109] the use of the term 'abuse' within EU law to describe illicit behaviour does not differ widely from the general understanding of the term in Article 102 TFEU within the German, English and French legal texts as well as in the general understanding of the term in everyday language.

2 Etymology and Linguistic Usage

415 In English dictionaries, the term 'abuse' – in line with its etymologic use since the fifteenth century[1110] – is translated as 'wrong or improper use' as well as 'bad or improper treatment'[1111] and circumscribed with 'to use wrongly, usually with harmful results'.[1112] This leaves *abuse* being 'the use of something in a way that is harmful or morally wrong'.[1113] In addition to this definition, the *Oxford Dictionary* further gives the motivation underlying abuse, stating that it can be the use of something either 'to bad effect or with a bad purpose'.[1114]

416 In legal language, *abuse* is specified as 'everything that is contrary to good order established by usage'.[1115] At least prima facie, the legal usage of the word 'abuse' in English seems to be in line with the general usage. Bringing the two together, the sanctioned behaviour in Article 102 TFEU would be understood as a use of the dominant position deviating from established standards of conduct to a bad effect or with a bad purpose.

1106. Regulation No 17/62/EEC, para. 2.
1107. Regulation No 17/62/EEC, para. 29.
1108. EC, *Press Release, Fair Taxation.*
1109. *See infra* at paras 415 ff.
1110. https://www.etymonline.com/word/abuse, accessed on 24 February 2020.
1111. http://www.dictionary.com/browse/abuse?s=t, accessed on 24 February 2020.
1112. http://dictionary.cambridge.org/dictionary/english-german/abuse_1, accessed on 24 February 2020.
1113. http://dictionary.cambridge.org/dictionary/english/abuse, accessed on 24 February 2020.
1114. https://www.lexico.com/definition/abuse, accessed on 24 February 2020.
1115. http://legal-dictionary.thefreedictionary.com/abuse, accessed on 24 February 2020.

417 The German translation of abuse in Article 102 TFEU, *missbräuchliche Ausnutzung*, consists of two separate words. *Miss-*, the prefix in the adjective *missbräuchlich*, indicates a defect or error, while the verb *brauchen* is translated as *to use*. In the current German language, *missbräuchlich* is thus the adjective used to indicate misuse. In legal language, where the noun *Missbrauch* has been used since the sixteenth century, the understanding is derived from the word root *Brauch*, which refers to a tradition. A tradition is a behaviour conducted by or within a plurality of people. *Missbrauch* was therefore understood as action against good tradition. In today's legal language *Missbrauch* is the use of an object contradicting reasonable, mutually accepted rules.[1116] Besides actual misuse, *missbräuchlich* also more generally indicates misconduct.

418 *Ausnutzung* stands for the full use of a possibility but can also mean the reckless, egoistic use of something for one's own purpose. Based on these results, Article 102 TFEU with its term *missbräuchliche Ausnutzung* penalises the reckless use of a 'potential', contrary to reasonable, mutually accepted rules. In cases of abuse of a dominant position, the 'potential' is given by the advantageous position in the market. With the plain linguistic understanding in Germany, dominant undertakings should thus be sanctioned for the breach of a behavioural norm for their own benefit.

419 In the French version of Article 102 TFEU, the sanctioned behaviour is translated as *d'exploiter de façon abusive*. The adjective *abusive* is mostly used to indicate insults or violent behaviour as in German and English. The noun *abus*, which can be translated as abuse, is also used to describe bad usage, again described as overly extensive or wrong usage. In the legal context, *l'abus* describes the breach of a rule or a reprehensible act against common practice.[1117] *Exploiter*, the French translation of exploiting, describes the conduct of someone using a situation to his or her advantage. Besides profiting, the meaning of *exploiter* also includes the usage of someone or something in an abusive manner.[1118]

420 The comparison reveals that the wording of Article 102 TFEU assumes a common starting point for the interpretation in all three languages. The passages describing the sanctioned behaviour in all three versions can be interpreted as 'using the dominant position beneficially while deviating from standard behavioural norms with a bad purpose or to a bad effect'. Even though 'bad effects' as a result of the conduct only explicitly appear in English dictionaries, they are also immanent in the German expression *missbräuchliche Ausnutzung* and the French *d'exploiter de façon abusive* at least in the sense of striving to gain an unjustified advantage. The same is true for the requirement of 'bad purpose' which in the English language appears as an alternative to showing 'bad effects'. The German word *Ausnutzung* which contains a component

1116. Köbler.
1117. http://www.larousse.fr/dictionnaires/francais/abus/314?q=abus#304, accessed on 24 February 2020.
1118. http://www.larousse.fr/dictionnaires/francais/exploiter/32282, accessed on 24 February 2020.

of recklessness and the French *exploiter* which implies intention do not contradict this finding.

421 The comparison of the texts provides guidance insofar as it implies that Article 102 TFEU requires behaviour to originate from an autonomous initiative by the undertaking to make the article applicable. If the national law imposes rules which mandate a specific behaviour, such conduct and the connected anticompetitive effects cannot – following the wording – be subject to competition law scrutiny. Limitation of competition in these cases is tolerated by competition law, which must recede. Indeed, as has been confirmed by the court practice, the application of Article 102 TFEU is not possible where the conduct by the undertaking is dictated by law or customs, or where alternative actions are not available to the undertaking.[1119]

422 Apart from these findings, the wording does not offer much guidance for the interpretation. The results do not contribute to resolving the fine line between holding a dominant position, which is not sanctioned, and the abuse of such a position. Transitions between 'using' the privileges resulting from a strong position in competition and 'abusing' the position so that an intervention becomes necessary can be smooth[1120] and cannot be defined with an analysis of the wording only.[1121] As the results of the analysis of the term 'abuse' have to be compliant with the systematics of EU law, the next chapter will evaluate the structure of Article 102 TFEU within competition law as well as its systematics.

III THE ROLE AND STRUCTURE OF ARTICLE 102 TFEU

1 The Role of Article 102 TFEU Within EU (Competition) Law

423 The goal of creating an undistorted internal market ranks high in the political aims of the Union and has been a core concern since the foundation of the European Community. The TFEU as a decree of constitutional rank within the EU is dedicated to ensuring this aim.[1122] Before the enactment of the TFEU, the principle was listed as a goal of the EU in Article 3(1)(g) of the TEEC. When amending the treaty, it was forced back into Protocol No 27 of the Treaty on the European Union. Owing to this systematic reconstruction, it was unclear whether the amendment meant a shift in the goals of the Union. In the literature, this question was answered in the negative. Even as part of the protocols, the goal of creating an internal market subject to free and undistorted competition is still an integral part of the treaties and therefore EU constitutional

1119. Implied in: ECJ, *Suiker Unie v. Commission*, C-40/73, para. 71; confirmed in: GC, *Irish Sugar*, T-228/97, para. 130.
1120. On the threshold for intervention, *see*: Jung, in: Grabitz et al., EUV/AEUV, Article 102, para. 131.
1121. For an approach that evaluates the term 'abuse' in everyday German language and contrasts it with use, *see*: Mestmäcker/Schweitzer, § 16, para. 1.
1122. ECJ, *Continental Can v. Commission*, C-6/72, paras 23 ff.

law.[1123] Following settled case law, the interpretation of EU competition law must progress within the limits of the goals expressed in the treaties.[1124] Article 3 of the TEU as well as the annexed Protocol No 27 therefore at the same time provide the aims of the provision and the boundaries for its interpretation.[1125]

424 Undistorted competition has many functions among which rank the fostering of innovation and technical progress as well as granting freedom and distributive justice.[1126] Freedom in this context is understood as absence of constraints by third parties and justice in choice and activity. Freedom is both the result and a fundamental prerequisite for competition. The problem with freedom in competition, however, is that it needs to be secured through law; otherwise, parties invoking their freedom extensively would impose constraints.[1127] In cartels, for example, the contracting parties use freedom of contract and business to fix prices or isolate sales regions with the result of excluding competition between the parties with respect to the specific parameter. It therefore comes as no surprise that the conduct or actions identified as abuse of a dominant position by the EU courts all concern restrictions to elements of the freedom to compete in the broader sense.[1128]

425 Competition law contributes to achieving the goals of an internal market and undistorted competition insofar as it is targeted towards reducing hurdles implemented by private parties. No participant on the market should be able to implement distortions that had been reduced by the legislature.[1129] Article 102 TFEU is the second pillar of EU competition law besides the prohibition of cartels (Article 101 TFEU) and merger control (Council Regulation (EC) No 139/2004). In this setting, it is the purpose of abuse control to identify particular conduct of dominant undertakings which affects the process of competition. It particularly targets conduct which results in hindering the maintenance of the current degree of competition (exit of competitors, a stagnation or decline in their market shares) or negatively influencing growth (as barriers to entry and exit[1130] or including the potential of current competitors to expand product range or geographical market).[1131]

426 Article 102 TFEU sets behavioural standards for undertakings holding a dominant position which therefore 'have a degree of immunity from the normal disciplining effects on the market' to 'bring about some of the results that would occur if

1123. *See also the jurisprudence referenced in* fn. 1125; some authors, however, saw a critical degrading of competition in this act. *See*: BEHRENS, EuZW 2008, 193; BRINKER, in: SCHWARZE ET AL., EU-Kommentar, Article 102, para. 16.
1124. ECJ, *Gaston Schul v. Inspecteur der Invoerrechten*, C-15/81, para. 33.
1125. *See*: ECJ, *Commercial Solvents*, Joined Cases C-6/73 and 7/73, para. 32; ECJ, *France Télécom*, C-202/07 P, para. 103.
1126. *See supra* at para. 44.
1127. *See supra* at paras 70 f.
1128. *See infra* at Part V, Chapter 15, section IV.
1129. *See supra* at para. 71.
1130. SCHMIDT/ENGELKE, WiSt 1989.
1131. BLUME HUTTENLAUCH/LÜBBIG, in: LOEWENHEIM ET AL., Kommentar Kartellrecht, Article 102, para. 218.

competition did exist'.[1132] Consequently, abuse control should prevent further weakening or vanishing of disciplinary effects.[1133]

427 Competition law in each case has to find the right balance between intervention and non-intervention, as both too much and too little interference in competition can have a negative effect and jeopardise the achievement of its goals.[1134] Conduct generally leaves pro-competitive as well as anticompetitive marks and identifying abusive behaviour in most cases requires an overall analysis. The general systematic of Article 102 TFEU as a provision of constitutional rank, however, provides no insights to answer this delicate point. Neither does the aim of the abuse control which is to ensure equal opportunities in the sense that the methods of all rivals, including those operating independently on the market, should be limited to competition on the merits.[1135,1136]

2 Systematics of Article 102 TFEU

428 Article 102 TFEU is divided into a general clause in section 1 and special clauses in section 2(a)-(d). As indicated by the wording, the catalogue of special clauses is only exemplary.[1137] It first and foremost displays a sample of the most immediate challenges competition law faces at the early stages of market integration.[1138] Therefore, despite their important contribution in the substantiation of the concept of abuse in EU competition law,[1139] the exemplary provisions are not of any definite significance. Scholars have nevertheless tried to approximate the term 'abuse' through identifying different common and distinguishing features in behaviours which were declared abusive by the courts. While elaborating a framework for the fine distinctions between abusive and non-abusive behaviour, scholars in EU law also borrowed the distinction between exclusionary and exploitative abuses from German law.[1140] Both categories have their legal basis in section 2(a)-(d) and were first mentioned by the Court of Justice in the case of *Continental Can*.[1141] Despite a lack of consensus in categorising

1132. O'Donoghue/Padilla, 3.
1133. *See* the definition of 'abuse' delivered by the ECJ, *infra* at para. 453 as well as: EC, *Guidance Paper*, para. 19; Blume Huttenlauch/Lübbig, in: Loewenheim et al., Kommentar Kartellrecht, Article 102, para. 218.
1134. Østerud, 2 and 14; on type 1 and type 2 errors with respect to the definition of relevant markets, *see:* Früh, 242.
1135. This term will be the focus of the analysis *infra* at Part V, Chapter 14, section IV, 3. For now, it is sufficient to understand competition on the merits as including achievements based on quality, service, etc.
1136. *See i.a.*: ECJ, *Hoffmann-La Roche v. Commission*, C-85/76, para. 91; ECJ, *AKZO*, C-62/86, para. 69; EC, *Report on Competition Policy 1997*, para. 62.
1137. ECJ, *Continental Can v. Commission*, C-6/72, para. 26.
1138. Schweitzer, in: Ehlermann/Marquis, European competition law annual 2007, 128 ff.
1139. Heinemann, Immaterialgüterschutz in der Wettbewerbsordnung, 446 f.
1140. Bellamy/Child, para. 10.072.
1141. ECJ, *Continental Can v. Commission*, C-6/72, para. 26.

abuses in the literature,[1142] the duo of exploitative and exclusionary abuses has commonly been mentioned in EU competition law by scholars and the courts.[1143]

3 Exclusionary and Exploitative Abuses

429 Exclusionary abuses consist of conduct targeted at reducing the opportunities for actual or potential competitors in the relevant market.[1144] Through limiting possibilities for competitors or contractors, exclusionary abuses impose indirect welfare losses on consumers.[1145] The object of protection is thus residual competition.[1146] The category of exclusionary abuses was first deduced from section 2(b) of Article 102 TFEU.[1147] After having pursued a successful exclusionary strategy, the dominant undertaking will most likely be in a position to impose exploitative conditions on contractors.[1148] This led AKMAN to conclude that abusive behaviour always includes exploitation.[1149]

430 The category of exploitative abuses aggregates all practices that include the imposing of unfair conditions in the competitive process.[1150] Exploitative abuses consist of behaviour which is targeted at forcing contracting parties to accept trading conditions that they would not accept in competition. The most common examples are high prices (section 2(a) of Article 102). The acceptance of these conditions by the weaker competitor then results in unjustifiably high profits for the dominant undertaking at the other party's expense. The relevant benchmark for the analysis is thus the condition (price) that would apply in the imaginary situation of undistorted competition.[1151]

431 By prohibiting exploitative abuses, the law seeks to protect competition in putting the trading conditions under scrutiny. The conditions addressed are those imposed by the dominant undertaking on direct contracting parties. It therefore addresses the opposite market side (players in upstream and downstream markets).[1152] Exploitative abuses also contribute to the protection of residual competition. This is by protecting actual and potential competitors from market-power-based distortions which occur as a side effect of the enforced unfair conditions.

1142. For further references on reprisal abuses where an undertaking retaliates against another for unappreciated behaviour in their own category *see*: O'DONOGHUE/PADILLA, 214 ff.
1143. *See i.a.*: ECJ, *Post Danmark*, C-209/10, para. 20; O'DONOGHUE/PADILLA, 237 ff.; WHISH/BAILEY, 207 ff.
1144. Similarly: BELLAMY/CHILD, para. 10.072; similarly: BLUME HUTTENLAUCH/LÜBBIG, in: LOEWENHEIM ET AL., Kommentar Kartellrecht, Article 102, para. 218; *see also the example in*: EC, *Guidance Paper*, para. 19.
1145. *See i.a.*: O'DONOGHUE/PADILLA, 215; SCHMIDT/HAUCAP, 161.
1146. FUCHS/MÖSCHEL, in: IMMENGA/MESTMÄCKER 2018, Article 102, para. 5.
1147. *See*: O'DONOGHUE/PADILLA, 239 ff.
1148. EC, *Guidance Paper*, para. 19.
1149. AKMAN, 301 ff.
1150. BELLAMY/CHILD, paras 10.064 and 10.072; FUCHS/MÖSCHEL, in: IMMENGA/MESTMÄCKER 2018, Article 102, para. 168.
1151. JUNG, in: GRABITZ ET AL., EUV/AEUV, Article 102.
1152. FUCHS/MÖSCHEL, in: IMMENGA/MESTMÄCKER 2018, Article 102, para. 4.

432 To sum up, a dominant undertaking when conducting an exploitative abuse exploits or instrumentalises an economic dependency in an abusive manner. When engaging in exclusionary abuse, it is motivated by the prospect of limiting a competitor's room to compete.[1153] The distinctive feature of the two types of abuse is the competitive relation affected by the abusive conduct. Exclusionary abuses[1154] contain practices that hamper actual or potential competitors (horizontal relation). Exploitative abuses have an adverse effect on buyers, consumers or suppliers (vertical relation).

433 The theory demands that the two categories should be separated accordingly. However, the systematics of Article 102 TFEU do not support such a separation, and neither does the corresponding classification provide the benefit of interpretation for the terminological vagueness in Article 102 TFEU.[1155] This is shown with respect to exclusionary abuses, where an intervention would need to be based on case-specific trading conditions.

434 Market intervention on such grounds leads to a result-oriented single case justice based on the principle of proportionality, but disregards the greater picture of competition as a dynamic process. Also, such interventions lead to the protection of competitors, rather than competition itself.[1156] As a result, interventions are motivated by the prospect of achieving a seemingly just market result, whereas the impact of the intervention on the market result is not predictable. The identification of sanction-worthy conduct is based on an underlying external fairness standard.[1157] Owing to the delicate balance of factors, attempts to reinstal undistorted competition with interventions entail a high risk of jeopardising it.[1158] The sanctioning of exploitative conditions can degenerate to merely combating symptoms. With this realisation comes the understanding that the boundaries between exploitation and exclusionary abuses are blurred. Symptomatically, the Commission has stressed that it does not examine the conditions of business transactions, but rather the attempts of a dominant undertaking to maintain its position in the market.[1159]

1153. *See i.a.*: BELLAMY/CHILD, para. 10.072; LAMPING, 163.
1154. The Commission emphasises their importance in the publication of their enforcement guidelines. EC, *Guidance Paper.*
1155. Similarly also: SCHRÖTER/BARTL, in: VON DER GROEBEN ET AL., Kommentar EU-Recht, Article 102, para. 173.
1156. It is therefore no surprise that the importance of exploitative abuses has remained miniscule. *See* references in: FUCHS/MÖSCHEL, in: IMMENGA/MESTMÄCKER 2018, Article 102, para. 172 The complexities of the challenges that occur with directly controlling trading conditions have resulted in a shift in the focus of competition law policy back to analysing the broader picture.
1157. In practice, it is common to determine a missing 'reasonable relation to the economic value of the product supplied'. *See among others*: ECJ, *United Brands*, C-27/76, para. 250; ECJ, *GT-Link v. DSB*, C-242/95, para. 39. This formula, however, leaves the problem of determining the economic value, providing yet another difficulty. *See this critique raised in*: EC, *Sundbusserne/Port of Helsingborg*, COMP/A.36.570/D3, para. 196; for an overview of the different attempts taken to resolve the problem over time, *see*: FUCHS/MÖSCHEL, in: IMMENGA/MESTMÄCKER 2018, Article 102, paras 174 ff.
1158. FUCHS/MÖSCHEL, in: IMMENGA/MESTMÄCKER 2018, Article 102, para. 170.
1159. EC, *Guidance Paper*, para. 63; EC, *Communication pro-active Competition Policy*, 6.

IV THE CONCEPT OF ABUSE IN ARTICLE 102 TFEU

1 Overview of the Section

435 The following search for the meaning of *abuse* in Article 102 TFEU will start with a look at the case groups on the abuse of a dominant position. In EU law, which is relatively young and to a great extent based on the case law of the Court of Justice, a search for the meaning of a provision cannot be done without a closer look at the court practice. It is not the aim of this book to provide an overall analysis of the case law on Article 102 TFEU, but rather to find a common denominator on which a test for analysing the conduct of applying blocking patents can be based. Therefore, the case law analysed is by no means comprehensive. The case law discussed in this chapter differs from the above cases in Chapter 12. There the book provides an analysis of the approach of the courts towards the acquisition of intellectual property rights. This part, however, focuses solely on the term 'abuse' itself.

436 Following the case law review, the frequently used concept of competition on the merits will be critically analysed with respect to its practical scope. Then, in the search for a conceptual foundation for the abuse of a dominant position, a bridge to the general principle of the abuse of rights will be built. After this, to present a test for analysing the application for patents under Article 102 TFEU, a closer look will be taken at the role of intent and the importance of anticompetitive effects. These sections will then provide the instruments to develop a test for the analysis of the blocking patents application under Article 102 TFEU and a prognosis of blocking strategies in the pharmaceutical industry.

2 Court Practice over Time

2.1 From the Beginning to Commercial Solvents

437 At first, Article 86 of the TEEC attracted little attention.[1160] To counteract the impending oblivion of the article and reduce insecurities regarding the application of the provision, the Commission created an advisory group. This group aimed to determine the theoretical basis of the provision. As a result, the group published a Memorandum in 1966, in which the concept of abuse was first concretised through two

1160. The struggle of EU economic policymakers to compete with large US companies as well as the reluctance of legal practitioners who were trained in civil law to interpret the vague provision were invoked as reasons for the oblivion. *See*: GERBER, Tulane Law Review 1987, 87; for early attempts to establish a functioning competition law system, *see* Regulation (EEC) No 17/1962 with which the Council in 1962 'laid down the system of supervision and enforcement procedures'. *See*: EC, *White Paper,* para. 3. Regulation (EEC) No 17/1962 was eventually amended by Regulation (EC) No 1/2003.

basic principles.[1161] Abuses were defined as *'comportement fautif au regard des objectifs fixés par le Traité'*[1162] (transl.: 'conduct running contrary to the principles of the treaty').[1163] With this linking of the abuse to the principles and goals of the treaty, the advisory group adhered to the basic methods of interpretation.[1164] Additionally, the Memorandum held that conduct which violated Article 86 of the TEEC involved using a powerful position in the market in order to receive benefits that would not have been possible under effective competition.[1165] The advisory group therefore concluded that a direct link between the abusive behaviour and the dominant position was required.

438 After the theoretical framework of the concept was established in the Memorandum, the Court of Justice in a next phase sought to establish basic principles for the interpretation of the provision.[1166] The court first came into contact with Article 86 when it was asked for its advisory opinion in a series of three cases. In *Parke/Davis*, *Sirena v. Eda* and *Deutsche Grammophon*, it had to deliver a preliminary ruling on the question of whether the use of an intellectual property right to raise prices was an abuse of a dominant position. The court held that the price level as such was not a general indication of an abuse. Extremely high and unjustified prices can indicate an abuse, however.[1167]

439 The first non-preliminary ruling, the *Continental Can* decision, set important groundbreaking standards. The Court of Justice had to decide whether a corporate acquisition could qualify as an abuse of a dominant position.[1168] The court concluded that structural measures, both those concerning the structure of the undertaking and those directly affecting the market, could influence conditions in the market.[1169] The corporate acquisition, according to the court, substantially influenced the supply situation in the market, so that 'the degree of dominance reached substantially fetters competition'[1170]. The court had concerns about the independence of the remaining

1161. *See also* the White Paper of 1999 where the Commission commented on the development of its role over time. EC, *White Paper*, para. 4.
1162. *Mémorandum sur la Concentration dans le Marché Commun*, 676; *see also*: PÉREZ/VAN DE SCHEUR, in: PATEL/SCHWEITZER, The historical foundations of EU competition law, 45. This wording was close to that of Article 66(7) of the Treaty of Paris and also found its way into certain national codes. *See*: SAMKALDEN/DRUKER, Common Market Law Review 1966, 176.
1163. *See also* the decision of the ECJ in *Continental Can* where it held that Article 86 TEEC was inseparable from the objectives of the TEC: ECJ, *Continental Can v. Commission*, C-6/72, para. 25.
1164. GERBER, Tulane Law Review 1987, 88.
1165. *Mémorandum sur la Concentration dans le Marché Commun*, 670 (overruled by the ECJ in the *Continental Can* decision: ECJ, *Continental Can v. Commission*, C-6/72, para. 27).
1166. GERBER identified three phases within the development process of the abuse concept. *See*: GERBER, Tulane Law Review 1987, 86 ff.
1167. *See*: ECJ, *Parke, Davis and Co. v. Probel and Others*, C-24/67, 72; ECJ, *Sirena v. Eda*, C-40/70, para. 17.
1168. The decision was influenced by concerns about excessive concentrations in markets as well as acquisitions of European companies by US entities for which the provision was seen as the only remedy. *See*: GERBER, Tulane Law Review 1987, 89.
1169. ECJ, *Continental Can v. Commission*, C-6/72, paras 20 ff.
1170. ECJ, *Continental Can v. Commission*, C-6/72, para. 26.

market players (economic coercion) and declared the acquisition as abusive under Article 102 TFEU.

440 Continental Can argued that it had not used its economic power for the acquisition and could therefore not have abused it. This understanding of abuse was supported by the results of the grammatical, systematic and historical interpretation conducted by Advocate General ROEMER.[1171] The Court of Justice did not follow Advocate General ROEMER and Continental Can.[1172] With the *Continental Can* decision, the court consequently favoured the results of teleological interpretation over the other topos and emphasised the importance of the objectives of the Treaty, namely the dedication of Article 86 to preventing competitive distortion.[1173] In the *Continental Can* decision, jurisprudence took account of the political atmosphere; at that time, there was growing concern about market concentration, and with a lack of legal mechanisms to control mergers and acquisitions, Article 86 presented the only legal remedy.

441 The importance of 'competitive distortion' for the concept of the abuse of a dominant position was confirmed in the *Commercial Solvents* case. Commercial Solvents had a monopoly as a supplier of amino-butanol, a raw material required to produce ethambutol, a drug for the treatment of tuberculosis.[1174] Commercial Solvents stopped supplying the raw materials to producers, and instead solely supplied the raw materials to its joint venture company which was a drug producer itself. The court found that the behaviour of Commercial Solvents resulted in vertical foreclosure as it eliminated the competitors from the downstream market and thus had an 'effect on the structure of supply of the market'[1175].[1176]

442 As effects on the structure of the market are accepted as long as they are based on meritocratic competition of the dominant undertaking, 'competitive distortion' taken separately is too broad and therefore does not qualify as a stand-alone standard for the analysis of potentially abusive behaviour. The Court of Justice in subsequent years further adapted the fundamentals of the concept of the abuse of dominance. The following years of court practice were thus marked by a search for principles to determine to what extent competitive distortion amounts to an abuse of dominance.

2.2 *United Brands: Refusal to Supply, Discriminatory and Unfair Prices*

443 Before the Court of Justice had to decide on the *United Brands* case, it made clear that in order to establish an abuse, the behaviour must eliminate a competitor from the market.[1177] In the *United Brands* case, the Court of Justice dissociated itself from this

1171. AG ROEMER, in: *Continental Can*, C-6/72, 254.
1172. ECJ, *Continental Can v. Commission*, C-6/72, para. 27.
1173. ECJ, *Continental Can v. Commission*, C-6/72, paras 23 ff.
1174. ECJ, *Commercial Solvents*, Joined Cases C-6/73 and 7/73, paras 9 ff.
1175. GERBER, 367.
1176. ECJ, *Commercial Solvents*, Joined Cases C-6/73 and 7/73, para. 25.
1177. *See supra* at para. 441.

necessity when it found a refusal to deal abusive because of the mere potential to drive competitors out of the market if repeated. The decisive element was concerns about the growing dependency of SMEs (banana ripeners) on the dominant undertaking, in that only undertakings supplied by United Brands could remain in the market.[1178]

444 United Brands refused to supply a former distributor because the distributor had engaged in an advertising campaign for a competitor. The court held that the refusal to supply[1179] was not justified and therefore was considered an abuse of the dominant position United Brands held.[1180] Even though a dominant undertaking must be able to protect its own commercial interests by reasonable means, such measures cannot be tolerated when disproportionate.[1181] The conduct interfered with the independence of SMEs, as it was capable of influencing other distributors in their actions and thereby potentially strengthening the position of United Brands in the market. Adopting conduct that interferes with the independence of SMEs 'is designed to have a serious adverse effect on competition on the relevant banana market by only allowing firms dependent upon the dominant undertaking to stay in business'.[1182]

445 In subsequent decisions on refusal to supply by vertically integrated dominant undertakings, the court has mainly focused on two factors when evaluating the conduct or proportionality of the refusal to supply. The first is whether the product refused is indispensable (objectively necessary) to compete in the downstream market,[1183] and the second, whether the resulting prevention of market access is likely to eliminate effective competition in the market.[1184] One factor influencing the proportionality of a refusal to supply is the economic strength of the undertakings involved.[1185] Additionally, the Commission listed:

1178. ECJ, *United Brands*, C-27/76, paras 192 ff.
1179. Note that the term 'refusal to supply' includes different practices 'such as a refusal to supply products to existing or new customers, refusal to license intellectual property rights, including when the licence is necessary to provide interface information, or refusal to grant access to an essential facility or a network'. EC, *Guidance Paper*, para. 78.
1180. A refusal to supply was first considered abusive in the case of *Commercial Solvent*, *see supra* at para. 441.
1181. *See i.a.*: ECJ, *United Brands*, C-27/76; EC, *BBI/Boosey & Hawkes*, IV/32.279, para. 19. Note that practice and doctrine both stress the careful balance needed when examining cases on refusal to supply, as dominant undertakings must also enjoy contractual freedom to choose trading partners and terminate business relationships in principle (*see also* the early decision by the US Supreme Court in *United States v. Colgate & Co.*: United States Supreme Court, *USA v. Colgate & Co.*, 250 US 300, 307 f.; as well as: AG Jacobs, *in: Oscar Bronner*, C-7/97, paras 57 f.). First, there are numerous legitimate reasons to end a business relationship or refuse to supply. Second, a too broad design of the case group, a pending threat of being obligated to supply, could harm the dominant undertaking's incentives to invest and competitors could profit from the investments of the dominant undertaking as free riders. *See*: Whish/Bailey, 713 f.
1182. ECJ, *United Brands*, C-27/76, paras 192 ff.
1183. GC, *Magill*, T-76/89, para. 58; ECJ, *Oscar Bronner*, C-7/97, para. 41; GC, *Tiercé Ladbroke SA v. Commission*, T-504/93, paras 132 ff.; EC, *Guidance Paper*, para. 83.
1184. ECJ, *Oscar Bronner*, C-7/97, para. 41; GC, *Microsoft*, T-201/04, para. 563; EC, *Guidance Paper*, para. 85.
1185. ECJ, *United Brands*, C-27/76, para. 190.

- less capacity pressures of the dominant undertakings relative to downstream competitors;
- closeness of the substitutability between the outputs of the dominant undertaking and those of its downstream competitors;
- the proportion of affected competitors; and
- the likelihood of a diversion from the demand served by the excluded competitors to the dominant undertaking

as factors influencing the proportionality of the conduct.[1186] In the opinion of the courts and the Commission, special attention should be paid to the potential of a refusal to deal in preventing new or improved products from being introduced onto the market.[1187]

446 A similar argument was applied with respect to the contractual obligation of not reselling green bananas and supplying foreign dealers. United Brands implemented these obligations in contracts with banana ripeners and distributors. The clauses were supposedly accepted by the ripeners and distributors owing to fear of sanctions.[1188] The ripeners thus obviously lacked economic independence. Consequently, the clauses unduly raised obstacles on trade and limited the market to the prejudice of consumers, as it resulted in an export ban on bananas.[1189]

447 In its argumentation, the court went on to provide another example of conduct it found to be designed to adversely affect competition - charging discriminatory prices. United Brands charged different prices to its distributors depending on the location of the end customer, even though it did not carry the risk of the conditions in the respective markets. The competitive disadvantage imposed on distributors was thus seen in the application of 'dissimilar conditions to equivalent transactions' which resulted in the partitioning of national markets.[1190] Whether United Brands had also abusively charged unfair prices was, however, negated by the court, owing to a lack of adequate legal proof. As a benchmark for the assessment of prices under Article 102 TFEU, the Court of Justice introduced a cost-price relationship. It held that prices which are unfair in themselves or result in an excessive profit margin through lacking relation to the value of the product result in competitive distortion and are thus abusive.[1191]

448 In ensuing decisions on unfair prices, the courts and the Commission have identified the following prerequisites for the assumption of unfair pricing which closely follow the wording of Article 102(2)(c) itself: the application of dissimilar conditions to equivalent transactions to the competitive disadvantage of competitors, without

1186. EC, *Guidance Paper*, para. 85.
1187. EC, *Guidance Paper*, para. 87; GC, *Magill*, T-76/89, para. 58; ECJ, *IMS Health*, C-418/01, para. 49.
1188. *See*: ECJ, *United Brands*, C-27/76, para. 155.
1189. ECJ, *United Brands*, C-27/76, paras 155 ff.
1190. ECJ, *United Brands*, C-27/76, para. 214.
1191. ECJ, *United Brands*, C-27/76, paras 248 ff.

justification for the difference in treatment and with the tendency to distort competition.[1192]

449 Despite not providing a benchmark or even an explanation for an excessive profit margin and indicating that various factors might influence the excessiveness of the price, the *United Brands* decision reflects a fundamental notion of the abuse of dominance concept, namely 'that a dominant firm acts abusively where it uses its economic power to achieve a gross disproportion between the respective performances required in a transaction'.[1193]

2.3 Hoffmann-La Roche *and* Intel*: Fidelity Rebates and Exclusive Dealing*

a Hoffmann-La Roche

450 The argumentation in *United Brands* reveals two approaches to measuring the abusiveness of conduct: transactional equivalence and economic coercion. In the *Hoffmann-La Roche* case, these approaches were unified.

451 The court held that Hoffmann-La Roche's exclusive dealing contracts and fidelity rebates were 'incompatible with the objective of undistorted competition within the Common Market, because [...] they are not based on an economic transaction which justifies this burden or benefit but are designed to deprive the purchaser of or restrict his possible choices of sources of supply and to deny other producers access to the market'.[1194] Additionally, fidelity rebates are designed to bind customers and cement the position of the dominant undertaking.[1195]

452 Competition in these cases is distorted, according to the court, as it is not based on supply and demand.[1196] In cases of exclusive dealing, the freedom from coercion in decision-making is of predominant concern.[1197] Already in a previous decision, in the case of *Suiker Unie v. Commission*, loyalty rebates had been declared abusive. The design of the rebate system left the purchaser with the potential to lose rebates when obtaining supplies from competitors. The decision was based on the argument that the system therefore possibly dissuaded purchasers from such acquisitions or at least made them financially disadvantageous.[1198] In applying this system of rebates, Suiker Unie charged different prices for equivalent transactions with other purchasers (Article

1192. For other decisions, *see i.a.*: ECJ, *Hoffmann-La Roche v. Commission*, C-85/76, para. 122; ECJ, *British Airways plc v. Commission*, C-95/04, para. 144.
1193. GERBER, Tulane Law Review 1987, 95.
1194. ECJ, *Hoffmann-La Roche v. Commission*, C-85/76, para. 90.
1195. Even more clear with respect to the abusive design of loyalty rebates and exclusive dealing contracts: GC, *BPB Industries*, T-65/89, para. 68, *see also*: GC, *Tomra Systems and Others v. Commission*, T-155/06, para. 208.
1196. ECJ, *Hoffmann-La Roche v. Commission*, C-85/76, para. 90.
1197. This understanding is also supported by the fact that the court did not accept the argument of justification that the purchaser willingly entered into the agreement. ECJ, *Gemeente Almelo and Others v. Energiebedrijf IJsselmij*, C-393/92, para. 44.
1198. ECJ, *Suiker Unie v. Commission*, C-40/73, paras 517 f.

102(c) TFEU) and additionally also restricted the possibilities for competitors to sell their supplies.[1199]

453 A year later, in the *Michelin* case[1200] as well as the *L'Oréal* preliminary ruling,[1201] the Court of Justice confirmed its findings in *Hoffmann-La Roche*, where it delivered a definition with substantive criteria for identifying abusive behaviour that has since been the foundation for analysis under Article 102 TFEU. With its definition, the court distanced itself from previous findings and the widely shared notion that the abuse of a dominant position in fact required an instrumentalisation of the dominant position itself:

> The concept of abuse is an objective concept relating to the behaviour of an undertaking in a dominant position which is such as to influence the structure of a market where, as a result of the very presence of the undertaking in question, the degree of competition is weakened and which, through recourse to methods different from those which condition normal competition in products or services on the basis of the transactions of commercial operators,[1202] has the effect of hindering the maintenance of degree of competition still existing in the market or the growth of that competition.[1203]

b Intel

454 In the following years, the courts continued to apply a strict standard towards loyalty rebates. Among the most noteworthy were the decisions in *BPB Industries plc and British Gypsum v. Commission* and *Irish Sugar v. Commission*. In both cases, the dominant undertakings were found guilty of having abused their dominant position because the rebate systems provided by them implied an intention to bind customers.[1204] The most famous case of a fine being imposed because of loyalty rebates, however, is the *Intel* case.

455 In *Intel Corp. v. Commission*, Intel was charged with a EUR 1.06 billion fine for having implemented loyalty rebates[1205] and 'naked restrictions'[1206].[1207] The Commission focused its argumentation on anticompetitive foreclosure. It argued that the rebates were likely to cause anticompetitive foreclosure, as a competitor who was as efficient would have to charge prices below the average avoidable costs.[1208] The

1199. ECJ, *Suiker Unie v. Commission*, C-40/73, paras 522 ff.
1200. ECJ, *Michelin I*, C-322/81, para. 70.
1201. ECJ, *L'Oréal v. De Nieuwe AMCK*, C-31/80, para. 27.
1202. The passage 'on the basis of transaction of commercial operators' was rewritten in the *Michelin I* case and replaced by 'based on trader's performance'. ECJ, *Michelin I*, C-322/81, para. 70.
1203. ECJ, *Hoffmann-La Roche v. Commission*, C-85/76, para. 91; recently confirmed in: ECJ, *AstraZeneca v. Commission*, C-457/10 P, para. 74.
1204. GC, *BPB Industries*, T-65/89, para. 71; GC, *Irish Sugar*, T-228/97, para. 197.
1205. *See summary in*: GC, *Intel*, T-286/09, paras 28 ff.
1206. GC, *Intel*, T-286/09, paras 32 f.
1207. EC, *Intel*, Case COMP/C 3/37.990, paras 917 and 1803.
1208. EC, *Intel*, Case COMP/C 3/37.990, paras 1002 ff.

rebates according to the Commission resulted in 'a reduction of consumer choice and in lower incentives to innovate'[1209]. On appeal, the General Court confirmed the results reached by the Commission, but rejected its analysis of effects on the market. 'Exclusivity rebates granted by an undertaking in a dominant position are by their very nature capable of restricting competition.'[1210]. With this argument, the court attached greater importance to the protection of the market structure than direct or indirect welfare considerations. This decision on exclusivity rebates marked a rejection of the *more economic approach* proclaimed by the Commission.[1211]

456 On appeal, the Court of Justice did not follow the Court of Justice. The Court of Justice rejected the General Court's strictly form-based approach and stressed that all circumstances of the case have to be examined whenever a dominant undertaking provides evidence that the conduct did not restrict competition:

> In that case, the Commission is not only required to analyse, first, the extent of the undertaking's dominant position on the relevant market and, secondly, the share of the market covered by the challenged practice, as well as the conditions and arrangements for granting the rebates in question, their duration and their amount; it is also required to assess the possible existence of a strategy aiming to exclude competitors that are at least as efficient as the dominant undertaking from the market.[1212]

457 Despite loyalty rebates in principle falling within the scope of Article 102, the Commission and courts have to assess exculpatory evidence, such as the aim to exclude less-effective competitors as argued by Intel. According to the Court of Justice, an analysis is only complete after weighing both the favourable and unfavourable effects. 'That balancing of the favourable and unfavourable effects of the practice in question on competition can be carried out in the Commission's decision only after an analysis of the intrinsic capacity of that practice to foreclose competitors which are at least as efficient as the dominant undertaking.'[1213] As the General Court failed to address Intel's criticism of the AEC-test (as-efficient-competitor test) conducted by the Commission, the Court of Justice referred the case to the General Court to complete the verification of facts.[1214]

458 With its recent *Intel* decision, the Court of Justice has adopted an interesting approach. The wording of the decision implies that fidelity rebates are presumptively abusive, but with a possibility for justification. The plea of 'inability to restrict competition' behoves the dominant undertaking. The Commission therefore does not have to prove foreclosing effects. This is despite the fact that it is obliged to assess objective factors such as the 'extent of the undertaking's dominant position', 'the share

1209. GC, *Intel*, T-286/09, para. 31.
1210. GC, *Intel*, T-286/09, para. 85.
1211. The Commission in its guidance declared the need to include considerations about the extent of the conduct. *See*: EC, *Guidance Paper*, paras 20 and 38.
1212. ECJ, *Intel*, C-413/14 P, para. 139.
1213. ECJ, *Intel*, C-413/14 P, para. 140.
1214. ECJ, *Intel*, C-413/14 P, paras 145 ff.

of the market covered by the challenged practice, as well as the conditions and arrangements for granting the rebates in question, their duration and their amount'[1215]. The understanding of abuse presented in the *Intel* case even contradicts the Commission's Guidance on Enforcement Priorities where the Commission self-imposed an obligation to analyse foreclosing effects.[1216]

459 Unfortunately, the court left other important questions open. Mention can be made of the burden of proof and the role of subjective elements. While it seems to be clear that proof of a foreclosing effect in the absence of an exclusionary strategy would qualify the rebates as abusive, the contrary is not obvious. Judging from the wording of the decision, it cannot be concluded whether proof of a strategy aimed at excluding competitors that 'are at least as efficient as the dominant undertaking'[1217] from the market would be sufficient.

2.4 AKZO: *Predatory Pricing*

460 In the *AKZO* case, a case of predatory pricing, the definition given by the Court of Justice in *Hoffmann-La Roche* was first applied in a horizontal relationship. The court declared that prices below average variable costs (AVC) were considered abusive. In applying them, the dominant undertaking could have no other motivation but to drive competitors out of the market. Prices below the average total cost (ATC) but above the average variable cost are, however, only abusive if applied as part of a plan to eliminate a competitor, as in these situations, they might result in an elimination of equally effective undertakings from the market with less financial power.[1218] The court found that AKZO's prices could not have been low to such an extent only to restore their own profit margins as the undertaking claimed, but were significantly lower than 'what was necessary to compete' and were therefore intended to damage the competitor ECS.[1219] The court continued to apply the test developed in the *AKZO* decision on predatory pricing in the following years.[1220]

2.5 Hilti *and* Microsoft: *Tying and Bundling*

461 Abusive contractual obligations may take various forms. Among the most observed is contractual tying.[1221] Tying refers to a practice of the supplier requiring the

1215. ECJ, *Intel*, C-413/14 P, para. 139.
1216. EC, *Guidance Paper*, paras 20 f.; *see also*: Haberer, WUW 2017, 528.
1217. ECJ, *Intel*, C-413/14 P, para. 139.
1218. ECJ, *AKZO*, C-62/86, paras 71 ff.; since then, this test has been applied several times by the ECJ, *see i.a.*: ECJ, *France Télécom*, C-202/07 P, paras 33 ff.
1219. ECJ, *AKZO*, C-62/86, para. 108.
1220. *As i.a. in*: ECJ, *France Télécom*, C-202/07 P, paras 33 ff.; ECJ, *Tetra Pak II*, C-333/94 P, paras 41 ff.
1221. *See also* the decision in the *Tetra Pak II* case: ECJ, *Tetra Pak II*, C-333/94 P, paras 34 ff., analysed in more detail *supra* at para. 327.

purchaser to buy a tying as well as a tied product.[1222] Through tying or bundling strategies, the dominant undertaking can influence demand and prices for the bound products. The bundling of the products leads to the charging of an overall price. As a consequence, consumers have to pay a higher (overall) price for the product demanded because they simultaneously purchase a second product without demanding it. By this means, the supplier binds demand, as both the consumers seeking to purchase product A and those demanding product B have to purchase the product bundling consisting of products A & B.[1223]

462 The basis for the analysis of contractual tying was set out in the case of *Hilti*. The tool manufacturer Hilti required purchasers of its patented nail cartridges to also purchase nails produced by itself. This conduct was not seen as a legitimate mode of competition, but 'liable to deter other undertakings from establishing themselves in the market'.[1224]

463 Tying, itself, can appear in various forms, as, for example, in the form of bundlings,[1225] where its abusive character is mainly dependent on the prices charged, or technical tying, where it is impossible to operate one product without the other owing to a physical integration of the tied product into the tying product. Technical tying was closely examined in the *Microsoft* decision.[1226] Microsoft did not offer licences for the Windows operating system without the Windows Media Player which was already pre-installed. Coercion to purchase the Windows Media Player was thus not only of a contractual nature but also technically driven. Anticompetitive foreclosure in the end was a result of the technical setting with the pre-installed player that required special efforts and the investment of consumers who did not wish to use the Media Player and the 'all-in-one licence'. As a result, the Windows Media Player profited from the wide distribution of the Windows operating system without having to compete with other media players.[1227] This led to the abusiveness of the conduct, as it left competitors only with methods that could not seriously jeopardise Windows Media Player's ubiquity.[1228] The strategy changed the balance of competition.

464 Tied sales are thus abusive under four conditions. First, the tying as well as the tied product need to have two separate markets.[1229] Second, the undertaking must be dominant in one of the markets, usually the tying product's market. Third, customers have no choice whether to buy the tied product or not when demanding the tying

1222. To analyse tying under Article 102 TFEU, the tying as well as the tied product need to be in two separate markets and the undertaking must be dominant in one of the markets, usually the tying product market. *See*: GC, *Microsoft*, T-201/04, paras 918, 842 and 869; EC, *Guidance Paper*, para. 48.
1223. EC, *Guidance Paper*, paras 55 ff.
1224. GC, *Hilti v. Commission*, T-30/89, para. 100.
1225. For an explanation of bundling *see*: EC, *Guidance Paper*, para. 48.
1226. *See supra* at paras 331 ff.
1227. There was also evidence that the product integration of the Windows Media Player in the Windows Operating System was primarily designed to promote the Media Player. GC, *Microsoft*, T-201/04, para. 937.
1228. GC, *Microsoft*, T-201/04, paras 1036 ff.
1229. *See*: GC, *Microsoft*, T-201/04, paras 921 f.; GC, *Hilti v. Commission*, T-30/89, para. 67.

product. Fourth, the conduct leads to foreclosure of competition.[1230] Anticompetitive effects can occur in the tied as well as in the tying market or even in both markets.[1231]

465 In its enforcement priorities, the Commission assumes technical tying to carry a greater risk of foreclosure, as it is costly to reverse and leaves only reduced opportunities for competitors to offer individual components. Generally, the durability and steadiness of the strategy are considered to increase the probability of anticompetitive foreclosure.[1232] The Commission also stressed that tying and bundling can generate positive effects such as efficiencies in the form of savings in production, distribution or transaction costs.[1233]

2.6 **Deutsche Telecom *and* TeliaSonera Sverige*: Margin Squeeze***

466 The strategy of a margin squeeze is closely connected to predatory pricing as well as a refusal to supply.[1234] Margin squeezes occur when a vertically integrated dominant undertaking charges prices for its services which restrict competition in the downstream market. This is because 'the difference between the retail prices charged by a dominant undertaking and the wholesale prices it charges its competitors for comparable services is negative, or insufficient to cover the product-specific costs to the dominant operator of providing its own retail services on the downstream market'.[1235] To determine whether a dominant undertaking's conduct results in a margin squeeze, courts only consider the scope of the dominant undertaking in terms of pricing.[1236] The courts have additionally based the finding of a violation of Article 102 on the establishment of potential anticompetitive effects, that is the potential exclusion of 'as efficient' competitors.[1237]

2.7 ***Findings***

467 Jurisprudence on the abuse of a dominant position under Article 102 TFEU is characterised by efforts of the courts and the Commission to provide guidelines and prerequisites to measure potentially abusive behaviour based on case-by-case judgments without decreasing predictability. The starting point is the fixed idea that dominant undertakings should only be allowed to compete 'by virtue of greater

1230. GC, *Microsoft*, T-201/04, paras 947 ff. *See also*: EC, *Guidance Paper*, para. 50.
1231. *See*: EC, *Guidance Paper*, para. 52.
1232. EC, *Guidance Paper*, para. 53.
1233. EC, *Guidance Paper*, para. 62.
1234. *See*: EC, *Guidance Paper*, para. 80.
1235. EC, *Deutsche Telekom*, COMP/C-1/37.451, 37.578, 37.579, para. 107; *see also*: ECJ, *TeliaSonera Sverige*, C-52/09, para. 32.
1236. *See i.a.*: GC, *Deutsche Telekom v. Commission*, T-271/03, paras 193 ff.; ECJ, *TeliaSonera Sverige*, C-52/09, paras 38 ff.
1237. ECJ, *TeliaSonera Sverige*, C-52/09, para. 64.

efficiency or superior performance'[1238]. The fundamental definition of abuse was delivered in the *Hoffmann-La Roche* case and included two factors:

(1) the quality to influence the structure of the market and having the effect of hindering the maintenance of the current degree of competition; as well as
(2) the recourse to methods different from normal competition (competition on the merits).[1239]

468 In the decisions of the EU courts, the aim of competition law is shown, which is to ensure transactions based on supply and demand and to create an environment where neither supply nor demand is shortened artificially.[1240] The court has presented various case-group-specific premises indicating competitive distortion resulting in non-meritocratic competition which influences the structure of the market. What the tests have in common is that their design already implies a high probability that the conduct, if applied and not justified, will have an adverse effect on competition.[1241] Depending on the conduct in question, the court, however, shifted its focus and adjusted the prerequisites constituting the assumption of an adverse effect on competition.

469 Appreciable differences in the case law presented exist with respect to the question of whether noticeable effects have to be manifested.[1242] In *Intel Corp. v. Commission*, the Court of Justice held that although fidelity rebates are presumptively abusive, the contrary might be demonstrated in a proof-founded objection by the dominant undertaking.[1243] In the case of margin squeezes, which are closely related to rebates with respect to their effect on the market,[1244] the court has, however, based its findings on actual evidence of potential anticompetitive effects.[1245] And yet, with predatory pricing, the necessity to prove anticompetitive foreclosure is dependent on the relative price applied.[1246] For this reason and since the other pillars of competition law - merger regulation and Article 101 TFEU - have been reassessed under the influence of the *more economic approach*, in legal practice, the conceptual design of the prohibition of the abuse of a dominant position is under discussion.[1247] The discourse outlined below in section IV thus concerns the question of whether the conceptual design is form based or effect based.

1238. *See*: EC, *ECS v. AKZO*, IV/30.698, para. 81.
1239. *See supra* at fn. 1203.
1240. Explicitly in: ECJ, *Hoffmann-La Roche v. Commission*, C-85/76, para. 90; inherent also in: GC, *Microsoft*, T-201/04, paras 1036 ff.
1241. *See supra* at paras 444 ff., 451, 456, 460, 462 and 466.
1242. *See also the analysis in*: AKMAN, World Competition 2009, 75 ff.
1243. *See supra* at paras 455 ff.
1244. *See*: EC, *Guidance Paper*, para. 80.
1245. *See supra* at fn. 1237.
1246. *See supra* at para. 460.
1247. *See the analysis in*: LOWE, in: HAWK, Annual proceedings of the Fordham Corporate Law Institute: international antitrust law and policy, 164 ff.

470 Closely connected to the question of form-based versus effect-based abuse concepts is the question of the role of intent. In some cases, the Court of Justice based its decision on evidence for a plan to exclude competitors.[1248] In other cases, the court assumed such an intent from the design of the conduct itself.[1249] Apart from certain forms of predatory pricing, it is also unclear whether the mere finding of a plan to exclude competitors in the absence of actual foreclosing effects is sufficient to subsume conduct under Article 102 TFEU. The role of intent will be examined in more detail in section IV, 4.2 below.

471 Over the years, discussions have also been raised with respect to the object of Article 102 TFEU. With the definition provided in the *Hoffmann-La Roche* decision and even more with its practice on predatory pricing, a strategy potentially resulting in lower prices for consumers,[1250] on tying and bundling[1251] and on refusal to supply,[1252] the Court cemented the responsibility of competition law on market structure and the competitive process, apparently irrespective of who profits. It is thus prima facie unclear why a teleological interpretation of Article 102 should focus on consumer welfare as a benchmark for evaluating abusive behaviour. The Commission with its Guidance Paper on the enforcement priorities, however, pronounced consumer welfare as the object of EU competition rules and also Article 102 TFEU.[1253] The Court of Justice at first rebuked the Commission for rushing ahead in this matter in the *British Airways* case[1254] and in the following cases stressed the importance of protecting the competition as such and not the 'immediate interests of individual competitors or consumers'[1255]. The Court of Justice only with its decision in *TeliaSonera Sverige* in 2011 and *Post Danmark A/S v. Konkurrencerådet* in 2012 followed the Commission.[1256] In EU law, therefore, consumer welfare has been chosen as the standard.[1257]

1248. *See*, for example, *supra* at para. 463.
1249. *See*, for example, *supra* at paras 454 and 460.
1250. *See supra* at fns 1218 ff.
1251. *See supra* at fns 1233 ff.
1252. *See supra* at paras 443 ff.
1253. EC, *Guidance Paper*, paras 5, 7, 19 ff. and 86 ff.; EC, *DG Competition discussion paper*, paras 4, 54 f. and 88.
1254. *See supra* at para. 67.
1255. ECJ, *T-Mobile Netherlands and Others*, C-8/08, paras 36 ff., esp. para. 38; confirmed in: ECJ, *GlaxoSmithKline Services and Others v. Commission*, Joined Cases C-501/06 P and others, para. 63.
1256. *See supra* at fn. 172.
1257. *See supra* at paras 65 ff. Note that AG KOKOTT in her recent opinion in the case *Generics (UK) and Others II* stressed the importance of the protection of the competitive process. The ECJ in its decision did not loose its focus on consumer welfare, however, and with respect to justifying a behaviour stated that 'the exclusionary effect [...] may be counterbalanced, or outweighed, by advantages in terms of efficiency that also benefit consumers'. AG KOKOTT, in: *Generics (UK) and Others II*, C-307/18, para. 174; ECJ, *Generics (UK) and Others II*, C-307/18, paras 156 f. and 165 ff., esp. para. 165.

3 'Competition on the Merits'

3.1 Appearance of the Principle

472 The development of jurisprudence on the abuse of a dominant position outlined above is inseparably linked to the concept of competition on the merits. The courts use competition on the merits as the conceptual basis to separate abusive from non-abusive behaviour.[1258] Competition on the merits is synonymous with 'methods of normal competition', the terminology used in the *Hoffmann-La Roche* decision.

473 The concept of competition on the merits was borrowed from German legal tradition. There, the term made its way into early legal practice. The German Imperial Court of Justice (ICJ) first used the concept in 1931[1259] to justify its finding that dumping prices is a form of unfair competition.[1260] The court introduced the concept based on the expert opinion NIPPERDEY gave for a party. Following his opinion, competition on the merits has been characterised by its sole reliance on superior performance to win other customers, such as better efficiency or higher level products. NIPPERDEY contrasted competition on the merits with competition of restraints.[1261]

474 The ICJ (Reichsgericht, RG) in 1931 adopted NIPPERDEY's expert opinion and held that fair competition contains all practices that are targeted to increase sales of the undertaking and that originate from one's own previous performance.[1262] One's own performance, as the Federal Court of Justice (Bundesgerichtshof, BGH) in consequence to this precedent later specified, is based on the strategic use of relevant factors such as quality and service.[1263] Conduct that is not performance based includes the breach of either law or contract or the abuse of the work of a third party.[1264]

475 In Germany, further developments included fairness standards as well. The extent of performance-based competition was developed by recourse to unfair competition law on a case-by-case basis.[1265] With the second amendment of the Act Against Restraints of Competition (ARC), the scope of competition on the merits was extended from unfair competition law to rules aimed at protecting the process of competition. Since then, the concept has been an integral part of competition law in Germany and is

1258. *See*, for example, the numerous references to case law in: EILMANSBERGER/KRUIS, in: STREINZ/MICHL, EUV/AEUV/GrCh, Article 102, para. 54, fn. 164; WURMNEST, 346, fn. 25.
1259. The ICJ was twenty-seven years earlier than the US Supreme Court which introduced the concept in 1958 in the *Northern Pacific Railway* case: UNITED STATES SUPREME COURT, *Northern Pacific Railway Co. v. USA*, 365 US 1, 6.
1260. RG, *Benrather Tankstelle*, RGZ 134, 342, 352 ff. Note that in Germany the scope of competition law scrutiny was not far-reaching in those days. Most cases were caught by the scope of the law against unfair competition.
1261. NIPPERDEY, 16 f.
1262. RG, *Benrather Tankstelle*, RGZ 134, 342, 352 ff.
1263. *See*: BGH, *Ersatzteile für Registrierkassen*, KZR 54/71, para. 22.
1264. NIPPERDEY, 28.
1265. ULMER, GRUR 1977, 565 ff.; *see also*: WURMNEST, 345 f.

especially relevant in the evaluation of unilateral conduct of dominant undertakings.[1266] Surprisingly, while 'performance on the merits' is frequently cited, it is rarely used to justify findings of abusive behaviour. Abuses are rather identified by weighing the interests involved and analysing the competitive conditions in the relevant market.[1267]

476 At Union level, the concept of competition on the merits first appeared in the above-cited passage of the *Hoffmann-La Roche* case.[1268] As a fixed component of the test of abusive behaviour presented in the decision, the concept was used as a measurement of potentially abusive behaviour. According to the wording, only 'the recourse to methods different from normal competition in products or services on the basis of the transactions of commercial operators, has the effect of hindering the maintenance of the degree of competition still existing in the market or the growth of that competition'[1269] and can be held abusive.

477 Even though competition on the merits has been an inherent part of assessing abusive behaviour of dominant undertakings since the *Hoffmann-La Roche* decision,[1270] the court has so far failed to provide guidance on what is understood as meritocratic competition. Only on one occasion, in the *Michelin I* judgment, was the description of competition on the merits as 'competition in products or services on the basis of the transactions of commercial operators' added as a characteristic. There the Court of Justice changed the wording slightly and included performance as a relevant characteristic of meritocratic competition: '[...] through recourse to methods different from those governing normal competition[1271] in products or services based on traders' performance, have the effect of hindering the maintenance or development of the level of competition still existing on the market'.[1272]

478 With the introduction of 'performance-based conduct' in *Michelin I*, the court got closer to the wording of the German translation of the *Hoffmann-La Roche* decision. There the translation of competition on the merits as *Leistungswettbewerb* suggests that the distinction has been performance related from the beginning.[1273] Whether the Court of Justice with the *Michelin I* decision tried to correct a translation error[1274] or responded to critiques on the vagueness of the concept remains unclear. In the following years, however, both the courts and the Commission adhered to that early wording and did not add further characteristics to specify the content of meritocratic

1266. *See i.a.*: SACK, in: LOEWENHEIM ET AL., Kommentar Kartellrecht, § 24 GWB, paras 59 ff.; WURMNEST, 345 f.; IMMENGA, in: IMMENGA/MESTMÄCKER, GWB Kommentar, § 24, para. 50.
1267. *See* with further reference to case law: WURMNEST, para. 346, fn. 23.
1268. The exact wording 'competition on the merits' has been used by the GC in *Irish Sugar*: GC, *Irish Sugar*, T-228/97, para. 111.
1269. ECJ, *Hoffmann-La Roche v. Commission*, C-85/76, para. 91.
1270. *See* with slight changes in the wording: ECJ, *Michelin I*, C-322/81, para. 70; ECJ, *AKZO*, C-62/86, para. 70; ECJ, *France Télécom*, C-202/07 P, para. 106.
1271. Normal competition and competition on the merits can be used as synonyms. *See*: ORGANISATION FOR ECONOMIC CO-OPERATION AND DEVELOPMENT, *Policy Roundtables*, 22.
1272. ECJ, *Michelin I*, C-322/81, para. 70.
1273. *Leistung* is the German translation of performance.
1274. As concluded by: KALLAUGHER/SHER, ECLR 2004, 270.

competition. To overcome the vagueness, the courts continued what the legislator with the sample catalogue had begun; they defined case groups and decided on the conformity of conduct with 'performance' and 'merits' based on immanent system values.[1275] The result of this practice is that several tests and reference points have emerged to evaluate whether conduct is performance related.[1276]

3.2 *Relevance in Practice*

479 The use of competition on the merits as a legal concept to evaluate the conduct of undertakings presumes that performance is a valid factor to separate conduct into two categories as well as being suitable to anticipate the effect of behaviour on competition. Both assumptions have, however, proved to be wrong.[1277] There is no clear-cut line between performance and non-performance. This can, for example, be seen with prices. Price was the first parameter to raise concerns that resulted in the creation of provisions to protect competition.[1278] High prices can be the result of superior performance of the product in terms of quality, exclusivity, etc., or a surplus of demand as a result of the market conditions. Scarcity can, however, also result in an artificial shortage conducted by the undertaking rather than superior performance. Whether and to what extent the high prices are the result of performance or other reasons is therefore difficult to distinguish.[1279]

480 Also, non-performance-based artificially high prices do not automatically imply resolutive effects on the functioning of competition. The missing relation between performance and illicit behaviour has already shown itself in the design and understanding of Article 102 TFEU. It only sanctions behaviour of dominant undertakings, while the same conduct by non-dominant undertakings is not considered a violation of competition law. Performance is thus not decisive. Furthermore, the article does not sanction the holding of a dominant position, nor the gaining of a dominant position based on superior performance. The unsuitability of performance as a stand-alone decisive factor has also been shown by the courts.[1280]

481 Unsurprisingly, therefore, the introduction of the concept of competition on the merits did not result in the implementation of general principles that would allow a more predictable outcome of competition law scrutiny.[1281] Likewise, legal scholars

1275. ØSTERUD, 42; WURMNEST, 346.
1276. *See supra* at Part V, Chapter 14, section IV.
1277. On the ambivalence of performance *see also*: EILMANSBERGER/KRUIS, in: STREINZ/MICHL, EUV/AEUV/GrCh, Article 102, para. 54; FUCHS, in: IMMENGA/MESTMÄCKER, GWB Kommentar, § 19, para. 28; WURMNEST, 347 f.
1278. *See supra* at paras 37 f.
1279. *See i.a.*: EILMANSBERGER, Common Market Law Review 2005, 140; O'DONOGHUE/PADILLA, 218 f.; WURMNEST, 347.
1280. *See in this respect*: ECJ, *TeliaSonera Sverige*, C-52/09, para. 24.
1281. This was due to the vagueness of competition on the merits and the fact that it had not been made clearer through court practice. ORGANISATION FOR ECONOMIC CO-OPERATION AND DEVELOPMENT, *Policy Roundtables*, 9 and 17. The same criticism was also raised in Germany, where the

were not able to detect a change in the approach of the courts after the introduction of the concept. Cases of abuse of dominance were and still are decided on a case-by-case basis,[1282] and the courts often substantiate their decisions detached from competition on the merits.[1283] The uselessness of the dichotomy between performance and non-performance-based conduct became apparent in the decisional practice of the court. The inability of the court to argue cases based on performance, as well as the mentioned difficulties, led ROUSSEVA to conclude that 'performance' amounts to an artificial decisive factor.[1284]

482 This leaves us with a concept which requires distinguishing good from bad competition based on 'performance' to determine the influence of misbehaviour on the market. Yet, the concept has, since its adoption, neither changed the analysis of competition law cases nor been consulted as an analytical tool. The concept was rather used in the argumentation of the court to substantiate the accuracy of a result already reached.[1285] Ultimately, adhering to competition on the merits meant arguing in circles. The conduct of a dominant undertaking is considered abusive when it consists of 'methods different from those govern[ing] normal competition', while the categorisation of conduct as abuse is justified if the conduct is beyond competition on the merits.

483 When the Court of Justice defines abuse as the conduct of dominant undertakings beyond performance with an effect on the structure of the market, it might as well paraphrase the objective purpose of competition law as the protection of competition as a regulatory principle.[1286] For the abuse of a dominant position, this means that 'competition on the merits' seemingly rephrases the legislative intent and broad consensus in academia that a dominant undertaking should not be deprived from engaging in competition and that competition as a process does not work without competitive pressure.[1287]

484 The execution of competitive pressure is therefore not a decisive factor for the finding of abuse of a dominant position. Yet, owing to their resources and supremacy on the market, dominant undertakings are more likely to increase competitive pressure unduly. The ordoliberals' conviction that dominant undertakings have a 'special responsibility' towards competition essentially therefore rephrases this realisation.[1288] Despite this harsh criticism outlined above, the concept of competition on the merits finds widespread acceptance,[1289] not only in case law[1290] but also in literature.[1291]

---

principle has its roots. *See*: LEISTNER, in: GLOY/LOSCHELDER/ERDMANN, Handbuch des Wettbewerbsrechts, paras 22 ff. For a summary of the criticism raised, *see also*: WUTTKE, 57 ff.

1282. For dominant undertakings, the legal situation remained highly unpredictable. This was officially noted as a serious shortcoming of the practice by the OECD in 2005: ORGANISATION FOR ECONOMIC CO-OPERATION AND DEVELOPMENT, *Policy Roundtables*, 9 and 17 f.
1283. ØSTERUD, 43.
1284. ROUSSEVA, Common Market Law Review 2005, 593 ff.
1285. *See*: ØSTERUD, 43 f.
1286. Similarly: SCHWEND, 74; as well as *supra* at fns 123 f.
1287. EILMANSBERGER, European Competition Journal 2006, 21 f.
1288. *See*: ECJ, *Michelin I*, C-322/81, para. 57; ECJ, *Post Danmark*, C-209/10, para. 23.
1289. *See also*: ORGANISATION FOR ECONOMIC CO-OPERATION AND DEVELOPMENT, *Policy Roundtables*, 17 f.
1290. For references to case law, *see supra* at fn. 1258 and paras 476 ff.

485 For the identification of abusive behaviour, the above allows two conclusions. First, competition on the merits has proved to be unsuitable to distinguish, or provide guidance on, the identification of abusive behaviour of dominant undertakings as, at its core, it is but a paraphrase of the legislative intent.[1292] Second, the degree of market concentration and the potential of the dominant undertaking to disturb the balance on the market must play an important role when assessing its behaviour – as with the 'as-efficient competitor' test[1293] – and consequently the factual circumstances of the case should always influence the decision finding.[1294]

4 Form-Based Versus Effect-Based Concepts

4.1 Anticompetitive Effects

a The Difficulty of Measuring Anticompetitive Effects

486 The court practice on the abuse of a dominant position outlined above has shown a certain inconsistency about the relevance of anticompetitive effects. The question of whether tests for the analysis of anticompetitive behaviour need to be effect based rather than form based has therefore gained increased attention in recent academic discourse.

487 The academic discourse has to be seen against the background of the general challenge in competition law to render competition comprehensible, as on the whole, it is a rather complex incomprehensible interplay of individual elements.[1295] In this discourse one should not forget that economic research is based on models. This entails an inherent simplification of the real world. Furthermore, these models and tests are all based on assumptions deduced from economic theories and their results are therefore affected by the underlying presumptions. Consequently, the economic theory which provides theoretical foundations for competition law evaluations is based on certain generalisations.[1296]

488 This must also apply under competition law. In order to become effective, the law must be applicable; otherwise, it will remain dead letters. Conducting a comprehensive

1291. HEINEMANN, for example, argues that competition on the merits allowed identifying conduct worthy of sanction in the *Microsoft* decision and supports the concept in general. HEINEMANN, Immaterialgüterschutz in der Wettbewerbsordnung, 116 f. and 446 f.; for commentators in favour of the concept, *see also*, for example, IMMENGA, in: IMMENGA/MESTMÄCKER, GWB Kommentar, § 24, para. 63; ULMER, GRUR 1977, 565 ff.; WUTTKE, 57 and 189 f. Generally in favour of the concept, despite conceding certain difficulties: FUCHS, in: IMMENGA/MESTMÄCKER 2018, Article 102, paras 201 f.; PAUL, 125 ff. and 138 ff.

1292. SCHWEND, 76.

1293. *See supra* at paras 457 f.

1294. *See i.a.*: ECJ, *Compagnie Maritime,* Joined Cases C-395/96 P and C-396/96 P, para. 114; ECJ, *Tetra Pak II,* C-333/94 P, paras 24 and 28.

1295. *See*: HEIDUK, in: HEIDUK/EMMERICH, Arzneimittelmarkt und europäisches Wettbewerbsrecht, 156 ff.

1296. *See supra* at para. 63 and esp. fn. 159.

analysis of the anticompetitive effects of a specific behaviour in a market therefore cannot become standard.[1297] In order to ensure the effectiveness of the law, the choice for a standard of proof must imply a willingness to generalise.[1298] WURMNEST rightly points out that without generalisation, resource expenditure borne by private market players as well as authorities would be unreasonably high, while at the same time the predictability of legal outcomes would be practically impossible.[1299] Applying such a standard would render the subsumption of conduct under legal provisions factually impossible because of difficulties in assessing the parameters and predicting their interaction. Generalisation does not, however, exclude effect-based case-by-case analysis per se.

489 The Court of Justice in the *Hoffmann-La Roche* decision explicitly mentioned that conduct qualifying as abuse must be 'such as to influence the structure of the market'.[1300] Additionally, it has been stated above that the problem in setting legal standards is that it requires an actual causally determined correlation between the market structure, behaviour on the market and the market result.[1301] In order to analyse the effect of certain behaviour on the market, an analysis of the market structure is thus the starting point.

b *The Elements of Market Structure*

490 The factors constituting market structure affect the nature of competition on the market and 'the way the firm operates'[1302].[1303] The market structure consists of all factors in a market which appear unchangeable to undertakings and are thus relatively robust in the short to medium term.[1304] The market structure in its broadest sense consists of 'every technological, institutional, geographical, legal and psychological characteristic of the selling firm [...], its buyers and the framework within which both [its buyer and the selling firm] operate [...]'.[1305] Among others, these include:

- the number of suppliers and demanders as well as their market shares;
- the degree of product homogeneity and market transparency as well as adjustment speeds;
- barriers to market entry and exit as well as the flexibility of production and sales; and

1297. This was explicitly mentioned by the Swiss Federal Court in its *Publigroupe* decision: BUNDESGERICHT, para. 8.3.2.
1298. *See*: HENN, 168, who holds that full evidence cannot be provided in competition law.
1299. WURMNEST, 255 f. and 267 f.; for other authors raising concerns with respect to the practicability of economic analysis, *see*, for example, SCHMIDT, WUW 2005.
1300. *See supra* at fn. 1203.
1301. *See supra* at Part I, Chapter 3, section III.
1302. KAYSEN/TURNER, 59.
1303. BAIN, 7; CARSTENSEN, U.C. Davis Law Review 1983, 498; SCHMIDT/HAUCAP, 71.
1304. BAIN, 295; KAYSEN/TURNER, 59; KERBER/SCHWALBE, in: BORNKAMM ET AL., MüKo, Einleitung, Die ökonomischen Grundlagen des Wettbewerbsrechts, para. 79.
1305. BAIN, 300.

- in certain circumstances, also intragroup factors (personal or monetary interdependence or integration).[1306]

491 Changes of factors relevant to the market structure thus *per definitionem* influence the operation of suppliers and demanders in the market.[1307] In markets characterised by the presence of a dominant undertaking, effects on the market structure which do not negatively affect the dominant undertaking's position always limit either residual or potential competition. The reason is that the mere existence of a dominant undertaking already implies an imbalance in the equilibrium of perfect competition.[1308] Unilateral conduct can influence the market structure directly, as, for example, when a market entry barrier in the form of a patent is established, or indirectly, for example, when products are tied or high prices charged.

c Changeability of Market Structure

492 Maintaining a dominant position in a given market over time is only possible if market entry and exit barriers are high.[1309] Another question regarding the analysis of unilateral behaviour thus concerns the timescale within which anticompetitive effects can occur and should be considered. Behavioural control, by definition, requires an *ex post* analysis. Yet, it is not apparent why the time of the analysis should define the relevant timescale within which effects are taken into consideration, particularly as the time of the assessment is coincidental. For reasons of legal certainty, dominant undertakings should already, from an *ex ante* perspective, be able to estimate at least the potential legal consequences of a behaviour. For the application of economic analysis on competition law, this leaves the problem of uncertainty with regard to specific outcomes when they have not yet shown at the time of the evaluation. The mere fact that effects on competition have not yet shown does not mean that they will not eventually do so.

493 This is mainly because disciplinary effects are not realised immediately.[1310] Just like efficiency gains, losses in efficiency caused by interference in the market structure can manifest themselves in the long run. Predatory prices, for example, which at first may just be observed positively as low prices, might in the end drive a competitor out

---

1306. Bain, 7 ff.; Kaysen/Turner, 71; Kerber/Schwalbe, in: Bornkamm et al., MüKo, Einleitung, Die ökonomischen Grundlagen des Wettbewerbsrechts, para. 79; Schmidt/Haucap, 72.
1307. Bain, 300; Carstensen, U.C. Davis Law Review 1983, 498.
1308. *See supra* at para. 46.
1309. That the threat of market entry (potential competition) can have a disciplinary effect on established players is the basis of the theory of contestable markets. With this theory, markets and thus established positions on the market are contestable when market entry and exit are possible at any time without losses (no sunk costs). Kerber/Schwalbe, in: Bornkamm et al., MüKo, Einleitung, Die ökonomischen Grundlagen des Wettbewerbsrechts, paras 95 ff.
1310. Of relevance for the effect of market entry barriers on competition is the (expected) reaction of established undertakings as well as the expected profits they can gain from establishing the barrier.

of the market or prevent a market entry in the long(er) run. After this change in the market structure, the undertaking charging predatory prices can raise prices above the market prices and negative effects will eventually occur.

494 The result of the assessment should therefore not depend on the moment in time when the evaluation takes place. To illustrate a Gedanken experiment: imagine two firms engaging in the same potentially abusive behaviour but judged at different times. One is judged when no effects can yet be seen, the other at a later stage when, for example, a competitor has been driven out of the market by predatory pricing. Of course, it is a theoretical scenario to imagine two different undertakings in the very same situation in the market with identical or equivalent relevant economic factors and having engaged in the same potentially unlawful behaviour. However, with the fundamental principles of equal treatment and the relative robustness of market structure in the short to medium term, these considerations must be raised.

495 If, theoretically, the same conduct in the same market situation was to be assessed, a difference in treatment depending on the timescale would result in an unfounded inequality in treatment of legal subjects. It is therefore not in the interests of effective law enforcement to deprive such conduct of competition law scrutiny from the outset because of 'bad timing'. A sole focus on the effects without considering the time factor is therefore not appropriate.

496 In competition law, discussions about the applicable time frame are mainly in the context of merger control. There the time frame within which market entries are likely is an important factor in the evaluation of a planned merger. The Commission in its horizontal merger guidelines provided assistance for the calculation of an appropriate time frame. Whether entry after the merger can indeed be expected is dependent on various factors such as 'the characteristics and dynamics of the market'[1311] and 'the specific capabilities of potential entrants'[1312].[1313] Generally, the Commission considered two years to be an appropriate time frame.[1314]

497 Analysis of the effects of mergers, unlike that of unilateral conduct in abuse control, is conducted under the assumption that a first structural change in the market, the merger of the two entities, has already taken place. Merger control is therefore limited to the question of consequential changes and effects. Abuse control starts with conduct whose effects on the market structure as well as its consequential changes and effects are (both) unclear. In order to meet the challenges of abuse control, it would therefore seem appropriate to apply at least a two-year assessment period where the unilateral conduct results in a direct change of market structure (e.g., the implementation of a market entry barrier)[1315] and an even longer period where the effects on

1311. EC, *Guidelines on the assessment of horizontal mergers*, para. 74.
1312. EC, *Guidelines on the assessment of horizontal mergers*, para. 74.
1313. An evaluation of the capability of entrants was made in: EC, *Metso/Svedala*, COMP/M.2033, paras 160 f.
1314. *See i.a.*: EC, *Alcoa/Reynolds*, COMP/M.1693, paras 31 f.; EC, *Guidelines on the assessment of horizontal mergers*, para. 74.
1315. *See supra* at fn. 1306.

market structure are as yet unclear because the conduct indirectly affects them (pricing strategies, conduct in a vertically integrated market). However, especially in innovation and technology markets, the relevant evaluation period when applying a merely effect-based test would have to be adjusted to the relevant innovation cycle, which is comparably long in the pharmaceutical industry,[1316] but much shorter in the case of electronic devices, for example.

498 Viewed against this background, the often criticised[1317] and seemingly inconsistent court practice becomes evident with respect to the question of whether the finding of abuse under Article 102 TFEU requires identifying anticompetitive effects. Unless anticompetitive effects have already been shown, one cannot avoid operating with estimations of such effects within the relevant time frame. Anticompetitive effects can therefore only be evaluated with respect to the likelihood of them appearing as a result of the particular behaviour. As the Court of Justice in *Post Danmark A/S v. Konkurrencerådet* held:

> In order to assess the existence of anti-competitive effects in circumstances such as those of that case, it is necessary to consider whether that pricing policy, without objective justification, produces an actual or likely exclusionary effect, to the detriment of competition and, thereby, of consumers' interests.[1318]

4.2 *Intent*

a The Problem with Identifying Intent

499 Intent is a 'subjective element that identifies the agent's state of mind'.[1319] When asking about intent, one asks about the underlying motivation or the actor's state of mind, before and during the conduct.[1320] While intent has always been an important factor in the assessment of agreements in competition law and is even a definitional element of the prohibited behaviour in Article 101 TFEU, its implications for cases of abusive unilateral conduct have been disputed in both EU competition[1321] and US antitrust law[1322].[1323]

1316. *See supra* at Part I, Chapter 5.
1317. Wernicke, EuZW 2015, 19-20 with further references.
1318. ECJ, *Post Danmark*, C-209/10, para. 44; similarly also: EC, *Guidance Paper*, paras 20, 39 and 85.
1319. Melícias, World Competition 2010, 570; Cass/Hylton, Southern Californian Law Review 2000, 657.
1320. On possible misunderstandings between economists and lawyers about the meaning of intent, *see*: Bavasso, European Competition Law Review 2005, 620.
1321. *See infra* at fn. 1337.
1322. *See*: 7th Cir., *A.A. Poultry Farms, Inc. v. Rose Acre Farms, Inc.*, 881 F.2d 1396, 1402; Fisher/MacGowan/Greenwood, 272; Hovenkamp, Ohio State Law Journal 2000, 1037 ff.
1323. Note that despite conceptual differences, section 2 Sherman Act and Article 102 TFEU both take a similar approach towards exclusionary conduct of dominant undertakings. Both legal systems allow dominant undertakings certain conduct, while other conduct is considered a breach of the competition law rules. Additionally, both systems are aimed at protecting consumers from the power of dominant undertakings. *See*, with respect to the consumer

500 In the USA, the courts have shown a rather ambivalent relationship with anticompetitive intent over the centuries.[1324] In 1985, the United States Supreme Court, like the Court of Justice in 1991,[1325] recognised that anticompetitive intent can be immanent in the conduct itself, when in *Aspen Skiing* it held that the conduct discussed suggested a dedication to achieving an anticompetitive end.[1326] In the same year, the Supreme Court confirmed its practice outlined in the *Aspen Skiing* case in another case, *Spectrum Sports*,[1327] where it declared that the finding of anticompetitive intent, no matter how contended and proven, does not, in the absence of a negative effect on consumers, represent a decisive factor to assume a violation of section 2 Sherman Act.[1328] Yet, in another case, similar to the practice in the EU, the Court of Appeals of the 6th Circuit (6th Cir.) heavily relied on evidence that displayed the intent of the dominant undertaking to exclude competitors.[1329]

501 The literature has tried to resolve this seemingly ambivalent approach of the US courts. The starting point was the finding that a reliance only on economic evidence may not be sufficient for competition law analysis, as in fact empirical data cannot reliably demonstrate market inefficiencies.[1330] With respect to patents and technology markets, where fostering innovation is equally important and protected by law, a reliance on strict static economic evidence may not allow a balanced decision to be reached that serves both aims.[1331] Thus, the focus shifted to the nature of the conduct, which is influenced by intent. Intent, however, as the United States Court of Appeals for the District of Columbia (D.C. Cir.) held, does not as such constitute an abuse of a dominant position.[1332] 'Evidence of the intent behind the conduct of a monopolist is relevant only to the extent that it helps us understand the likely effect of the monopolist's conduct.'[1333]

502 A similar discrepancy appears in EU law. In the EU, also, there has been criticism of including subjective factors in the analysis of an objective concept such as the abuse of dominance.[1334] The law provides protection from the conduct of dominant undertakings irrespective of the underlying motivation. The only factors relevant for the

welfare standard: Hovenkamp, Ohio State Law Journal 2000, 1043, as well as *supra* at paras 64 ff. It is thus possible to consider the US literature and case law on intent as well. However, conceptual differences have to be considered. An analogy is thus not per se indicated.

1324. Note that in the USA, depending on the claim, another intent standard is required.
1325. *See infra* at paras 504 ff.
1326. United States Supreme Court, *Aspen Skiing Co. v. Aspen Highland Skiing Corp.*, 472 US 585, 610 f.; confirmed in: United States Supreme Court, *Spectrum Sports, Inc. v. McQuillan*, 506 US 447, 459.
1327. *See supra* at fn. 1326.
1328. United States Supreme Court, *Brooke Group v. Brown & Williamson Tobacco Corp.*, 509 US 209, 230; Melícias, World Competition 2010, 574.
1329. *See*: 6th Cir., *Conwood Co., LP. v. US Tobacco Co.*, 290 F.3d 768, paras 43 and 53.
1330. Khan, Harvard Law Review 1953, 49 f.; Lao, American University Law Review 2004, 178; *see also supra* at paras 487 ff.
1331. Melícias, World Competition 2010, 578.
1332. D.C. Cir., *United States v. Microsoft*, 253 F.3d 34, para. 21; Turner, 25.
1333. D.C. Cir., *United States v. Microsoft*, 253 F.3d 34, para. 21.
1334. *See infra* at fn. 1337. Separate from this dispute is the role of intent with respect to the possibility of imposing sanctions and justification.

evaluation are those having an impact on competition.[1335] Additionally, the suitability of a subjective element to determine the abusive nature of behaviour has been questioned. Since competition is always aimed at outperforming rivals,[1336] any intent not going beyond the mere gain of market shares can, a priori, be ruled out as a factor contributing to the abusive character of conduct. Therefore, applying a broad understanding of anticompetitive intent is unsuitable for the evaluation of abusive conduct under Article 102 TFEU.[1337] A rash assumption of abuse on the basis of intent would risk cooling activities that should be protected and encouraged by the law because competitors are driven by the intent to outperform rivals.[1338] Furthermore, relying on intent raises legal questions not only from a substantive point of view but also with respect to more practical issues. Intent as a subjective element is hard to recognise and prove.[1339]

503 Despite criticism, intent has often been considered by the EU courts when analysing anticompetitive behaviour. The case law will be analysed in more detail below.[1340] A starting point for the analysis is the impression that the role of intent in cases of Article 102 TFEU seems to be lacking a consistent concept. Judging from the wording, evidence of anticompetitive intent is not required to establish an abuse of a dominant position,[1341] but in certain cases evidence of intent is an important, sometimes even constitutive,[1342] factor in assuming an abuse of dominance.[1343] In other cases, anticompetitive intent is even understood as being immanent in the behaviour itself.[1344]

1335. GC, *AstraZeneca v. Commission,* T-321/05, para. 356; ECJ, *Tomra and Others v. Commission,* C-549/10, paras 22 ff.
1336. In the US also, this issue was a source of concern: 7TH CIR., *A.A. Poultry Farms, Inc. v. Rose Acre Farms, Inc.,* 881 F.2d 1396, 1402; HOVENKAMP, Ohio State Law Journal 2000, 1039.
1337. EILMANSBERGER/BIEN, in: BORNKAMM ET AL., MüKo, Article 102, para. 507; HOVENKAMP, Ohio State Law Journal 2000, 1039; WURMNEST, 345; POSNER, 214; 7TH CIR., *A.A. Poultry Farms, Inc. v. Rose Acre Farms, Inc.,* 881 F.2d 1396, 1402.
1338. *See argumentation in*: UNITED STATES SUPREME COURT, *Verizon Communication Inc. v. Law Offices of Curtis V. Trinko, LLP,* 540 US 398, 414.
1339. On the difficulties of recognising intent: MELÍCIAS, World Competition 2010, 576 ff.; POSNER, 214; O'DONOGHUE/PADILLA, 309; on the recognition of intent in cases involving defensive trademarks in Switzerland, *see*: CHERPILLOD, sic! 2000, 360.
1340. *See infra* at paras 504 ff.
1341. Since the *Hoffman-La Roche* case, the Court of Justice referred to the abuse as objective concept. *See*, for example, FUCHS/MÖSCHEL, in: IMMENGA/MESTMÄCKER 2018, Article 102, para. 149, fn. 678 with further references; O'DONOGHUE/PADILLA, 279 ff.; *see also supra* at para. 453.
1342. Similarly: EILMANSBERGER, Common Market Law Review 2005, 136 and 138; JUNG, in: GRABITZ ET AL., EUV/AEUV, Article102, paras 126 f.; critical: WURMNEST, 344.
1343. *See infra* at fn. 1387; on the importance of direct intent evidence in practice: O'DONOGHUE/PADILLA, 307 ff.
1344. JUNG, in: GRABITZ ET AL., EUV/AEUV, Article 102, paras 126 f.; AG MENGOZZI, *in: Post Danmark,* C-209/10, paras 95 ff. Immanence of anticompetitive intent is often expressed through the finding that the conduct can have no other meaning but the restriction of competition.

b Case Law on the Role of Intent in EU Competition Law

504 In EU law, the significance of anticompetitive intent in connection with the abuse of a dominant position is mainly discussed in cases of predatory pricing.[1345] In its *AKZO* decision, the leading case on predatory pricing,[1346] the Court of Justice analysed the importance of anticompetitive intent dependent on the character of the conduct.[1347] In the analysis, a cost/price ratio allowed the distinguishing of two categories. Only in a second step did intent become relevant.[1348] The Court of Justice decided that in cases where prices are below the AVC[1349] the conduct is illegal in the absence of justification.[1350] The Court of Justice thus set the threshold[1351] to distinguish anticompetitive from competitive intent at the point where every item sold would generate a loss.[1352] The court concluded that such a strategy could have no other end but to eliminate competitors.[1353] Although the threshold was criticised,[1354] the *AKZO* decision made it clear that certain conduct cannot be motivated by any other ends but to drive competitors out of the market. This finding was later applied in the case of *Deutsche Post*. Even though internal documents did not reveal intentions targeted against the

---

1345. *See i.a.*: Pries, 120 ff.; as well as the case law cited hereinafter.
1346. Later this practice was confirmed in the *Tetra Pak II* judgment. *See infra* at fn. 1359.
1347. ECJ, *AKZO*, C-62/86, para. 72; AG Mengozzi, *in: Post Danmark*, C-209/10, para. 87; Posner had already named these two approaches as possible ways to tackle predatory pricing: Posner, 214.
1348. ECJ, *AKZO*, C-62/86, paras 70 ff.; the approach was confirmed in the case of *Tetra Pak II:* ECJ, *Tetra Pak II*, C-333/94 P, paras 41 ff.
1349. Note that in certain cases (e.g., seasonal products, products with expiration dates or to enter the market), it is rational to sell at a loss. A static evaluation of prices thus leads to an overinclusive application of Article 102 TFEU (risk of type I errors). The Commission in its Guidelines suggested using the average avoidable costs (AAC) as the benchmark. The AAC is preferable as it allows including a dynamic perspective. The AAC are understood as the 'the average of the costs that could have been avoided if the company had not produced a discrete amount of (extra) output'. EC, *Guidance Paper*, paras 26 and 64; ECJ, *Post Danmark*, C-209/10, para. 44; Whish/Bailey, 734.
1350. ECJ, *AKZO*, C-62/86, para. 72.; yet, the holding of the court does not go as far as to assume an abuse per se as was indicated with the argumentation in the *Tetra Pak II* case: ECJ, *Tetra Pak II*, C-333/94 P, para. 41; ECJ, *France Télécom*, C-202/07 P, para. 109.
1351. A similar test was introduced by Areeda/Turner, therefore also called the *Areeda/Turner test*, to assess the abusive character of pricing strategies under US law. Areeda/Turner, however, based their test exclusively on an analysis of costs and prices, *see*: Areeda/Turner, Harvard Law Review 1975, 697 ff.; on the differences between the *Areeda/Turner test* and the judgment in AKZO, *see*: Østerud, 133 ff.
1352. Posner tried to address this by proposing to understand predatory pricing as pricing below long-run marginal costs. Posner, 215. Similarly, the ECJ in *Post Danmark* evaluated the price level with respect to the question of whether a competitor as efficient as the dominant undertaking would be capable of competing with the prices: ECJ, *Post Danmark*, C-209/10, paras 35 ff.; EC, *Guidance Paper*, para. 64.
1353. ECJ, *AKZO*, C-62/86, paras 70 ff.; *see also*: Posner, 215. In rebate systems, an abusive character is assumed when the rebates are based on a countervailing advantage.
1354. The standard of the AVC is not appropriate for all industries. An example where the AVC fails to provide a useful characteristic is the telephone sector, where initial costs (infrastructure) are high, but actual production costs (phone calls) are not, *see*: Whish/Bailey, 762 f.; EC, *Deutsche Post AG*, COMP/35.141, para. 35.

competition, the pricing strategy did not make any sense, considering the circumstances, if it was not for hampering competitors.[1355]

505 Intent in cases where the conduct lacks any economic rationale is thus not explicitly mandated but implicitly assumed by the court as immanent in the conduct itself (objective intent).[1356] A similar objective approach is taken in cases of Article 101(1) TFEU. Evidence of actual effects on the market is not required to categorise the agreement as a violation of Article 101 TFEU if the nature of the agreement is such as to have a high potential of distorting competition.[1357] Also, where the potential for distorting competition is not immanent in the conduct itself, objective criteria are used to evaluate the subjective element. For the assumption of an anticompetitive practice, it is sufficient that the negative impacts of a concerted practice are expected and that the undertaking is nevertheless willing to engage in the conduct.[1358]

506 In cases where prices were between the AVC but below the ATC, the court only understood the conduct as abusive if the low prices were 'part of a plan for eliminating competitors',[1359] that is, if the company was acting with the intention of driving competitors out of the market.[1360] Evidence for such an anticompetitive intention can be provided directly as well as indirectly. Direct evidence includes internal documents containing threats against competitors. Indirect evidence is seen in circumstantial evidence such as the dedication towards implementing the strategy as well as the duration of the low pricing strategy.[1361] This approach was taken in the *Tetra Pak II* case.[1362] After applying the cost/price ratio to identify the category of the conduct, direct evidence of intent as well as circumstantial evidence played a role in substantiating the existence of a plan to exclude competitors.[1363]

1355. EC, *Deutsche Post AG*, COMP/35.141, paras 36 ff.
1356. Eilmansberger/Bien, in: Bornkamm et al., MüKo, Article 102, paras 509 ff.; Jung, in: Grabitz et al., EUV/AEUV, Article 102, para. 224; Melícias, World Competition 2010, 571; ECJ, *AKZO*, C-62/86, paras 64 and 79; GC, *Compagnie maritime belge transports and Others v. Commission*, T-24/93, para. 147; AG Mengozzi, *in: Post Danmark*, C-209/10, para. 87; critical: Wurmnest, 345.
1357. Schroeder et al., in: Grabitz et al., EUV/AEUV, Article 101, paras 142 ff.; in Switzerland, the Federal Supreme Court recently applied the same reasoning as regards agreements fulfilling legal presumptions set out in Article 5(3) and (4) KG: BGE 143 II 297, para. 5.2.5; for an in-depth analysis of Article 5(3) and (4) KG *see*, for example, Hager/Murer, recht: Zeitschrift für juristische Weiterbildung und Praxis 2015.
1358. Schroeder et al., in: Grabitz et al., EUV/AEUV, Article 101, para. 142.
1359. ECJ, *AKZO*, C-62/86, para. 72; ECJ, *Tetra Pak II*, C-333/94 P, para. 41; for detailed argumentation on signs of intent: GC, *Tetra Pak II*, T-83/91, para. 151.
1360. Note that abusive conduct can also be targeted at preventing market entrance, irrespective of whether the behaviour is targeted against actual or future competitors. *See*: Pries, 126; Schuhmacher, ZWeR 2007, 366.
1361. ECJ, *AKZO*, C-62/86, paras 146 ff.
1362. The combination of direct intent and circumstantial evidence was also confirmed in the case of *Wanadoo (France Télécom)*. There the authorities could refer to actual anticompetitive effects that were noticeable on the market: For a summary of the argumentation, *see*: Pries, 126 ff.
1363. GC, *Tetra Pak II*, T-83/91, paras 120 ff., 190 and 212.

507 In the case of *Compagnie Maritime*, intent also had importance in the assessment of the behaviour. The revelation of a plan to deter competition was decisive for the conclusion on the anticompetitiveness of the conduct.[1364] This conclusion was reached despite the fact that the conduct assessed did not result in the elimination of competitors as was intended.[1365]

508 Besides predominance in predatory pricing cases, intent has also played a role in the assessment of other conduct under Article 102 TFEU. In the case of *ITT Promedia,* the General Court had to evaluate a case of potentially abusive litigation. The court considered that access to courts is a fundamental right protected by Articles 6 and 13 of the ECHR (European Convention of Human Rights) and a general principle of EU law. Therefore, an abuse of a dominant position through calling upon courts, or exercising a fundamental right, can only be abusive in most exceptional cases. The rules of competition cannot render such a fundamental principle invalid.[1366] The Commission implemented a test consisting of two cumulative criteria. To be abusive conduct, first, 'it cannot reasonably be considered as an attempt to establish the rights of the undertaking concerned and can therefore only serve to harass the opposite party' and second, 'it is conceived in the framework of a plan whose goal is to eliminate competition'.[1367] This means that even in cases where taking proceedings can have no other outcome but the harassment of competitors, the conduct is only abusive if it is also part of a broader plan. In theory, the court established a double intent standard for cases where the exercise of a statutory right is at question. In practice, however, at least in cases of potentially abusive litigation where expenses are required, actions taken only to harass the opposite party are presumptively at the same time also part of a plan to at least hamper competition through the opposite party.

509 With respect to the acquisition and execution of intellectual property rights, which as property rights also enjoy protection as fundamental rights, there is evidence that intent plays an important role in categorising the conduct as abusive.[1368] A possible scenario is the execution of an intellectual property right that leads to the market exit of competitors or imposes an even higher barrier to entry than the intellectual property right already does. Among the first and most famous cases where such conduct was under scrutiny is the case of *Magill* which concerned a refusal to license.[1369] The court

1364. ECJ, *Compagnie Maritime,* Joined Cases C-395/96 P and C-396/96 P, paras 74 ff.; *see also i.a.*: EC, *ECS v. AKZO,* IV/30.698, para. 81; EC, *AstraZeneca,* COMP/A.37.507/F3, paras 632 ff., 648 and 789.
1365. ECJ, *Compagnie Maritime,* Joined Cases C-395/96 P and C-396/96 P, paras 97 and 119 f.; *see also*: EC, *Wanadoo Interactive,* COMP/38.233, paras 110 ff.; GC, *AstraZeneca v. Commission,* T-321/05, paras 360 ff.
1366. GC, *ITT Promedia v. Commission,* T-111/96, para. 61.
1367. GC, *ITT Promedia v. Commission,* T-111/96, paras 30 and 55; similarly, in the US on sham litigation: United States Supreme Court, *Professional Real Estate v. Columbia Pictures,* 508 US 49, 60 f.
1368. The same conclusion has been drawn by Dolmans: Dolmans, Antitrust Law Journal 1998, 467.
1369. Previously, in the cases of *Volvo v. Veng* and *CICRA/Renault,* an abuse of a dominant position was denied with reference to the specific subject matter doctrine. ECJ, *Volvo v. Veng,* C-238/87, paras 8 ff.; ECJ, *CICRA v. Renault,* C-53/87, para. 16.

concluded that the execution of the intellectual property right was aimed at securing a monopoly and therefore reaching a goal going beyond the aim of both intellectual property and competition law.[1370] The judgment was only based on the circumstances of the case. Evidence of intent was not found. In the literature, this led to the comment by JUNG that refusals to license are wilful acts within which the exclusionary potential manifests itself.[1371]

c The Role of Intent in EU Competition Law: A Comment Based on Case Law

510 EU case law does not imply that the presence of anticompetitive intent per se renders conduct abusive. Likewise, neither the wording of Article 102 nor its purpose suggests that proof of intent qualifies conduct as abusive.[1372] It is thus impermissible to equate the presence of anticompetitive intent with the emergence of anticompetitive effects.[1373] Anticompetitive effects are not the result of intents but actions put into practice with or without the mere intention to cause anticompetitive effects. However, anticompetitive intent can influence the likelihood of an anticompetitive effect.[1374]

511 This was acknowledged by the Commission when it held that, as a result of the presence of anticompetitive intent, otherwise permissible conduct could be rendered abusive.[1375] The courts have followed the Commission with this assumption. An example is the position of the General Court in its *AstraZeneca* decision. According to the court, conduct put into practice when motivated by anticompetitive means is likely to be a threat to undistorted competition.[1376] This conclusion has a certain rationale. Indeed, there is a higher likelihood that conduct which is part of a strategy will be pursued with greater effort and more determination compared with conduct which is not part of such a strategy.[1377] Therefore, it seems understandable that a plan to distort competition, if put into practice, also has the capability to distort competition and can, as the case of *Compagnie Maritime* shows, qualify as an abuse overall, even if no anticompetitive effects have shown. Yet, the mere plan to distort competition taken for itself would not be enough to find an abuse.[1378]

1370. GC, *Magill*, T-76/89, paras 58 ff.; as well as in: GC, *BBC v. Commission*, T-70/89, paras 58 ff.
1371. JUNG, in: GRABITZ ET AL., EUV/AEUV, Article 102, para. 226.
1372. Critical: ØSTERUD, 129; LAO, American University Law Review 2004, 157.
1373. AG COLOMER, in: *Sot Lelos v. GlaxoSmithKline*, Joined Cases C-468/06-478/06, para. 76; critical: LAO, American University Law Review 2004, 157.
1374. Similarly: ØSTERUD, 129; *see also*: GC, *Michelin II*, T-203/01, paras 239 ff.; ECJ, *Tomra and Others v. Commission*, C-549/10, para. 20.
1375. EC, *AstraZeneca*, COMP/A.37.507/F3, para. 327 with further references; *see also*: ØSTERUD, 156.
1376. GC, *AstraZeneca v. Commission*, T-321/05, para. 359; EC, *AstraZeneca*, COMP/A.37.507/F3, para. 327; GC, *Michelin II*, T-203/01, para. 241.
1377. GC, *Michelin II*, T-203/01, para. 241.
1378. SCHRÖTER/BARTL, in: VON DER GROEBEN ET AL., Kommentar EU-Recht, Article 102, para. 164.

512 In most cases, it is difficult to distinguish anticompetitive from competitive intent.[1379] Engaging in competition always comes with the intention to outcompete others. This must be mitigated by a less subjective understanding of intent since punishing the mere intention to outperform cannot be the goal of competition law. Such a rule would rather hamper economic activities and therefore competition.[1380] ØSTERUD thus suggests assuming anticompetitive intent only in cases where conduct, judging from objective criteria, would be irrational if it was not for the exclusion of competitors or market foreclosure.[1381]

513 The pervasive analysis model in case law involves a combination of direct with circumstantial evidence to prove the existence of an anticompetitive intent (overall strategy).[1382] When asking about anticompetitive intent, the authorities ask about the possibility that any rationale other than foreclosure motivates the conduct.[1383] A dominant firm's behaviour is unlawfully 'exclusionary' or 'predatory' if the conduct would not make economic sense but for its elimination or softening of the competition. With this definition intent becomes objectifiable.[1384] Such an objective perspective on intent is also important in cases where direct evidence of anticompetitive intent is available.[1385] In practice, internal documents showing anticompetitive intent function like other objective factors, but are highly conclusive for the existence of a plan.[1386] Consequently, otherwise permissible conduct can be rendered abusive as a result of the presence of documents proving anticompetitive intent culminating in a plan directed against actual or future market participants.[1387] However, direct evidence of intent should only be considered if the prospect of distorting competition is the decisive motivation for engaging in a practice.[1388] A greater significance of anticompetitive intent would bear the risk of burdening authorities disproportionately.[1389]

1379. *See comments by*: BAVASSO, European Competition Law Review 2005, 620; HOVENKAMP, Ohio State Law Journal 2000, 1039.
1380. O'DONOGHUE/PADILLA, 307 ff.; ØSTERUD, 149; 7TH CIR., *A.A. Poultry Farms, Inc. v. Rose Acre Farms, Inc.*, 881 F.2d 1396, 1402.
1381. ØSTERUD, 156 f. This test which has been named the 'objective justification test' was also applied by the Commission in its decision in *GVG v. FS*: EC, *GVG/FS*, COMP/37.685, para. 145.
1382. *See supra* at paras 337 ff. and 365 ff.
1383. ØSTERUD, 143 ff.; in the US, this argument culminated in the so-called no economic sense test, *see*: WERDEN, Antitrust Law Journal 2006, 413 ff.
1384. *See similarly in*: ECJ, *AKZO*, C-62/86, para. 71; ECJ, *France Télécom*, C-202/07 P, para. 107; on the importance of finding objective standards for identifying plans to block competitors: ZECH, ZWeR 2011, 328; on problems with subjective versus objective standards: CASS/HYLTON, Southern Californian Law Review 2000, 697 ff.
1385. ECJ, *France Télécom*, C-202/07 P, paras 107 ff.; O'DONOGHUE/PADILLA, 309; similarly in US practice, *see*: CASS/HYLTON, Southern Californian Law Review 2000, 715 ff.
1386. ECJ, *France Télécom*, C-202/07 P, paras 97 ff.; GC, *BPB Industries*, T-65/89, para. 69; EC, *Guidance Paper*, para. 20.
1387. EC, *AstraZeneca*, COMP/A.37.507/F3, para. 327.
1388. Similarly: O'DONOGHUE/PADILLA, 309, fn. 66; even more restrictive: ØSTERUD, 146.
1389. BAVASSO, European Competition Law Review 2005, 618; EILMANSBERGER, Common Market Law Review 2005, 171; *7TH CIR., A.A. Poultry Farms, Inc. v. Rose Acre Farms, Inc., 881 F.2d 1396, 1402.*

514 Let us consider an imaginary scenario in which a company decided to apply for a patent rather than keeping its invention a trade secret. The critical factor, as displayed in the internal documentation revealed in the examination, was the consideration that the patent would not only allow for the commercial exploitation of the technology through launching the product on the market but also in all probability would hinder a competitor who wanted to launch a similar product using a partially identical technology. While the obvious intention to hinder the competitor from entering the market would, following a wide definition of anticompetitive intent including 'the intent to compete vigorously',[1390] be a decisive criterion for the assessment of the conduct, the fact that the exclusionary intent was only a concomitant to the main purpose, which is the successful exploitation of a company's intangible asset, would not in itself contribute to the abusive character of the conduct.[1391] To classify behaviour as abusive solely based on the presence of a direct anticompetitive intent would fall too short.[1392]

515 Case law suggests that in the EU an equally narrow concept of anticompetitive intent dominates. To establish direct intent, the authorities request proof that the conduct is 'part of a plan to eliminate competitors'.[1393] Within the 'plan' this conduct should mainly serve a specific aim. With respect to cases where direct evidence is missing, the authorities apply the standard that distorting competition is the only rational explanation to engage in the conduct.

516 This so-called no economic sense test as presented by ØSTERUD is preferable to the 'sacrifice test', which appears to be the test advocated and applied by the DOJ in recent cases. The basis for the 'sacrifice test' is the assumption that exclusionary conduct normally involves the sacrifice of short-term profits or goodwill in order to maintain or obtain long-term monopoly power. As BAVASSO rightly points out, accepting short-term losses is not suitable as a standard for assuming anticompetitive effects. This is because anticompetitive behaviour does not always include the necessity to sacrifice short-term profits,[1394] and also because sacrificing short-term profits can be economically justified.

517 The case law on the role of intent with respect to Article 102 TFEU allows the conclusion that the influence of anticompetitive intent is dependent on the nature of the conduct.[1395] Where direct evidence of intent is missing, the question has to be asked whether the circumstances allow ascribing the conduct any motivation to compete legitimately. If not, the presence of an anticompetitive intent, irrespective of

1390. UNITED STATES SUPREME COURT, *Spectrum Sports, Inc. v. McQuillan*, 506 US 447, 458 f.
1391. Note that following the EU case law, the proof of anticompetitive intent and the lack of objective justification for the conduct directly leads to the assumption of an abusive character. *See the analysis in*: ØSTERUD, 151 ff.
1392. EILMANSBERGER, Common Market Law Review 2005, 147.
1393. ECJ, *AKZO*, C-62/86, para. 72.
1394. BAVASSO, European Competition Law Review 2005, 620.
1395. EILMANSBERGER/BIEN, in: BORNKAMM ET AL., MüKo, Article 102, para. 508.

direct evidence, has to be assumed. In cases where conduct can have other underlying motivations, achieving an anticompetitive effect has to be the main goal.[1396]

518 With intent, the courts have therefore applied a similar approach as with anticompetitive effects. In most cases, the authorities did not provide evidence for actual effects on competition.[1397] In cases where, judging from objective circumstances, the conduct is not in any respect based on legitimate interests and thus implicitly only motivated by anticompetitive intent, the courts and the Commission have held that it is sufficient to conclude on the basis 'of the economic or regulatory context' that the conduct is capable of restricting competition.[1398] The courts have also declared that it is not necessary to prove actual effects on competition in cases where the emergence of anticompetitive effects is dependent on the reactions of third parties.[1399] This leads to the conclusion that in cases where the dominant undertaking has executed a plan objectively liable to distort competition, a violation of competition law cannot be established independently of the reaction of third parties. Another conclusion would allow dominant undertakings to avoid sanctions depending on the conduct of third parties. Such a regulation, however, would not meet the character of Article 102 TFEU as an absolute offence.[1400]

5 Results

519 Legal analysis cannot rely on general robust economic models which would allow an accurate case-by-case analysis but must serve the regulatory goal of providing the environment for competition to unfold most effectively by juggling with approximations and applying them on a case-by-case basis.[1401] The above insights therefore suggest that effective competition law enforcement which seeks to combine single case justice, practicability and predictability would be inconceivable without creating case groups. The results of available empirical studies allow for the creation of such groups and tailored analysis patterns.[1402] The finding of abuse is ultimately nothing more than a comparison of the estimated market results when the conduct in question occurs in one scenario but not in another ('what-if-analysis').[1403]

520 Thereby, it must be considered that the mere definition of case groups as with legal presumptions in the case of Article 101 TFEU or abstract strict liability torts in

1396. *See similarly*: Perinetto, European Competition Journal 2019, 161.
1397. Differently in the *Wanadoo* case: *see supra* at fn. 1362.
1398. GC, *AstraZeneca v. Commission*, T-321/05, para. 376; *see also*: Perinetto, European Competition Journal 2019, 171 f.
1399. GC, *AstraZeneca v. Commission*, T-321/05, para. 377; *see also*: Kadar, Journal of European Competition Law & Practice 2019, 443 ff.
1400. In this respect, *see*: Emmerich/Lange, § 10, para. 5; Fuchs/Möschel, in: Immenga/Mestmäcker 2018, Article 102, para. 144; ECJ, *Tetra Pak II*, C-333/94 P, para. 44.
1401. *See supra* at paras 385 ff.
1402. *See similarly*: EC, *Oracle/Peoplesoft*, COMP/M.3216, paras 193 f.
1403. GC, *O2 v. Commission*, T-328/03, paras 71 and 73; Röller/Friederiszick, in: Baudenbacher C., Neueste Entwicklungen im europäischen und internationalen Kartellrecht, 7.

criminal law does not ensure single case justice. An unlimited application of presumptions would therefore contradict the aim of Article 102 TFEU. In order to foster the functioning of the process of competition, excessive regulatory inventions have to be avoided. The path adopted by the Court of Justice in the *Intel* case therefore meets these concerns and criteria when it predicates the finding of an abuse on a form-based approach with the potential to prove the absence of or justify distorting effects. Contrary to what the wording of the *Intel* case suggests, the absence or presence of distorting effects should be proved by the authorities and not the undertakings under scrutiny. In this respect it should be borne in mind that negative effects cannot be proved when they have not yet occurred. Therefore, in competition law cases, a reduced standard of proof has to be accepted in as much as the whole body of evidence presented must not leave any doubts that distorting effects will occur. The General Court in its *AstraZeneca* decision held that 'the ability of the practice in question [which is beyond competition on the merits] to restrict competition may be indirect, provided that it is shown to the requisite legal standard that it is actually liable to restrict competition'.[1404]

521 Case law on the role of intent in Article 102 TFEU cases is by no means comprehensive. As in the history of US case law, the courts of the EU also showed a somewhat incomprehensive handling of the intent factor. As an objective concept, the finding of an abuse does not require the finding of anticompetitive intent. Yet, anticompetitive intent is an important factor in assessing behaviour. In cases where anticompetitive intent has not (yet) manifested itself, anticompetitive intent is sometimes established based on objective criteria. As has been seen with regard to anticompetitive effects, a reliance on merely economic evidence may not be sufficient from the perspective of the undertakings which should be able to assess potential violations of competition law beforehand as well as from a policy perspective, as empirical data cannot in all cases reliably demonstrate anticompetitive effects. Consequently, decisions are found by extrapolation from the nature of the conduct to its effect on competition. Likewise, intent is assumed if the conduct lacks any rational if it was not for distorting competition.

522 The finding of an abuse of a dominant position does not happen without difficult legal assessments including value judgments. Yet, the method is preferable to strict effect-based standards, as it means that sanctioning is not dependent on the reactions of third parties and allows for a more foreseeable application of competition law. However, the conclusion drawn by JUNG with regard to the refusal to license that, as a wilful act, exclusionary potential is manifested within the refusal itself[1405] cannot be fully supported and goes too far. Generally speaking, all conduct is the expression of a certain will. The expression of a will cannot be enough to assume a specific intent. Additionally, most conduct which has been qualified as abusive could, in other constellations, be perfectly pro-competitive. Therefore, the role of intent cannot be

1404. GC, *AstraZeneca v. Commission*, T-321/05, para. 376.
1405. JUNG, in: GRABITZ ET AL., EUV/AEUV, Article 102, para. 226.

understood in this broad sense but should rather be considered when distorting competition is the only rational explanation to engage in the conduct. As has been pointed out above, 'neither the suitability of conduct to distort competition, nor the intent to distort competition would, taken separately, be enough to find an abuse. The finding of an abuse requires the presence of both'.[1406]

523 For cases where the conduct of the dominant undertaking consists of exercising a given fundamental right, as, for example, the right to seek legal protection in court proceedings, the courts have established two cumulative criteria. The first is that the exercise cannot reasonably be justified as an attempt to establish the right and is therefore a means to harass the opposite party and, second, that the right is exercised as part of a plan to eliminate the competition.

V CONCLUSION

524 The historical, textual and structural interpretation of Article 102 TFEU does not reveal specific guidance, although some indications are revealed. Article 102 TFEU was not drafted as a directly applicable provision, but marked a compromise between the members of the Union. Its aim was to contribute to undistorted competition on the internal market by sanctioning behaviour deviating from standard behavioural norms with a bad purpose or to a bad effect. A bad purpose can be seen in the limiting of a competitor's room to compete (exclusionary abuse) or in the use of economic dependency in an abusive manner (exploitative abuse). Further guidance has to be gained by conducting a teleological interpretation.

525 The analysis of case law has shown that the courts have approached abuse as defined in the *Hoffman-La Roche* case by building case groups which show a certain pattern. The Court of Justice has mainly adopted two-staged tests consisting of a 'hard fact' and a circumstantial analysis. The following table lists the 'hard fact' in the first and the circumstantial analysis in the second row for each type of conduct:

Refusal to Supply	*Fidelity Rebates*	*Unfair Pricing*	*Predatory Pricing*	*Tying/Bundling*	*Margin Squeeze*
product is indispensable	fidelity rebate	dissimilar conditions for equivalent transactions	price below ATC but above AVC	customers have no choice but to buy both products	price difference insufficient to cover costs

1406. *See supra* at para. 511.

Refusal to Supply	*Fidelity Rebates*	*Unfair Pricing*	*Predatory Pricing*	*Tying/Bundling*	*Margin Squeeze*
prevention is likely to eliminate effective competition	capacity to foreclose competition	tendency to distort competition	plan to eliminate competition	foreclosure of competition	establishing anticompetitive effects (potential exclusion of an efficient competitor)

526 The circumstantial analysis requires a comprehensive look at different factors, but, judging from the case law, it has remained unclear whether anticompetitive effects in fact have to be proved and how anticompetitive intent fits within the analysis. On the importance of showing anticompetitive effects, it has been concluded that anticompetitive effects do not show immediately and therefore one has to operate with estimations when they have not yet shown. Similarly, evidence of anticompetitive intent should be used as circumstantial evidence. However, the presence of anticompetitive intent is a strong factor that suggests conduct likely to be distorting the competition.

527 What still remains unclear is the answer to the question of when conduct which has not yet been identified as potentially abusive by the court, namely conduct for which no case group has yet been created, amounts to an abuse of a dominant position. Legal practice and scholars have used the concept of competition on the merits. However, this concept does not offer much guidance, as has been seen. The historical analysis has shown that the drafters of the first provision prohibiting the abuse of a dominant position understood the abuse as a general principle or guideline. Abuse as a general principle is known from the abuse of rights principle. Therefore the hypothesis follows that the abuse of dominance is borrowed from the abuse of rights principle and implicitly prohibits the abuse of the freedom to compete. Chapter 15 will focus on this hypothesis.

CHAPTER 15

Abuse of a Dominant Position as a Manifestation of the Abuse of Rights?

I OVERVIEW OF THE CHAPTER

528 The approach of finding an answer to what makes up the substance of *abuse* in Article 102 TFEU within the general principle of the abuse of rights has two aspects. The results of the study of Article 102 TFEU conducted above show many conceptual similarities of the abuse of a dominant position compared with the abuse of rights principle. Therefore section II will first provide an overview of the results of the analysis conducted in the previous chapter.[1407] Second, it will be shown that both the abuse of a dominant position and the abuse of rights seek to limit power.

529 Section III focuses on the development and relevance of the abuse of rights principle within the EU. After a quick look at the origins of the abuse of rights principle in Europe and a more in-depth outline of the abuse of rights principle in French and German law, the book moves on to the establishment of the abuse of rights principle as a fundamental legal principle on an EU level.

530 In section IV, the insights gained in the previous chapters to provide an answer to the substance of *abuse* in Article 102 TFEU will be combined. This chapter closes with section V, which provides an interim conclusion on the meaning of abuse in Article 102 TFEU and the relevance of the findings for the course of the book.

1407. *See supra* at Part V, Chapter 14.

II SIMILARITIES BETWEEN THE ABUSE OF RIGHTS AND THE ABUSE OF A DOMINANT POSITION

1 Recapitulation of the Analysis

1.1 Historical Perspective

531 Historically, in adopting Article 86 of the TEEC, the founders did not want to create a directly enforceable prohibition, but rather included general principles within the treaty to create a common conceptual foundation. As a newly founded union originating from different cultural and legal heritages, the founders could not automatically draw on common legal standards. The idea of including the abuse of a dominant position was therefore born from a commonly agreed upon necessity of establishing limits to the use of private power in order to achieve the goals of the Union.[1408]

1.2 Textual Analysis

532 The use of the term 'abuse' within the EU in contexts ranging from economic law (tax abuse, market abuse) to substance abuse indicates a general nature rather than a specific misconduct. The above analysis of the legal text of Article 102 TFEU in English, German and French enabled the working out of a common denominator understanding of the term 'abuse' in the relevant legal and everyday language.

533 In English, the word 'abuse' stands for the use of something in a manner deviating from established standards of conduct to a bad effect or with a bad purpose.[1409] The German *Missbrauch* sanctions the breach of a behavioural norm for one's own benefit.[1410] The French *d'exploiter de façon abusive* also expresses the breach of a rule for personal advantage.[1411] Bringing these understandings together, the term 'abuse' in Article 102 TFEU is used to describe the use of something differently from defined or immanent standards to a bad effect or with a bad purpose.[1412] Therefore there is not only a linguistic similarity between the abuse of a dominant position and the general abuse of rights.[1413]

1408. *See supra* at paras 405 ff.
1409. *See supra* at para. 416.
1410. *See supra* at para. 418.
1411. *See supra* at para. 419.
1412. *See supra* at para. 410.
1413. *See also*: FISCHER, who understands the term 'abuse' as legal concept in both the abuse of rights and the abuse of a dominant position. FISCHER, ZGR 1978, 248.

1.3 *The Role and Structure of Article 102 TFEU*

534 A closer look at the structure and microstructure of Article 102 TFEU reveals the provision's dedication to establishing undistorted competition in the internal market. Article 102 TFEU serves this aim by disciplining dominant firms. In the absence of disciplining effects from competitors, dominant firms do not face constraints and are not prevented 'by external factors' from breaking defined or immanent standards to a bad effect or with a bad purpose.[1414]

1.4 *The Courts' Understanding of Abuse in Article 102 TFEU*

535 The case law on the abuse of a dominant position has revealed that abuses are established where the freedom of competitors is curtailed. Article 102 TFEU is understood as contributing to the freedom of competition and is applied by the courts to serve this end. Article 102 TFEU is therefore dedicated to preventing dominant undertakings from further weakening competition through either curtailing actual or potential competitors' economic freedom, or by weakening the remaining sources of disciplining effects for the dominant undertaking itself.[1415]

1.5 *Results of the Interpretation*

536 With Article 102 TFEU, we therefore have a provision which:

- at first was nothing but a codification of general principles;
- is of a general nature and sanctions conduct that deviates from immanent behavioural standards with a bad effect or purpose;[1416]
- is dedicated to implementing obstacles for undertakings which are potentially endangering undistorted competition but which do not face discipling external effects from competition on the market; and
- sanctions *abuse* as the central behaviour under scrutiny. Conduct is abusive when the dominant undertaking either weakens sources of disciplining effects or curtails competitors' freedom to compete[1417].

1414. *See supra* at paras 428 ff.
1415. In this category, for example, is the breach of law which has been identified as being potentially abusive under early German competition law. *See supra* at para. 474.
1416. Guski, 585 ff. According to Gerber, however, the term 'abuse' was not implemented to describe a specific behaviour, but rather 'used to code particular kinds of harmful effects'. Gerber, 174.
1417. Curtailing freedom to compete in this broad definition also includes the implementation of unfair trading conditions (exploitation). The competitor is limited in its ability to negotiate these conditions.

537 Conceptually, Article 102 TFEU therefore curtails the right of a dominant undertaking to compete unrestrictedly where this freedom has results contradicting the aim of the law.[1418] Similarly, the abuse of rights, as a closer look at its origins will reveal,[1419] also restricts the use of a right or privilege when the conduct results in unwanted effects.[1420] With respect to the limitation of the right of the state to prevent tyranny, LASOK drew the following conclusion: 'The concept of abuse of right (or power) is ultimately concerned with the exercise of a right (or power) either for ends different from the legal purpose served by the right (or power) or in an excessive or disproportionate way.'[1421]

2 Limiting 'Power' to Prevent Failure

538 The provision of the abuse of a dominant position is based on the fundamental understanding originating from ordoliberalism that entrepreneurial freedom has to be limited when market players use their freedom to implement restrictions on competition which ultimately lead to an inefficient allocation of resources.[1422] From a policy perspective, the provision is the result of a balance of interests[1423] between the importance of strong undertakings for competition and their power to significantly hamper it. The abuse as an offence is based on the understanding that rights are dedicated to an individual for a specific purpose and are therefore limited.[1424] This limitation must be implemented by the law, as holders of the rights do not face other constraints.[1425] The abuse of rights, according to ZENKER, limits the scope for 'all rights, legal situations, legal institutions and legal norms'[1426].

539 RAISER, with respect to the principle of the abuse of rights, held that 'in a legal community based on the principles of freedom and self-determination of its members it is not sufficient to simply determine the boundaries of these principles with prohibitions. The boundaries of the freedom and self-determination of the members are rather immanent in the legal community itself'.[1427] This is expressed through the principle of the abuse of rights, since 'those who abuse a right given by the legal community to enjoy on the basis of self-determination act illegally and shall lose the protection of the law'.[1428]

1418. GUSKI, 585.
1419. *See infra* at Part V, Chapter 15, section III.
1420. In this regard *see also*: BAUR, 102 f.
1421. LASOK, 8 f.; similarly: AG TESAURO, *in: Kefalas a.o.*, C-367/96, para. 24.
1422. *See supra* at paras 53 f.
1423. This balance of interests is not specific to competition law, but general. Remember the justification of the patent right in particular and intellectual property rights in general, for other examples of these considerations. *See supra* at paras 90 ff.
1424. *See*: BAUDENBACHER, 26.
1425. On the rationale to sanction the abuse of a dominant position, *see supra* at Part I, Chapter 4, section I.1.
1426. ZENKER, 19 (German original, translated by the author).
1427. RAISER, JZ 1972, 732 (German original, translated by the author); similarly: GUSKI, 585.
1428. RAISER, JZ 1972, 732 (German original, translated by the author).

540 Similarly, the prohibition of the abuse of a dominant position is bound to limit business activities of dominant undertakings where their activities amount to constraints of competition. Factually, the abuse of a dominant position therefore restricts the dominant undertaking's freedom to compete, where the actions lead to unjust results. Yet, other than the abuse of rights, the abuse of a dominant position does not result in the loss of the protection by law, but rather the implication of boundaries through law. Additionally, the abuse of a dominant position and the abuse of rights differ in that the abuse of a dominant position does not concern the use of a legally granted right, but the extensive use of competitive freedom, or, in other words, of the privilege of being able to move independently on the market.[1429]

541 Despite the differences in the concept, based on the abovesaid, the question of whether the abuse of a dominant position has its conceptual foundations within the general principle of the abuse of rights can be raised.[1430] The following sections will examine this issue.

III ABUSE OF RIGHTS IN EU LAW

1 Origins of the General Principle of the Abuse of Rights

542 The principle of the abuse of rights is a general concept known in many jurisdictions.[1431] It evolved from principles of Roman law tradition. The most important foundations are the defences of the *exceptio doli*[1432] and the *aemulatio* (chicanery). Furthermore, the later developed *aequitas* (equity[1433]) also contributed to the abuse of rights principle as it is understood nowadays.

543 The *exceptio doli* used to be the most important defence in Roman law. It permitted the defendant to assert fraudulent behaviour of the plaintiff at the moment of the acquisition of the right claimed. The defence was also available to the defendant in

1429. GUSKI, 585 ff.; *see infra* at paras 567 ff. *See also* the authors who therefore reject a conceptual bond between the abuse of rights and the abuse of a dominant position, as, for example, FLEISCHER, JZ 2003, 871. *See also*: GHESTIN/GOUBEAUX who argue that abusing a given freedom is not comparable to abusing a right. GHESTIN/GOUBEAUX, paras 767 ff.
1430. Note that the relationship between the abuse of rights and the abuse of a dominant position is also central in the analysis of ZENKER. ZENKER analyses whether the abuse of rights principle would provide a remedy for market inefficiencies below the scope of the prohibition of the abuse of a dominant position. *See*: ZENKER, 18 ff.
1431. In her thesis, L. BAUDENBACHER focused on the development of the understanding of the abuse of rights principle within the European states. For a fundamental analysis, *see* therefore: BAUDENBACHER.
1432. *See* hereinafter at para. 543.
1433. The classical equity was not a principle used in court and had a similar importance to justice. GÄCHTER thus proposed an understanding of *aequitas* as appropriateness rather than equity. *See*: GÄCHTER, 29 ff.

cases where claiming the right constituted a fraudulent or unfaithful conduct.[1434] The *exceptio doli* was also the legal remedy to enforce the prohibition of chicanery.[1435]

544 The *aemulatio*, the state when the execution of a right brings no use to the holder but harm to others, goes back to narratives of Gaius and the statement '*male enim iure uti non debemus*' (understood as: we may not use our rights in a bad way).[1436] In Roman property law, these maxims found expression in the principle '*sic utere iure tuo ut alterum non laedas*' (understood as: use your own [property] in a way which does not harm others).[1437] This principle, however, conflicted with another maxim, '*neminem laedit qui suo utitur*':[1438] He who exercises his legal rights harms no one.[1439] The latter maxim provided the basis for the application of the abuse of rights in case law under the French Code Civil of 1804.[1440]

545 From the Roman law tradition, abuse of rights principles found their way into many jurisdictions. Though varied in their manifestations, the abuse of rights in civil law systems is generally applied to limit the execution of a formally existing right to a socially tolerable degree and therefore as a corrective tool. Depending on the jurisdiction, the degree of tolerance differs, however. Social or economic interests serve alike as limits.[1441] Independently of which interests should be protected by prohibiting the abuse of rights, the principle can be interpreted differently jurisdiction-wise; the narrowest interpretation of the abuse of rights principle exists in jurisdictions where only chicanery is forbidden. Chicanery is understood as the execution of a right guided by the sole idea of imposing damage on others.[1442] The broadest application is guaranteed if the element of malicious intent is eliminated from the prerequisites needed to determine an abuse of rights. The abuse of rights in jurisdictions with a broad understanding is generally seen as a specific application of the principle of acting in good faith.[1443] In between these extremes, variants exist.[1444]

546 In common law systems, the existence of the abuse of rights principle is controversial. Opinions of scholars range from a denial of the existence to a full acknowledgement of the principle as in civil law tradition.[1445] Most jurisdictions acknowledge that the exercise of rights must be limited where it would interfere with

1434. Honsell, 35 and 47 f.; Kaser/Knütel/Lohsse, § 33, paras 18 f.
1435. Kaser/Knütel/Lohsse, § 4, para. 15.
1436. Falcón y Tella, 190; Kaser/Knütel/Lohsse, § 4, para. 15.
1437. Kiss, Max Planck Encyclopedia of Public International Law [MPEPIL] December 2006, para. 2.
1438. On early disputes in doctrine: Trüeb, 27 ff.
1439. For this translation *see*: http://definitions.uslegal.com/n/neminem-laedit-qui-jure-suo-utitur/, accessed on 27 February 2020.
1440. *See*: Fleischer, JZ 2003, 865.
1441. For examples *see*: Byers, McGill Law Journal 2002, 393.
1442. Byers, McGill Law Journal 2002, 393 f.
1443. Byers, McGill Law Journal 2002, 393.
1444. *See*: Byers, McGill Law Journal 2002, 394 ff. with examples.
1445. Byers, McGill Law Journal 2002, 395 ff.

the laws and interests of society to a great extent.[1446] However, concluding that the abuse of rights as a general principle is also acknowledged in common law still goes too far.

547 That there is a common acknowledgement of the abuse of rights as a limitation to the exercise of a right is supported by the fact that the abuse of rights is also known as a concept in international law. There it applies to two situations: first, to circumstances where one state exercises a given right 'in a way which impedes the enjoyment by other states of their own rights', and second, to the exercise of a state's 'own right for an end different from that for which the right was created, to the injury of another state'.[1447]

2 Development in Early French and German Law

548 As has been stated above, the Roman maxim according to which the exercise of legally existing rights never harms others was the basis for the French[1448] Code Civil of 1804.[1449] It was therefore remarkable that the Court of Appeal in Colmar in 1855 in the case of *Doerr c. Keller* mandated a property owner to tear down a chimney that was only built to obstruct the view of the neighbour.[1450] This judgment was followed by other decisions in which the French courts all held that malice is not protected by the law. Therefore, the courts did not protect the exercise of the right.[1451] Some scholars, however, adopted a critical attitude towards this line of jurisprudence that was soon called 'l'abus de droit'. However, these critics did not prevent the abuse of rights from becoming a fundamental principle of French law.[1452]

549 Prussian law included the prohibition of chicanery from the eighteenth century and also accepted the *exceptio doli* as a tool for courts to restrict malice.[1453] In the course of the enactment of the German Civil Code (GCC) in 1896, the legislator however decided not to include a provision on the abuse of rights and the *exceptio doli* was thereafter no longer allowed to justify restrictions on the execution of rights. Yet, the prohibition of chicanery survived the codification of civil law and was incorporated in § 226 GCC. As things developed, § 226 GCC soon failed to meet the standards, and the courts developed the abuse of rights doctrine mainly with reference to another provision of the GCC: the obligation of the debtor to perform in good faith (§ 242 GCC).

1446. Byers, McGill Law Journal 2002, 396 ff.
1447. Kiss, Max Planck Encyclopedia of Public International Law [MPEPIL] December 2006, para. 1.
1448. On the influence of German and French law on the development within the EU, *see*: Tridimas, 24 f.
1449. *See supra* at para. 544.
1450. Cour de Colmar, *Doerr v. Keller*, 9; cited after: Baudenbacher, 27. Today, this issue is known as spite housing. *See*, for example, the references to the so-called Hollensbury Spite House or the spite house in Alexandria: Paschall, Curbed 27 September 2013; Bailey, The New York Times 29 February 2008.
1451. For a brief summary of the case law *see*: Baudenbacher, 27 ff.
1452. Fleischer, JZ 2003, 865 f.
1453. Haferkamp, in: Falk/Mohnhaupt, Das Bürgerliche Gesetzbuch und seine Richter, 1 ff.

As in French law, the abuse of rights was soon accepted as a general principle in German law.[1454]

550 As the above insights into the origins of the principle of the abuse of rights in general, and in France and Germany specifically, show, general principles and their acceptance within a jurisdiction have to develop from the inside over a long period of time. This also applies, at least concerning their substance, when the principle itself or similar values have been laid down in legislation. What does this finding mean for the EU, where:

- general principles were not incorporated into written law;
- there is no long-term legal tradition to look back to, as the Union is a construct of post-war Europe; and
- different jurisdictions and different legal traditions clash?

3 Adoption of a General Principle of Law at the Union Level

3.1 Prerequisites for the Acknowledgement of a General Principle Within the Law of the Union

551 General legal principles in the law of the EU are principles either intrinsic to the legal order of the Union or common to the law of the Member States.[1455] While principles of the first category can directly be deduced from primary and secondary Union law, principles of the second category are generated by comparing the laws of the Member States[1456].[1457] With such analysis, the Court of Justice has already acknowledged good faith[1458] as well as various other principles and guarantees, including fundamental rights, as general principles of EU law.[1459] The decisive factor is not whether a comprehensive standard can be identified in all Member States, but whether the principle would fit within the legal system of the Union.[1460] Once acknowledged as a general principle, the rules are immanent in the legal order of the Union and have constitutional status. Thus, any breach of the general principle is an infringement of community law in the sense of Article 263 TFEU.[1461]

552 The status of the abuse of rights doctrine as a general principle of law is still a matter of hot debate,[1462] despite widespread acknowledgement of the principle as an

1454. A summary of the development in Germany can be found in: BAUDENBACHER, 33 ff.; TRIDIMAS.
1455. LENAERTS, European Review of Private Law 2010, 1124; TRIDIMAS, 2 f.
1456. As indicated by Article 340(2) TFEU for non-contractual liability.
1457. OESCH, paras 409 ff.
1458. Mentioned early by the ECJ: ECJ, *von Lachmüller, Peuvrier, Ehrhardt v. Commission*, Joined Cases C-43/59, 45/59 and 48/59, 474. On the development as a general principle, *see*: LENAERTS, European Review of Private Law 2010, 1146 ff.
1459. *See* the summary in: OESCH, para. 411; FLEISCHER, JZ 2003, 871.
1460. This is due to the limitations on the interpretation of community law given in Article 19 TEU.
1461. LENAERTS, European Review of Private Law 2010, 1124.
1462. The monography by L. BAUDENBACHER is representative: *see especially*: BAUDENBACHER, 494 ff.

interpretative tool.[1463] For the abuse of rights doctrine to reach the status of a general principle at EU level, it has to fall within the second category, and thus be present in Member States' law as well as fit within EU law.[1464]

3.2 The Common Denominator in the Member States

553 The principle of the abuse of rights cannot fall back on a common basis in the legal systems of the Member States. The common law does not know the principle of the abuse of rights. The same is true for the Scandinavian countries, among which Sweden does not even have chicanery.[1465] This, however, does not mean that the idea of sanctioning the consumption of a right contradicting the very purpose of the law is unknown to these legislations.[1466] In order to prevent unwanted outcomes, the Swedish legislator, for example, enacts detailed provisions. Swedish law does not refrain from sanctioning the abuse of rights, but the legislator wanted to reduce the power of the court to fill loopholes.[1467] In common law, the idea of limiting the execution of formal rights found its expression in the principles of equity which have a long tradition.[1468]

554 Different understandings of the abuse of rights also exist among the Member States following the civil law tradition. While some states only prohibit chicanery, others acknowledge two possible forms of the abuse of rights: first, the exercising of personal rights to the harm of others, and second, the exercising of a right to either circumvent a provision that would apply or to compel application of a non-applicable provision (subreption). This second, wide interpretation of the abuse of rights is often linked with the understanding of the abuse of rights as a specific application of the principle of acting in good faith (Article 281 of the Greek Civil Code).

555 Despite the named differences, the underlying ideas of limiting the execution of rights in certain situations are quite similar among the Member States. Therefore, the widely recognised understanding that the execution of a formal right does not always lead to just results, which is the common denominator of the EU Member States, provides the basis for the development of the abuse of rights principle.[1469]

1463. Supportive: AG Trstenjak, in: *Budějovický Budvar*, C-482/09, para. 119; critical: Baudenbacher, 494 ff.
1464. Lenaerts, European Review of Private Law 2010, 1125 ff.; for other general principles, *see*: Tridimas, 5.
1465. The concept of chicanery is alien to Swedish law, but not to the Norwegian and Finnish legal systems. Cottier/Sychold, in: Cottier/Widmer, Abus de droit et bonne foi, 336.
1466. Lenaerts, European Review of Private Law 2010, 1125.
1467. Cottier/Sychold, in: Cottier/Widmer, Abus de droit et bonne foi, 339 ff.
1468. Lasok, 4.
1469. Lenaerts, European Review of Private Law 2010, 1128.

3.3 Findings from Case Law

556 The principle of the abuse of rights emerged within the jurisprudence on the freedom of movement. There the Court of Justice used it in cases where an undertaking insisted on its freedom of movement to circumvent the application of a national provision.[1470] In various cases, the court held that national legislators must be given the power to prevent circumvention of national provisions by invocation of fundamental freedoms[1471] and that 'EU law cannot be relied on for abusive fraudulent ends.'[1472] The same is true when fundamental freedoms are used to benefit from more advantageous national law.[1473]

557 Besides cases on the abusive invocation of fundamental freedoms, another line of cases developed. In these cases, 'Community law provisions are abusively relied upon in order to gain advantages in a manner that conflicts with the purposes and aims of the provisions.'[1474] The first two of such cases concern company law. The court recognised that referring to a provision is not permitted where it results in undue advantages that do not conform to the aim of the provision.[1475] The approach was confirmed in the decision of *Emsland-Starke* where the court provided a two-part test for the finding of an abuse by national courts.[1476]

558 According to the Court of Justice, the finding of an abuse of community law requires:

- 'first, a combination of objective circumstances in which, despite formal observance of the conditions laid down by the Community rules, the purpose of those rules has not been achieved';[1477] and
- 'second, a subjective element consisting of the intention to obtain an advantage from the Community rules by creating artificially the conditions laid down for obtaining it'.[1478]

1470. For a summary of the jurisprudence *see*: ECJ, *Centros Ltd v. Erhvervs- og Selskabsstyrelsen*, C-212/97, para. 24; also: ECJ, *Diamantis*, C-373/97, para. 33.
1471. For the first time in: ECJ, *van Binsbergen v. Bedrijfsvereniging*, C-33/74, para. 13.
1472. ECJ, *Torresi*, C-58/13 and C-59/13, paras 42 ff.; *see also*, for example, AG Maduro, *in: Halifax and Others*, C-255/02, paras 62 and 64.
1473. To receive higher social benefits, for example, *see*: ECJ, *Brennet v. Paletta*, C-206/94, para. 24; also with respect to undue payments on imports into the Union: ECJ, *General Milk Products v. Hauptzollamt Hamburg-Jonas*, C-8/92, para. 21. Note that the decision in the case of *Centros Ltd.* is not in line with these decisions. There the court had to answer the question of whether the founding of a foreign company to avoid legislation requiring the payment of a minimum of share capital is covered by the freedom of movement. Despite the undisputed intention of the founder to circumvent national provisions, the court protected the action as being covered by the purpose of the freedom of movement. *See*: ECJ, *Centros Ltd v. Erhvervs- og Selskabsstyrelsen*, C-212/97.
1474. AG Maduro, *in: Halifax and Others*, C-255/02, para. 63.
1475. ECJ, *Kefalas and others*, C-367/96, paras 20 and 28; ECJ, *Diamantis*, C-373/97, para. 33.
1476. According to the ECJ, it is the duty of the national courts to deliver evidence within the national jurisdiction and applicable rules. ECJ, *Emsland-Stärke*, C-110/99, para. 54; ECJ, *Halifax and Others*, C-255/02, para. 76.
1477. ECJ, *Emsland-Stärke*, C-110/99, para. 52.
1478. ECJ, *Emsland-Stärke*, C-110/99, para. 53.

Central to the abuse, following this definition, is thus 'the distorted use of the finality and function of the relevant rule'[1479] to the harm of others without legitimate interest. Since the *Emsland-Starke* case, the application of this two-staged test has been confirmed by the Court of Justice on several occasions.[1480]

559 While the first and objective element causes almost no difficulties,[1481] the second and subjective element raises many more controversial issues.[1482] Of great importance is the intended degree of deviation from the aim of the provision required as a minimum threshold for the finding of an abuse.[1483] The Court of Justice's decision in the 2008 case of *Ministero dell'Economia v. Part Service* concretised this. The court held that conduct primarily aimed at the mere attainment of an undue advantage fulfilled the minimum threshold of an abuse. The finding of an abuse thus does not preclude that the fulfilling of an economic purpose comes with abusive conduct. The main aim is decisive.[1484] This finding for cases where the circumvention of a provision was to be analysed also applies for cases of subreption. It is necessary for there to be an intention to achieve an undue advantage. Implicit in the court's silence in *Torresi* and explicit in the statement in *SICES* is the attitude that the parallel achievement of economic purposes does not justify intention. The 'apparent' intention is sufficient. Practices that for objective reasons cannot have another principal aim or underlying intention but the attainment of an advantage not covered by the purpose of the law are therefore also abusive.[1485] The aim and intent can either be established circumstantially or factually.[1486]

560 With the reasoning in the *Emsland-Stärke* case, the Court of Justice could have provided a legislative answer in the search for the meaning of abuse in Article 102 TFEU. Much like its predecessor in France and the Member States following the French model in applying the abuse of rights principle, the term 'abuse', as used by the Court of Justice, functions as a limit to the execution of a legally granted right if the execution would lead to unsustainable results not covered by the rationale of the provision (*contra rationem legis*).[1487] The court thereby seemed to apply a rather narrow

1479. Osti, in: Pitruzzella/Muscolo, Competition and patent law in the pharmaceutical sector, 99.
1480. Among the latest are the cases of *ÖBB Personenverkehr v. Gotthard Starjakob* and *WebMindLicenses* in 2015. ECJ, *ÖBB Personenverkehr v. Gotthard Starjakob,* C-417/13, para. 56; ECJ, *WebMindLicenses,* C-419/14, para. 36.
1481. The purpose of the provision has ever since been the centre of all considerations. *See*, for example, ECJ, *Halifax and Others,* C-255/02, paras 74 and 86; ECJ, *Torresi,* C-58/13 and C-59/13, paras 35 ff.
1482. *See the analysis in*: Sørensen, Common Market Law Review 2006, 456 ff.
1483. *See also*: Deacon Neil: http://www.euroblawg.com/eu-law-2/the-eu-law-doctrine-of-abuse-ofrights-should-it-be-a-general-principle-of-eu-law-and-is-it/, accessed on 28 December 2015 (no longer available).
1484. ECJ, *Part Service,* C-425/06, paras 40 ff.
1485. ECJ, *Torresi,* C-58/13 and C-59/13, para. 46; ECJ, *SICES and Others,* C-155/13, para. 33. Note that in the *SICES* case, the Court of Justice references the *Halifax* case. The cited provision was concretised in *Ministero dell'economia v. Part Service* and has to be read in the light of that decision. *See supra* at fn. 1484.
1486. Baudenbacher, ZfRV 2008, 216.
1487. *See*: Lenaerts, European Review of Private Law 2010, 1122.

approach where only behaviour leading to obviously unjust results could constitute an abuse of rights.

561 In the *Halifax* case, which concerned an alleged attempt to circumvent the obligation to pay VAT taxes, the court argued with recourse to the general notion of abuse of rights. According to the court, community law does not protect 'abusive practices by economic operators, that is to say transactions carried out not in the context of normal commercial operations, but solely for the purpose of wrongfully obtaining advantages provided for by Community law'.[1488] Even more clear is the statement in the *Diamantis* case, which concerned company law. 'Community law cannot be relied on for abusive or fraudulent ends',[1489] that is, the exercise of a right which contradicts the aim of that right.[1490]

562 Yet, at a Union level, a clear recourse to the abuse of rights principle in a court decision was missing for a long time,[1491] and its recognition as a general principle was controversial. The Court of Justice did not explicitly recognise the abuse of rights as a general concept for quite some time.[1492] However, in its recent decisions in the cases of *Altun and others v. Openbaar Ministerie* in 2017 and *Cussen and others v. T.G Brosnan* in 2018, the Court of Justice for the first time explicitly declared the abuse of rights to be a general principle of EU law.[1493]

563 In the case of *Cussen and others v. Brosnan*, the Court of Justice clarified the status of the abuse of rights and acknowledged it as a fundamental principle of EU law which is applicable to all fields of law:

> [...] the principles that abusive practices are prohibited is applied to the rights and advantages provided for by EU law irrespective of whether those rights and advantages have their basis in the Treaties [...], in a regulation [...] or in a directive [...].[1494]

564 With respect to the fundamental freedoms, the court referred to its decision in the case of *van Binsbergen*, where it held that Member States have the right to take measures when the freedom of services is used to avoid the application of another rule.[1495]

1488. ECJ, *Halifax and Others*, C-255/02, paras 68 f.
1489. ECJ, *Diamantis*, C-373/97, para. 33.
1490. ECJ, *Diamantis*, C-373/97, para. 33.
1491. However, *see* the opinions delivered by different AGs, for example, AG TRSTENJAK who on several occasions argued based on the abuse of rights principle, first in: AG TRSTENJAK, *in: Stringer and Others*, C-520/06, para. 80; AG TRSTENJAK, *in: Budějovický Budvar*, C-482/09, para. 119.
1492. *See*, for example, the analysis of L. Baudenbacher: BAUDENBACHER, 494 ff.
1493. ECJ, *Cussens and others*, C-251/16, paras 27 ff.; ECJ, *Altun and others*, C-359/16, para. 49; on the recognition of the concept in EU law, *see also*: SCHUBERT, in: SÄCKER ET AL., Münchener Kommentar BGB, § 242, para. 155; ZENKER, 21 ff.
1494. ECJ, *Cussens and others*, C-251/16, para. 30.
1495. ECJ, *van Binsbergen v. Bedrijfsvereniging*, C-33/74, para. 13.

565 The principle of the abuse of rights is therefore without doubt applicable to economic and thus competition law as well. Not only did the Court of Justice accept the abuse of rights as a fundamental principle[1496] but the court also developed it in case law, which partly concerned the fundamental freedoms and thus the economic constitution competition law seeks to protect, even more so as the question submitted to the Court of Justice in the *Halifax* case asked about the doctrine 'as developed by the court'.[1497] A further argument in favour of this conclusion is the fact that the Court of Justice has already applied the abuse of rights principle to intellectual property law.

566 In the famous *Budweiser* case, a Czech (Budějovický Budvar) and a US (Anheuser Busch) brewer had a dispute over the brand 'Budweiser'. Both manufacturers had 'Budweiser' registered as a trademark in 2000 according to British law. Then, after four years and 364 days, Anheuser Busch applied for the declaration of invalidity of Budějovický Budvar's 'Budweiser' trademark based on Article 4(1) and (2) as well as Article 9 of Directive 89/104. Anheuser Busch claimed that the date of application of its trademark was earlier than the application of Budějovický Budvar's 'Budweiser' and that the five-year period of acquiescence, which limits the right to apply for the declaration of invalidity, was not yet over.[1498] During the proceedings, the question of a potentially abusive enforcement of rights immanent in the trademark right was raised by both the Czech and Slovakian governments, who accused Anheuser Busch of having abused its right to raise absolute grounds for refusal under trademark law because it filed the claim only one day before the expiration of the acquiescence period. Advocate General TRSTENJAK, the Advocate General in the case, affirmed the application of the principle of the abuse of rights to the Union's trademark law and applied the definition and requirements laid down by the Court of Justice in *Emsland-Stärke*[1499].[1500] In the opinion of the Advocate General, an abuse of rights was not given in this case as the execution of the right did not contradict the goal of the trademark directive. Unfortunately, the Court of Justice did not address the accusation of a possible abuse of rights in its considerations. We therefore lack argumentation by the court in this matter.

IV ABUSE OF RIGHTS PRINCIPLE WITHIN THE ABUSE OF A DOMINANT POSITION

1 Theoretical Foundation

567 The above considerations[1501] allow for the assumption that the abuse of a dominant position and the general principle of the abuse of rights as recognised in

1496. In this regard *also*: LENAERTS, European Review of Private Law 2010, 1138.
1497. ECJ, *Halifax and Others*, C-255/02, para. 43.
1498. AG TRSTENJAK, *in: Budějovický Budvar*, C-482/09, paras 12 ff.
1499. *See*: ECJ, *Emsland-Stärke*, C-110/99, paras 52 f.; confirmed in: ECJ, *Eichsfelder Schlachtbetrieb*, C-515/03, para. 39.
1500. AG TRSTENJAK, *in: Budějovický Budvar*, C-482/09, para. 119.
1501. *See supra* at Part V, Chapter 15, sections II and III.

many civil law jurisdictions are rooted in similar considerations.[1502] Both sanction the excessive use of a given power with an 'unwanted' outcome.[1503] While the abuse of a dominant position sanctions the excessive use of economic freedoms[1504] enjoyed by dominant undertakings, the abuse of rights sanctions the excessive use of a right[1505] (e.g., property[1506]).[1507]

568 Yet, despite similar conceptual roots, it would not be correct to equate the abuse of a dominant position and the general abuse of rights principle.[1508] With the abuse of a dominant position, competition law sanctions the use of the privileges enjoyed as a result of the supremacy position on the market (ability to behave independently on a market) when the usage of those privileges results in unsustainable outcomes. Unlike the general abuse of rights, the abuse of a dominant position does not sanction the use of a legally granted right against its purpose.[1509] The common conceptual ground is therefore limited to the essence of the concepts. The aim of both *abuses*, the general principle of law in civil as well as the codified abuse of a dominant position in competition law, is to provide limitation where private parties exceed their freedoms unbearably.[1510] The *abuse* within the abuse of rights principle stands for an excess of the competences conferred by a given right which is limited by the aim of the right.[1511] The *abuse* within the abuse of a dominant position by contrast is the expression of an

1502. Different authors in literature reject this conclusion. *See*: FLEISCHER, JZ 2003, 871; GHESTIN/GOUBEAUX, para. 767. Stressing a structural difference, also: SGANGA/SCALZINI, IIC 2017, 407 and 424. The notion of ULLRICH/HEINEMANN that the abuse of a dominant position is a concept specific to competition law and cannot be confused with the abuse of intellectual property rights might also be interpreted as a critical voice against the positioning of the abuse of a dominant position within the conceptual framework of the abuse of rights principle. The statement was made in order to differentiate the abuse of a dominant position by means of intellectual property rights from the abuse of intellectual property rights. Its consequences for the understanding of the abuse of a dominant position presented here are not straightforward therefore. *See*: ULLRICH/HEINEMANN, in: IMMENGA/MESTMÄCKER 2018, Teil GRUR B, para. 44. Similarly, AKMAN finds that the Spanish Tribunal Supremo (Spanish Supreme Court, *see* the reference hereinafter at fn. 1507) has added a different concept to the concept of abuse in Article 102 TFEU when understanding the abuse of a dominant position as abuse of rights based on the 'anti-social exercise of exceptional economic freedom'. AKMAN, in: KËLLEZI ET AL., Abuse of dominant position and globalization & protection and disclosure of trade secrets and know-how, 12.
1503. Similarly: RAISER, JZ 1972, 732.
1504. Occupational freedom (Article 15), entrepreneurial freedom (Article 16) and the right to property (Article 17) form the foundation of the economic constitution of the EU. WOLLENSCHLÄGER, in: VON DER GROEBEN ET AL., Kommentar EU-Recht, Article 17, para. 1.
1505. *See supra* at paras 558, 560, 563 and 566.
1506. *See* the references to spite housing *supra* at fn. 1450.
1507. In early German literature: BAUR, 92 ff.; FISCHER, ZGR 1978, 248; more recently, GUSKI, 585. For a concretisation of the Spanish equivalent to Article 102 TFEU based on the abuse of rights, *see*: TRIBUNAL SUPREMO, *Tandem Transportes y Ruta Sur*, No 0805/2003, para. 12.
1508. OSTI therefore goes too far, when he states that 'the abuse is not seen, or not anymore, as an abuse of a dominant position – i.e., of significant market power. It is merely an abuse of a right – whether an IP, or a property, or even a contract right'. OSTI, in: PITRUZZELLA/MUSCOLO, Competition and patent law in the pharmaceutical sector, 101.
1509. *See* the therefore critical voices: FLEISCHER, JZ 2003, 871; GHESTIN/GOUBEAUX, paras 767 ff.
1510. *See*: RAISER with respect to the abuse of rights: RAISER, JZ 1972, 732.
1511. BAUR, 93, PEDRAZZINI, in: BRÜGGER, FS Troller, Der Rechtsmissbrauch im Patentrecht, 209.

imbalance between the possibilities immanent in a privilege (possibility to exploit the freedom of competition due to the ability to behave independently) and the result as intended by the legal system and society (undistorted competition).[1512] These differences do not diminish the similarities, however.[1513]

569 Freedom of competition was initially understood as part of the freedom of profession. However, nowadays, it is rather understood as part of entrepreneurial freedom;[1514] both entrepreneurial freedom and freedom of profession cover freedom of competition.[1515] Either way, the scope of protection of the economic fundamental rights is overlapping. This can be shown with respect to the third fundamental economic right, the right to property. Since private property is a fundamental prerequisite of free competition,[1516] the acquisition and disposal of property as an inherent part of competition is protected by the freedom to conduct business and the freedom of profession[1517] rather than the right to property, which grants the substance of the acquired as such. A clear separation can be difficult in this relation.[1518] The dominant undertaking's right to compete freely in the Union's market as noted above must therefore include a comprehensive understanding of all fundamental economic rights. The fundamental economic rights in relation to the provisions of competition law have a double function, in as much as competition law secures freedom of competition[1519] by restricting freedom of competition.[1520]

2 Limitations to the Freedom of Competition

570 The adoption of an abuse of rights, like the abuse of a dominant position, results in the question of how and to what extent fundamental rights can be abused or forfeitured, based on the initial determination of the scope within which an abuse can occur.[1521] Executive powers immanent in a given right are limited by internal and external boundaries. This is also true for fundamental rights. As with other legal privileges, fundamental rights are granted to secure the holder's position among society and its members. The scope of the right is thereby narrowed by its social, legal

1512. Similarly: GUSKI, 586.
1513. KÄHLER even understands the abuse of a dominant position as codification of the abuse of rights principle. KÄHLER in: GSELL ET AL., Beck-online Grosskommentar, § 242 BGB, para. 298. Similarly: SCHUBERT, in: SÄCKER ET AL., Münchener Kommentar, § 242 BGB, para. 155; AG GULMANN, *in: RTE and ITP v. Commission,* Joined Cases C-241/91 P and C-242/91 P, fn. 36.
1514. FRENZ, paras 2501 and 2505 ff.
1515. *See*: NOWAK, in: HESELHAUS/NOWAK, Handbuch der europäischen Grundrechte, § 35, para. 35; in this respect also: FRENZ, para. 2717. NOWAK, however, considers that freedom of competition is not an independent guarantee, but contained in the freedom of profession.
1516. EMMERICH/LANGE, § 1, para. 9.
1517. In this respect: FRENZ, para. 2502.
1518. FRENZ, paras 2502 ff. and 2890.
1519. This aspect is frequently stressed in the literature on fundamental rights. *See*, for example, FRENZ, para. 2501, *see also supra* at para. 53.
1520. In this respect also: EVERLING, in: SCHWARZE, Wirtschaftsverfassungsrechtliche Garantien für Unternehmen im europäischen Binnenmarkt, 24.
1521. GALLWAS, 31.

and ethical value. Improper usage beyond these boundaries is not covered by the protection of the right and is considered an excess (internal boundaries, ger. *Innentheorie*). In the case of fundamental rights, other than in civil law, internal boundaries beyond the scope of the fundamental right do not exist. The scope of the fundamental right is rather defined by its social and legal ethical value within society. Reif therefore concludes that there is no internal value to fundamental rights that would require a restriction, as realisations of freedom only require limitations when they clash with other opposing interests.[1522] This conclusion follows from the character of fundamental rights as representative of a society's fundamental values.

571 Limitations to fundamental rights are thus only implemented through external boundaries in the case of opposing legal interests. External boundaries are given through legal rules outside the scope of the fundamental right. Conflicts can occur in relation to legitimate interests of other bearers of fundamental rights, of society or the state.[1523] In cases of abuse of fundamental rights, the owner, through engaging in conduct formally within the scope of the fundamental right (e.g., when acquiring property), shifts the balance of interests, as laid down by the legislator, to limiting either the third parties' interests or freedom, to demand greater commitment than intended by the legislator.[1524]

572 The relevant perspective is society. The legislator, with Article 102 TFEU, created a legal reservation for dominant undertakings to execute their economic fundamental rights, when societal interests in guaranteeing undistorted competition are opposed. Societal interests can only proceed where restrictions of fundamental rights meet the requirements of Article 52(1) ECHR. In Article 52(1) ECHR, boundaries for justifications of restrictions of fundamental rights are set by the principle of proportionality. Article 52(1) ECHR expresses the fact that competition law as authoritative interference into the rights of private entities has to comply with the fundamental rights granted within a jurisdiction.[1525]

573 Article 52(1) ECHR, according to consistent case law, first requires any intervention by legal authorities to be founded on a legal basis and justified 'on the grounds laid down by law'.[1526] Second, any limitations of fundamental rights must also be compliant with the public interest.[1527] Third, limitations of fundamental rights must comply with the principle of proportionality, which, according to German standards, holds that the authoritative interference with fundamental rights has to be suitable, necessary as well as proportionate to the specific legal purpose. However, Germany with this triad of elements almost stands alone compared with the practice in other Member States. At

1522. Reif, 62 ff.
1523. Gallwas, 33.; *see supra* at para. 70.
1524. Gallwas, 32.
1525. At the Union level, these boundaries are set by the Charter (Article 52(1) of the Charter) as well as the general principles of EU law which consist of the ECHR as well as the fundamental freedoms resulting from the traditions of the Member States (Article 6(3) EUV). *See*: Kamann, in: Kamann/Ohlhoff/Völcker, Kartellverfahren und Kartellprozess, paras 26 ff.
1526. ECJ, *Hoechst AG v. Commission*, Joined Cases C-46/87 and 227/88, para. 19.
1527. ECJ, *Nold v. Commission*, C-4/73, para. 14.

a European level, the status of the element of proportionality in the narrow sense is especially unclear.[1528] Article 52(1) ECHR only lists suitability and necessity as relevant criteria.

574 With Article 102 TFEU a provision is given that meets the requirements of both the first and second prerequisites. As a provision at constitutional level, the prohibition of the abuse of a dominant position is founded on an equal legal basis to the fundamental rights.[1529] Furthermore, the functioning of competition is among the most important interests promoted within the EU. Fostering competition within the EU also included strengthening the internal market, which resulted in the granting of the four fundamental freedoms: the free movement of goods, persons and capital and the freedom to provide services. The four fundamental freedoms are also recognised as public interests which can justify the limitation of fundamental economic rights.[1530] In the following considerations, therefore, the focus will be on the principle of proportionality.[1531]

575 First, however, the applicability of the fundamental right has to be established. This requires an analysis of whether the conduct is protected by the dominant undertaking's own legitimate interests.[1532] The question can only be answered in the affirmative if the conduct is covered by the protection afforded by the fundamental right.[1533] Second, in analysing proportionality of the behaviour, in the context of competition law, the applicable perspective is whether the conduct was suitable and necessary to fulfil the protected interest of the dominant undertaking as well as whether it was proportionate to the specific legal purpose (proportionality in the narrow sense).[1534] Proportionality in the narrow sense asks whether the conduct was adequate from the perspective of the market participants. These fundamentals refer to the early decision in the case of *Volvo/Veng.*[1535]

1528. HESELHAUS, in: HESELHAUS/NOWAK, Handbuch der europäischen Grundrechte, § 36, paras 77 ff., esp. paras 83 f.
1529. Article 102 TFEU has, for example, served as a legal basis independent of patent law to impose compulsory licences, therewith curtailing the right to property. *See infra* at para. 696.
1530. *See*, for example, L. BAUDENBACHER who within the jurisprudence of the ECJ sees a weighting of interests in favour of the four fundamental freedoms when opposed to fundamental (economic) rights. BAUDENBACHER, 93 and 117.
1531. *See infra* at Part VI, Chapter 18.
1532. With legitimate business interests, the analysis addresses one of the sources which are regularly put forward as sources of objective justifications by dominant undertakings. On the relevance of objective justifications for this analysis, *see supra* at para. 21. A lucid overview over objective justifications in Article 102 TFEU cases can be found in: VAN DER VIJVER, Journal of European Competition Law & Practice 2013, 121 ff.
1533. *See infra* at Part VI, Chapter 18, section III.
1534. *See infra* at Part VI, Chapter 18, section II.
1535. ECJ, *Volvo v. Veng*, C-238/87, paras 8 f.; *see also*: KEMPEL, 60.

3 Findings from the Analysis of the Drafting History of Article 102 TFEU in Comparison with Section 2 Sherman Act

576 Further insight about the nature of 'abuse' in Article 102 TFEU can be gained by comparing the provision to section 2 of the US Sherman Act. Although the role of US scholars within the drafting process is debated today, US thought undoubtedly influenced the establishment of many of the European treaties. This was due to the position of the USA as an occupying power of West Germany and owing to its influence on other European countries through the Marshall Plan.[1536] With the Sherman Act, the USA set an important model for competition law legislation in the modern age and influenced many legislators worldwide. Yet, the approaches taken towards dominant undertakings within the EU differ from the US approach. Apart from section 2 Sherman Act which prohibits certain attempts at monopolisation, the competition law provisions of the ECSC and the subsequent treaties do not contain such a prohibition.

577 Above, it has been pointed out that the first competition law provisions at a supranational level in Europe, Articles 65 and 66 § 7 of the Treaty of Paris, were based on an initiative of the USA.[1537] Even though Article 66 § 7 remained a dead letter,[1538] the founders of the EEC later shared the idea that private economic power needed to be limited in order to secure the goals of the Community.[1539] While the understanding of the importance of restricting private economic power was mutual among the founding states,[1540] it was all but clear that the abuse of dominance would find entrance into the TEEC. The Spaak Report within which the Intergovernmental Committee on European Integration (Spaak Committee) elaborated a basis for the drafting of the TEEC proposed measures against monopolisation similar to the Sherman Act, in addition to the behavioural control mechanisms.[1541] The thoughts of the Spaak Report were outlined during the negotiations. The French delegation took the position that monopolies, like cartels, should be prohibited. Yet, remarkably, the prohibition of monopolies did not survive the negotiations and EU competition law, therefore, took a different path from the Sherman Act.

578 An important difference between the USA and the EU is the motivation initiating the genesis of competition law. European states were forced by the idea of building peace through market integration and dismantling trade barriers between Member States. The goal of the founders of the EEC was to foster economic strength. The means for achieving this goal were market integration and thereby the removal of trade

1536. On the US influence in the drafting of the Treaty of Rome, *see*: AKMAN, Oxford Journal of Legal Studies 2009, 289; more critical: GERBER, 431.
1537. *See supra* at paras 38 and 405.
1538. SAMKALDEN/DRUKER, Common Market Law Review 1966, 162; VON DER GROEBEN, 259.
1539. *See supra* at para. 405.
1540. SCHWEITZER, in: EHLERMANN/MARQUIS, European competition law annual 2007, 128.
1541. AKMAN, Oxford Journal of Legal Studies 2009, 280 f.; SCHWEITZER, in: EHLERMANN/MARQUIS, European competition law annual 2007, 135 ff.

barriers and the development of fundamental freedoms.[1542] By implementing behavioural rules, the founders wanted to make sure that the endeavours were not thwarted by private players on the market.[1543] Yet, it was also brought up that striving for a superior market position was the core of competition. Dominant positions can be reached by simply outperforming others and are not against competition per se as long as the markets are kept open.[1544]

579 US policymakers in the late nineteenth century, however, wanted to break down conglomerates that had an adverse effect on consumers because of being too powerful.[1545] According to THORELLI, established competition theory was based on the idea of a direct correlation between the removal of monopolistic elements and free competition.[1546] Furthermore, the prohibition of monopolisation also had a political background. Large quantities of wealth being controlled by a few were seen as a threat to democracy.[1547] Therefore, the US Sherman Act prohibited monopolisation.

580 Likewise, the competition law provisions at EU level were the result of a political compromise.[1548] A prohibition of monopolisation along the lines of section 2 Sherman Act did not find enough support. Additionally, there was the fear of a regulatory overreach resulting in yet another impediment to free competition.[1549] Consequently, prohibiting abusive behaviour with such a vague provision was seemingly the lowest common denominator.[1550] As GERBER points out, after World War II, many national competition laws emerged as well. The norms restricting the conduct of powerful firms within these new legislations were quite vague and rather than providing guidance on the characteristics of the sanctioned behaviour they operated 'as administrative authorizations'.[1551] Therefore, it comes as no surprise that the compromise reached when building the EEC followed this tradition. The provisions were thought to be general principles and guidelines. Direct applicability was not foreseen,[1552] but the founding states shared the legal conviction that unilateral conduct should not amount to being abusive.

581 This section shows that the design of the law was dependent on its aim as well as the political and societal structures at the time of drafting and amending the provisions. Within the EU there was a fear of implementing competitive restraints. Therefore, neither clear behavioural instructions which bore the risk of overregulation nor the

1542. MÜLLER-GRAFF, in: DAUSES/LUDWIGS, Handbuch des EU-Wirtschaftsrechts, para. 18.
1543. SCHWEITZER, in: EHLERMANN/MARQUIS, European Competition Law Annual 2007, 128 and 137.
1544. SCHWEITZER, in: EHLERMANN/MARQUIS, European Competition Law Annual 2007, 137.
1545. PERITZ, 11 f.; THORELLI, 160 ff.; UNITED STATES SUPREME COURT, *Standard Oil v. USA*, 221 US 1, 50.
1546. THORELLI, 227.
1547. SCHWEITZER, in: EHLERMANN/MARQUIS, European Competition Law Annual 2007, 126.
1548. *See* the insights from the contract negotiations at: VON DER GROEBEN, 281 ff.
1549. SCHWEITZER, in: EHLERMANN/MARQUIS, European Competition Law Annual 2007, 137; with respect to the competition law provisions in the Treaty of Paris: VON DER GROEBEN, 252 and 260.
1550. SCHWEITZER, in: EHLERMANN/MARQUIS, European Competition Law Annual 2007, 135.
1551. GERBER, 173 ff.
1552. *See supra* at fn. 1101.

prohibition of monopolisation which could result in lowering competitive activities of successful market players was wanted.

4 Understandings from Italy's *Pfizer* Decision

582 In Italy, the national courts have interpreted the abuse of a dominant position as analogous to the general abuse of rights. Pfizer was found guilty of having abused its dominant position. Pfizer allegedly delayed generic entry for latanoprost - an active ingredient to treat ocular pressure - in Italy, where patent protection expired sooner than in other Member States. Pfizer applied for a divisional patent in Italy and an supplementary protection certificate to align the patent term. Though legitimate under patent law, the Consiglio di Stato (state council[1553]) held that Pfizer was guilty of having abused its dominant position. The court stated that Pfizer's conduct was not prohibited under patent law, but was an abuse of the dominant position, as Pfizer had exploited the patent system in order to gain anticompetitive advantages.[1554]

583 On the relationship between the abuse of rights and the abuse of a dominant position, the Consiglio di Stato held:

> 'Del resto, l'abuso di posizione dominante, imputato a Pfizer, non è che specificazione della più ampia categoria dell'abuso del diritto, della quale presupposto è, appunto, l'esistenza di un diritto, del quale si faccia un uso strumentale, non coerente con il fine per il quale l'ordinamento lo riconosce: nel caso di specie, l'esclusione dal mercato dei concorrenti.'[1555]
>
> '[...], the abuse of a dominant position, [...] is nothing more than a specification of the general principle of the abuse of rights, the requirements of which are the existence of a right instrumentalised in a way which is not consistent with the aim dedicated by the law: in this specific case, the exclusion of competitors from the market' [translated by the author].

584 The court understood the abuse of a dominant position as a specific category of the general abuse of rights principle, the use of a right by a dominant undertaking not in line with its aim. Incoherency with the aim was seen in the fact that Pfizer did not use the divisional patent to produce additional products, but allegedly to delay generic entry.[1556]

585 In the *AstraZeneca* case, the Commission reasoned similarly to the Consiglio di Stato in the *Pfizer* case, though the Commission was less explicit in addressing the general abuse of rights. Deregistration of a specific product is generally compliant with

1553. The Consiglio di Stato is the highest administrative court in competition matters in Italy.
1554. Consiglio di Stato, *Pfizer Italia,* No 693/2014, para. V C); *see also,* for example, Galimbertt/Marchesoni.
1555. Consiglio di Stato, *Pfizer Italia,* No 693/2014, para. V C); similar also: Tribunal Supremo, *Tandem Transportes y Ruta Sur,* No 0805/2003, para. 12.
1556. Consiglio di Stato, *Pfizer Italia,* No 693/2014, para. V C). On the relevance of intent, *see supra* at paras 510 ff.

the rights of an undertaking in competition. Undertakings are entitled to request the withdrawal of market authorisations for their products. However, in the case of the drug Losec, the deregistration was allegedly not requested based on genuine industrial interests, such as health concerns or poor demand, but to hamper generic entry. It was therefore understood as an abuse of the right to withdraw a product from the market, because it was pursuing no goals other than anticompetitive effects.[1557]

V CONCLUSION

586 Despite missing common ground, various aspects of the principle of using a right *contra rationem legis* are known in the jurisdictions of the Member States. Unsurprisingly therefore, the idea of denying legal protection to the right holder in cases where their behaviour leads to obviously unjust results has also found its way into the jurisprudence of the Court of Justice. It was only recently, however, that the court acknowledged the abuse of rights as a fundamental principle of EU law. Yet, in previous cases, the Court of Justice had gone as far as to introduce a two-stage test whereby the intent to use the right against its aim was decisive in declaring conduct abusive.[1558]

587 The principles elaborated with respect to the general principle of the abuse of rights apply to the abuse of a dominant position as well. The abuse of rights seeks to prevent right holders from using their right with a fraudulent end. It is the aim of Article 102 TFEU to prevent dominant undertakings from using their competitive freedom to trim competitive constraints without legitimate cause. To meet the threshold of an abuse of rights, the behaviour has to be directed towards causing effects contrary to its aim, as the case law shows.[1559] In other words, causing fraudulent effects has to be the main aim of the conduct. Whether this threshold is also in line with the case law as well as with the aim of the provision against the abuse of a dominant position will be elaborated in detail in the next part.[1560]

588 Critics might argue that with the presented understanding of placing the abuse of a dominant position in the tradition of the general abuse of rights, yet another unclear, open concept has been created. However, a balancing of interests as well as uncertain legal concepts are immanent in law.[1561] The mere fact that a concept requires such a balancing act cannot be held against it.[1562] In contrast to the concept of competition on the merits, the evaluation based on the principle of the abuse of rights enables a

1557. EC, *AstraZeneca*, COMP/A.37.507/F3, paras 870 f. For a more detailed analysis of the case, *see supra* at paras 334 ff.
1558. *See supra* at paras 504 ff.
1559. *See supra* at paras 583 ff.
1560. *See infra* at Part VI, Chapter 18 section 2.3 and section III.4.
1561. Contradicting (fundamental) rights always requires a delicate balance. Delicacy as such cannot therefore be used as an argument against arguing cases based on fundamental rights considerations. GEIGER in this respect points out that it is precisely fundamental rights which allow a careful balancing of involved interests. GEIGER, IIC 2004, 278; *see also* at fn. 1562.
1562. *See also* BAUR, who understands balancing of interests as part of judicial methods: BAUR, 104.

balancing of interests[1563] based on known and experienced concepts. The origins of the abuse of rights principle go back to Roman and Greek law traditions. Its elaboration has since been part of judicial work. A common area of application of abuse of rights considerations in the everyday legal profession is General Business Terms (GBTs) in contracts. Despite GBTs being mutually agreed on contractual terms, the undertaking issuing them has more weight, as it produces the content. It is therefore required to give adequate consideration to the interests of third parties. Failure to do so is understood as abuse of the freedom to contract.[1564] Likewise, when conducting business, a dominant undertaking has to consider residual competition and must not weaken it inadequately.

589 The concept of the abuse of a dominant position as presented here only differs from the established use of the concept within legal practice in as much as the indeterminate term of competition on the merits is considered to be unsuitable.[1565] Taking the definition of the Court of Justice in the *Hoffmann-La Roche* case, to which competition on the merits dates back,[1566] as a starting point, the following amendments would be necessary:

> The concept of abuse is an objective concept relating to the behaviour of an undertaking in a dominant position which is such as to influence the structure of a market where, as a result of the very presence of the undertaking in question, the degree of competition is weakened and *[... where the undertaking, through exhausting its competitive freedoms strives to hinder the maintenance of the ...]* degree of competition still existing in the market or the growth of that competition.[1567]

590 The concept of abuse presented in this book does not contradict the absolute character of the EU competition law rules in Articles 101 and 102 TFEU. EU competition law follows the 'prohibition principle' (*Verbotsprinzip*), which is opposed to the abuse principle. A consequence of the prohibition principle is that the provisions are directly applicable (*see* Article 1 of Council Regulation (EC) No 17/2003) and authorities can directly impose sanctions.[1568] After the prohibition principle, the sanctioned conduct is a violation of competition law irrespective of whether competition authorities have in fact declared the conduct as abusive.[1569] This is not the case under the abuse principle (*Missbrauchsprinzip*); in legislation following the abuse principle, a conduct is only a violation of competition law if declared abusive by an authority or court because the

1563. On the balancing of interests required when fundamental rights are at stake, *see*: Reif, 77.
1564. With reference to the decision of the German Federal Court: Baur, 103.
1565. Zech also addresses difficulties with competition on the merits with respect to patents: Zech, ZWeR 2011, 318 f.
1566. *See supra* at para. 453.
1567. ECJ, *Hoffmann-La Roche v. Commission*, C-85/76, para. 91 (emphasis added).
1568. On the direct applicability and the absolute character of Article 102 TFEU, *see*: Kling/Thomas, § 6, para. 3; Fuchs/Möschel, in: Immenga/Mestmäcker 2018, Article 102, para. 2; Jung, in: Grabitz et al., EUV/AEUV, Article 102, para. 12.
1569. On the difference between the abuse and the prohibition principle with respect to the effect of the law: Heinemann, ZSR 2016, 443 f.; Jung, in: Grabitz et al., EUV/AEUV, Article 102, para. 12.

threshold of the respective prohibition is met. Cartel agreements and unilateral conduct of dominant undertakings are therefore initially permissible, until the authorities step in.[1570]

591 The adjustments proposed do not render the provision more vague and do not change its direct applicability. Legal certainty does not suffer merely because the conceptual roots have been located within the general abuse of rights principle. The interpretation furthermore does not change the absolute character of the provision as intended by the legislator. Any assumption that the author proposed a change from the prohibition to the abuse principle would therefore only be based on semantics.

1570. HEINEMANN, ZSR 2016, 443 f.

Part VI Blocking Patents as Abuse of a Dominant Position

CHAPTER 16

Synthesis of the Preceding Analysis

I ARTICLE 102 TFEU

592 The conduct of dominant undertakings only in the rarest cases amounts to an abuse. The finding of an abuse requires a major disproportion between the respective performances.[1571] In order to qualify as an abuse, the conduct, following the established abuse concept,[1572] has to be beyond competition on the merits and also has to have the capacity to distort competition.

593 To identify whether the conduct is beyond competition on the merits, legal practice has provided case groups. However, outside the framework of known case groups, competition on the merits has shown imperfections as a standard to distinguish sanctionable from unproblematic behaviour. The previous analysis when analysing the core of the abuse concept in Article 102 TFEU revealed that the prohibition of the abuse of a dominant position has its roots within the general principle of the abuse of rights.[1573] In fact, Article 102 TFEU in its historical form was just an expression of the consistent will of the contracting parties to limit unilateral behaviour to a tolerable degree. The abuse of a dominant position is in its essence a limitation of entrepreneurial freedom where exercising this freedom would amount to a distortion of competition.[1574] Identifying an abuse based on this understanding requires an analysis of all the factors and interests involved.

594 Further analysis has revealed that the actual anticompetitive effects of the conduct do not have to be shown. It does need to be shown, however, that the conduct under

1571. GERBER, Tulane Law Review 1987, 95.
1572. *See supra* at Part V, Chapter 14, sections IV.2 and 3.
1573. *See supra* at Part V, Chapter 15, section IV.
1574. That the freedom to conduct business is not granted limitless within the EU has constantly been held by the ECJ with respect to fundamental rights and freedoms. *See*, for example, ECJ, *Sky Österreich*, C-283/11, para. 45 with further reference to previous case law.

analysis would probably result in anticompetitive effects. Although proof of anticompetitive intent is not required, it is a weighty factor in the analysis of whether the behaviour is abusive.[1575]

II RELATIONSHIP BETWEEN PATENTS AND ARTICLE 102 TFEU

595 Besides an isolated analysis of Article 102 TFEU, this book has also provided an insight into previous cases of Article 102 TFEU involving patents. In the early case of *CICRA/Renault*, the court held that the mere fact of enjoying benefits granted by law does not qualify as an abuse of a dominant position. This ruling stood in the tradition of the separation doctrine that allowed competition law scrutiny under the TFEU only with regard to the exercise of property rights. The existence of property rights, however, belonged to the jurisdiction of property law and any effect resulting from property law itself did not open up competition law to scrutiny. The application for a patent could not therefore be analysed under competition law. As previously noted, the doctrine of separation between the existence and exercise was heavily criticised and lost its importance.[1576] Yet, despite a transition in doctrine, the courts adhered to the principle for a relatively long time. Only in recent cases, namely the Court of Justice in the *AstraZeneca* decision and the Commission in its *Boehringer Ingelheim/Almirall* and *Servier* inquiries, has practice distanced itself from the separation doctrine. In these cases, the court and the Commission identified abusive behaviour within patent filing strategies. In their reasoning, the court and Commission, however, always found additional conduct besides 'just' acquiring a patent, which rendered the strategies abusive 'overall'.[1577]

III OUTLINE OF FURTHER ANALYSIS

596 After the recapitulation of the preceding analysis, the application of blocking patents has to be analysed in two respects. First, it has to be analysed regarding whether the application of blocking patents is likely to distort competition. It has been seen that patents in general make market entry more difficult in terms of eliminating competition by imitation. The entrant has to either enter with a substituting or non-infringing technology or bear the costs of infringement or annulment proceedings. Patent grants therefore affect market structure and, as such, competition.[1578] In the hands of dominant undertakings, patents strengthen the dominant position, as they entail a competitive advantage by providing access to the protected technology. The hindering effect on market entrants is even bigger in the presence of blocking patents.

1575. *See supra* at paras 519 ff.
1576. *See supra* at Part I, Chapter 4, section II.2.2.
1577. *See supra* at Part IV.
1578. *See also*: VOLKMANN, 207.

The question therefore is whether, and under what conditions, the strengthening effect of patents on the market results in a distortion of competition.

597 Second, it has to be analysed regarding the cases in which the dominant undertakings applying for blocking patents were found to be overusing their freedom on the market. Article 102 TFEU limits the economic rights granted to a dominant undertaking. As fundamental rights, economic rights are not granted limitless, but are restricted by the overarching goals of the Union to which Article 102 TFEU is dedicated. For the finding of an abuse of a dominant position, the relevant conduct has to be analysed with respect to whether the aim of competition law and the interests protected therewith allow for a restriction of the fundamental economic rights. Therefore the competing legitimate interests of society and the dominant undertaking need to be weighed up. Qualitatively an abuse can only be found in cases where prohibiting the conduct would involve a justifiable impact on the fundamental rights of the dominant undertaking. The approach taken here allows for an analysis of the fundamental interests and characteristics of each field, without recourse to doctrines.

598 The following chapter will start with an analysis of the expected effects of blocking patents on the market (Chapter 17, section I). The subsequent analysis of the potential overuse of freedom on the market is divided into two parts. Section II provides an analysis of the weighting of the fundamental rights involved, and whether applying a blocking patenting strategy can result in limitations to the right to property. Section III will analyse whether and how unused patents can fulfil the aim of patent law.

CHAPTER 17

Distortion of Competition Through Patent Application

I OUTLINE OF THE CHAPTER

599 The privileges obtained with a patent application are crucial to an understanding of the power an applicant can seize. In order to grasp the rights and privileges given to a patent applicant and the effect of patent applications on competition, it is important to understand the application process in detail. The rights and privileges given to the applicant at each step of the process are inseparable from the application itself.

600 This section will therefore give an overview of the application process as well as the power and privileges provided to the patent applicant. While in practice the characteristics of the application process have to be analysed in accordance with the relevant (national) patent law, this section will provide a general insight and reference to the particularities of certain national laws only where such a mention would provide additional benefit. The section is divided into the different stages of the patent application process: before the publication of the submitted application; after the publication of the application; and after the grant of the patent. The goal of the latter subsection is to analyse the impact of registered patents on access to a technology. As we lack data on the effect of patents, other insights in the patent system have to serve as a proxy measurement. Data on the effect of patents are, however, available for different technologies and concern licensing and negotiations.

601 The section starts not with an analysis of the effect of the patent application process on competition, but with a section on the difficult relationship between innovation and competition. This is because, in the case of patents, distortions of competition are inherent in the system, as long as it is for the benefit of fostering innovation. An analysis of the distortions of competition cannot therefore be undertaken in isolation from the effect on innovation.

II THE INFLUENCE OF PATENTS ON INNOVATION AND DIFFICULTIES REGARDING THE MEASUREMENT OF INNOVATION

602 From the economic literature, we know that the incentive to innovate depends on the increase in profits after the innovation. The higher the expected post-innovation profits compared with the profits made with the current technology, the higher the incentive to innovate.[1579] The current competition, however, must allow the potential innovator to gain enough profits for reinvestment into R&D. Fostering innovation therefore cannot only involve a mere reduction of pre-innovation profits.

603 The relationship between innovation and competition has been described as an inverted U-form in the literature. According to this figure, pre-innovation profits need to be high enough for the firms to accumulate sufficient capital for investment. Yet, to avoid complacency, an optimal balance of competition, which reduces pre-innovation profits, is required. An undertaking's incentive to innovate and escape competition grows after an intensification of competition and declines with further growing intensity owing to the presence of sufficient capital to invest.[1580] After the innovation, the undertaking will replace part of its own profits made with the former technologies through the shift of demand to the newly established technology.[1581] From the described relationship, it is evident that a general answer about the optimal degree of competition in order to yield maximal innovation is not possible. The optimal degree of competition and innovation is specific to the sector and product and also dependent on the current situation in the market.

604 In addition to the difficulties in determining the optimal level, measuring innovation is generally a difficult, if not impossible, task.[1582] The problems start with developing a mutual understanding of 'innovation' in a specific field. It is clear that a surplus to existing knowledge or standards is intrinsic to innovation. Innovations either satisfy actual unmet, inadequately met or potential needs. Measurements of innovation therefore take the status quo as a starting point and track the surplus compared with the current level of solutions and demands.

605 In the pharmaceutical sector, innovations concerning drugs would, considering the above, consist of new therapies for formerly incurable diseases and improvements on existing treatments. Such improvements can be seen in new therapies with first-in-class drugs[1583] or further developments of existing drug classes, such as the

1579. Chowdhury/Gaigl, in: Pitruzzella/Muscolo, Competition and patent law in the pharmaceutical sector, 8.
1580. On this correlation, *see*: Chowdhury/Gaigl, in: Pitruzzella/Muscolo, Competition and patent law in the pharmaceutical sector, 10 f.
1581. Chowdhury/Gaigl, in: Pitruzzella/Muscolo, Competition and patent law in the pharmaceutical sector, 9.
1582. *See supra* at paras 266 ff.
1583. Heiduk, in: Heiduk/Emmerich, Arzneimittelmarkt und europäisches Wettbewerbsrecht, 69 f.

development of galenic and retard (sustained release) forms as examples.[1584] With these types of developments, a cautious analysis is required, however. Different galenic or retard forms do not necessarily add a surplus to existing therapies or even open new fields of application.[1585]

606 Conversely, following the definition above,[1586] novel drugs without additional benefits to existing therapies are not considered innovations. For this reason, methods that measure innovation by using the number of drugs approved containing NCEs[1587] do not necessarily provide viable figures. However, the above economic definition is also too narrow. NCEs which substitute existing therapies add to the known technology as well, as pharmaceuticals cannot always be supported by all people. Therefore, NCEs provide an alternative in cases of incompatibility. Considering analgesics, different chemical entities not only relieve pain and have anti-inflammatory effects but can also cause allergies and incompatibility, as, for example, with paracetamol and ibuprofen. Incremental innovations and NCEs could therefore both qualify as innovation.

III THE EFFECT OF PATENTS ON COMPETITION AND INNOVATION WITHIN THE APPLICATION PROCESS

1 Before the Publication of the Application

607 In most jurisdictions, a patentable invention is generally under no special protection before filing the patent application.[1588] Thus, all privileges related to general material properties apply to the invention as well. Consequently, the inventor holds general property rights to all tangible assets of the invention. An inventor can forbid others from using a specific item such as a prototype machine but cannot prevent copying. Additionally, the inventor can decide when and how the invention will be displayed. In any case, as discussed in depth in the first part,[1589] it holds that in order to economically profit from an invention, it either has to be kept in secret or protected by patent right. Registering a patent is thus primarily a way to engage in competition and not distort it.[1590]

1584. *See*: HEIDUK, in: HEIDUK/EMMERICH, Arzneimittelmarkt und europäisches Wettbewerbsrecht, 67 ff. with further examples.
1585. Imagine, for example, a drug administered by capsule instead of pill. Such a change in the galenic form is not as such beneficial but only if additional benefits such as for example better therapeutic effects come along.
1586. *See supra* at para. 604.
1587. *See supra* at fn. 397.
1588. Noteworthy in this case is Article 35 of the Swiss Patent Act. It protects a third party that used the technology before the patent application in good faith. Also, in cases where a third party planned for the use of the technology before the patent application was filed, the patent cannot be held out to the party.
1589. *See supra* at paras 86 ff.
1590. *See i.a.*: ENCAOUA/MADIÈS, in: MADIÈS/GUELLEC/PRAGER, Patent markets in the global knowledge economy, 126; ULLRICH, in: DREXL/LEE, Pharmaceutical innovation, competition and patent law, 251; ULLRICH/HEINEMANN, in: IMMENGA/MESTMÄCKER 2018, Teil GRUR B, para. 42.

608 Submitting the relevant documents to the patent office is a private process and not open to the public. As a commonly used standard in many jurisdictions,[1591] patent applications are published only after eighteen months from the submission.[1592] This is the patent system's mechanism to secure the information function of the patent while at the same time leaving the applicant time to reconsider.[1593] Through delaying the publication in relation to the filing, a time-limited legal limbo is introduced which continues until the grant of the patent. The submission itself is without immediate consequences for the public or the patent applicant. A patent applicant's power is dependent on the ultimate granting of the exclusive right. From the above, it follows that the publication of the application allows the public to see the patented subject matter after eighteen months and thus to steer their own R&D efforts before the granting of the patent.[1594]

2 After the Publication of the Application

609 Through the publishing of the filed claim, the invention is revealed to the market participants in detail. Publication creates prior art. Through provisional rights, publication also strengthens the position of the applicant with regard to compensation rights. The strengthening of the position is related to the right of the patent holder to ask for compensation. Publication itself does not give the applicant the right to exclude others, but gives grounds for receiving monetary compensation, and in some jurisdictions even to claim damages retrospectively for use of the patented technology during the time gap between the publication and the grant from the time of the publication (provisional protection).[1595]

610 Research data suggest that the possibility of claiming damages is not considered great.[1596] The limited protection available for the patent applicant means that unauthorised use of applied-for patent claims can be an economically advantageous

1591. Note that in the USA the revelation of information in a patent is only a recent development.
1592. Examples are the EPC (Article 93(1)(a) EPC), Switzerland (Article 58a(1)(a) PatA) and Japan (Article 64 of the Japanese Patent Law), but the USA 35 U.S.C. § 122 also allows an opt-out of the publication requirement if the applicant refrains from filing a foreign counterpart. The practice is common in most industrialised countries. *See*: Tegernsee Group, paras 113 ff and 129 ff.
1593. The reason for imposing an eighteen-month period before the publication is that the invention could turn out to be unpatentable. With the 'waiting period' the applicant gets the chance to withdraw the application before the publication. *See*: Tegernsee Group, paras 113 ff.
1594. Tegernsee Group, para. 116.
1595. *See*: 35 U.S.C. § 154 (d); EPO, *National Law Relating to the EPC*, III. A.
1596. This conclusion also applies in jurisdictions in which the legislator or case law have provided the inventor with privileges before filing a patent application, as, for example, in Germany. There the exploitation of an invention, as a consequence of natural law being a historical and conceptual foundation of intellectual property law, is seen as a privilege of the inventor themselves. Against this background, the Federal Constitutional Court accepted an inventor's right along the lines of a 'technical copyright'. This privilege makes the inventor eligible for defence and damage claims. Additionally, the inventor can deduce a claim under public law to be rewarded with the patent grant. However, the inventor's right in this situation is not

option.[1597] Furthermore, a relatively high number of patent applicants have reported that their competitors invented around after the publication of the patented claims.[1598] However, the imminent danger that the patent applicant will prohibit and sanction the use of the technology after the patent grant makes this investment risky. It could be argued that barriers to enter the market are not that high during this period. This is because the infringer in a personal worst-case scenario has to pay a substantial fee for the use of the technology after the grant and potentially the costs of proceedings. Thus, some surveys found evidence that disclosure tends to keep innovators from patenting their innovations rather than motivating them.[1599]

611 From the mid-1990s, the number of patent grants did not grow as fast as the total of patent applications.[1600] Not all pending applications result in granted patents. Nevertheless, the likelihood that a patent will be granted after the publication is high.[1601] It has therefore been argued that the application for a patent has an information effect on the market.[1602] A pending, published application pitches the applicant's claims. Although these claims may be narrowed by the patent office, the publication describes the potential maximum of the scope of the patent. Even if the applicant later withdraws the application, the technology becomes state of the art, leading to un-patentability.[1603]

612 Another argument is that publication, apart from creating state of the art, secures freedom to operate for the applicant. This is owing to the fair chance of receiving a patent grant.[1604] Influenced by the knowledge of an existing patent application, competitors might refrain from developing a technology (further) or abstain from introducing a new product to the market. However, even if certain authors as well as the Commission[1605] have addressed a possible deterrence of innovation through the

exclusive. An exclusive right covering the invention can only be obtained through the patent application (BVerfGE, *Patentanmeldungen*, 1 BvL 5, 6, 9/7, B.I., paras 31 ff.). In practice, however, these inventors' privileges show full effects only between employers and employees. Therefore, and especially due to the fact that Germany follows the first-to-file principle, the position of inventors before filing the patent application in Germany only differs at first sight, and the wording of the Federal Constitutional Court, despite being remarkable, is of reduced importance.

1597. Anton/Yao, RAND Journal of Economics 2004, 2 and 14.
1598. *See infra* at para. 612.
1599. *See*: Duguet/Kabla, Économie et Économétrie de l'innovation 1998, 291, 304 and 318 with further references.
1600. *See*: WIPO statistics database: https://www3.wipo.int/ipstats/index.htm?tab=patent, accessed on 21 January 2020.
1601. Harhoff/Engel/Möschel 2007, 8.
1602. *See*: Burr et al., 39 f.; Jell, 17; Stierle, 29 f.; Aoki/Spiegel point to the potential use of patent applications to mislead rivals. Aoki/Spiegel, International Journal of Industrial Organization 2009, 342.
1603. Jell, 18 ff.
1604. Servier seemed to have planned the application of its blocking patents to ensure the obligatory publication was at a time convenient for the overall strategy. EC, *Servier*, AT.39612, para. 2770.
1605. The EC acknowledged that the insecurity about which claims would eventually protect Servier's products and processes made it more challenging for potential entrants to find out which patents their products might infringe. EC, *Servier*, AT.39612, para. 2770.

design of the current patent system, such an effect has not (yet) been proven.[1606] On the contrary, economic literature suggests that a system where pending patent applications are published is preferable over non-disclosure until the grant. Based on a general model implemented by AOKI/SPIEGEL, publication even enhances the probability of new products.[1607] Through early publication of the patent claims, competitors can adjust their strategy prior to the patent grant and invent around the patented technology.[1608] Additionally, the information revealed can add value to current research all over the industry. Thus, needless R&D expenditure can be reduced.[1609]

613 Summing up the facts, the publication requirement on the one hand imposes a threat for competitors. If granted, the patent holder is allowed to retrospectively claim compensation or even damages for the use of the technology after the publication. Through revealing the technology earlier, the publication also allows competitors to adapt to the developments early and adjust their own efforts. The information published can furthermore contribute to the research of rivals.[1610] Despite the threat of a possible grant and the connected consequences for competitors, the publication itself seems to improve the position of competitors. Admittedly, in the studies cited, publication had only been compared with non-publication. Yet, SCOTCHMER/GREEN found evidence that in systems with weak novelty requirements, firms sometimes refrain from patenting interim developments because of the mandatory disclosure and the positive effect on competitors.[1611] The information function of the patent therefore seems to be of great importance in fostering R&D.[1612] In reaching this conclusion, however, comparison was only made between early and late publication. Studies on the effects of patenting compared with keeping an invention a trade secret or just unravelling the invention without applying for property rights protection are still missing. The conclusions therefore have to be taken with a pinch of salt.

614 Although showing that patent applications affect competition, the effects identified have tended to be positive rather than negative for both competition and innovation. So far, no study appears to have identified a distorting effect of patent applications on the market that could distort competition, which suggests that distortion of competition is unlikely to stem from the publication of pending patent claims.

1606. WALSH/ARORA/COHEN find little evidence that a considerable number of prospering projects were abandoned due to existing property rights, as more than one factor will influence a company's R&D planning. WALSH/ARORA/COHEN, in: MERRILL/COHEN, Patents in the knowledge-based economy, 303 ff.
1607. AOKI/SPIEGEL, International Journal of Industrial Organization 2009, 341; with similar results also: SCOTCHMER/GREEN, The RAND Journal of Economics 1990, 144 f.
1608. Respondents to a survey by the TEGERNSEE GROUP reported a high number of incidents of inventing around and copying after the publication. TEGERNSEE GROUP, paras 116 and 122.
1609. TEGERNSEE GROUP, para. 114; SCOTCHMER/GREEN, The RAND Journal of Economics 1990, 144.
1610. SCOTCHMER/GREEN, The RAND Journal of Economics 1990, 134 f.
1611. SCOTCHMER/GREEN, The RAND Journal of Economics 1990, 144 f.
1612. '[...] the "best fences" are likely to be "low and penetrable"'. DAVID, Journal of Institutional and Theoretical Economics 2004, 30.

3 After the Grant of the Patent

3.1 The Power of the Patent Holder

615 After the grant, a patent endows its holder with many privileges.[1613] The most powerful in relation to the effects on competition is the right to exclude others from using the technology.[1614] The second most concerning for undistorted competition is the possibility to demand compensation for the use of the invention. This exclusive right is part of the reward system that underlies patent law. It should allow the patent holder to receive a decent return on R&D investments.

616 In practice, the patent is only of value for the patent holder if a licence can be sold or sales increased due to the monopoly right. As such, the patent generally strengthens the position of its holder. A patent is, however, far from returning a well-defined value that can be measured. Patents are rights that bring many uncertainties, even after the grant.[1615] Patents compared with other forms of property are probabilistic rights.[1616]

617 Even though results of surveys conclude that protecting one's own invention is typically the main reason for a patent holder to patent rather than blocking, preventing third parties' access to the technology is another often-wanted benefit of seeking protection for the invention.[1617] If a patent holder does not want to prevent others from using its technology, it should not apply for a patent. It is therefore in the nature of the patent to limit the possibilities of competitors in that it excludes competition by imitation. The extent of this effect is, however, dependent on the patent holder's behaviour as well as the characteristics of the technology and the product market. Valid patents cannot limit competitive opportunities per se,[1618] but they complicate residual competition because the use of the protected technology is dependent on the 'approval' of the patent holder. If the patent holder in this situation does execute the blocking power, it diminishes competitive opportunities of actual or potential competitors with the technology as well as the final product market.[1619] Patent law, however, leaves it to the patent holder to decide whether to realise their rewards through licensing or their own use of the technology. This leads to the assumption that the mere presence of a patent in general does not distort either competition or innovation.

1613. The impact of these privileges on competition is based on the patent's (or the portfolio's) merit. The EC held that all threats resulting from the merits of the patent are to be considered within competition on the merits. EC, *Servier*, AT.39612, para. 2793.
1614. Shapiro strongly relativises this power. As only a limited number of granted patents have commercial relevance, he attests that the patent holder has only been given a possibility to exclude. Shapiro, RAND Journal of Economics 2003, 395.
1615. Lemley/Shapiro, Journal of Economic Perspectives 2005, 95.
1616. *See supra* at para. 216.
1617. *See supra* at paras 201 ff.
1618. Patented innovations can still be used for trials and their information used to invent around. *See*, for example, Straus, GRUR Int 2009, 97 ff.
1619. Lamping, 228 ff.

3.2 *Distorting Effect of Patents*

618 The distorting effect addressed here could also be circumscribed as a signalling effect to competitors instead of investors, as the term 'signalling effect' is generally used.[1620] The question is whether the mere presence of a patent changes a competitor's attitude towards their own R&D projects. If a higher number of patents does not result in lower competition or innovation activities, then the distorting effect of additional patents can be considered generally low. The assumption is that as long as competitors have sufficient access to the patented technology, even in cases of a technology being protected by additional property rights, competition is not distorted.

619 Without further knowledge of industries and technologies, one would assume the distorting effect to be bigger when the blocking power immanent in the patent is bigger. This is assumed under the following conditions: first, the broader the patent and the more features covered, the harder it is to invent around. Both access to the technology and possibilities for further research are narrowed.[1621] Second, patents on basic innovations (basic patents) have more blocking power, as further developments are dependent on the underlying basic patent.[1622] The holder of the basic patent has the power to hamper all further developments as long as they depend on the basic technology. Third, patents on further developments (secondary patents) have more blocking power when the patent holder already holds the basic patent and when development of alternatives is costly, lengthy or difficult.[1623]

620 Nowadays, more than one intellectual property right protects the technology behind most products.[1624] Sometimes various licensing litigation with different parties precedes the development of a marketable product. A patent holder holding a patent to a necessary part of the technology thus has the potential to block the whole development. Additionally, the high costs of negotiating various different licences may discourage competitors from developing and launching a product. Addressing these concerns, in 1998 HELLER formulated the theory of the tragedy of anticommons.[1625] It states that if too many owners (partly) own a technology and can block others from using it, the danger exists that the technology will be underused due to mutual blocking.[1626]

1620. *See*, for example, BURR ET AL., 40 f.; LAMPING, 142 f.; STIERLE, 30 f.
1621. Concerns addressed in: WALSH/ARORA/COHEN, in: MERRILL/COHEN, Patents in the knowledge-based economy, 296 f.
1622. On basic patents, *see supra* at paras 229 ff.
1623. On secondary patents, *see supra* at paras 240 ff.
1624. Smartphones are a frontrunner with allegedly about 250,000 active patents involved. HECKENDORF, Süddeutsche Zeitung 30 August 2011.
1625. Anticommons refers to 'a property regime in which multiple owners hold effective rights of exclusion in a scarce resource'. HELLER, Harvard Law Review 1998, 673. The 'tragedy of anticommons' is an adaption of the tragedy of commons introduced by HARDIN to explain overuse of common resources. HARDIN, Science 1968, 1243.
1626. HELLER, Harvard Law Review 1998, 677 ff.; HELLER/EISENBERG, Science 1998.

621 The tragedy of anticommons has been challenged on various occasions. WALSH ET AL. evaluated R&D in the biomedical industry where the tragedy of anticommons, according to HELLER/EISENBERG,[1627] is likely to occur. The study did not find much evidence supporting the concerns of HELLER/EISENBERG. WALSH ET AL. found that even if more patents cover a technology, it is not more likely that bargaining breakdowns will occur. Other studies including data from the field of biotechnology have even identified a positive effect of multiple patents. According to the hypothesis of the authors GALASSO/SCHENKERMANN, the more patents that are needed for a product, the lower the contribution of each and therefore the bargaining power of each holder. This effect is enhanced when intellectual property rights overlap. Thus, the incentives of each patent holder to sue the infringer decrease. Settlements on technologies with fragmented protection were found to be reached quicker.[1628] The same can be said for licensing agreements. Standard-setting organisations even convince their members to give royalty-free licences. Pursuing infringements in these cases is often not economical.[1629] A negative effect of patent applications has so far been identified, as a large number of registered patents can reduce the pace of the negotiation process due to the large number of patents that need to be considered.[1630]

622 Another reason why registered patents might not deter competition is seen in the number of patents used for a marketable product. Though initially many patents may seem to be related to a product, in the end, often only a handful would be infringed through a product or research.[1631]

3.3 *Patent Pools as a Remedy to Counteract the Deterrent Effect of the Presence of Patents?*

623 An evaluation of the effect of patent pools might provide further information about whether patents, through their mere presence, can hamper competition. If many patents held by different holders might distort competition and reduce innovation, patent pools could provide a remedy. For their members, patent pools reduce blocking and transaction costs as well as the risk of costly infringement litigation. Patent pools simulate joint ownership of technology.[1632]

624 Results of studies on the effect of patent pools with respect to the costs associated with fragmented patent holders are mixed. For one thing, licensing fees are reduced

1627. HELLER/EISENBERG, Science 1998, 701.
1628. GALASSO/SCHANKERMAN, The RAND Journal of Economics 2010, 501; LICHTMAN, U Chicago Law and Economics, Olin Working Paper No 292 2006, 7 f.
1629. On the whole *see*: LICHTMAN, U Chicago Law and Economics, Olin Working Paper No 292 2006, 2 and 6.
1630. GALASSO/SCHANKERMAN, The RAND Journal of Economics 2010, 499 ff.; on patenting strategies including several patents, *see* paras 240 ff.
1631. WALSH/ARORA/COHEN, in: MERRILL/COHEN, Patents in the knowledge-based economy, 294.
1632. Note that the findings of this subsection are mainly based on the findings of LAMPE/MOSER and their study on the sewing machine patent pool (1856-1877). *See* hereinafter at fns 1633 ff.

and members of a patent pool face fewer threats from lawsuits.[1633] Due to the joint litigation risk for members, however, the risk of outsiders getting involved in a lawsuit is raised.[1634] In order to match the patent pool, outsiders' patenting activities increase, while the insiders patent less. Overall, patent pools reduce the number of patents in an industry.[1635] This may not necessarily be negative. The parties in the patent pool may stop patenting defensively, as threats to get involved in litigation are reduced and their bargaining position is strengthened. Patent pools thus address one threat of patents on effective competition in that they seem to reduce the overall licensing costs in an industry. As such, they guarantee easier access to technologies. Outsiders, however, face an increased threat of litigation and pooling patents does not encourage innovation; it rather slows it down.[1636]

3.4 Patent Invalidation

625 While the above-mentioned studies have focused on the effect of patents held by different patent holders in cumulative industries, the effect of individual patents on follow-on innovation has not yet been considered. In order to develop an understanding of the impact of individual patents on innovation, GALASSO/SCHANKERMAN examined the effect of judicial patent invalidation on follow-on innovation, using citations as a measurement of knowledge spillovers.[1637] The results presented by the authors show a great differentiation with respect to specific sectors. In most sectors, no effect resulting from the invalidation of a patent could be identified. Where the effects did show, the sectors were characterised by complexity of products and high fragmentation of ownership, namely in the biotechnology, electronics and medical instruments industries.[1638] In addition, the invalidation of stronger patents generally had a greater effect on follow-on innovation than the invalidation of weaker patents, but weaker patents showed a higher probability of being invalidated compared with strong patents. Of general interest with respect to the abuse of a dominant position was the finding that invalidations of patents held by SMEs did not show an effect, while the invalidation of a large undertaking's patent caused significantly more citations by small- and medium-sized firms.[1639]

626 GALASSO/SCHANKERMAN did not identify a spurt of innovation caused by patent invalidation in the drug and chemical industry. The authors concluded that in the drug sector, generic companies, which do not generally engage in R&D, primarily challenge the validity of patents. The authors thus suggested that follow-on innovation was not

1633. For example, in the case of the sewing machine patent pool in the USA: LAMPE/MOSER, The Journal of Economic History 2010, 901 ff.
1634. LAMPE/MOSER, The Journal of Economic History 2010, 907 f.
1635. LAMPE/MOSER, The Journal of Economic History 2010, 911 f.
1636. LAMPE/MOSER, The Journal of Economic History 2010, 915 ff.
1637. GALASSO/SCHANKERMAN, The Quarterly Journal of Economics 2015, 319 ff.
1638. GALASSO/SCHANKERMAN, The Quarterly Journal of Economics 2015, 321 f.
1639. GALASSO/SCHANKERMAN, The Quarterly Journal of Economics 2015, 322.

the motivation for challenging the validity of drug patents in the drug industry.[1640] Data from the Commission's sector inquiry of the pharmaceutical industry indeed shows that in approximately nine out of ten disputes, it was the originator who initiated the dispute (mostly infringement claims).[1641] Yet, only 54 per cent of the litigation cases concerning the validity of the patent were launched by originator companies. These numbers indicate that generic companies mainly engage in disputes to clear generic entry.[1642] The hypothesis is supported by the fact that litigation cases between originator and generic companies are far more frequent than between originators (only sixty-six out of seven hundred cases[1643]). Litigation between originators largely concerned only a handful of INNs (International Nonproprietary Names)[1644], and in most cases, both originator companies had an R&D programme in the same ATC3 class, thus conducting similar R&D activities.[1645] In disputes which ended in a final judgment (thirteen cases), the patent was only upheld in one case and annulled in seven cases, while the remaining five cases concerned infringement cases only.[1646]

IV CONCLUSION

627 Patents as means to compete *per definitionem* affect competition and have, as has been outlined, the potential to influence the market structure.[1647] Owing to the mechanisms of the application process, distortion is, however, unlikely to originate from the mere filing of a patent.

628 The application process itself is a non-public event. Even though the patent unfolds certain effects retrospectively, access to the patented technology can only be blocked after the grant.[1648] The grant is the end of the process, out of the sphere of the patent holder. As seen above, the right of an inventor to receive a patent is in most cases granted by law and is part of the property regimes.[1649] A prerequisite is having a patentable invention. Patent law provides that a grant follows the patent application if the legal requirements are met. The act of submitting the documents is the only part of the patent application process that is subject to the will of the applicant. If it was just the application under scrutiny, the submission of the documents would be the sole act that could be qualified as an abuse of a dominant position but only if it resulted in a distortion of competition.

1640. GALASSO/SCHANKERMAN, The Quarterly Journal of Economics 2015, 349 ff.
1641. EC, *Sector Inquiry, Final Report,* para. 564.
1642. EC, *Sector Inquiry, Final Report,* paras 586 and 597.
1643. EC, *Sector Inquiry, Final Report,* paras 698 and 1174.
1644. The INN is an international standard used to identify pharmaceutical ingredients. *See*: https://www.who.int/medicines/services/inn/en/, accessed on 27 April 2020.
1645. EC, *Sector Inquiry, Final Report,* paras 1176 and 1198.
1646. EC, *Sector Inquiry, Final Report,* para. 1194.
1647. *See supra* at paras 341, 381 f. and 595.
1648. *See supra* at para. 615.
1649. *See supra* at paras 190 ff.

629 It has further been shown that the interpretation of the effects of patent applications on the market is highly delicate and robust general findings are rare. The effect of a patent is situational. Certain indications have been given that the effect is dependent on factors such as the type of invention (basic, follow-on or cumulative innovation), the breadth of the patent as well as the market and technology situation or the position of the patent holder within the market and technology. Yet, it follows that the mere fact that a patent has been granted is unlikely to distort competition.

630 The granted patent does, however, affect competition and has the potential to strengthen positions in the market and therewith a dominant position. Therefore, it could theoretically amount to a distortion of competition but only in very rare cases. A distorting effect might occur when:

- a dominant undertaking patents several minor developments within a field of research where competitors are present;
- a dominant undertaking patents the further development of the only technology competing with its own products, or
- a dominant undertaking patents in response to patents of competitors.

631 In the pharmaceutical sector, this might be the case when only two therapies that meet a medical demand exist and the dominant undertaking supplying therapy A patents a development of therapy B.[1650] In these situations, as has been argued by the General Court for secondary acquisitions in the case of *Tetra Pak I*, a distortion might arise, since competition with respect to the medical demand is controlled by the dominant undertaking, even if the dominant undertaking does not refuse to license the technology.[1651] A distortion can therefore only occur based on the application of a patent if as an additional element competition is factually eliminated or severely hampered.[1652] In these cases, it might also be concluded that the conduct lacks justification and that therefore abusive intent is immanent in the behaviour itself (objective intent).

632 In most situations, however, a distortion of competition will only arise as a result of the patent holder's behaviour.[1653] That is, if the patent applicant does not respect the legal rules and acts fraudulently or beyond the scope of patent law (breach of contract

1650. Note that the loss of market shares because of a new entrant is only one concern of undertakings in the pharmaceutical industry. In countries (such as, e.g., Switzerland) where the price for a drug is set by the state based on a comparison with other drugs already on the national market that have a comparable therapeutic effect, the entrance of a substitute does not only potentially erode market shares but might also result in a lower selling price set by the state. A dominant undertaking has therefore additional interests to prevent competitors from launching substitute therapies.
1651. GC, *Tetra Pak I*, T-51/89, paras 23 f.
1652. Berg/Köbele propose that the factual elimination of competition is taken as a precondition for the finding of an abuse of a dominant position through the primary acquisition of patents. Berg/Köbele, PharmaR 2009, 590.
1653. Notable in this regard is the finding of Reiss, according to which offensive and defensive patents cannot be distinguished based on the patent claims or the portfolio but only on the motivation and conduct of the patent holder. Reiss, 326.

with society).[1654] As case law indicates, such behaviour might, at the time of applying for a patent, occur through providing fraudulent information to authorities or knowingly patenting unpatentable subjects.[1655] Since using an invention in competition always includes a strategic decision, evaluating the intention of a patent applicant would allow a more precise estimation of the potential effects of the patent. It could therefore be suggested that a patent applicant's intention of how the property right will be executed should be considered at the time of application. This argument is not convincing, however. If it is the use of the patent and not the property position itself which causes the distortion of competition, there is little need to analyse the application as separate conduct, as the behaviour will show eventually. The patent claim itself does not represent the full threat to competition. Whether a patent is distorting competition can only be judged on how it is used.

633 Concluding on the above, one cannot help but agree with GALASSO/SCHANKERMAN on their comment concerning the effect of patents on cumulative innovation: 'The main conclusion from these studies is that anything can happen – patent rights may impede, have no effect, or even facilitate subsequent technological development. It depends critically on assumptions about the bargaining environment and contracting efficiency between different generations of innovators.'[1656]

634 Certain fundamental conclusions can still be drawn, however. The first was discussed with respect to broad basic patents, but applies for many secondary patents accumulated in one portfolio as well: the broader the subject matter of the patent or patents held by one entity, the harder to invent around and therefore the higher the detrimental impact on competition and innovation. Other important factors in determining the detrimental impact are the value of the innovation itself (key to follow-on) and the availability of different lines of innovation. Additionally, a time-related factor influences the blocking power. The blocking power of secondary patents is highest at the end of the exclusivity period of the basic patent. A vast number of patents can hamper innovation owing to the difficulty of evaluating potential infringements.[1657]

635 Other than these fundamental mechanisms, the analysis of the effects of patents on competition has led to the result that the immediate effect of a patent appearing on the market only rarely amounts to a distortion of competition. More important than the number and breadth of patents on a market is the conduct of the patent holder. Acquisitions of portfolios or exclusive licences are forms of competitive behaviour which occur when the publication of the patented information has already occurred and where neither the allocation of resources for further development nor the protection of one's own inventions can be cited as justification. In fostering innovation and competition, it is essential to keep markets open and reduce market entry barriers

1654. This is the same understanding underlying the US patent misuse doctrine. *See supra* at paras 397 ff.
1655. *See supra* at paras 338 ff.
1656. GALASSO/SCHANKERMAN, The Quarterly Journal of Economics 2015, 319.
1657. On flooding strategies, *see supra* at paras 240 ff.

to allow entry.[1658] Therefore, the accumulation of patent rights in the hands of a few should not gain prevalence, as the data on patent pools has shown. Primary and secondary acquisitions cannot be measured equally.

1658. SCHERER/ROSS, 660.

CHAPTER 18

Balancing Interests

I THE RELEVANCE OF FUNDAMENTAL RIGHTS FOR THE ANALYSIS

636 The analysis of Article 102 TFEU has revealed that the abuse of a dominant position seeks to limit the competitive freedom of dominant undertakings where the conduct in question would pose a threat to competition. The phrase 'competitive freedom' is used to describe the opportunities of an undertaking within the competitive process. While the number of actual opportunities is dependent on the situation in the market and the undertaking's position therein, competitive freedom as the fundamental freedom of action is protected by fundamental rights. Fundamental rights are not granted limitless but can be restricted where public interest demands limitations. Fundamental rights therefore face external limitations in the form of public interest. One of these public interests - the functioning of competition - has been codified within competition law.

637 Within the terminology of fundamental rights, an undertaking's freedom of action is known as the freedom to conduct business and is granted under Article 16 of the European Charter of Fundamental Rights ('the Charter'). This fundamental freedom is rather broad and 'covers the freedom to exercise an economic or commercial activity, the freedom of contract and free competition [...]'.[1659] The core elements of entrepreneurial freedom, as granted within Article 16 of the Charter, are the right to start, end and conduct one's own entrepreneurial activity, freedom of contract, freedom of advertising, freedom of trade as well as the freedom to merge with other companies.[1660] Freedom of competition is often mentioned as an element of entrepreneurial freedom as well. Yet, the individual right immanent in the freedom of competition is situated within the freedom of profession rather than entrepreneurial freedom.[1661] The freedom

1659. ECJ, *Sky Österreich*, C-283/11, para. 42.
1660. NOWAK, in: HESELHAUS/NOWAK, Handbuch der europäischen Grundrechte, § 35, paras 30 ff.
1661. NOWAK, in: HESELHAUS/NOWAK, Handbuch der europäischen Grundrechte, § 35, para. 35.

of profession is granted in Article 15 of the Charter and covers the personal right to choose and pursue a career.[1662] The two fundamental economic rights are entangled, however. This can also be seen in the case law of the Court of Justice. According to the interpretation of the Court of Justice as presented by NOWAK, entrepreneurial freedom is seen as part of the freedom of profession.[1663]

638 The conduct analysed within this book concerns the acquisition of blocking patents. Patents as intellectual property rights,[1664] like property rights in general, are also subject to protection by fundamental rights.[1665] The fundamental right to property is granted through Article 17 of the Charter and was also recognised by the Court of Justice as a fundamental principle of the Union law in 1979.[1666] The article grants the right to own, sell, abandon and exploit legitimately acquired property. The right to property therefore protects the holder's right to own the property, to use and to dispose of it. The acquisition of property generally falls within the scope of entrepreneurial freedom as granted in Article 16 of the Charter rather than within the right to property, which protects the acquired (owned) in its substance (possession).[1667] Furthermore, Article 17 provides the right to defend oneself against interference with the property by the state or by private persons. With Article 17(2) the Charter expands the property rights' protection to intellectual property rights as well. The fundamental right to property has a protective element with respect to status as well as disposition. In this regard, ULLRICH writes of a dual autonomy granted to businesses.[1668] Despite the minimal guarantee of the fundamental right to property, property rights are only guaranteed up to a 'socially acceptable' degree, which is defined by the objectives of general interest pursued by the community.[1669]

639 Since the enactment of the Charter, restrictions and deprivations of property rights have to meet the standards stated in Article 17. According to this provision, interference with the property right in the form of expropriation or restriction of the property requires a legal basis as well as public interest to be justified. Additionally, expropriation, in contrast to restrictions on the property, is subject to compensation.[1670] In the context of restrictions, public interest is evaluated with regard to the principle of proportionality. The Court of Justice when analysing proportionality attaches high importance to the goals pursued by the Union.[1671] The court has already accepted

1662. JARASS, Article 15, para. 8; NOWAK, in: HESELHAUS/NOWAK, Handbuch der europäischen Grundrechte, § 34, paras 37 ff.
1663. NOWAK, in: HESELHAUS/NOWAK, Handbuch der europäischen Grundrechte, § 34, para. 2.
1664. PIEPER, in: DAUSES/LUDWIGS, Handbuch des EU-Wirtschaftsrechts, para. 96.
1665. In case law, the ECJ expressly assigned intellectual property rights to the property rights system as well. ECJ, *Generics (UK) and Others I*, C-368/96, paras 78 ff. *See also* Article 17(2) of the Charter.
1666. First in: ECJ, *Nold v. Commission*, C-4/73, paras 13 f. It was not only property rights that were accepted as fundamental rights by the ECJ before the enactment of the Charter. For an overview, *see*: ZÄCH/HEIZMANN, paras 37 ff.
1667. *See*, for example, JARASS, Article 17, para. 4.
1668. ULLRICH, in: DREXL/LEE, Pharmaceutical innovation, competition and patent law, 251.
1669. ECJ, *Germany v. Council*, C-280/93, para. 78.
1670. SONNEVEND, in: GRABENWARTER, Europäischer Grundrechteschutz, paras 70 f.
1671. SONNEVEND, in: GRABENWARTER, Europäischer Grundrechteschutz, paras 75 f.

far-reaching interference with property rights, such as the slaughtering of whole fish populations to prevent an epidemic, as a restriction to the execution of a property right in the interest of the goals of the Union.[1672]

640 With Article 345 TFEU, there is a second norm concerning the protection of property rights in EU law.[1673] According to its wording, the Treaty shall in no way prejudice the rules in Member States governing the system of property ownership. Historically, Article 345 TFEU had the function of granting autonomy to the Member States in designing their property rights regimes.[1674] It originated from the problem that, while the founding members decided to build the Union on free competition, certain national economies were shaped by the presence of nationalised enterprises in the aftermath of World War II. Article 345 TFEU therefore does not grant fundamental rights to private property but is limited to regulating competences of the Union and the Member States in the field of property rights.[1675] The scope of Article 345 TFEU has been concretised in extensive case law. Contrary to what the wording might indicate, the article does not exempt property law from the influence of the Union's law. The General Court held: '[...] notwithstanding the provision in question, other provisions of the Treaty empower the Community to adopt sanctions or preventative measures influencing the right of individuals to property. That is the case, in particular, in the fields of competition (article 83 of the Treaty establishing the European Community) [...]'.[1676] In the case of *Konle*, the Court of Justice concluded that Member States are only allowed to exercise their powers within the limits of the law of the Union.[1677] Competences of the Member States have the reservation that they do not contradict the goals of the Union.

641 Unlike Article 17 of the Charter, Article 345 TFEU is not a fundamental guarantee, but the legal basis regulating the competences of the Union and the Member States in the field of property rights. According to Article 345 TFEU, the assignment of property rights is within the competence of the Member States (assignment of private and public

1672. ECJ, *Booker Aquaculture and Hydro Seafood*, C-20/00 and C-64/00, paras 67 ff.
1673. HARACOGLOU even claims that Article 345 TFEU marks the starting point of all evaluations of the position of intellectual property rights in the legal structure of EU legislation. HARACOGLOU, 103. Note that despite the wording which only refers to property rights, it is widely acknowledged that Article 345 TFEU also concerns intellectual property rights. *See*: AG ROEMER, in: *Parke/Davis*, C-24/67, 77; GASTER, Computer und Recht 2005, 248.
1674. KINGREEN, in: CALLIESS/RUFFERT, EUV/AEUV, Article 345, para. 2; KÜHLING, in: STREINZ/MICHL, EUV/AEUV/GrCh, Article 345, para. 3.
1675. KINGREEN, in: CALLIESS/RUFFERT, EUV/AEUV, Article 345, para. 5. Article 345 TFEU is what is called a competence norm. *See*: BÄR-BOUYSSIÈRE, in: VON DER GROEBEN ET AL., Kommentar EU-Recht, Article 345, para. 2. It leaves the classification of property rights in either public or personal rights to the Member States, as long as this categorisation does not interfere with the objectives of the Union. Dissenting opinions are mainly from previous doctrines that interpreted the article more broadly. Yet many of these have adopted a narrower approach as well. *See* references and conclusion in: KÜHLING, in: STREINZ/MICHL, EUV/AEUV/GrCh, Article 345, para. 10.
1676. GC, *Minin v. Commission*, T-362/04, para. 77. With respect to competition law, *see*: ECJ, *Consten/Grundig*, Joined Cases C-56/64 and 58/64, 345; GC, *Ufex and Others v. Commission*, T-613/97, para. 77.
1677. ECJ, *Konle*, C-302/97, para. 38; ECJ, *British American Tobacco*, C-491/01, para. 147.

property) as long as this assignment does not interfere with the objectives of the Union. Generally, property rights are restricted when they interfere with the goals of the Union.[1678] One of these goals – the object of protection of competition law – is undistorted competition.[1679] Both Article 345 TFEU and Article 17 of the Charter therefore provide the basis for restrictions of property rights in order to guarantee the functioning of competition.[1680] An analysis will require balancing the right to property and the fundamental right of freedom of competition against the greater aim of society that competitors compete by virtue of performance only.

642 The Court of Justice's definition of the abuse of a dominant position makes clear that 'means to an end' are not relevant. Considering the wording of the judgment, the court therefore did not exclude the use of legally guaranteed privileges. The right to apply for a patent to keep it as a blocking position, rather than use it, has to be weighed against the aim of undistorted competition and the fostering of innovation immanent in competition law. Thereby, it should be noted that patents are primarily means to allow competition and not to block it.[1681] The delicate weighing of interests needed when working out the lines between rightful and potentially abusive patent applications therefore has to respect the functions of patent law detached from its mere usage. These two elements will thus be subject to the final analysis of balancing of interests. The starting point is an analysis of whether the right to acquire a patent can be limited based on economic considerations. The second part of the analysis will shed light on whether and to what extent unused patents (still) fulfil the aim of patent law.

II LIMITATIONS TO THE FUNDAMENTAL RIGHT TO PROPERTY

1 Outline of the Section

643 As property rights, patents face not only external but also internal limitations.[1682] Patents are only provided if certain preconditions are met and can only be invoked against competitors who make use of the protected technology. Since patents are a socially designed form of rewarding an inventor for their contribution to innovation, the requirements and expectations of the system are specified in each jurisdiction. In designing the patent law, policymakers can decide on the range, the privileges and the preconditions of patent protections, tailored to the specific economic environment. For example, policymakers can steer which contributions are mandatory to earn the merit of a patent grant and the connected privileges. They can include legal facts and their

1678. *See supra* at para. 640.
1679. *See supra* at paras 423 ff.
1680. *See also supra* at paras 121 ff. Deprivations of property are principally allowed in the Union. *See*: von Danwitz, in: von Danwitz/Depenheuer/Engel, Bericht zur Lage des Eigentums, 271.
1681. Ullrich, in: Drexl/Lee, Pharmaceutical innovation, competition and patent law, 251.
1682. The terminology of internal and external limitations to property rights by fundamental rights is used by Geiger in a 2004 article on fundamental and property rights. *See*: Geiger, IIC 2004, 270 and 275.

consequences. Yet inefficiencies of the patent system result in patents being granted despite not meeting the patentability criteria.

644 Property is only protected by the fundamental right to property if it was lawfully acquired. Formally existing rights which have not been legally acquired and have no materially founded reason for existence are not protected. Lawfulness thereby requires a protectable subject matter as well as a lawful assignment thereof, via either patent application or contractual acquisition.[1683] Patents not meeting the patentability requirements do not enjoy the protection of Article 17 of the Charter, as they do not cover protectable subject matter.[1684] The question with respect to blocking patents is whether the feared negative effects on competition resulting from the use of a blocking position can render a patentable subject matter unpatentable, and further, whether and to what extent economic concerns raised by patenting strategies can result in a loss of the claim to a patent. If a dominant undertaking loses the claim to the patent based on its conduct, the behaviour is not legitimate and where it is likely to result in the distortion of competition it constitutes an abuse of the dominant position. This section will start with an analysis of the potential limitations in patentability requirements and then proceed to analyse whether a failure to use the patent in trade results in a loss of the claim to the patent.

2 Patentability Requirements

2.1 General Considerations

645 A side effect of the broad and relatively detailed harmonisation of substantive patent law on an international level is that it leaves little need for harmonisation within the EU. The intellectual property rights regime of the EU is characterised by the parallel existence of national legislation and the laws of the Union. As seen above,[1685] the Union's primary law with Article 345 TFEU not only contains a provision which obliges the EU legislator to accept the property rights regimes of the Member States but also provides a basis for intervention when the goals of the Union are at stake.

646 However, EU constitutional law does not contain substantive intellectual property law. For the internal market, the EU lacks far-reaching harmonisation of patent law in the Union's legal instruments.[1686] The predominant legal provision of the law of patents in Europe is the EPC. This convention, despite being signed by all Member

1683. Frenz, para. 2886.
1684. Frenz, para. 2884.
1685. *See supra* at paras 638 ff.
1686. To date in EU law, there are only two directives that harmonise patentability: Directive 98/44, which harmonises the patentability of biotechnological inventions, and Directive 1768/92, which regulates the grant of SPCs, only concern specific sectors, however. With the introduction of the European patent with unitary effect (EPUE), the EU sought closure of legal loopholes with respect to the effect of patents. The EPUE is based on two regulations of the European Parliament (Regulation (EU) No 1257/2012 and Regulation (EU) No 1260/2012) and thus on secondary EU legislation. The harmonisation resulting after the creation of the

States, is a multilateral treaty and not issued by the EU as legislator. With respect to patentability, the EPC in Article 52 has copied Article 27 TRIPS.[1687] Arguably due to the high and common standard set by the TRIPS Agreement, the EU legislator felt little need to harmonise patentability requirements. With respect to patentability, this means that Articles 52 and 53a EPC and thus international law are the relevant provision securing a minimal standard at Union level. With Article 53a EPC, the exclusion from patentability where 'the commercial exploitation of [the patented invention] would be contrary to *ordre public* or morality' has also found its way into European patent law.

2.2 Limitations to Patentability

647 Article 53a EPC acknowledges the necessity to refuse patent protection to certain innovations at an early stage to protect *ordre public* and morality and therewith legitimate societal interests. With the term '*ordre public*', or public policy as is often used in the English legal terminology,[1688] one refers to a jurisdiction's fundamental values.[1689] *Ordre public* is especially important in international private law with regard to the question of whether the law of another country must be applied in international matters. It functions as a corrective where the applicable foreign law would contradict the fundamental values acknowledged, such as the fundamental rights.[1690]

648 At Union level, *ordre public* and morality are codified in Article 36 TFEU which holds that Member States can prohibit or restrict the import, export or transit of goods on grounds of public morality, public policy or public security ('triad of the ordre public'[1691]). Therefore, a concretisation of the terms has only taken place in the context of the free movement of goods in relation to the interests of the Member States. In this context, balancing the free movement of goods with the exclusive right of the patent holder has resulted in the principle of EU-wide exhaustion.[1692] Fundamentally, the lawful use of a right as guaranteed by the Member State finds its limits where it results in the 'artificial partitioning of the markets'.[1693]

EPUE, however, concerns neither patentability requirements nor the application process. Receiving an EPUE is dependent on the grant of a European Patent based on the EPC.

1687. Patents according to Article 27(1) TRIPS have to be granted for inventions 'whether products or processes, in all fields of technology, provided that they are new, involve an inventive step and are capable of industrial application'.
1688. *See*: HAY, in: BAETGE ET AL., FS Kropholler, Comments on public policy in current American conflicts law, 89 f.
1689. PIRES DE CARVALHO, The TRIPS Regime of Patents and Test Data, para. 27.112.
1690. FREY/PFEIFER, EuR 2015, 726 ff.
1691. *See*: BRIGOLA, in: DAUSES/LUDWIGS, Handbuch des EU-Wirtschaftsrechts, paras 243 ff.
1692. *See supra* at paras 125 f.
1693. MÜLLER-GRAFF, in: VON DER GROEBEN ET AL., Kommentar EU-Recht, Article 36 AEUV, para. 79.

649 The Court of Justice has left the Member States with large discretion in defining the national understanding of *ordre public* and morality.[1694] Yet, national understandings must follow the fundamentals of the law of the Union.[1695] Although the Court of Justice in general limits itself to an assessment of proportionality when the interpretation of public morality is disputed, it has commented several times on the interpretation of public policy or public security. Public policy or public security must, according to the court, be understood as narrow as securing the basic interests of a jurisdiction.[1696] At EU level, such a fundamental interest has been found in the functioning of the economy.[1697]

650 The understanding of *ordre public* within Article 27 of the TRIPS Agreement differs, however. Article 27(2) TRIPS, like Article 53a EPC, is understood as reserving the right of the Member States to refuse patent law protection of inventions when the commercial exploitation thereof is prohibited and would endanger the *ordre public* or morality.[1698] According to a common understanding, non-patentability can only be established if commercial exploitation of the patented invention would endanger either the public order or a society's attitude to morality. The existence of another national legal prohibition not addressing *ordre public* or morality of the commercial exploitation itself is not sufficient to allow the refusal of patentability.[1699]

651 Yet, in certain cases, fundamental societal interests can be endangered at the time of establishing the property right.[1700] One could also conclude that the TRIPS Agreement recognises the importance of giving its Member States the opportunity not only to refuse protection to the execution of patent rights in certain cases but also to refuse patent protection itself. The WTO Panel with its reasoning in the case of *Canada – Patent Protection of Pharmaceutical Products* also supports this interpretation. The panel based its decision on Article 27 in conjunction with Article 30 TRIPS which allows for limited exceptions to the rights conferred by a patent,[1701] while respecting the fundamentals in Articles 7 and 8.[1702]

1694. ECJ, *Henn and Darby*, C-34/79, paras 15 f.
1695. LEIBLE/STREINZ, in: GRABITZ ET AL., EUV/AEUV, Article 36, para. 17; MÜLLER-GRAFF, in: VON DER GROEBEN ET AL., Kommentar EU-Recht, Article 36 AEUV, para. 57.
1696. ECJ, *Omega*, C-36/02, para. 30; BRIGOLA, in: DAUSES/LUDWIGS, Handbuch des EU-Wirtschaftsrechts, para. 244, especially fn. 602 with further references.
1697. ECJ, *Campus Oil*, C-72/83, para. 34.
1698. CORREA, EIPR 1994, 328; dissenting: STRAUS, in: BEIER/SCHRICKER, From GATT to TRIPS – the agreement on trade-related aspects of intellectual property rights, 181.
1699. CORREA, in: CORREA/YUSUF, Intellectual property and international trade, 267 f.
1700. Within the TRIPS Agreement, this thought was expressed most clearly in the Anell Draft of 1990. There it was discussed whether the mere publication of the invention should be qualified as violation of the *ordre public*. *See*: VON SAINT-ANDRÉ/TAŞDELEN, in: BUSCHE ET AL., TRIPS Kommentar, Article 27(2), para. 59.
1701. Of importance for exceptions under Article 27 TRIPS is that they meet the three conditions set out in Article 30 TRIPS. Any exception has to be limited ('narrow curtailment' of legal rights granted in Article 27 TRIPS), and not unreasonably conflict with normal exploitation, or prejudice legitimate interests of the patent owner. *See*: WTO, *Canada – Patent Protection of Pharmaceutical Products*, WT/DS114/R, paras 7.20 ff.
1702. On the relationship between Articles 7, 8, 27, 28 and 30 TRIPS, *see*: WTO, *Canada – Patent Protection of Pharmaceutical Products*, WT/DS114/R, paras 7.26 and 7.92.

652 In practice, as was the case in *Canada – Patent Protection of Pharmaceutical Products*, Article 27 is mainly used as a basis for applying more restrictive standards to patentability with respect to selected areas of technology. Some developing countries, above all India, have implemented more strict rules for the patentability of pharmaceuticals.[1703] However, not only developing countries have claimed legitimate interests but also members of the EPC have relied on the said regulations when implementing reservations[1704] with respect to the patentability of software.[1705] Yet, one of the most important decisions on patentability and TRIPS-compliance concerned pharmaceuticals. It was the decision by the Indian Supreme Court where the pharmaceutical company Novartis claimed the incompatibility of section 3(d) IndPA with the TRIPS Agreement.[1706] Section 3(d) IndPA denies patentability for saline forms of already known active substances.[1707] Its aim is the prevention of a patent strategy known as evergreening.[1708]

653 Evergreening is a strategy which generally results in the delayed market entry of generic producers if applied.[1709] Despite the conceptual differences between blocking patent strategies and evergreening, the mention of evergreening in connection with section 3(d) IndPA is still relevant for this book, as it is another patenting strategy raising competition law concerns, and the prevention of evergreening through patentability requirements can only be explained in the interests of influencing competition. Unsurprisingly, the strengthening of the generic drug industry is a major concern of developing countries due to their dependence on affordable health care.

654 In a previous case, Novartis challenged the provision as incompliant with the TRIPS Agreement as well as the Indian constitution before the Madras High Court. The court held that the provision was aimed at creating checks and balances against abusive conduct.[1710] It declared the provision as compliant with the Indian constitution but considered itself incapable of analysing TRIPS-compliance of the provision.[1711] The

1703. It is not intended to discuss the compatibility of the Indian Patent Act, especially section 3(d) in this book. *See*: BERTHOLD, 174 ff.
1704. A more protection-friendly approach towards the patentability of software was taken by the US courts. However, in the US also, the authorities struggle to reconcile software and patent protection. *See the overview in*: GOLDSTEIN/TRIMBLE, 408 ff.
1705. BOA, Case Law, A. 2.4.2.
1706. SUPREME COURT OF INDIA, *Novartis v. India*, No 2706-2716.
1707. On the patentability requirements in Indian law, *see*: KANKANALA/NARASANI/RADHAKRISHNAN, Chapter 2.
1708. For an explanation of the strategy of evergreening, *see supra* at para. 255.
1709. *See supra* at para. 255.
1710. The Madras High Court in the case of *Novartis v. Union of India* apparently declared that the sole purpose of the strict patentability requirements for pharmaceuticals in section 3(d) IndPA was the prevention of evergreening. MADRAS HC, *Novartis v. India*, 4 MLJ 1153, 2007, paras 8 and 12, cited after SEN/RAMANUJAN, IIC 2010, 171; the case was not appealed, but Novartis took the decision by the Indian patent office to the Supreme Court of India. The Supreme Court did not address the question of the compliance of section 3(d) IndPA with the TRIPS Agreement, however.
1711. SUPREME COURT OF INDIA, *Novartis v. India*, No 2706-2716.

subsequent, mainly positive, reaction in the literature[1712] as well as the fact that the WTO was not asked to evaluate the compliance of section 3(d) IndPA with the TRIPS Agreement[1713] suggest that the TRIPS Agreement in principle accepts exclusion from patent protection in cases where greater public interests such as fostering innovation – the aim of the patent law itself – are affected and where greater interests can be seen in the creation of checks and balances against abusive conduct.[1714]

655 In Europe, the EPO is critical with respect to the requirement for analysing potential economic effects when granting a patent. It stated that it 'has not been vested with the task of taking into account the economic effects of the grant of patents in specific areas of technology and of restricting the field of patentable subject-matter accordingly'.[1715] Consequently, in its decision on the patentability of a breast and ovarian cancer susceptibility gene, the Board of Appeal of the EPO (BoA) refused arguments concerning the socio-economic consequences of a patent grant. It rightly pointed out that the analysis of economic consequences was beyond its scope.[1716]

656 In accordance with the strict wording of the TRIPS Agreement, the BoA further underlined that Article 53a EPC must be understood narrowly insofar as it is the exploiting of the invention and not the patent itself which must be compatible with the *ordre public*. It denied the argument of one of the opponents that the use of the patent included the use of the invention in the case of breast cancer genes. The BoA did not see any basis to distinguish between different technological fields and to equate the use of the patent with the use of the invention for certain fields.[1717]

2.3 Comment

657 In order to deny patentability for patents which cover patentable claims but, as mere property rights, endanger competition and thus violate *ordre public*, the patent offices would have to undertake impossible *ex ante* considerations of potential economic effects. This is neither within the competence of the patent office nor the task of patent law. Patent law only provides property protection to technical teachings covering patentable subject matter. Likewise, it is not within the ability of competition

1712. *See i.a.*: Correa, Economic an Political Weekly 2013, 49 ff.; Sen/Ramanujan, IIC 2010, 186; Dhar/Joseph, in: Liu/Racherla, Innovation, Economic Development, and Intellectual Property in India and China, 302 ff. Note, however, that some of the voices in the literature may have been influenced by their Indian heritage. Denying TRIPS-compliance: Berthold, 210 ff.
1713. The question of whether section 3 (d) of the Indian Patent Act is compliant with the TRIPS Agreement was not brought to the WTO, but the WTO mentions the Indian Patent Act as example for a narrow interpretation of the patentability criteria in the TRIPS Agreement. *See*: https://www.wto.org/english/tratop_e/trips_e/trilatweb_e/ch3d_trilat_web_13_e.htm, accessed on 6 July 2020.
1714. This was not the case, for example, with respect to the 'mailbox rule'. AB WTO, *India – Patent Protection for Pharmaceuticals*, WT/DS50/AB/R, paras 50 ff.
1715. EPO, *Guidelines for Examination*, G. II. 4.1.3.
1716. BoA, *Breast and ovarian cancer/University of Utah*, T 1213/05, paras 52 ff.
1717. On the paragraph, *see*: BoA, *Breast and ovarian cancer/University of Utah*, T 1213/05, para. 53.

authorities to decide whether a patented subject matter is in fact novel, non-obvious or inventive in the specific field of technology. The development of the concept 'patentable' is the task of the patent law. It is not the task of competition law to correct erroneous protection from a scientific point of view, but to intervene if the conduct of market players is distorting competition.[1718] This also answers the question of why the legislator has chosen not to assign the control of patentability requirements to other authorities but the patent office and why patentability requirements only concern technical patentable subject matter and not secondary effects emanating from the grant of the patent.

658 It is questionable not only whether the narrow conception of exceptions to patentability as presented by the BoA is useful but also whether a distinction between the patented subject matter and the patent is reasonable. In answering the first question, it is important to reconsider the technical fields which have been denied patentability so far, for example, software. In Article 52(2)(c) EPC, the patentability of programs as such is denied. Even though the inventiveness of certain programs can indeed be doubted, the exclusion of a whole area per se cannot be justified other than for economic reasons. In fact, as HILTY/GEIGER point out, the decision to implement an exception for software programs was economically motivated. Europe was behind the USA in the field of software development, and as the USA did not authorise patentability of programs, the EPC followed the US model. Software programs were consequently banned from patent protection. There were fears of a hampering effect on innovation resulting from different levels of intellectual property law protection.[1719] As indicated by the design of the patent law, which was created to engage with competition, the legislator thus included socio-economic considerations when defining patentability standards.

659 The notion of *ordre public* in Article 27(2) TRIPS is the catch-all element in the balancing of interests between the innovator on one side and the interests of society in terms of economy and morals on the other side. This means that *ordre public* is only invoked when the patentability requirements, as set out by the legislator, fail to rule out certain substance matter from being patented. Exclusions of whole categories of inventions from patent protection are, however, argued based on the margin for argumentation with regard to the patentability requirements and not on the level of exceptional cases and catch-all provisions. Patented subject matter which would in general raise economic or other *ordre public* issues is therefore excluded from patentability in national laws by means of defining the patentability requirements narrowly. This is persuasive. It is neither in the patent office's ability nor in its responsibility to analyse potential (future) economic effects of patents when granting them, but is rather the legislator's duty to adopt a design that does not raise reservations with respect to potential endangerment of the aim of the law. The patent system, as ULLRICH points out,

1718. ENCAOUA/MADIÈS, in: MADIÈS/GUELLEC/PRAGER, Patent Markets in the Global Knowledge Economy, 162.
1719. HILTY/GEIGER, IIC 2005, 619, especially fn. 15.

is designed as a 'one size fits all' concept and does not provide remedies for individual inefficiencies.[1720]

2.4 Implications

660 The analysis has shown that economic considerations resulting from the use of the patent as a blocking position cannot result in losing the claim to the patent based on patentability requirements. The basic claim to fundamental rights protection remains. Yet, as seen above, the fundamental notion that the property rights, like any other privilege, can be restricted in order to serve a legitimate higher cause still holds. The Court of Justice in the 1970s in the cited cases of *Nold v. Commission* and *Hauer v. Land Rheinland Pfalz* held that property rights are only granted within the limitations of the social functions of the property and the overall objectives pursued by the Union.[1721] For this purpose, the use of the property can be regulated in the general interest.[1722] The question raised with respect to blocking patents is whether the right to not use a property right can be limited based on analogous grounds to the right to use a property.

3 The Right to Not Use the Patent

3.1 General Considerations

661 The question addressed in this section is whether a failure to implement a patent in a product to sell it or to license the technology can result in a loss of the right, that is, whether a failure to use the patent can amount to a limitation on patentability.

662 The failure to use an intellectual property right in trade has resulted in losses of the property right. The ECHR in settled case law refused fundamental right protection to those property right positions which had been impossible to exercise for a long period. 'By way of contrast, the hope of recognition of the survival of an old property right which it has long been impossible to exercise effectively cannot be considered as a "possession" [...].'[1723] This exclusion, however, does not capture property rights which could be exercised but were left unused by choice.

663 Restrictions on the general right to intellectual properties are expressions of the social component of intellectual goods when they leave the mind of their creators and enter the public sphere.[1724] General public interest is thereby understood broadly, and first and foremost includes legitimate economic goals as set out in the Union's primary

1720. ULLRICH, in: DREXL/LEE, Pharmaceutical innovation, competition and patent law, 254 ff.
1721. *See supra* at fns 1666 f.
1722. In this respect *see* previous court law in Germany: BVERFGE, *Kirchenmusik*, 1 BvR 352/71, paras 5 f.
1723. ECTHR, *Malhous v. Czech Republic*, No 33071/96, para. B.2.d.
1724. In this respect also: TIMMANN, 212 f.

law.[1725] The right to use as well as the right not to use a property must therefore be measured on the same principles. The foundation for this analysis is provided by the TRIPS Agreement which grants an international minimal standard for intellectual property right protection. Any restriction of intellectual property rights based on economic considerations has to be TRIPS-compliant.

3.2 Implications from the TRIPS Agreement

664 Article 8 TRIPS, together with Article 7, was implemented in the Uruguay Round due to concerns of developing countries. Those countries feared negative influences of strong intellectual property rights on their interests, especially with respect to public health, economic and technical development.[1726] Articles 7 and 8 TRIPS were drafted to allow measures which restrict the execution of intellectual property rights where public policy objectives are at stake.[1727] Rights and obligations should be balanced.[1728] In applying these measures, Member States are committed to granting intellectual property rights only within certain limits. As a result of the compatibility clause, however, Article 8 cannot serve as justification for restricting rights granted by the TRIPS Agreement, but only to prevent abuses thereof.[1729]

665 The TRIPS Agreement does not concretise the content of the abuse of intellectual property rights. Contrary to what the term 'principles' would suggest, Article 8 does not contain any 'rule, law or doctrine' or in other words any 'authoritative, widely adhered to standard'[1730] to define the scope of the provisions set out in the agreement.[1731] The article thus gives no indication with respect to an understanding of what constitutes an abuse. Guidance for the interpretation provides Article 5A of the Paris Convention. According to Article 5A(4), an abuse of patent rights consists in refraining not only from exercising a right but also through the insufficient exercising of the property right. A property right, following the example given in the Paris Convention, is insufficiently exercised when it blocks industrial development.[1732]

666 The TRIPS Agreement takes account of this in paragraph 5 of the preamble where it recognises developmental and technical objectives as important public interests

1725. HESELHAUS, in: HESELHAUS/NOWAK, Handbuch der europäischen Grundrechte, § 36, para. 79.
1726. For a summary of the opposition of developing countries to the implementation of IP protection in the Uruguay Round, *see*: PACÓN, GRUR Int. 1995, 875 ff.
1727. Public policy objectives worthy of protection are either derived from legitimate public interests in Article 8(1) or conduct in 8(2) TRIPS. *See*: BRAND, in: BUSCHE ET AL., TRIPS Kommentar, Article 8, para. 30.
1728. PIRES DE CARVALHO, The TRIPS Regime of Antitrust and Undisclosed Information, para. 7.46.
1729. HEINEMANN, Immaterialgüterschutz in der Wettbewerbsordnung, 585; HEINEMANN, GRUR Int. 1995, 536; PIRES DE CARVALHO, The TRIPS Regime of Patents and Test Data, para. 8.1.
1730. For the definition of 'legal principle', *see*: GARNER, Black's Law Dictionary.
1731. Article 8 differs from Articles 3 and 4 TRIPS which do contain principles with respect to the scope of the provisions in the TRIPS Agreement. PIRES DE CARVALHO, The TRIPS Regime of Patents and Test Data, paras 8.1. and 8.23; HÖHNE, in: BUSCHE ET AL., TRIPS Kommentar, Article 7, para. 1.
1732. BODENHAUSEN, Article 5, para. (g).

warranting the establishment of a patent system. That the TRIPS Agreement allows for exceptions in the protection of intellectual property rights when the fundamental aim of the law is at stake can also be seen with respect to the goal of the TRIPS Agreement. The agreement resulted from the desire to reduce distortions and impediments to international trade. Thus, in keeping the balance between providing effective and adequate protection of intellectual property rights and mitigating distortions of competition, Article 8(2) TRIPS acknowledges the need for measures whenever intellectual property rights implement trade barriers. It does not set requirements with regard to the means to address such inefficiencies, however.

667 The nature of Article 8(2) TRIPS, like the general principle of the abuse of rights, is that of a corrective.[1733] Member States of the TRIPS Agreement only commit to grant and protect intellectual property rights within the limit of the minimal standard granted through the TRIPS Agreement.[1734] This indicates that in general using a patent as an instrument to reach goals disfavoured by the legal system qualifies as an abuse of patent rights under the TRIPS Agreement.[1735] The minimal standards in the TRIPS Agreement, however, simultaneously restrict the means available to obtain a balanced intellectual property rights regime. All property rights fulfilling the minimal requirements have to be granted. The abusive use of such a property right can thus never result in the revocation of the right.[1736]

668 At the same time, Article 8(2) TRIPS has to be read not only as a defence of a minimal guarantee but also as implementing the principle of proportionality.[1737] In the case of patents, this leads to the situation where the forfeiture of valid patents is not compliant with the TRIPS Agreement in principle.[1738] Yet, Pires de Carvalho concludes that a revocation of a patent is not contrary to the TRIPS Agreement in cases of violations of competition law, when a forfeiture of the patent is in line with the principle of proportionality (suitable, necessary and least stringent).[1739] Article 5(A)(3) of the Paris Convention also opens the door for exceptions 'where the grant of the compulsory licenses would not have been sufficient'. It is thus compliant with TRIPS Agreement to categorise behaviour targeted at blocking innovation as abusive and denying it legal protection, even if it includes a rightfully held intellectual property right.

1733. Brand, in: Busche et al., TRIPS Kommentar, Article 8, para. 1; the Member States have to execute their right carefully (in good faith). *See*: AB, *USA – Shrimps*, WT/DS58, para. 158.
1734. This also applies to measurements taken to prevent the abuse of rights, as they have to be consistent with the provisions of the agreement (compatibility clause).
1735. *See generally*, without reference to the TRIPS Agreement: Wolff, 113.
1736. Pires de Carvalho, The TRIPS Regime of Antitrust and Undisclosed Information, para. 7.46.
1737. Pires de Carvalho, The TRIPS Regime of Antitrust and Undisclosed Information, para. 8.4.
1738. The strongest evidence for this position of the Member States is the communication Switzerland delivered in the draft of the TRIPS Agreement: Switzerland, *Communication*, Article 233 (6).
1739. Pires de Carvalho, The TRIPS Regime of Antitrust and Undisclosed Information, paras 32.11 ff.

669 From case law, it can also be derived that a legitimate societal interest can be seen in the provision of checks and balances to prevent the abuse of rights.[1740] This prima facie supports the conclusion that the TRIPS Agreement would allow measures denying patentability in cases where the acquisition of a patent would not comply with fostering innovation or undistorted competition. The starting point for this reasoning is the premise that it is a waste of resources to grant an exclusive right which cannot be exploited.[1741] Such an interpretation is supported by the primary aim of the TRIPS Agreement as stated in the preamble: the reduction of distortion and of impediments to international trade. Since exclusionary rights immanent in a property generally bear the risk of imposing barriers to trade, it has to be in the interests of Member States to grant exclusionary rights only within the limits where the holding or execution of the privileges granted is generally accepted and encouraged.[1742] As held in the preamble, the TRIPS Agreement further seeks to establish an effective and adequate intellectual property rights regime and to remove barriers from international trade. The maintenance of purely formal rights is thus not protected by the aim of the agreement as they require resources and implement barriers to trade unnecessarily.

670 Examples of provisions where this basic idea is expressed can be found in many trademark laws. For example, Article 22(2) of the Italian Royal Decree No 929 on trademarks reads: 'A trademark registration may not be obtained by anyone who has made the application in bad faith.' The Italian legislator not only enacted this provision to prevent bad faith in cases where the applicant knows of specific interests of third parties (Article 6bis of the Paris Convention) in the same trademark but also bad faith aimed at causing foreclosure effects.[1743] This is typically the case when the registrant of the trademark has no intention of using the sign in trade but aims to withhold it from the market.[1744]

671 Yet, according to the wording in the TRIPS Agreement, it is the exploitation of the invention (patented subject matter) which must be non-compliant with *ordre public* and morality and not the exploitation of the patent as a property right.[1745] This would suggest that economic reasons stemming from the use of the patent itself, such as the prevention of the use of the technology or the impeding of further development through blocking patents, would not justify a restriction of patentability under the TRIPS Agreement. Demanding compulsory licences in order to counteract the blocking of innovation would be in accordance with the TRIPS Agreement, however.

1740. *See supra* at fns 1710 and 1714.
1741. Seuba, in: Correa/Yusuf, Intellectual property and international trade, 408 (this reference can no longer be found in the 3rd edition).
1742. This is supported by the wording of the Preamble of the TRIPS Agreement which states that intellectual property rights should 'not themselves become barriers to legitimate trade' and has already been acknowledged by Article 5 A (2) of the Paris Convention which allows for a neutralisation through compulsory licences.
1743. Vanzetti, in: Lange, Internationales Handbuch des Marken- und Kennzeichenrechts, para. 1923.
1744. Vanzetti, in: Lange, Internationales Handbuch des Marken- und Kennzeichenrechts, para. 1926.
1745. *See*: von Saint-André/Taşdelen, in: Busche et al., TRIPS Kommentar, Article 27(2), para. 60.

3.3 *Implications from Trademark Law*

672 The starting point for the analysis is the fact that legislation based on the existence of patents being dependent on good intentions for using the patent in trade (bona fide) does not exist. This is different with trademarks. Article 17 TRIPS introduced unfair competition law as a limitation to the execution of rights granted with trademarks. Members may provide limited exceptions to the rights conferred by a trademark, such as the fair use of descriptive terms, if such exceptions take account of the legitimate interests of the owner of the trademark and of third parties.

673 The EU was prominently involved in the enactment of this provision. The effort was probably motivated by the idea of promoting the approach of Directive 89/104/EEC on the approximation of the trademark law in the Member States.[1746] Article 3(2)(d) thereof leaves it open whether bad faith at the time of the registration qualifies as grounds for refusal or forfeiture. Through the inclusion of unfair competition law in the TRIPS Agreement, bad faith at the time of the registration is thus accepted as grounds for invalidity of trademarks within the minimal guarantee the agreement seeks to establish in its Member States. In the absence of bad faith at the time of the registration, Member States can demand that the failure to use a trademark for at least three years can cause the loss of the property right (Article 19(1)).[1747]

674 The importance of good faith in trademark law can best be understood by studying history. In common law, unfair competition and trademark law both have their origin in the prevention of misrepresentations in trade. In the sixteenth century, the tort of passing-off was developed to protect traders who owned well-established signs in goodwill, from the use by other parties in trade. The most important cases concerned the misleading of consumers about relevant factors of the good. Misrepresentations were thus seen as a form of deception and sometimes even fraud. Later, such misrepresentations liberated themselves from their conceptual basis. As an independent tort, the passing-off was aimed at protecting 'honesty and fair dealing' and preventing 'deception of the public'. The idea of a doctrine of unfair competition was born. The precondition for committing the tort of passing-off was fraudulent intent.[1748] In Germany, the courts have acknowledged since 1909 that the modalities of a trademark registration can violate morals and fair practice.[1749] A violation of the principles of morals and fair practice through the registration of trademarks was thus accepted as a valid claim for the cancellation of the property right out of general considerations. Applicable legal bases for the conclusion were seen in § 242 and 826 of the GCC as well as in the law against unfair competition, depending on the circumstances of the case. Both trade-related and general societal considerations were thus considered valid reasons for the limitation of the property right to good faith.[1750]

1746. PETER, in: BUSCHE ET AL., TRIPS Kommentar, Article 17, para. 3.
1747. For an example, *see* the Italian Trademark law as referenced *supra* at para. 670.
1748. CHRONOPOULOS, 5 ff.; REULEN, 139 ff.
1749. RG, *Böttchers Echter Malzkaffee,* RGZ 106, 250, 254.
1750. On this development, *see*: EIKEL, 15 ff.

675 Although different emphases in the jurisdictions exist, both good faith and the usage requirement limit the protection of trademarks to the degree required by the market.[1751] After all, the usage requirement only applies retrospectively and includes a five-year 'transition period'. A registration with the intention of keeping the trademark as a blocking position technically cannot qualify as an abuse of trademark rights, owing to the five-year period. Legislators have therefore addressed concerns relating to registration for merely blocking purposes in trademark law. In trademark law, bad faith itself is a possible obstacle to the registration of trademarks.[1752]

3.4 Is Bad Faith Relevant in Patent Law after All?

676 Bad faith of an applicant also found its way into patent law, although not at Union level. In 1890, the Swiss Federal Court, despite the absence of an explicit provision, held that the right of joint use[1753] (Articles 35 and 48 PatA) is only due for the prior user who uses the invention in good faith.[1754] Bad faith was thereby seen as the logic consequence when the claimant had illegally gained knowledge of the invention.[1755] Swiss literature lists cases where the prior user knew of the intention of the inventor to apply for a patent as well as situations where the prior user gained their knowledge about the invention illegally, as examples of bad faith.[1756] As in trademark law, a general approach applies which focuses on the intentions of the applicant and the circumstances of the acquisition.

677 The Swiss approach towards joint use, in respect of the acquisition of a right for joint use, focuses on those aspects that could question the claim to acquire the patent rights rather than the usage of them. These limitations on the right to the patent are part of the balance of interests which, according to PEDRAZZINI, would have to be analysed following the general abuse of rights principle, if they were not regulated.[1757] Bad faith in Swiss patent law can therefore be placed within the context of the general abuse of rights, in respect of an instrument to gain a right without being entitled to it.

678 What blocking trademarks and blocking patents have in common is that the applicant or registrant makes use of a given entitled right to realise a competitive advantage. While in trademark law, the conduct results in a violation of trademark law and the factual registration of a non-right, the intent to use the right in trade is not constitutive in patent law. The wilful application for blocking patents therefore results in the granting of a valid patent right from a patent law perspective. It has been argued

1751. SPUHLER, in: BENDER ET AL., MarkenR, § 26, para. 1.
1752. ECJ, *Schokoladenfabrik Lindt & Sprüngli*, C-529/07, paras 34 ff.
1753. The right of joint use allows use of the patented invention under the patent holder.
1754. BGE 16, 418 ff., 422; cited after: STIEGER, in: BERTSCHINGER/GEISER/MÜNCH, Schweizerisches und europäisches Patentrecht, para. 12.245, fn. 306.
1755. STIEGER, in: BERTSCHINGER/GEISER/MÜNCH, Schweizerisches und europäisches Patentrecht, para. 12.246.
1756. STIEGER, in: BERTSCHINGER/GEISER/MÜNCH, Schweizerisches und europäisches Patentrecht, paras 12.246 f.
1757. PEDRAZZINI, in: BRÜGGER, FS Troller, Der Rechtsmissbrauch im Patentrecht, 209 f.

above that the submission of documents within the application process is the unilateral behaviour which results in the granting of the patent. However, the submission of documents is not the moment when the patent unfolds its blocking power.[1758] Likewise, the submission is not the moment when a blocking patent fails to fulfil its aim. Rather, because of the publication requirement, the patent application fulfils the information function and provides society with additional information which then allows competitors to invent around or adjust their own innovation projects.

679 However, when applying for a patent with the intention of keeping it as a blocking position, an applicant instrumentalises the blocking power of the patent which it will receive after the grant. It is the first step in a plan of taking advantage of effects which materialise later. Whether the effects will materialise only shows when the patent holder in fact denies the benefits of using the protected invention to society. A blocking intention taken separately cannot therefore be held as a decisive factor, but proves the abusive character of the patent application together with the later conduct of not using the technology.

680 Therefore, it must be kept in mind that blocking motives are hardly verifiable in the absence of clear evidence. The lack of intention to launch a product or develop an invention further could, for example, be indicated by the absence of R&D spending. Both the development and launch of a product would require R&D spending before and after the filing of the patent. A lack of such expenditure related to the patented technology before and after the filing could thus indicate the existence of a plan to use the patent strategically rather than for direct economic purposes. Yet, as ZECH points out, such an investigation will quickly reach its limitations. Uncertainties with respect to the time and extent to which R&D expenses must be made would not provide certainty.[1759]

681 Whether good faith at the time of the application also includes the intention to use the patent in trade is another question. If answered in the affirmative, patent law would factually imply a usage requirement. Patents indeed have functions within the system of competition which are not realised until the use of the patented technology in competition.[1760] The actual question is therefore not whether the absence of clear usage intentions is abusive because such plans may not be realised in the end. The question is rather whether there was a clear intention of not making the technology available to the market from the start, and whether such behaviour is abusive.

682 To tackle the problem of patent registration with the mere intention to block, an approach following the US model in the case of trademarks could be implemented. According to section 1(b) of the Trademark Act (15 USC 1051), the registrant has to deliver a verified statement declaring their intention to use the trademark in commerce. This statement expressing the bona fide intention of the registrant is needed in cases where the trademark has not yet been used commercially, that is, in cases where there

---

1758. *See supra* at paras 628 ff.
1759. ZECH, ZWeR 2011, 328; similarly: DOLMANS, Antitrust Law Journal 1998, 468.
1760. *See supra* at paras 90 ff.

is a danger that the trademark will never be put to use. The reason for this prerequisite is that in US trademark law bad faith does not exist as an independent basis to oppose a trademark registration. Bad faith can be raised to support the opposition of fraud, however.[1761] Since every registrant has to declare their bona fide intention, wilful false statements are considered fraudulent.[1762] By implementing the requirement of a declaration of intentions, the US trademark law moved 'bad-faith registrations' away from a violation of bona fide intentions to fraudulent behaviour. The conduct of delivering false statements appears in the case law of Article 102 TFEU with the *AstraZeneca* case and is popular among scholars with respect to the analysis of broken FRAND commitments as well.[1763]

683 Following the above analysis, any patent right acquired while patentability requirements are not met results in the granting of a factual non-right which is not protected by the fundamental right to property and which does not have a reason for existence founded in material law. Therefore, in cases when patent applicants knowingly deliver information to the patent office which does not qualify them to be awarded with a patent grant, they engage in acquiring non-rights or instrumentalising patent law against its purpose. In accordance with settled case law, fraudulent and abusive ends are conterminously understood as a reason to deny legal protection.[1764] This also applies expressly for misrepresentations of facts in contract law in many Member States.[1765]

684 It follows from this analysis that any pretence of meeting the patentability requirements qualifies as an abuse of patent law, as the patent applicant is not seeking to gain property rights protection by virtue of their own achievements in competition, but by fraudulently creating the impression of such an achievement. Economic freedom is not granted such as to enable the acquisition of rights through fraudulent behaviour. Especially within patent law, where the validity of granted patents is assumed and invalidity must be claimed by means of judicial proceedings, indications for the balancing of interests in the evaluation of proportionality are thus clear. The abuse of patent law conducted by a dominant undertaking in these cases qualifies as abuse of a dominant position.

4 Conclusion

685 The above analysis has shown that a patent applicant does not lose their claim to the patent based only on economic considerations. Whether the conduct of keeping the

1761. Fraud can be raised against a trademark registration (15 U.S.C. § 1120).
1762. *See*, for example, Fed. Cir., *In re Bose Corp.*, 91 U.S.P.Q.2d 1938, 2009, 6.
1763. ECJ, *AstraZeneca v. Commission*, C-457/10 P, paras 95 ff.; Picht, GRUR Int. 2014, 11; Geradin/Rato, European Competition Journal 2007, 159 ff. who find conceptional obstacles to apply Article 102 TFEU to breaches of FRAND commitments.
1764. *See*: ECJ, *Centros Ltd v. Erhvervs- og Selskabsstyrelsen*, C-212/97, para. 24 for further reference.
1765. Fleischer, Informationsasymmetrie im Vertragsrecht, 593 f., 690 ff. and 765 f.

patent as a blocking position could still amount to an abuse of the dominant position will be answered after the final analysis. This asks whether the prevention of the purpose of patents qualifies as a reason to deny the conduct of applying for blocking patent protection.

III UNUSED PATENTS AND THE PURPOSE OF PATENT LAW

1 The Goal of This Section

686 When outlining the analysis in Part VI, Chapter 18, section II, it was stated that the interests protected by patent law were crucial when conducting an analysis of potentially abusive behaviour involving patents. This section therefore aims to elucidate how and in what manner unused patent laws challenge the patent system. This section, like Chapter 18, section II, will include an analogy to trademark law. Some of the above considerations will be used again in the analysis either to provide a better understanding or because they are also applicable here.

687 This section starts with a recapitulation of the aim of patent law and proceeds with an analysis of whether patents include an implied usage expectation as trademarks do. Section 4 of this section addresses the question of whether and when the interest of securing one's own innovation (with blocking patents) should recede against the interests of society to use the patented technology. Section 5 will address the problem of patents failing to meet the patentability requirements and their impact on competition.

2 The Purpose of Patent Law

688 When justifying patent law, economic considerations collide with aspects of personal rights of the inventor.[1766] Patents protect technical teachings, which in theory can only be concretised after substantial mental and financial efforts. The protected information adds to the technical knowledge available for a society and therefore gets published. Even an unused patent therefore does not fail to fulfil its information function.[1767] Likewise, registered patents do not fail to establish the marketability of intangible assets and reward the inventor with the property right. Following libertarian theories, which approve of patents based on moral and ethical arguments,[1768] the actual usage of a patent in trade is not fundamental to achieving the aims associated with the patent system. In addition, unused patents reward the inventor for their labour and reward society with new technologies as well as theoretically allowing for competition with the technologies (e.g., licensing). According to utilitarian and

1766. *See supra* at para. 92.
1767. On the information function *see supra* at para. 200.
1768. On libertarian theories *see supra* at para. 92.

modern patent theories, the patent system aims to ensure a more efficient allocation of resources.[1769]

689 The question therefore has to be asked as to whether unused patents fulfil their purpose, and whether the granting of a patent involves an implied expectation that the patent holder will exploit the patented technology either internally (own products) or externally (licences). If the answer is no, the patent system factually allows and encourages the patent holder to invest resources in R&D and deliver innovations from which society cannot profit other than by mere knowledge of the technology.

690 When patent applications cover a patentable invention, applicants always have a legitimate interest in protecting their intellectual assets with a patent.[1770] Patents are not granted for their own sake but to fulfil a function in terms of competition. These underlying weightings have to be carefully considered when analysing potential infringements of competition law by patent applicants or holders.[1771] Measures against effects originating from factual circumstances that are expressly and exhaustively regulated in patent law are unlikely to be justifiable.[1772]

691 When arguing cases at the intersection between intellectual property and competition law, it is important to take into consideration the fundamentals of each field of law as well as the interests of the involved parties and balance the relevant interests.[1773] Therefore, an in-depth analysis of the relevant interests, the degree of their restrictions as well as alternative conduct to reach the same goal has to be conducted when analysing potentially abusive behaviour under Article 102 TFEU.

692 Blocking patents endanger the functioning of competition but not based on their design, their general nature as exclusive rights, or their subject matter. The decisive factor is rather the internal motivation of the patent applicant in not giving access to the technology to third parties other than by disclosing the patent claims. The balancing of interests, when analysing the proportionality of a restriction on the right to property, has to answer the question of whether and how the interest in securing one's own innovation must recede against the interest of undistorted competition.[1774] An evaluation of abusive behaviour therefore has to take patent law and the legitimate interests

1769. On utilitarian and modern patent law theories *see supra* at paras 93 ff.
1770. HAEDICKE, in: HAEDICKE/TIMMANN, Patent law, para. 162. *See also the analysis in* Part VI, Chapter 18, section II.
1771. *See*: ZECH, ZWeR 2011, 317 ff.
1772. In Switzerland, Article 3(2) Swiss Cartel Act (SCA) regulates the relationship between competition and intellectual property law. It holds that competition law cannot apply effects solely based on legislation governing intellectual property. The article was introduced into the SCA in 1995 on the occasion of its revision. Owing to the introduction of a prohibition of vertical agreements, competition law scrutiny was expanded to licensing agreements. It was feared that competition law scrutiny would also involve an analysis of contractual terms which reflect the privileges granted under the relevant intellectual property laws. *See*: BBl 1995 I 468, 542.
1773. *See also*: BEJRANANDA, 124.
1774. Similarly, the conclusions drawn by JUNG: JUNG, ZWeR 2004, 392.

protected with it as the starting point. This will allow a careful consideration of the peculiarities of both patent and competition laws.

3 Usage Requirement Analogous to Trademark Law

693 Trademark law might provide an answer to the question of implied usage expectations in patent law. With trademark rights, any use of the intellectual property right contrary to its purpose has an effect on competition. The reason lies within the justification for creating a right to trademarks. The underlying rationale for establishing a system of trademark law is the efficiency increase in consumer decisions as well as the upholding of quality standards. This is secured through a system whereby with products labelled with trademarks, consumers face reduced costs when choosing goods. Trademarks 'serve as information tools' to 'foster the flow of information in markets'.[1775] At the same time, producers are forced to maintain the quality standard consumers are used to, so that they in turn can rely on the label.[1776] The rationale of the trademark is thus purely based on economic considerations. The core of trademarks is to provide the proprietor with a sign that 'he alone can use, permit or prohibit its use on the products or services [...], or on products or services which the consuming public would think were connected to him if that sign were used on or in connection with them'[1777]. The law does not protect products, but rather the sign itself with which products of the proprietor can be labelled. The only privilege conveyed with the right is therefore its use as a label in trade.

694 Apart from being used in competition, trademarks are of no value.[1778] This is also reflected in the modalities needed to find protection under trademark laws. Only signs capable of distinguishing the goods or services of one undertaking from those of other undertakings (Article 15(1) TRIPS) can become trademarks in the legal sense. Beyond these formal criteria, trademarks, unlike patents, copyrights or designs, do not have to fulfil qualitative protection requirements. The trademark has no intellectual value. Its purpose is not the promotion of an activity of societal interest that would not be competitive without protection.[1779] All grounds for refusal of trademark registrations therefore concern criteria which would render the fulfilment of its purpose impossible.[1780]

695 The same is true for the grounds for cancellation or revocation, of which only a failure to use and bad faith will be mentioned here. Unused trademarks fail to perform a commercial function and thus the aim of the trademark itself. Furthermore, unused trademarks present a latent inconvenience for current and future market participants. Therefore, many trademark law codes, including the major European codes (Directive

1775. DOGAN/LEMLEY, Houston Law Review 2004, 777 f.
1776. LANDES/POSNER, 167.
1777. PHILLIPS, para. 1.15.
1778. THOUVENIN, 346.
1779. LANDES/POSNER, 166.
1780. This can best be seen in Article 16(1) sentence 2 as well as 16(3) TRIPS.

89/104 and Regulation 40/94), hold the possibility of revoking a trademark which has been unused for a continuous period of five years. In addition, trademark laws often include bad faith of the registrant as grounds for cancellation or revocation. Bad faith may be established on the grounds that an unauthorised agent has registered the trademark or that the filing violates an earlier trademark. Within the acknowledged grounds of bad faith, for example, in German trademark law, one can also find the misuse of rights which includes the application for blocking trademarks.[1781] The fear of failing to control the trademark system, which is characterised by easy access, and the desperate need to keep the trademark registries as lean as possible in order to guarantee the functioning of the system, forced legislators to include fundamentals of the principles of the abuse of rights in the codes.

696 National patent laws and the EPC do not have comparable mechanisms in general. Patent laws, as VESALA puts it, are 'relatively hands-off when it comes to behavioural aspects of patenting and the effects of exercising rights under the patent law'.[1782] This was different in German law. The German Patent Law Code of 1877 had a take-back regulation similar to the provisions in trademark law as well as an indirect force to grant licences (§ 11). The grounds for implementing these provisions were seen in the protection of the national industry. The use of the patent at that time was synonymous with producing a good using the patented technology within Germany and marked a compromise with opponents of the patent system.[1783] As with trademark law, the usage requirement was not a precondition for the granting of the patent, but rather a potential cause for forfeiture.[1784] The current German patent law still has licensing requirements. Yet this only applies if the national economy is not sufficiently supplied with the patented technology and in cases where the interested party endeavours to be granted a licence and where a compulsory licence would serve public interests (§ 24 (5) PatG). With this provision, the legislator seeks to prevent abuses through blocking patents.[1785]

697 That patent laws are generally ill-equipped when it comes to sanctioning unwanted behaviour, compared with trademark laws, could be explained by recourse to the aim and conception of the two intellectual property rights. The subject matter of trademark law differs widely from the subject matter of patent law. The very aim of trademark law makes clear that non-usage, unfair usage or a plethora of registered trademarks would either raise the likelihood of confusion or torpedo the aim through not fostering the information flow.[1786] What endangers fulfilling the purpose of patent law (fostering innovation) and sometimes simultaneously competition law (securing undistorted competition) is not the mere existence of an exclusionary right. What is problematic is rather that the invention will never be commercially exploited as long as the patent holder acts according to its purpose. This intention might already be present

1781. BGH, *EQUI 2000*, I ZR 283/97, 2000, 9 f.
1782. VESALA, in: BALLARDINI/BRUUN/NORRGÅRD, Transitions in European patent law, 275.
1783. KRASSER/ANN, § 5, paras 16 f.; LÜHRS, 134 f.
1784. On the development, *see*: STIERLE, 45 ff.
1785. STIERLE, 66 f.
1786. *See supra* at paras 694 ff.

at the time of the application for the patent, but knowledge on such subjective intentions can – if at all – only be achieved retrospectively.

698 Failure to directly exploit the patent economically does not result in losing the right. Therefore, expectations of actual usage of the patent cannot be deduced from patent law itself.[1787] There is no general obligation to address economic concerns by means of the relevant specific intellectual property law. The TRIPS Agreement, for example, which addresses the abuse of intellectual property rights in Article 8, leaves it to Member States to address inefficiencies of intellectual property law systems with other legislation, such as competition law.[1788]

4 The Interests of Securing One's Own Innovation

699 Unused patents factually represent R&D efforts which did not result in a marketable technology, but only in 'making knowledge public'. This is not necessarily economically inefficient. Public knowledge can spur innovation and there are many economically justifiable reasons for neither marketing a certain technology nor using it in further innovations. Inefficiencies occur when demand for the technology cannot be satisfied due to the failure to use the patent. In this case, resources have been spent by the patent holder who is not willing to let society share the results, even if a third party would invest in the delivery of a marketable product.

700 Failures to use a patent are thus economically worrisome when licences are refused without the intention of the patent holder to commercialise the innovation or when competitors refrain from further activities (research, commercialisation) because of the distorting effect of the patent, such as when the competitor assumes an unwillingness to patent from the behaviour of the patent holder.

701 For a competitor already in the market, a blocking patent impedes innovation rather than hindering market entry. The question must be asked as to what keeps competitors from engaging in activities aimed at inventing around the patent of the dominant undertaking. Relevant factors that keep companies from innovating around a patent are switching costs for consumers, the presence of patents for alternative technical solutions and the costs of inventing around as well as, depending on the industry, regulatory requirements in the course of receiving market approvals.

702 If barriers to innovation are high and entry into the innovation race unlikely, effective competition on the level of innovation cannot occur. In the absence of competition of innovation, with the innovation market being upstream to the product market,[1789] effective competition on the product market also cannot occur. If in these

1787. KÄSEBERG, however, is in favour of including rules against detrimental effects of patenting within patent laws, for example, by including an obligation to use the patent. KÄSEBERG, 108.
1788. On the fact that competition law complements intellectual property laws, *see supra* at para. 356 and Part I, Chapter 4, section III.
1789. *See supra* at paras 254 ff.

situations a potential demand for the technology exists and evidence of a plan to use the technology cannot be found, the interests of the patent holder holding a blocking position to protect their assets should be of subordinate importance compared with potential demand for the technology. The right not to use the patent should rank lower than the interests of making the technology available to society. Because of the social component of patents, the interests of competitors and society to customise or further develop the patented technology when other sources are inaccessible weigh higher than the claim of the patent holder to request a withdrawal of the technology.

703 The reason for this position is that the patent holder cannot justify the blocking with the need to recoup R&D expenses. A patent application with the intention of blocking factually implies a waiver of the legitimate claim to secure one's own innovation. The recouping of R&D costs through licensing or commercialisation or the potential recouping through further innovation will not follow.[1790] The same has to apply for secondary acquisitions irrespective of whether intent at the time of the acquisition can be proved. The undertaking acquiring a patent from a former patent holder cannot put forward the amortisation of R&D or securing their own innovation as justification. As a non-inventor, the second acquirer cannot put forward a legitimate interest in the ownership position.[1791] Yet, it should be kept in mind that in order for society to benefit, the information must be made public. Potential patent applicants, as seen above,[1792] are sometimes hesitant to apply for a patent owing to the publication requirement. Sanctioning the mere application of a patent is therefore highly delicate. In order not to scare off applicants further, such measures are only justified in extreme cases.

704 This same result, namely that the patent holder cannot be protected in executing his or her right conferred by the property in competition, applies in the event of the patent being used in strategies to renew patent protection of related technologies. Patents do not serve as a means to compensate for the R&D costs of related innovation.[1793] In industries where the general patent term is not considered enough from an economic point of view, for example, where an extension is economically sound, this need is met by supplementary protection, such as the supplementary protection certificate in the pharmaceutical sector.[1794] In other industries, the strategy of applying for blocking patents to factually renew the patent term of a related patent will most likely amount to an abuse of the dominant position. In applying for a blocking patent when the market entry of competitors is likely, the dominant undertaking unduly

1790. Zech, ZWeR 2011, 331.
1791. Critical with respect to potential innovation-hampering effects of usage requirements: Stierle, 267 and 270 f., whereby Stierle focuses on general usage requirements and not on blocking patents held by dominant entities.
1792. *See supra* at paras 612 f.
1793. Critical, especially with respect to follow-on innovation by the holder of the basic patent: Stierle, 267 and 270 f.
1794. *See supra* at para. 99.

strengthens the effect of the patent as a market entry barrier, without justification.[1795] Further weighting of the relevant interests would compromise the patent system's aspiration to foster innovation since a patent applicant would theoretically be allowed to block entire research areas.

705 The situation in the market in these cases is comparable to situations where market entry is dependent on access to a technology. This justifies a look at the considerations made with regard to the issuing of compulsory licences under competition law.[1796] Compulsory licences are granted according to the essential facility doctrine. Following this doctrine, competitors have to be granted access to the technology if the blocking of the patented technology is keeping competitors from competing in the downstream market. This is the case when the technology has evolved to become a de facto standard or is factually indispensable. The criteria defined by the Court of Justice are that access to the technology must be indispensable for accessing the market and that 'the refusal [to license] is preventing the emergence of a new product for which there is a potential consumer demand, that it is unjustified as well as such as to exclude any competition on a secondary market'.[1797]

5 The Effect of Weak Patents on the Market

706 A specific problem of patent clusters with respect to innovation is that they often include rather weak patents as blocking positions.[1798] For example, reference can be made to the *Servier* case and the maze of weak patents applied for.[1799] These so-called trivial patents fail to satisfy the criteria of novelty and inventiveness. Irrespective of the strategy used, invalid or weak patents are a constant barrier to undistorted competition and a potential harm to innovation.[1800] Other than in the case of valid or strong patents, society does not profit from the innovation revealed in the patent claim. It therefore grants a property right without being rewarded in the form of a contribution to the current state of the art. From a socio-economic perspective, there is no reason to propertise the public good. Furthermore, seeking to prevent market failure is not a valid argument as, owing to an apparent lack of profitably invested R&D, there is no risk of making investment in R&D unattractive.

707 Unlike with strong unused patents, the information, reward and propertisation functions are not fulfilled[1801] if the protected information does not meet the patentability requirements. For such information, the legislator has decided that they are not worth being rewarded with a property right since they do not provide additional

1795. This situation should not be confused with situations where the patent holder applies for a development at the end of the life cycle to in fact use this advanced technology further.
1796. Similarly: Zech, ZWeR 2011, 329 ff.
1797. ECJ, *IMS Health*, C-418/01, para. 37; GC, *Microsoft*, T-201/04, para. 332.
1798. *See evidence in*: EC, *Sector Inquiry, Final Report*, paras 498 ff.
1799. *See supra* at paras 360 ff.
1800. *See*: FTC, *Report: To Promote Innovation*, 5.
1801. *See considerations supra* at paras 688 f.

intellectual value for society. Patents covering technology not meeting the patentability requirements therefore constitute barriers to entry and provide the patent holder with the power to exclude others from using the technology without adding protection-worthy knowledge in return. The patent holder profits from the property rights and rewards regime - a betterment in competition - without being entitled to such a reward.[1802] As well as risking litigation with the holder of the weak patent or the potential of paying unjustified royalties, the presence of an invalid patent raises the costs of innovation, can force competitors to refrain from R&D and deters innovation while cementing the patent holder's position in the market.[1803]

708 If the patent is granted despite lacking patentability, most jurisdictions provide for the possibility of claiming nullity of the patent (Article 138 EPC) or having it re-examined (US Patent Reexamination Act of 1999). Automatic mechanisms do not - to the author's knowledge - exist, and therefore opponents have to seek legal actions and bear the costs accompanying them. Patent laws thus include a presumption in favour of the validity of registered patents. The need to prevent the overcrowding of registrations, as occurs in trademark law, does not exist with patents. Owing to the high likelihood of patents being granted,[1804] the applicant, when applying for a patent with trivial scope, instrumentalises the patent application process to gain an undue advantage.

709 In the pharmaceutical industry, the presence of secondary patents of disputable quality has resulted in widespread conduct by originators. In so-called pay-for-delay agreements, originators holding a weak secondary patent pay generic producers so that they delay their entry and do not oppose the weak patent.[1805] Thus, the regulation mechanism of the patent system fails to recognise patents not worthy of protection.[1806] Facing the problem of delayed generic entry, questionable secondary patents and high prices for drugs, India has even gone as far as to prohibit secondary patents in the pharmaceutical industry (section 3(d) of the Indian Patent Act).[1807]

710 However, in the pharmaceutical industry, incremental innovations can have substantial positive impacts on the tolerability and efficiency of a drug.[1808] Their actual value only shows after clinical trials, or even continuing trials, in the search for new

1802. *See supra* at paras 694 ff.
1803. For the biotech industry, this reaction of competitors has been verified in: FTC, *Report: To Promote Innovation,* 5.
1804. *See supra* at paras 611 ff.
1805. On the struggles of pharmaceutical undertakings with regard to the life cycle of drugs and patents, *see supra* at para. 153. On pay-for-delay agreements in case law, *see supra* at para. 153.
1806. *See*: HAEDICKE, ZGE 2011, 276 ff.
1807. KANKANALA/NARASANI/RADHAKRISHNAN, 19.
1808. Note that incremental innovations are not only important in the pharmaceutical sector. Many innovations develop based on micro-inventions. *See*: CORNISH, in: SCHRICKER/DREIER/KUR, Geistiges Eigentum im Dienst der Innovation, 13; ULLRICH, in: SCHRICKER/DREIER/KUR, Geistiges Eigentum im Dienst der Innovation, 99; WERTHEIMER/LEVY/O'CONNOR, in: FARQUHAR/SUMMERS/SORKIN, Investing in health, 80 ff.

medical indications.[1809] Accordingly, their value can only be determined retrospectively. Although drug development with regard to modifications is less risky compared with fundamental developments based on basic patents, uncertainty as to whether market approval will be granted still exists.[1810] For undertakings conducting further innovation, the situation is even worse, since after the disclosure of the basic patents, the pressure among competitors to invent around the patent and provide a valuable modification of the molecule increases.[1811] FACKELMANN points out that even minor development of drugs requires a significant monetary effort to pass clinical tests and reach market approval and that patent protection is an important factor in the calculation of pre- and post-innovation profits and R&D expenses. He indicates that, following this premise, patentability requirements have to be quite low for pharmaceuticals - for basic innovations (basic patents) because of their high likelihood of technical failure, and for further developments (secondary patents) due to the high expense of clinical trials.[1812]

711 However, despite the above detrimental effects and potential inefficiencies in allocating resources, the importance of patentability requirements and the negative effect of trivial patents should not be neglected in the pharmaceutical industry.[1813] This conclusion is further supported by sector-specific factors. As has been shown above, most of the costs in the development process of drugs arise from clinical trials.[1814] Securing R&D expense is not the direct aim of the patent system, which means that low patentability requirements cannot be justified for an easier way of providing the means to recover R&D expenses. The legislator in the pharmaceutical sector has met its specific needs by implementing supplementary protection mechanisms, for example, document protection, the supplementary protection certificate or market exclusivity, as in the case of orphan drugs,[1815] and not through sector-specific adjustments to the patentability requirements.[1816]

6 Implications

712 Patent laws, other than trademark laws, do not impose an obligation on the right holder to use the property right in trade. Yet, in order to fulfil their aim within competition and not to raise the barriers to both competition and innovation unduly, it can be necessary to demand that the dominant right holder uses the patent when potential demand for the technology exists.

1809. *See supra* at paras 158 ff.
1810. *See supra* at paras 161 ff.
1811. On the whole paragraph, *see*: UNGER, Medizinische Klinik 2006, 257 ff.
1812. FACKELMANN, 436 f.
1813. With the same result also: FACKELMANN, 438 f.
1814. *See supra* at paras 161 ff.
1815. On the remedies implemented by the legislator, *see*: GASSNER, GRUR Int. 2004, 983 f.
1816. FACKELMANN, 438 f.

713 If the patent holder cannot resort to protection from the fundamental right to property, as the patentability requirements are not met, the interest of securing undistorted competition outweighs the interest of a dominant undertaking to secure their own 'innovation'.

714 This leads to the conclusion that three types of blocking patents have to be distinguished. The distinction is made based on the legitimacy of the ownership of the property right. The following table provides an overview:

	Valid Blocking Patents	*Invalid Blocking Patents*	*Secondary Acquisition of Blocking Patents*
Securing own Innovation	✔	✖	✖
Recouping R&D	✖	✖	✖

715 The problem that remains, in practice, is not that the blocking patent is an unjustified property right that changed the market structure unduly through the applicant or holder not complying with the patentability requirements, but rather that of the anticompetitive intent, which raises concerns. It is 'the 100 per cent anti-competitive intent' combined with the lack of intention to develop the technology or launch the product that makes blocking patents so highly delicate.[1817] Thus, it is the subjective motivation at the time of the filing or while holding the patent that is decisive, paired with intentions directed towards future conduct (not using the technology in trade). Without the plan to combine the non-usage with the refusal to make the invention available beyond publication, competition law concerns would probably not be raised. In these cases, the conclusion drawn by JUDGE HOLMES more than a century ago seems to apply: it is the plan that makes the parts unlawful.[1818] This carries the problem that competition authorities, in the absence of direct evidence, would have to evaluate the intention of future behaviour. To be of relevance in determining the nature of the patent application, the intent therefore, either objectively immanent or expressed through direct evidence, has to provide information on future behaviour. To erase the problems addressed above with respect to the fine line between competitive and anticompetitive intent as well as being up to par with the required standard of proof, direct or circumstantial evidence has to leave no doubt with regard to the anticompetitive nature of the conduct. Rather than a lack of interest in receiving legal protection when evaluating the primary acquisition of patents, the first criterion should be to consider the intent of the applicant to exploit the right in competition.[1819]

1817. DREXL, in: DREXL/LEE, Pharmaceutical innovation, competition and patent law, 309.
1818. JUDGE HOLMES, in: UNITED STATES SUPREME COURT, *Swift & Co. v. United States*, 196 US 375; cited after LERNER, 235.
1819. Similarly: BERG/KÖBELE, PharmaR 2009, 590.

IV CONCLUSION

716 It has been seen that the mere filing for a patent does not qualify as abuse of a dominant position. If the applicant applies for patents with the intention of using them as blocking patents, he or she does not instrumentalise the power granted by the patent within the application process or through the application as such; the blocking power is immanent in the granted patent. The blocking power of a patent is determined not only by the breadth of the patent as well as the diffusion of other patents in the same area among patent holders and similar factors but to a great extent also through the conduct of the patent holder. The abuse only starts after the patent holder withholds the technology from the market. If the patent has been filed with the intention of keeping it as a blocking position, this conduct theoretically starts after the grant of the patent. The prerequisite is that demand for the technology has already been controlled by the patent applicant before the application and potential demand for the technology exists.

717 The evaluation of whether the holding of blocking patents amounts to an abuse of a dominant position requires a balancing of interests. This balance tips against the patent holder if he or she sets up a barrier to innovation without justification, that is when the right not to use the patent is not protected by law. This is the case when the barrier raised by the patent holder renders entry into the innovation race unlikely for competitors and the patent holder cannot prove an actual or potential future plan for using the patented technology in trade.[1820]

718 The conclusion that an undertaking abused its dominant position in the market by holding blocking patents therefore requires:

(a) an actual unused patent;
(b) a lack of legitimate interest in the non-usage,[1821] which is affirmed if:
    (i) the patent implements a barrier which makes entry into the innovation race unlikely for competitors; and
    (ii) evidence of actual or potential future plans for using the patent cannot be found; or
    (iii) the property right itself has not been rightly established.

Ultimately, however, it is the specific collusion of multiple factors that changes the nature of the conduct.[1822]

719 If the patent holder applies for a patent with unpatentable scope, these considerations and conclusions do not apply. In these cases, patent applicants are making use of the high chance of receiving a patent grant, even if patentability requirements are

1820. *See supra* at paras 689 ff; similarly: HEINEMANN, in: MATHIS/TOR, New developments in competition law and economics, 163 ff.
1821. *See also in this regard*: JUNG, ZWeR 2004, 392.
1822. KHAN, Harvard Law Review 1953, 52.

either only partially met or not at all. They are therefore factually instrumentalising inefficiencies of the system for undue profit. Granted patents, owing to the presumption of validity, convey a competitive advantage despite sometimes protecting non-patentable subjects. As has been seen, society in such cases is betrayed by not being rewarded with the disclosure of an invention in turn for providing a property right. An intention to use the patent as a blocking position does not need to be shown in these cases. Where a right has knowingly (in *bad faith*) been invoked without entitlement to it, objective circumstances can lead to the conclusion that the applicant was motivated solely by the idea of procuring an illegal advantage. Anticompetitive intent can thus be assumed. Owing to the lack of interests worthy of protection, there are also no grounds for objectively justifying the behaviour. In these cases, a revocation of the property right could, depending on the circumstances, be a proportional sanction.[1823] A revocation cannot be justified in cases where valid patents are involved, however.[1824] Then compulsory licences must serve as a remedy to remove the blocking position in competition.[1825]

1823. The same can be true for secondary acquisitions.
1824. *See supra* at paras 667 ff., 685 and 712 ff.
1825. Article 31(k) TRIPS establishes the conditions for the grant of a compulsory licence after an anticompetitive behaviour has been determined anticompetitive in a judicial or administrative process.

Findings

720 *Chapters 1 and 2 of Part I* show that there has been a constant shift in the understanding of competition. These changes in the understanding of competition have influenced the interpretation of competition law. Competition law contributes to safeguarding competition so that it can fulfil the aims attributed to it by competition policy. The field of competition law consists of a bundle of laws, above all competition law in the narrow sense (also referred to as antitrust law), unfair competition law and intellectual property laws, including patent law. Owing to the pursuit of seemingly conflicting goals, patent and competition law in the narrow sense have had a rocky relationship in the past. In recent years, scholars have, however, worked out the conflicts and stressed the common goals of fostering innovation. According to the current natural understanding of competition and intellectual property laws, it has become conceivable to analyse the compatibility of intellectual property acquisitions and therefore to measure the application of blocking patents against the standard of competition law.

721 *Chapter 5 of Part I* introduces the competitive environment of pharmaceutical markets. The drug market is characterised by cost-intensive and highly risky R&D projects. Patent protection is crucial to guarantee survival in the market. Originators feel the pressure of competition from other originators as well as generic companies at the end of the patent term. Carefully considered patent management is therefore important to pharmaceutical undertakings.

722 *Chapter 6 of Part II* shows that patenting strategies are an integral part of management decisions. The management of patents is especially relevant for undertakings engaging in R&D activities. While the traditional motive of seeking protection for developed technology still ranks the highest among companies, an interest in using patents to block competitors is another frequently mentioned motive to patent. *Chapter 7 of Part II* holds that the effect of blocking patents on competition is highly circumstantial and generalised findings are difficult. However, as a general rule, broad patent claims or several patents held by the same patent holder increase the blocking effect on competition. Although strategies involving blocking patents result in negative effects on competition, patent law itself does not provide remedies such as the withdrawal of the property or similar as, for example, trademark law does.

723 *Part III* is dedicated to analysing the impact of patents on the definition of the relevant market as well as the establishment of a dominant position. Patent-protected technologies create demand in vertically integrated markets, the product and the technology as well as the innovation market. The relevance and importance of defining innovation markets are controversial in competition law. Defining innovation markets is appropriate when concerted practices or mergers are under scrutiny, but innovation markets are not relevant when the abuse of dominance is being analysed since a dominant position cannot be established in innovation markets. Future effects of shifts within the R&D landscape are only relevant when analysing the situation on technology markets as a factor of potential competition.

724 Owing to the fact that patents function as market entry barriers and provide their holder with the ability to prevent others from using the patented technology, they are an important factor when analysing the market position of an undertaking. That an undertaking is already dominant in the relevant market when applying for the patent is rarely the case. Patent acquisitions which open the scope of Article 102 TFEU are therefore most likely to involve either the application for secondary patents or patent acquisitions.

725 The evaluation of previous case law with Article 102 TFEU and intellectual property rights in *Part IV, Chapter 12* reveals that the courts have so far been hesitant to declare the mere application for a blocking patent as abusive. Convictions have only been made based on sets of different strategies 'overall', though the secondary acquisition of blocking patents has been acknowledged as an abuse of the dominant position. This has led to the conclusion that secondary acquisitions should follow an evaluation pattern different from those of a primary acquisition (application). Such a differentiation is justified based on the legitimate interests of the patent acquirer. When applying for a patent, a patent applicant has to disclose a patentable innovation from which society can profit and that he or she invested certain resources in developing. The acquirer when purchasing a patent or exclusive licence does not have to disclose novel technology.

726 Since further insights could not be gained from case law, the book in *Part IV, Chapter 13* briefly addresses the patent misuse concept of US antitrust law. Owing to fundamental differences in the conceptions of US antitrust and EU competition law as well as the limitations of the patent misuse concept itself, it is not considered suitable as a concept to work out the lines between the rightful use of patents and the abuse of Article 102 TFEU in using them.

727 The analysis of the history of Article 102 TFEU, its textual and structural aspects, conducted in *Chapter 14 of Part V*, shows that the provision was created to stress the common agreement on the necessity to restrict the usage of private power. The wording adds to the general character. The term 'abuse' represents behaviour deviating from standards to bad effect or with a bad purpose. The role of Article 102 TFEU is to discipline dominant undertakings which are not otherwise hindered where they are breaking behavioural standards to bad effect or with a bad purpose.

728 *Part V, Chapter 14, section IV* further shows that the courts differentiate abusive from non-abusive behaviour based on the concept of competition on the merits. Despite a failure to provide a more detailed understanding of meritorious competition, the courts have used a two-stage test when deciding cases. The elements of the test are a 'hard fact' on the one hand and circumstantial analysis on the other hand.

729 *Part V, Chapter 14, section IV* also holds that important questions concerning Article 102 TFEU centre around the extent to which a distortion of competition disadvantages for consumers must be evident. It has been concluded that estimations have to be employed when anticompetitive effects are yet to show. Similarly, anticompetitive intent does not need to be shown, but proof of anticompetitive intent can be a strong factor showing an indication of conduct likely to distort competition.

730 Based on the analysis in Chapter 14 of Part V, *Chapter 15 of Part V* addresses the hypothesis that the abuse of a dominant position has conceptual similarities with the general abuse of rights principle. The abuse of rights principle, despite only recently being acknowledged by the Court of Justice, is known to the Member States in that the use of a right in contradiction to its purpose cannot be protected. The summary of the abuse of rights principle in Article 102 TFEU means that the concept of competition on the merits does not need to be used to measure behaviour and to conduct a balancing of the relevant interests alongside known patterns.

731 After a recapitulation of the analysis in *Part VI, Chapter 15*, in *Chapter 17 of Part VI*, it is shown that a patent grant always has an effect on competition. The detrimental impact on competition and innovation is high for broad patents or patent families held by one entity if only a few lines of innovation are available and the patented innovation is valuable (key to follow-on). A distortion could only occur in very rare cases, however. An example might be flooding strategies or patent applications in reaction to the patenting activities of competitors in order to complicate these. The mere application for a patent (primary acquisition) will only in the rarest cases amount to an abuse of dominance. Possible scenarios where the threshold could be met involve the use of patent applications to control the demand in a market. Yet in most cases, a distortion of competition will only arise as a result of the patent holder's behaviour (keeping the patent as a blocking position) after the grant of the patent.

732 The conclusions drawn in *Part VI, Chapter 18* start with the realisation that higher societal interests impose limitations on patent rights. Economic considerations resulting from the patent as a property right itself do not limit the right to the patent, and neither does a failure to use the patent in trade result in a loss of the right. Patents thereby differ from trademark laws. However, states are not obliged to grant patents unrestrictedly. The TRIPS Agreement allows for limitations to the right to property when public interests are at stake. Blocking industrial development has been recognised as an important public interest, which justifies counteractions. The TRIPS Agreement thus accepts that patents can be abusively used to block development.

Patent laws, also based on their fundamental aim, do not imply an expectation on the patent holder to use the patent in trade. However, if the demand for certain technology cannot be met due to a patent being held as a blocking position by a dominant undertaking, the right not to use the patent is outweighed by the interests of undistorted competition.

733 The findings of this book culminate in the conclusion that a dominant undertaking abuses its position by holding blocking patents if it sets up a barrier to innovation without justification, that is, if it lacks interest in using a patent worthy of protection. It is deemed to represent an abuse of a dominant position if the patent makes entry into the innovation race less likely for competitors and the property right has either not been rightly established or the dominant undertaking fails to provide actual or potential future plans to use the patented technology.

Outlook: Global Shortages and the Role of Patents

I PATENTS AND THEIR BARRIERS

734 This book has shown that patents as man-made privileges have always been exposed to discussions about their role in society, their scope and above all their justification. The reasons to implement a patent system are diverse. They range from the idea to protect a natural connection between an inventor and its 'fruits of mental labour'[1826] to the more economic assumption that patents are the reward of society issued to an inventor for the contribution to knowledge[1827]. Nowadays, the justification of patents includes an overall cost-benefit assessment.[1828] This is reflected in the objectives of the protection and enforcement of intellectual properties as stated in Article 7 of the TRIPS Agreement.[1829]

735 Owing to this background, it does not come as a surprise that the limitations of patent law are subject to heated discourses. As with property rights in general, patents face both internal and external limitations.[1830] By answering a question on the intersection between competition and patent law, this book focused on external boundaries implied onto patents. The central question concerned the limits competition law imposes on the exploitation of patents. More precisely, the analysis examined the circumstances under which the right of the patent holder to exploit the patent has to take a back seat to preventing a distortion of competition.

736 Since the manuscript for this book was finished, patents have prominently appeared on the agenda of world politics. The spotlight hit patents after the successful development of vaccines against the currently raging coronavirus SARS-CoV-2. The

1826. *See supra* at paras 91 f.
1827. *See supra* at para. 93.
1828. *See supra* at paras 94 f.
1829. *See supra* at fn. 265.
1830. *See supra* at paras 120, 263, 570 ff., 636 and 643.

debate concerning patent protection for COVID vaccines has culminated in the request of India and South Africa to waive patents on COVID. The request was brought forward to the council for the TRIPS Agreement in October 2020. The two countries proposed to instal a waiver of patents on COVID vaccines until 'the majority of the world's population has developed immunity'[1831].

737 This request is based on the concern that patents might impose 'barriers to the timely access to affordable medical products'. The countries fear that patents and any other intellectual property right protecting the vaccines could be responsible for shortages in the supply of costly vaccines. They hope that by waiving the intellectual property rights, access to affordable medicine could be granted worldwide and production could be diversified and scaled up.[1832]

II ARE PATENTS RESPONSIBLE FOR THE SHORTAGE?

738 In this book, it has been stated on several occasions that patents can function as barriers to market access.[1833] In the context of competition law, market entry barriers are important factors when analysing the likelihood of a market entry. In the same context, it has been noted that patents also provide their holders a certain degree of freedom in their behaviour on the market. The presence of patents is not the sole factor allowing the holding of a dominant position and preventing market entries. Such an equation would fall too short.[1834]

739 In the same vein, it falls too short to equate the problem that the demand for COVID vaccines exceeds the supplied capacities with the presence of patents. A patent does not make a launchable product.

740 While this is generally true for complex product industries, where a product is based on more than one patent,[1835] it is certainly true for products in highly regulated industries. In the pharmaceutical industry, patents are generally applied for at an early stage of the product development process.[1836] At this time, it is neither known whether the protected compound or composition will pass the required trials nor whether it is suitable for upscale production.[1837] Additionally, the technologies, processes or also APIs developed can have several different fields of application.[1838]

741 mRNA technology, which is the technology used in the COVID vaccines developed by Moderna and Pfizer/Biontech, is not limited to its application in vaccines, but

1831. WTO, IP/C/W/669/Rev.1, para. 5.
1832. WTO, IP/C/W/669/Rev.1, 3 f.
1833. *See supra* at paras 234, 266, 286, 317, 609, 669, 707, 712 and 724.
1834. *See supra* at paras 286, 308, 311 and 491.
1835. *See supra* at para. 207.
1836. *See supra* at paras 147 and 152.
1837. On 12 August 2021, *The New York Times* vaccine trackers report that ninety-nine vaccines are currently being tested in clinical trials. *See*: https://www.nytimes.com/interactive/2020/science/coronavirus-vaccine-tracker.html, accessed on 12 August 2021.
1838. *See*, e.g., on second medical use *supra* at para. 172.

research also focuses on its use in cancer therapy.[1839] The technology has been studied since the early 1990s where at the University of Wisconsin scientists have been able to inject mRNA in mice. It took fifteen more years until scientists were able to modify the transport pathway with which the mRNA is delivered to the cells by embedding mRNA in lipid nanoparticles. They therewith laid the foundations for the application of mRNA in the human body and an additional fifteen years until Moderna and Pfizer/Biontech were able to market the first vaccine.[1840] Needless to say that during these more than thirty years of development, several milestones were achieved and patented long before the virus was in the process of spreading globally. These technologies were not developed to be used in the fight against a global pandemic.

742 Furthermore, the development of the COVID vaccine only started after the publication of the gene sequence of the virus in January 2020. Given that it takes twenty-eight months on average from the patent application to the grant with the EPO,[1841] it does not come as a surprise that all patentable developments made since January 2020, i.e., in the process of developing the COVID vaccine have not resulted in granted patents yet. At this time, it is not even possible to get an idea of how many patents have been applied for in the course of the development of the vaccine. Pending patent applications are only published after eighteen months.

743 From a regulatory perspective, a pharmaceutical can only be launched after the successful completion of clinical trials and after obtaining a marketing authorisation.[1842] A marketing authorisation can only be obtained if clinical data showing the safety of the product is submitted. In many jurisdictions including the EU[1843], these documents are protected by regulatory data protection (RDP). During the time that RDP is in place, other applicants cannot rely on the data in support of obtaining a marketing authorisation, but have to deliver the necessary data themselves. Even if no patents existed at all, path to market would not be cleared unless all the regulatory requirements are met by the new competitor.

744 From a practical perspective, customers can only enjoy a product if the holder of the marketing authorisation is able to ensure supply. Operating a successful supply chain starts with a manufacturing site able to produce the product in the required quantities and further includes the delivery of raw materials and equipment to the production site and the transportation of the final product.[1844] While this may sound practicable, one has to keep in mind that operating a supply chain for a pharmaceutical involves a complex network of suppliers. Such multi-tier supply chains consist of several players delivering basic and highly specialised as well as bespoke materials and

1839. *See*, for example, https://www.cancernetwork.com/view/messenger-rna-vaccines-beckoning-of-a-new-era-in-cancer-immunotherapy, accessed on 12 August 2021.
1840. *See* the review by Cagigi/Lore on the use of mRNA in mice, monkey and humans.
1841. EPO News, 14 January 2021, Patent grants up 5.9% at IP5 offices in 2019: https://www.epo.org/news-events/news/2021/20210114.html, accessed on 14 August 2021.
1842. *See supra* at paras 134, 136, 164 f., and 710 f.
1843. *See* Article 14(11) of Regulation (EC) No 726/2004.
1844. *See*: https://www.swr.de/wissen/so-funktioniert-die-produktion-von-corona-impfstoffen-100.html, accessed on 22 August 2021.

equipment. To make matters even more complicated, high standards have to be guaranteed alongside the whole production and supply chain. Additionally, the number of suitable sub-tier suppliers that can deliver the required products at the required quality is limited.

745 The production of vaccines requires highly sophisticated production facilities. These facilities and the companies operating them are limited in numbers.[1845] Production of the COVID mRNA vaccine has proven to be especially difficult. Even those pharmaceutical companies that conducted research for some time had no infrastructure to produce these vaccines in large quantities a year ago. To supply as many people as possible with the vaccine, the pharmaceutical companies enter into collaboration with manufacturers. But also such partners are limited in numbers because shifting production to a new product requires the reorganisation of the factory and the building of new production lines.[1846] Taking Moderna's vaccine as example, there has initially only been one manufacturer in Europe able to produce the vaccine on a large scale, Lonza in Switzerland. Only in June 2021, the EMA approved an additional site for production in Europe. Around the same time, additional manufacturing sites were also opened in the USA.[1847]

746 Consequently, there are only limited production facilities that can produce vaccines in general and in particular COVID vaccines. Additionally, market access is not cleared for other pharmaceutical companies – not only because of patents that may have been applied for but also because of regulatory restrictions. These practical issues clash with an unseen demand. The whole world requires the COVID vaccine. Irrespective of patents, the market is not ready to supply the world on short notice.

III COMPULSORY LICENCES AS INTERNAL LIMITATIONS TO PATENTS

747 The international minimum standards of intellectual property protection have been set out in the TRIPS Agreement. As described above for patent systems in general,[1848] also the provision implemented in the TRIPS Agreement has to strike a balance between protection and omitting blocking positions in order to fulfil their task of promoting technological innovation and the transfer of technology. The TRIPS Agreement is the result of a compromise reached in long rounds of negotiations.[1849] In

1845. *See*, e.g., https://www.interpharma.ch/blog/massenproduktion-und-versorgung-mit-einem-impfstoff/, accessed on 22 August 2021.
1846. *See*: https://www.swr.de/wissen/so-funktioniert-die-produktion-von-corona-impfstoffen-100.html, accessed on 22 August 2021; https://www.chemistryworld.com/news/why-manufacturing-covid-vaccines-at-scale-is-hard/4013429.article, accessed on 22 August 2021.
1847. EMA Press Release, 11 June 2021, Additional manufacturing capacity for Moderna's COVID-19 vaccine: https://www.ema.europa.eu/en/news/additional-manufacturing-capacity-modernas-covid-19-vaccine, accessed on 14 August 2021.
1848. *See supra* at paras 94 f.
1849. RIDDER, 27 f.

these negotiations, remedies for situations where patents do create unwanted blocking positions have been discussed as well.

748 The TRIPS Agreement allows for the granting of compulsory licences if certain conditions are met.[1850] Compulsory licences may only be granted in individual cases (Article 31(a) TRIPS) for a limited time and cause (Article 31(c) and (g) TRIPS) and if a licence could not be obtained on reasonable commercial terms, unless in cases of national emergency or extreme urgency (Article 31(b) TRIPS). Compulsory licences are granted only on an unexclusive basis and are not transferable (Article 31(d) and (e) TRIPS). Issuing a compulsory licence further requires an adequate remuneration of the patent holder (Article 31(h) TRIPS).

749 Following Article 31(f) TRIPS, compulsory licences have to be 'predominantly' granted for the supply of the national market. This licence thus in general includes manufacturing.[1851] While predominantly does not mean exclusively, scholars have interpreted Article 31(f) in that exports under such a licence are allowed if the national market is too small for profitable production.[1852] This provision has proven to be problematic for countries that do not have sufficient capacities to manufacture pharmaceuticals.[1853]

750 Therefore, Article 31bis TRIPS was introduced in 2017 to expand the system of compulsory licences to supply developing or least developed countries with pharmaceutical products they cannot produce themselves.[1854] It allows for the issuing of a compulsory licence for the export to such countries. A compulsory licence request of a company willing to take over the supply in the country of destination has to be preceded by negotiations with the patent owner and accompanied by a notification of the relevant country to the council of the TRIPS Agreement.[1855]

751 Article 31bis TRIPS thus addresses the problems that led to the request of waiving patents during the pandemic and guarantee a fair allocation of vaccines on a global scale.

752 However, while the TRIPS Agreement has implemented mechanisms to react to a situation such as the current, it is also the first time that they could get tested in practice and on a global scale after the case between Canada and Rwanda that initiated the amendments to the TRIPS Agreement in the first place.[1856] Another request with the

---

1850. Above, the possibility to obtain a licence in cases of insufficient use has been introduced. *See* paras 261 ff.
1851. HÖHNE, in: BUSCHE ET AL., TRIPS Kommentar, Article 31, para. 28.
1852. RIDDER, 98 ff. Note that § 36 (4) of the Austrian Patent Act as well as § 24 of the German Patent Act do not state that the compulsory licence has to be granted to predominantly supply the national market.
1853. HÖHNE, in: BUSCHE ET AL., TRIPS Kommentar, Article 31, para. 29.
1854. HÖHNE, in: BUSCHE ET AL., TRIPS Kommentar, Article 31, para. 29.
1855. WTO, Analytical Index, TRIPS Agreement, Article 31bis.
1856. WTO, Notification of Rwanda, 19 July 2007, IP/N/9/RWA/1.

Indian patent office to export an anticancer drug to Nepal has not been successful because Nepal never notified the WTO about intentions to import the said drug.[1857]

753 It must be acknowledged that the issuing of compulsory licences is not a well-established practice in general. In many countries requests have been rare. In 2017, the German BGH issued a compulsory licence for the production of the HIV drug Isentress® based on a request for preliminary measures.[1858] In Switzerland, there are still no known cases of issued compulsory licences. Thus, case law still has to be developed.

754 Critics argue that the established system implemented several hurdles and procedural burdens and would need amendments to enhance access to medicine.[1859] However, even if that were the case, the reluctance shown through the missing requests does not prove them right. Given that the provisions on the compulsory licences are a compromise reached by the WTO members while considering and weighing all the different involved interests, it seems unlikely that the system will be amended without having been tested and thus also without clear knowledge about alleged strengths and weaknesses.

IV LEARNINGS

755 It has been shown that patents are not the reason for the current shortage on COVID vaccines[1860] and thus a waiver of patents does not seem to be a suitable remedy for the problems faced currently. However, the idea that patents could block access to a technology is not new, and remedies to react to certain situations have found their way into patent laws in the form of compulsory licences.

756 The compulsory licences in the TRIPS Agreement address two situations of supply shortage; one is for the situation where a domestic market is not supplied despite manufacturing in this state is possible (Article 31(f) TRIPS), and the other provides remedy in case a country does not have the necessary production facilities and is dependent on imports (Article 31bis TRIPS). Despite that such licences have only been issued on rare occasions, the adopted regulation represents a broadly discussed compromise reached on an international level by the members of the WTO. It thus prima facie provides a solution which weighs and balances involved interests to the best extent possible. The current pandemic offers chances to test the system for strengths and weaknesses.

1857. Correa, South Centre Policy Brief, 57, 5.
1858. BGH, *Raltegravir,* X ZB 2/17. In 2019, the same court has denied a compulsory licence to produce Praluent® because the applicant did not show sufficient efforts to obtain a licence from the patent holder. The licence was again requested in a case concerning preliminary measures. BGH, *Praluent®*, X ZB 2/19.
1859. Correa, South Centre Policy Brief, 57, 5.
1860. *See also*: AIPPI, Position Paper on the waiver of certain provisions under the TRIPS, 12 May 2021, para. 6.

757 In the current situation, rather than discussing a waiver of the patents, it may be more beneficial to discuss a fair allocation of the actually produced vaccines. VON BOGDANDY/VILLARREAL in this regard held that 'even if the compulsory licensing system in the TRIPS Agreement allows overcoming patent protection, it certainly does not by itself contribute to towards a fair and equitable global distribution of COVID-19 vaccines, particularly in low income countries'.[1861]

1861. VON BOGDANDY/VILLARREAL, ZAöRV, 91.

Bibliography

ACKERMANN THOMAS, § 21 Europäisches Kartellrecht, in: RIESENHUBER KARL (ED.), Europäische Methodenlehre, Berlin 2014, 473 ff.

AGRANAT ISRAEL/WAINSCHTEIN SILVYA R., The Strategy of Enantiomer Patents of Drugs, Drug Discovery Today 2010, 163 ff.

AHN HYEWON, Second Generation Patents in Pharmaceutical Innovation, Baden-Baden 2014, Doctoral Thesis Univ. Augsburg 2013.

AKMAN PINAR, Consumer Welfare and Article 82 EC; Practice and Rhetoric, World Competition 2009, 71 ff.

AKMAN PINAR, Searching for the Long-Lost Soul of Article 82 EC, Oxford Journal of Legal Studies 2009, 267 ff.

AKMAN PINAR, Abuse of a Dominant Position and Globalization, International Report, in: KËLLEZI PRANVERA/KILPATRICK BRUCE/KOBEL PIERRE (EDS), Abuse of Dominant Position and Globalization & Protection and Disclosure of Trade Secrets and Know-How, Cham 2017, 3 ff.

AKMAN PINAR, The Concept of Abuse in EU Competition Law, Law and Economic Approaches, 2nd ed., Oxford Etc. 2015.

ALBERS MICHAEL, Der 'More Economic Approach' bei Verdrängungsmiss-bräuchen, Zum Stand der Überlegungen der Europäischen Kommission (Beitrag zu einem in Hamburg gehaltenen Kartellrechtssymposium) 2006, https://ec.europa.eu/competition/antitrust/art82/albers.pdf, accessed on 4 February 2020 (cit. ALBERS M., Kartellrechtssymposium).

ALBERS REGINA, Die neue Waffe gegen Prostatakrebs, Hilfe bei Potenzproblemen, Focus Magazin, 24 May 2015 (cit. ALBERS R., Focus Magazin, 24 May 2015).

ALBERT CARSTEN F., Patente in der Fusionskontrolle, Tübingen 2011, Doctoral Thesis Univ. Bayreuth 2010.

ALMUNIA JOAQUIN, Converging Paths in Unilateral Conduct, Speech Delivered at the ICN Unilateral Conduct Workshop in Brussel 3 December 2010, https://ec.europa.eu/commission/presscorner/detail/en/SPEECH_10_722, accessed on 3 March 2020.

AMSTUTZ MARC, Urteilsanmerkung zum Bundesgerichtsentscheid vom 11. April 2011 – Terminierungspreis im Mobilfunk, sic! 2011, 520 ff.

AMSTUTZ MARC/REINERT MANI (eds), Kartellgesetz, Basler Kommentar 2010 (cit. AUTHOR, in: BSK KG, Article XY).

ANTON JAMES J./YAO DENNIS A., Little Patents and Big Secrets: Managing Intellectual Property, RAND Journal of Economics 2004, 1 ff.

AOKI REIKO/SPIEGEL YOSSI, Pre-grant Patent Publication and Cumulative Innovation, International Journal of Industrial Organization 2009, 333 ff.

AREEDA PHILLIP/TURNER DONALD F., Predatory Pricing and Related Practices under Section 2 of the Sherman Act, Harvard Law Review 1975, 697 ff.

ARORA ASHISH, Patents, Licensing, and Market Structure in the Chemical Industry, Research Policy 1997, 391 ff.

ARORA ASHISH/FOSFURI ANDREA/GAMBARDELLA ALFONSO, Markets for Technology, the Economics of Innovation and Corporate Strategy, Cambridge (MA) 2002.

ARUNDEL ANTHONY/PATEL PARI, Strategic Patenting, Background Report for the Trend Chart Policy Benchmarking Workshop New Trends in IPR Policy, European Trend Chart on Innovation 2003.

ATHANASIADOU AMALIA, Patent Settlements in the Pharmaceutical Industry under US Antitrust and EU Competition Law, Alphen aan den Rijn 2018.

BABEY FABIO/RIZVI SALIM, Die Frand-Selbstverpflichtung: Fair, Reasonable and Non-discriminatory Terms (FRAND) im Lichte des Kartellrechts, WUW 2012, 808 ff.

BAETGE DIETMAR/VON HEIN JAN/VON HINDEN MICHAEL (eds), Die richtige Ordnung, Festschrift für Jan Kropholler zum 70. Geburtstag, Heidelberg 2008 (cit. AUTHOR, in: BAETGE ET AL., FS Kropholler, Titel).

BAILEY STEVE, A Tiny, Beloved Home That Was Built for Spite, The New York Times 29 February 2008, https://www.nytimes.com/2008/02/29/travel/ escapes/29away .html, accessed on 27 April 2020.

BAIN JOE S., Industrial Organization, 2nd ed., New York 1968.

BAKER SCOTT/MEZZETTI CLAUDIO, Disclosure as Strategy in the Patent Race, Journal of Law and Economics 2005, 173 ff.

BAKER MCCLANAHAN JOHN, Copyright Misuse as a Defense in an Infringement Action: Lasercomb America, Inc. v. Reynolds, Washington and Lee Law Review 1992, 213 ff.

BARTH ULI, Innovationsmärkte in der Fusionskontrolle, Eine rechtsvergleichende Untersuchung nach deutschem, europäischem und US-amerikanischem Recht, Baden-Baden 2004, Doctoral Thesis Univ. Tübingen 2003.

BARTON JOHN H., Antitrust Treatment of Oligopolies with Mutually Blocking Patent Portfolios, Antitrust Law Journal 2001, 851 ff.

BASEDOW JÜRGEN, Konsumentenwohlfahrt und Effizienz: Neue Leitbilder der Wettbewerbspolitik?, WUW 2007, 712 ff.

BASEDOW JÜRGEN, Das Sozialmodell von Lissabon: Solidarität statt Wettbewerb?, EuZW 2008, 225.

BAUDENBACHER CARL (ed.), Lauterkeitsrecht, Kommentar zum Gesetz gegen den unlauteren Wettbewerb (UWG), Basel 2001 (cit. AUTHOR, in: BAUDENBACHER, UWG Kommentar, Article XY).

BAUDENBACHER LAURA MELUSINE, Überlegungen zum Verbot des Rechtsmissbrauchs im Europäischen Gemeinschaftsrecht, ZfRV 2008, 205 ff.

BAUDENBACHER LAURA MELUSINE, Vom gemeineuropäischen zum europäischen Rechtsmissbrauchsverbot, Baden-Baden 2016, Doctoral Thesis Univ. Zürich 2015.

BAUER HANS H./FISCHER MARC, Product Life Cycle Patterns for Pharmaceuticals and Their Impact on R&D Profitability of Late Mover Products, International Business Review 2000, 703 ff.

BAUR JÜRGEN F., Der Missbrauch im deutschen Kartellrecht, Tübingen 1972 (Habil. Univ. München 1970-1971).

BAVASSO ANTONIO, The Role of Intent under Article 82 EC: From 'Flushing the Turkeys' to 'Spotting Lionesses in Regent's Park', European Competition Law Review 2005, 616 ff.

BEHRENS PETER, Der Wettbewerb im Vertrag von Lissabon, EuZW 2008, 193.

BEIER FRIEDRICH-KARL, Das Patentwesen und seine Informationsfunktion: gestern und heute, GRUR 1977, 282 ff.

BEJRANANDA KANSAK, Die kartellrechtliche Beurteilung unternehmerischer Strategien gegen den Markteintritt konkurrierender Arzneimittel 2016, Doctoral Thesis Univ. Regensburg 2016.

BELLAMY CHRISTOPHER/CHILD GRAHAM D., European Union Law of Competition, 8th ed., Oxford 2018.

BENDER ACHIM/EKEY FRIEDRICH L./FUCHS-WISSEMANN GEORG (eds), Markengesetz und Markenrecht ausgewählter ausländischer Staaten, 4th, Heidelberg, Hamburg 2019 (cit. AUTHOR, in: BENDER ET AL., MarkenR, Article XY).

BENKARD GEORG/ASENDORF CLAUS DIETRICH (eds), Patentgesetz, Gebrauchsmustergesetz, Patentkostengesetz, 11th ed., München 2015 (cit. AUTHOR, in: BENKARD/ASENDORF, Münchener Kommentar PatG, Article XY).

BENKARD GEORG/EHLERS JOCHEN/KINKELDEY URSULA (eds), Europäisches Patentübereinkommen, 3rd ed., München 2019 (cit. AUTHOR, in: BENKARD ET AL., EPÜ, § XY).

BENNET DAVID E., The Power of Patents and Their Strategic Use, Business in North Carolina, 64 f.

BENTLY LIONEL ET AL., Intellectual Property Law, 5th ed., Oxford 2018.

BERG WERNER/KÖBELE MICHAEL, Grenzen kartellrechtmässigen Handelns nach der EU-Untersuchung des Arzneimittelsektors, Risiken und Chancen für betroffene Unternehmen, PharmaR 2009, 581 ff.

BERTHOLD GESINE, Evergreening von Arzneimittelpatenten, Schutzverlängernde Patentstrategien und die Möglichkeiten ihrer Begrenzung im Recht der WTO, Baden-Baden 2011, Doctoral Thesis Univ. Lausanne 2010.

BISHOP SIMON/WALKER MIKE, The Economics of EC Competition Law, Concepts, Application and Measurement, 3rd ed., London 2010.

BLIND KNUT ET AL., Motives to Patent: Empirical Evidence from Germany, Research Policy, 655 ff.

BLIND KNUT ET AL., Erfindungen kontra Patente, Schwerpunktstudie 'zur technologischen Leistungsfähigkeit Deutschlands' 2003.

BLIND KNUT/CREMERS KATRIN/MÜLLER ELISABETH, The Influence of Strategic Patenting on Companies' Patent Portfolios, Research Policy, 428 ff.

BLOCKX JAN, The Limits of the 'More Economic' Approach to Antitrust, World Competition 2019.

BODENHAUSEN GEORG HENDRIK CHRISTIAAN, Pariser Verbandsübereinkunft zum Schutz des gewerblichen Eigentums, Kommentar, 2nd ed., Köln 1971.

BODEWIG THEO, Neue Guidelines für Lizenzverträge in den USA, GRUR Int. 1997, 958 ff.

BÖHM FRANZ, Wirtschaftsordnung und Staatsverfassung, Tübingen 1950.

BÖHM FRANZ, Die Forschungs- und Lehrgemeinschaft zwischen Juristen und Volkswirten an der Universität Freiburg in den dreissiger und vierziger Jahre des 20. Jahrhunderts, Das Recht der Ordnung der Wirtschaft, in: WOLFF HANS JULIUS/WÜRTENBERGER THOMAS (EDS), Aus der Geschichte der Rechts- und Staatswissenschaften zu Freiburg im Breisgau, Freiburg im Breisgau 1957, 95 ff.

BÖHM FRANZ, Demokratie und ökonomische Macht, in: Institut für ausländisches und internationales Wirtschaftsrecht, Kartelle und Monopole im modernen Recht, Karlsruhe 1961, 1 ff.

BÖHM FRANZ, Wettbewerb und Monopolkampf, Eine Untersuchung zur Frage des wirtschaftlichen Kampfrechts und zur Frage der rechtlichen Struktur der geltenden Wirtschaftsordnung, 246, Baden-Baden 2010 (cit. BÖHM, Wettbewerb und Monopolkampf).

BOLDRIN MICHELE/LEVINE DAVID K., The Case Against Patents, Journal of Economic Perspectives 2013, 3 ff.

BORK ROBERT H., The Antitrust Paradox: A Policy at War with Itself, 2nd ed., New York 1993.

BORNKAMM JOACHIM/MONTAG FRANK/SÄCKER FRANZ JÜRGEN (eds), Münchener Kommentar: Europäisches und Deutsches Wettbewerbsrecht, Europäisches Wettbewerbsrecht; Kartellrecht, Missbrauchs- und Fusionskontrolle, 2nd ed., München 2015 (cit. AUTHOR, in: BORNKAMM ET AL., MüKo, Article XY).

BOUCHARD RON A., Patently Innovative, How Pharmaceutical Firms Use Emerging Patent Law to Extend Monopolies on Blockbuster Drugs, Cambridge (UK) 2012.

BOWMAN WARD S., Patent and Antitrust Law: A Legal and Economic Appraisal, Chicago 1973.

BRIGOLA ALEXANDER, Warenverkehr, in: DAUSES MANFRED A./LUDWIGS MARKUS (EDS), Handbuch des EU-Wirtschaftsrechts, München 2019.

BROCKHOFF KLAUS, Forschung und Entwicklung, Planung und Kontrolle, 5th ed., München 1999.

BRÜGGER PAUL (ed.), Homo creator, Festschrift für Alois Troller, Basel, Stuttgart 1976 (cit. AUTHOR, in: BRÜGGER, FS Troller, Titel).

BÜCHI JAKOB, Grundlagen der Arzneimittelforschung und der synthetischen Arzneimittel, Basel 1963.

BUCK CARSTEN, Über die Auslegungsmethoden des Gerichtshofs der Europäischen Gemeinschaft, Frankfurt am Main, Berlin, Bern, New York, Paris, Wien 1998, Doctoral Thesis Univ. Münster (Westfalen) 1997.

BÜHLER STEFAN/LEHMANN URS, Zusammenarbeit in Forschung und Entwicklung im neuen Kartellgesetz, AJP 1997, 651 ff.

BURK DAN L./LEMLEY MARK A., The Patent Crisis and How the Courts Can Solve It, Richmond (Virg.) 2009.

BURR WOLFGANG ET AL., Patentmanagement, Strategischer Einsatz und ökonomische Bewertung von technologischen Schutzrechten, Stuttgart 2007.

BUSCHE JAN/RÖHLING ANDREAS (eds), Kölner Kommentar zum Kartellrecht, Köln 2017 (cit. AUTHOR, in: BUSCHE/RÖHLING, Kölner Kommentar GWB, Article XY).

BUSCHE JAN/STOLL PETER T./WIEBE ANDREAS (eds), TRIPS, Internationales und europäisches Recht des geistigen Eigentums; Kommentar, 2nd ed., Köln 2013 (cit. AUTHOR, in: BUSCHE ET AL., TRIPS Kommentar, Article XY).

BYERS MICHAEL, Abuse of Rights: An Old Principle – A New Age, McGill Law Journal 2002, 389 ff.

CAGIGI ALBERTO/LORE KARIN, Immune Responses Induced by mRNA Vaccination in Mice, Monkeys and Humans, Vaccines 2021, 61 ff.

CALLIESS CHRISTIAN/RUFFERT MATTHIAS (eds), EUV/AEUV, Das Verfassungsrecht der Europäischen Union mit Europäischer Grundrechtecharta: Kommentar, 5th ed., München 2016 (cit. AUTHOR, in: CALLIESS/RUFFERT, EUV/AEUV, Article XY).

CANAPA DAMIANO, Trademarks and Brands in Merger Control: An Analysis of the European and Swiss Legal Orders 2016, Doctoral Thesis Univ. Zurich 2016.

CARSTENSEN PETER C., Antitrust Law and the Paradigm of Industrial Organization, U.C. Davis Law Review 1983, 487 ff.

CASS RONALD/HYLTON KEITH, Antitrust Intent, Southern Californian Law Review 2000, 657 ff.

CHERPILLOD IVAN, Marques défensives, de réserve, et dépôts frauduleux, sic! 2000, 359 ff.

CHOWDHURY AVANTIKA/GAIGL ALEXANDER, The Economics of Competition Law and of Pharmaceutical Patents, in: PITRUZZELLA GIOVANNI/MUSCOLO GABRIELLA (EDS), Competition and Patent Law in the Pharmaceutical Sector, Alphen aan den Rijn 2016.

CHRONOPOULOS APOSTOLOS, Das Markenrecht als Teil der Wettbewerbsordnung, Köln 2013, Doctoral Thesis Univ. München 2011-2012.

CLAPHAM ROLAND, Das wettbewerbspolitische Konzept der Wettbewerbsfreiheit, in: COX HELMUT/JENS UWE/MARKERT KURT (EDS), Handbuch des Wettbewerbs, München 1981, 129 ff.

CLARK JOHN MAURICE, Toward a Concept of Workable Competition, The American Economic Review 1940, 241 ff.

CLARK JOHN MAURICE, Competition as a Dynamic Process, 45, Westport (CT) 1980.

COCKBURN IAIN, Is the Pharmaceutical Industry in a Productivity Crisis?, Innovation Policy and the Economy 2006, 1 ff.

COHEN WESLEY M. ET AL., R&D Spillovers, Patents and the Incentives to Innovate in Japan and the United States, Research Policy 2002, 1349 ff.

COHEN WESLEY M./NELSON RICHARD R./WALSH JOHN P., Protecting Their Intellectual Assets: Appropriability Conditions and Why US Manufacturing Firms Patent (or Not), NBER Working Paper Series.

COLLINS HUGH, EC Regulation of Unfair Commercial Practices, in: COLLINS HUGH (ED.), The Forthcoming EC Directive on Unfair Commercial Practices, The Hague 2004, 1 ff.

CONDE GALLEGO BEATRIZ, Die Anwendung des kartellrechtlichen Missbrauchsverbots auf 'unerlässliche' Immaterialgüterrechte im Lichte der IMS Health- und Standard-Spundfass-Urteile, GRUR Int. 2006, 16 ff.

CORNISH WILLIAM, The Expansion of Intellectual Property Rights, in: SCHRICKER GERHARD/DREIER THOMAS/KUR ANNETTE (EDS), Geistiges Eigentum im Dienst der Innovation, Baden-Baden 2001, 9 ff.

CORREA CARLOS MARÍA, The GATT Agreement on Trade-Related Aspects of Intellectual Property Rights: New Standards for Patent Protection, EIPR 1994, 327 ff.

CORREA CARLOS MARÍA, Chapter 8, Patent Rights, in: CORREA CARLOS MARÍA/YUSUF ABDULQAWI (EDS), Intellectual Property and International Trade, Alphen aan den Rijn 2016, 263 ff.

CORREA CARLOS MARÍA, Will the Amendment to the TRIPS Agreement Enhance Access to Medicines?, South Centre Policy Brief 2019, 57, .

COSCELLI ANDREA/EDWARDS GEOFF, Dominance and Market Power in EU Competition Law Enforcement, Chapter 8, in: LIANOS IOANNIS/GERADIN DAMIEN (EDS), Handbook on European Competition Law 2013, 350 ff.

COSCELLI ANDREA/OVERD ALAN, Market Definition in the Pharmaceutical Sector, European Competition Law Review 2007, 294 ff.

COTTIER BERTIL/SYCHOLD MARTIN, Qu'en est-il de 'l'abus de droit' dans le pays qui ignorent cette institution?, in: COTTIER BERTIL/WIDMER PIERRE (EDS), Abus de droit et bonne foi, Fribourg 1994.

COX HELMUT/HÜBENER HARALD, Wettbewerb. Eine Einführung in die Wettbewerbstheorie und Wettbewerbspolitik, in: COX HELMUT/JENS UWE/MARKERT KURT (EDS), Handbuch des Wettbewerbs, München 1981, 1 ff.

CRISAND MARCEL, Pharma-Trends und innovatives Pharma-Marketingmanagement, Strategische Neuausrichtung einer ärztegerichteten Marketingkonzeption, Wiesbaden 1996.

DAVID PAUL A., Can 'Open Science' Be Protected from the Evolving Regime of IPR Protections?, Journal of Institutional and Theoretical Economics 2004, 9 ff.

DAVIS RICHARD/ST QUINTIN TOM/TRITTON GUY, Tritton on Intellectual Property in Europe, London 2018.

DE BRONETT KLAUS, Der 'More Economic Approach' bei der Anwendung des europäischen Kartellverwaltungsrechts und Kartellstrafrechts, EWS 2013, 1 ff.

DEACON NEIL, The EU Law Doctrine of Abuse of Rights: Should It Be a General Principle of EU Law; and Is It?, http://www.euroblawg.com/eu-law-2/the-eu-law-doctrine-of-abuse-ofrights-should-it-be-a-general-principle-of-eu-law-and-is-it/, accessed on 28 December 2015 (not available anymore).

DEDERICHS MARIELE, Die Methodik des EuGH, Häufigkeit und Bedeutung methodischer Argumente in den Begründungen des Gerichthofes der Europäischen Gemeinschaften, Baden-Baden 2004, Doctoral Thesis Univ. Münster 2003.

DHAR BISWAJIT/JOSEPH REJI K., The Challenges, Opportunities and Performance of the Indian Pharmaceutical Industry Post-TRIPS, in: LIU KUNG-CHUNG/RACHERLA UDAY S. (EDS), Innovation, Economic Development, and Intellectual Property in India and China, Singapore 2019, 299 ff.

DICKSON MICHAEL/GAGNON JEAN PAUL, The Cost of New Drug Discovery and Development, Discovery Medicine 2009, 172 ff.

DIMASI JOSEPH A./GRABOWSKI HENRY G./HANSEN RONALD W., Innovation in the Pharmaceutical Industry, New Estimates of R&D Costs, Journal of Health Economics 2016, 20 ff.

DOGAN STACEY L./LEMLEY MARK A., Trademarks and Consumer Search Costs on the Internet, Houston Law Review 2004, 777 ff.

DOLMANS MAURITS, Restrictions on Innovation: An EU Antitrust Approach, Antitrust Law Journal 1998, 455 ff.

DOMEIJ BENGT, Pharmaceutical Patents in Europe, The Hague 2000.

DRABINSKI THOMAS/ESCHWEILER JAN/SCHMIDT ULRICH, Preisbildung von Arzneimitteln im internationalen Vergleich, Berlin 2008.

DREHER MEINRAD, Die Kontrolle des Wettbewerbs in Innovationsmärkten, ZWeR 2009, 149 ff.

DREWS JÜRGEN, Die verspielte Zukunft, Wohin geht die Arzneimittelforschung?, Basel 1998.

DREXL JOSEF, Die neue Gruppenfreistellungsverordnung über Technologietransfer-Vereinbarungen im Spannungsfeld von Ökonomisierung und Rechtssicherheit, GRUR Int. 2004, 716 ff.

DREXL JOSEF, Anticompetitive Stumbling Stones on the Way to a Cleaner World, Protecting Competition in Innovation Without a Market, Journal of Competition Law and Economics 2012, 507 ff.

DREXL JOSEF, AstraZeneca and the EU Sector Inquiry: When Do Patent Filings Violate Competition Law?, in: DREXL JOSEF/LEE NARI (EDS), Pharmaceutical Innovation, Competition and Patent Law, Cheltenham 2013, 290 ff.

DUGUET EMMANUEL/KABLA ISABELLE, Appropriation Strategy and the Motivations to Use the Patent System: An Econometric Analysis at the Firm Level in French Manufacturing, Économie et Économétrie de l'innovation 1998, 289 ff.

EBENROTH CARSTEN TH./BOHNE MICHAEL, Gewerbliche Schutzrechte und Article 86 EG-Vertrag nach der Magill-Entscheidung, EWS 1995, 397 ff.

EIKEL CONSTANTIN, Die Sperrmarke, Markenrechtliche Einordnung und Verteidigungsmöglichkeiten, Hamburg 2014.

EILMANSBERGER THOMAS, Der Umgang marktbeherrschender Unternehmen mit Immaterialgüterrechten im Lichte des Article 86 EWGV, EuZW 1992, 625 ff.

EILMANSBERGER THOMAS, How to Distinguish Good from Bad Competition under Article 82 EC: In Search of Clearer and More Coherent Standards for Anti-competitive Abuses, Common Market Law Review 2005, 129 ff.

EILMANSBERGER THOMAS, The Essential Facilities Doctrine under Article 82: What Is the State of Affairs after IMS Health and Microsoft?, King's Law Journal 2005, 329 ff.

EILMANSBERGER THOMAS, Dominance: The Long Lost Child? How Effects-Based Rules Could and Should Change Dominance Analysis, European Competition Journal 2006, 15 ff.

ELLERY TONY/HANSEN NEAL, Pharmaceutical Lifecycle Management, Making the Most of Each and Every Brand, Hoboken 2012.

EMMERICH VOLKER, Europarechtliche Aspekte, in: HEIDUK GÜNTER/EMMERICH VOLKER (EDS), Arzneimittelmarkt und europäisches Wettbewerbsrecht, Baden-Baden 1985.

ENCAOUA DAVID/MADIÈS THIERRY, Chapter 6, Dysfunctions of the Patent System and Their Effects on Competition, in: MADIÈS THIERRY/GUELLEC DOMINIQUE/PRAGER JEAN-CLAUDE (EDS), Patent Markets in the Global Knowledge Economy, Cambridge 2014, 125 ff.

ENGEL CHRISTOPH, Die soziale Funktion des Eigentums, in: VON DANWITZ THOMAS/DEPENHEUER OTTO/ENGEL CHRISTOPH (EDS), Bericht zur Lage des Eigentums, Berlin, Heidelberg 2002, 9 ff.

ERNST HOLGER, Strategisches Intellectual Property Management, in: HOMMEL ULRICH/KNECHT THOMAS C. (EDS), Wertorientiertes Start-up-Management, München 2002, 292 ff.

EUCKEN WALTER, Grundsätze der Wirtschaftspolitik, 7th ed., Tübingen 2004.

EVANS DAVID S., How Economists Can Help Courts Design Competition Rules: An EU and US Perspective, World Competition 2005, 93 ff.

EVERLING ULRICH, Wirtschaftsfreiheit im europäischen Binnenmarkt, Anspruch und Realität, in: SCHWARZE JÜRGEN (ED.), Wirtschaftsverfassungsrechtliche Garantien für Unternehmen im europäischen Binnenmarkt, Baden-Baden 2001, 11 ff.

FACKELMANN CHRISTIAN ROGER, Patentschutz und ergänzende Schutzinstrumente für Arzneimittel im Spannungsfeld von Wettbewerb und Innovation, Köln 2009.

FAIX AXEL, Patentmanagement, WiSt 2001, 517 ff.

FALCÓN Y TELLA MARÍA JOSÉ, Equity and Law, Boston 2008.

FAULL JONATHAN/NIKPAY ALI, The EU Law of Competition, 3rd ed., Oxford 2014.

FELDMAN ROBIN C., The Insufficiency of Antitrust Analysis for Patent Misuse, Hastings Law Journal 2003, 399 ff.

FELDMANN CHRISTOPH, Strategisches Technologiemanagement, Wiesbaden 2007.

FIKENTSCHER WOLFGANG, Das Verhältnis von Kartellrecht und Recht des unlauteren Wettbewerbs, GRUR Ausl. 1966, 181 ff.

FIKENTSCHER WOLFGANG/HACKER PHILIPP/PODSZUN RUPPRECHT, FairEconomy, Crises, Culture, Competition and the Role of Law, Berlin, Heidelberg 2013.

FISCHER DAGMAR/BREITENBACH JÖRN, Die Pharmaindustrie, Einblick: Durchblick – Perspektiven, 4th ed., Berlin 2013.

FISCHER ROBERT, Der Missbrauch einer marktbeherrschenden Stellung (§ 22 GWB) in der Rechtsprechung des Bundesgerichtshofes, ZGR 1978, 235 ff.

FISHER FRANKLIN M./MACGOWAN JOHN J./GREENWOOD JOEN E., Folded, Spindled, and Mutilated, Economic Analysis and US v. IBM, 2nd ed., Cambridge (MA) 1983.

FLEISCHER HOLGER, Informationsasymmetrie im Vertragsrecht, Eine rechtsvergleichende und interdisziplinäre Abhandlung zu Reichweite und Grenzen vertragsschlussbezogener Aufklärungspflichten, München 2001 (Habil. Univ. Köln 1998-1999).

FLEISCHER HOLGER, Der Rechtsmissbrauch zwischen Gemeineuropäischem Privatrecht und Gemeinwirtschaftsprivatrecht, JZ 2003, 865 ff.

FOX ELEANOR M., We Protect Competition, You Protect Competitors, World Competition 2003, 149 ff.

FOX HAROLD G., Monopolies and Patents: A Study of the History and Future of the Patent Monopoly, Toronto 1947.

FRAKES MICHAEL D./WASSERMAN MELISSA F., Is the Time Allocated to Review Patent Applications Inducing Examiners to Grant Invalid Patents?, Evidence from Micro-Level Application Data, The Review of Economics and Statistics 2017, 550 ff.

FREISSMUTH MICHAEL/OFFERMANNS STEFAN/BÖHM STEFAN, Pharmakologie & Toxikologie, Von den molekularen Grundlagen zur Pharmakotherapie, Berlin, Heidelberg 2012.

FRENZ WALTER, Handbuch Europarecht, Band 4: Europäische Grundrechte, Berlin, Heidelberg 2009.

FREY MICHAEL/PFEIFER LAURA, Der ordre public: die öffentliche Ordnung - derselbe Begriff, verschiedene Funktionen - ein Rechtsprinzip?, EuR 2015, 721 ff.

FRITSCH MICHAEL, Marktversagen und Wirtschaftspolitik, Mikroökonomische Grundlagen staatlichen Handelns, 9th ed., München 2014.

FRÜH ALFRED, Immaterialgüterrechte und der relevante Markt, Eine wettbewerbsrechtliche und schutzrechtliche Würdigung technologischer Innovation, Köln 2012, Doctoral Thesis Univ. Zürich 2011.

GÄCHTER THOMAS, Rechtsmissbrauch im öffentlichen Recht, Unter besonderer Berücksichtigung des Bundessozialversicherungsrechts; ein Beitrag zu Treu und Glauben, Methodik und Gesetzeskorrektur im öffentlichen Recht, Zürich, Basel, Genf 2005 (Habil. Univ. Zürich 2002).

GALASSO ALBERTO/SCHANKERMAN MARK, Patent Thickets and the Market for Innovation, Evidence from Settlement of Patent Disputes, The RAND Journal of Economics 2010, 472 ff.

GALASSO ALBERTO/SCHANKERMAN MARK, Patents and Cumulative Innovation, Causal Evidence from the Courts, The Quarterly Journal of Economics 2015, 317 ff.

GALIMBERTT GIOVANNI/MARCHESONI EVELINA, Italy: The Abuse of a Dominant Position by Pfizer in Xalatan Case, https://www.twobirds.com/en/news/articles/2014/global/life-sciences-may/italy-the-abuse-of-a-dominant-position-by-pfizer-in-xalatan-case, accessed on 14 February 2020.

GALLWAS HANS-ULLRICH, Der Missbrauch von Grundrechten, Berlin 1967.

GARNER BRYAN A., Black's Law Dictionary, 11th ed., St. Paul (MN) 2019.

GASSMANN OLIVER/BADER MARTIN A., Patentmanagement, Innovationen erfolgreich nutzen und schützen, 4th ed., Berlin, Heidelberg 2017.

GASSNER ULRICH M., Unterlagenschutz im Europäischen Arzneimittelrecht, GRUR Int. 2004, 983 ff.

GASTER JENS L., Kartellrecht und geistiges Eigentum: Unüberbrückbare Gegensätze im EG-Recht?, Computer und Recht 2005, 247 ff.

GAUSS NICOLAS, Die Anwendung des kartellrechtlichen Missbrauchsverbots nach Article 82 EG (Article 102 AEUV) in innovativen Märkten, Baden-Baden 2010.

GEIGER CHRISTOPHE, Fundamental Rights, a Safeguard for the Coherence of Intellectual Property Law?, IIC 2004, 268 ff.

GERADIN DAMIEN/RATO MIGUEL, Can Standard-Setting Lead to Exploitative Abuse? and the Meaning of FRAND: A Dissonant View on Patent Hold-Up, Royalty Stacking and the Meaning of FRAND, European Competition Journal 2007, 101 ff.

GERALD MICHAEL C., The Drug Book, from Arsenic to Xanax, 250 Milestones in the History of Drugs, New York (NY) 2013.

GERBER DAVID J., Fairness in Competition Law: European and US Experience, Prepared for Presentation at a Conference on Fairness and Asian Competition Laws held on 5 March 2004, in Kyoto, Japan (cit. GERBER, Fairness in Competition Law: European and US Experience).

GERBER DAVID J., Law and the Abuse of Economic Power in Europe, Tulane Law Review 1987, 57 ff.

GERBER DAVID J., Authority, Community and the Civil Law Commentary: An Example from German Competition Law, The American Journal of Comparative Law 1994a, 531 ff.

GERBER DAVID J., Constitutionalizing the Economy: German Neo-Liberalism, Competition Law and the 'New' Europe, The American Journal of Comparative Law 1994b, 25 ff.

GERBER DAVID J., Law and Competition in Twentieth Century Europe, Protecting Prometheus, Oxford 1998.

GHESTIN JAQUES/GOUBEAUX GILLES, Traité de Droit Civil, Introduction Général, 4th ed., Paris 1994.

GILBERT RICHARD J./NEWBERY DAVID M.G., Preemptive Patenting and the Persistence of Monopoly, The American Economic Review 1982, 514 ff.

GLAZIER STEPHEN C., Patent Strategies for Business, 3rd ed., Washington D.C. 2000.

GLÖCKNER JOCHEN, Europäisches Lauterkeitsrecht, München 2006 (Habil. Univ. St. Gallen 2002-2003).

GODT CHRISTINE, Eigentum an Information, Patentschutz und allgemeine Eigentumstheorie am Beispiel genetischer Information, Tübingen 2007 (Habil. Univ. Bremen 2005).

GOLDSTEIN PAUL/TRIMBLE MARKETA, International Intellectual Property Law, Cases and Materials, 4th ed., St. Paul (MN) 2012.

GORDON WENDY JANE, Systematische und Fallbezogene Lösungsansätze für Marktversagen bei Immaterialgütern, in: v. OTT CLAUS/SCHÄFER HANS-BERND (EDS), Ökonomische Analyse der rechtlichen Organisation von Innovationen, Tübingen 1994, 328 ff.

GOVAERE INGE, The Use and Abuse of Intellectual Property Rights in E.C. Law, Including a Case Study of the E.C. Spare Parts Debate, London 1996.

GOYDER DANIEL G./GOYDER JOANNA/ALBORS-LLORENS ALBERTINA, Goyder's EC Competition Law, 5th ed., Oxford 2009.

GRABITZ EBERHARD/NETTESHEIM MARTIN/HILF MEINHARD (eds), Das Recht der Europäischen Union, Kommentar, 68th ed., München 2019 (cit. AUTHOR, in: GRABITZ ET AL., EUV/AEUV, Article XY).

GRABOWSKI HENRY G./VERNON JOHN M., Brand Loyalty, Entry, and Price Competition in Pharmaceuticals after the 1984 Drug Act, The Journal of Law & Economics 1992, 331 ff.

GRANSTRAND OVE, The Economics and Management of Intellectual Property, Towards Intellectual Capitalism, Cheltenham Etc. 2000.

GRAVENGAARD MARTIN ANDREAS/KJAERSGAARD NIELS, The EU Commission Guidance on Exclusionary Abuse of Dominance: And Its Consequences in Practice, European Competition Law Review 2010, 285 ff.

GREFERMANN KLAUS, Patentwesen und technischer Fortschritt, Kritische Würdigung der Zusammenhänge in ausgewählten Branchen der Bundesrepublik Deutschland anhand empirischer Untersuchungen, Göttingen 1974.

GREIF SIEGFRIED, Ausübungszwang für Patente, Ökonomische Möglichkeiten und Grenzen unter besonderer Berücksichtigung der Entwicklungsländer, GRUR Int. 1981, 731 ff.

GRINDLEY PETER C./TEECE DAVID J., Managing Intellectual Capital: Licensing and Cross-licensing in Semiconductors and Electronics, California Management Review 1997, 1 ff.

GRUBB PHILIP/THOMSEN PETER R./WRIGHT GORDON/ HOXIE, THOMAS, Patents for Chemicals, Pharmaceuticals and Biotechnology, Fundamentals of Global Law, Practice and Strategy, Oxford 2016.

GRUBER UTTA/KLEBER MICHAELA, Grundlagen der Volkswirtschaftslehre, 4th ed., München 2000.

GSELL BEATE/KRÜGER WOLFGANG/LORENZ STEPHAN/REYMAN CHRISTOPH (eds), Beck-online.Grosskommentar, Zivilrecht, München (cit. AUTHOR, in: GSELL ET AL., Beck-online Grosskommentar, § XY).

GUELLEC DOMINIQUE/MARTINEZ CATALINA/ZUNIGA PLUVIA, Pre-emptive Patenting: Securing Market Exclusion and Freedom of Operation, Economics of Innovation and New Technology 2012, 1 ff.

GUSKI ROMAN, Rechtsmissbrauch als Paradoxie, Negative Selbstreferenz und widersprüchliches Handeln im Recht 2019.

HABERER ANNO, Die Intel-Entscheidung des EuGH, WUW 2017, 526 ff.

HAEDICKE MAXIMILIAN, Pay – for – Delay – Vergleichsvereinbarungen im Spannungsfeld zwischen Patent- und Kartellrecht, ZGE 2011, 263 ff.

HAEDICKE MAXIMILIAN, § 1 Introduction, in: HAEDICKE MAXIMILIAN/TIMMANN HENRIK (EDS), Patent Law, München 2014.

HAFERKAMP HANS-PETER, Die exceptio doli generalis in der Rechtsprechung des Reichsgerichts vor 1914, in: FALK ULRICH/MOHNHAUPT HEINZ (EDS), Das Bürgerliche Gesetzbuch und seine Richter, Frankfurt am Main 2000, 1 ff.

HAGEN WOLFGANG, Das Radio, Zur Geschichte und Theorie des Hörfunks – Deutschland/USA, München 2005.

HAGER PATRICIA M./MURER ANGELIKA S., Wie hast du's mit der Erheblichkeit? Zur kartellrechtlichen Gretchenfrage vor dem Bundesverwaltungsgericht, recht: Zeitschrift für juristische Weiterbildung und Praxis 2015, 197 ff.

HALL BRONWYN H., Exploring the Patent Explosion, Journal of Technology Transfer, 35 ff.

HALL BRONWYN H./ZIEDONIS ROSMARIE H., The Patent Paradox Revisited: An Empirical Study of Patenting in the US Semiconductor Industry, 1979-1995, RAND Journal of Economics, 101 ff.

HALLADAY CASEY W., The Origins of Canada's Cartel Laws, Canadian Competition Law Review 2012, 157 ff.

HARACOGLOU IRINA, Competition Law and Patents: A Follow-On Innovation Perspective in the Biopharmaceutical Industry, Cheltenham (UK), Northampton (MA) 2008.

HARDIN GARRETT, The Tragedy of the Commons, Science 1968, 1243 ff.

HARHOFF DIETMAR/HALL BRONWYN/VON GRAEVENITZ GEORG/HOISL KARIN/WAGNER STEFAN, The Strategic Use of Patents and Its implications for Enterprise and Competition Policies, 2007, http://ec.europa.eu/DocsRoom/documents/3427/attachments/1/translations/en/renditions/pdf, accessed on 14 February 2020.

HARHOFF DIETMAR/ENGEL CHRISTOPH/MÖSCHEL WERNHARD, Patentschutz und Innovation, Gutachten, Wissenschaftlicher Beirat beim Bundesministerium für Wirtschaft und Technologie 2007, https://www.bmwi.de/Redaktion/DE/Publikationen/Ministerium/Veroeffentlichung-Wissenschaftlicher-Beirat/patentschutz-und-innovation.pdf, accessed on 14 February 2020.

HÄUSSER ERICH, Mehr Innovation Durch Bessere Information, in: OPPENLÄNDER KARL HEINRICH (ED.), Patentwesen technischer Fortschritt und Wettbewerb, Berlin 1984, 133 ff.

HAUSMANN HANS-CHRISTIAN, Das Microsoft-Urteil: Zwischen Kartellrecht und gewerblichen Schutzrechten, MMR 2008, 381 ff.

HECKENDORF KATHARINA, Wer hat's erfunden?, Krieg um Patente für Smartphones, Süddeutsche Zeitung, 30 August 2011, https://www.sueddeutsche.de/wirtschaft/krieg-um-patente-fuer-smartphones-wer-hat-s-erfunden-1.1134483, accessed on 27 April 2020.

HEERMANN PETER W./SCHLINGLOFF JOCHEN, Münchener Kommentar zum Lauterkeitsrecht, 3rd ed., München 2020 (cit. AUTHOR, in: HEERMANN/ SCHLINGLOFF, Münchener Kommentar Lauterkeitsrecht, Article XY).

HEIDUK GÜNTER, Ökonomische Aspekte, in: HEIDUK GÜNTER/EMMERICH VOLKER (EDS), Arzneimittelmarkt und europäisches Wettbewerbsrecht, Baden-Baden 1985, 10 ff.

HEINE H.G., Monopolistischer Patentmissbrauch, GRUR 1948, 170 ff.

HEINEMANN ANDREAS, Die Freiburger Schule und ihre geistigen Wurzeln, München 1989 (cit. HEINEMANN, Freiburger Schule).

HEINEMANN ANDREAS, Das Kartellrecht des geistigen Eigentums im TRIPS-Übereinkommen der Welthandelsorganisation, GRUR Int. 1995, 535 ff.

HEINEMANN ANDREAS, Immaterialgüterschutz in der Wettbewerbsordnung, Eine grundlagenorientierte Untersuchung zum Kartellrecht des geistigen Eigentums, Tübingen 2002 (cit. HEINEMANN, Immaterialgüterschutz in der Wettbewerbsordnung).

HEINEMANN ANDREAS, Kartellrechtliche Zwangslizenzen im Patentrecht: Die Spundfassentscheidung des BGH vom 13. Juli 2004, ZWeR 2005, 198 ff.

HEINEMANN ANDREAS, Compulsory Licences and Product Integration in European Competition Law: Assessment of the European Commission's *Microsoft* Decision, IIC 2005, 63 ff.

HEINEMANN ANDREAS, Gefährdung von Rechten des geistigen Eigentums durch Kartellrecht? Der Fall 'Microsoft' und die Rechtsprechung des EuGH, GRUR 2006, 705 ff.

HEINEMANN ANDREAS, Die Relevanz des 'More Economic Approach' für das Recht des geistigen Eigentums, GRUR 2008, 949 ff.

HEINEMANN ANDREAS, The Contestability of IP-Protected Markets, in: DREXL JOSEF (ED.), Research Handbook on Intellectual Property and Competition Law, Cheltenham (UK), Northampton (MA) 2008, 54 ff.

HEINEMANN ANDREAS, Intellectual Property Rights and Merger Control: How to Secure Incentives to Innovate in the Long Run, in: DREXL JOSEF (ED.), Technology and Competition, Bruxelles 2009, 601 ff.

HEINEMANN ANDREAS, Immaterialgüterrecht und Wettbewerbsrecht: Divergenz oder Konvergenz?, MR-Int. 2014, 1 ff.

HEINEMANN ANDREAS, Behavioural Antitrust: A 'More Realistic Approach' to Competition Law, in: MATHIS KLAUS (ED.), European Perspectives on Behavioural Law and Economics, Cham et al. 2015, 211 ff.

HEINEMANN ANDREAS, Marktwirtschaft und Wettbewerbsordnung: Der Zweck des Kartellrechts, Zeitschrift für Schweizerisches Recht (ZSR) 2016, 431 ff.

HEINEMANN ANDREAS, Abusive Filing of IP Rights, in: MATTHEWS DUNCAN/ZECH HERBERT (EDS), Research Handbook on Intellectual Property and the Life Sciences, Cheltenham, Northampton 2017.

HEINEMANN ANDREAS, Blocking Patents and the Process of Innovation, in: MATHIS KLAUS/TOR AVISHALOM (EDS), New Developments in Competition Law and Economics, Cham, Switzerland 2019, 149 ff.

HEINRICH PETER, PatG/EPÜ, Schweizerisches Patentgesetz, Europäisches Patentübereinkommen, Kommentar in synoptischer Darstellung, 3rd ed., Bern 2018.

HEIZMANN RETO A., Der Begriff des marktbeherrschenden Unternehmens im Sinne von Article 4 Abs. 2 in Verbindung mit Article 7 KG, Zürich 2005, Doctoral Thesis Univ. Zürich 2005.

HEIZMANN RETO A./LOACKER LEANDER D. (EDS), Bundesgesetz gegen den unlauteren Wettbewerb (UWG), Kommentar, Zürich 2018 (cit. AUTHOR, in: HEIZMANN/LOACKER, UWG Kommentar, Article XY).

HELLER MICHAEL A., The Tragedy of the Anticommons: Property in the Transition from Marx to Marktes, Harvard Law Review 1998, 621 ff.

HELLER MICHAEL A./EISENBERG REBECCA S., Can Patents Deter Innovation?, The Anticommons in Biomedical Research, Science 1998, 698 ff.

HELLMANN VANESSA, Der Vertrag von Lissabon, Vom Verfassungsvertrag zur Änderung der bestehenden Verträge – Einführung mit Synopse und Übersichten, Berlin/Heidelberg 2009.

HENN FLORIAN, Strafrechtliche Verfahrensgarantien im europäischen Kartellrecht, Implikationen und Grenzen der Strafrechtsähnlichkeit von Kartellbußgeldern, Berlin 2018.

HERDZINA KLAUS, Wettbewerbspolitik, 5th ed., Stuttgart 1999.

HESELHAUS SEBASTIAN/NOWAK CARSTEN (eds), Handbuch der europäischen Grundrechte, 2nd ed., München 2020 (cit. AUTHOR, in: HESELHAUS/NOWAK, Handbuch der europäischen Grundrechte, Article XY).

HILTY RETO M., The Law Against Unfair Competition and Its Interfaces, in: HILTY RETO M./HENNING-BODEWIG FRAUKE (EDS), Law Against Unfair Competition, Berlin, Heidelberg 2007, 1 ff.

HILTY RETO M./FRÜH ALFRED, Lizenzkartellrecht, Bern 2017.

HILTY RETO M./GEIGER CHRISTOPHE, Patenting Software? A Judicial and Socio-Economic Analysis, IIC 2005, 615 ff.

HONSELL HEINRICH, Römisches Recht, 8th ed., Berlin 2015.

HOPPMANN ERICH, Das Konzept der optimalen Wettbewerbsintensität, Jahrbuch für Nationalökonomie und Statistik 1966, 286 ff.

HOVENKAMP HERBERT, The Monopolisation Offense, Ohio State Law Journal 2000, 1035 ff.

HOVENKAMP HERBERT, Innovation and the Domain of Competition Policy, Alabama Law Review 2008-2009, 103 ff.

HOVENKAMP HERBERT, Federal Antitrust Policy: The Law of Competition and Its Practice, 4th ed., St. Paul (MN) 2011 (cit. HOVENKAMP, Federal Antitrust Policy).

IMMENGA ULRICH, Ökonomie und Recht in der europäischen Wettbewerbspolitik, ZWeR 2006, 346 ff.

IMMENGA ULRICH/MESTMÄCKER ERNST-JOACHIM (eds), GWB, Kommentar zum Deutschen Kartellrecht, 4th ed., München 2007 (cit. AUTHOR, in: IMMENGA/MESTMÄCKER, GWB Kommentar, § XY).

IMMENGA ULRICH/MESTMÄCKER ERNST-JOACHIM (eds), Wettbewerbsrecht, 5th ed., München 2012 (cit. AUTHOR, in: IMMENGA/MESTMÄCKER 2012, Article XY).

IMMENGA ULRICH/MESTMÄCKER ERNST-JOACHIM (eds), Wettbewerbsrecht, 6th ed., München 2018 (cit. AUTHOR, in: IMMENGA/MESTMÄCKER 2018, Article XY).

JACOB ROBIN, Pharmaceutical Patents: Competition Law Goes Too Far, in: PITRUZZELLA GIOVANNI/MUSCOLO GABRIELLA (EDS), Competition and Patent Law in the Pharmaceutical Sector, Alphen aan den Rijn 2016, 85 ff.

JAFFE ADAM B./LERNER JOSH, Innovation and Its Discontents, How Our Broken Patent System Is Endangering Innovation and Progress, and What to Do About It, Princeton 2011.

JARASS HANS D., Der grundrechtliche Eigentumsschutz im EU-Recht, NVwZ 2006, 1089 ff.

JARASS HANS D., Charta der Grundrechte der Europäischen Union, Unter Einbeziehung der vom EuGH entwickelten Grundrechte, der Grundrechtsregelungen der Verträge und der EMRK: Kommentar, 3rd ed., München 2016.

JELL FLORIAN, Patent filing strategies and patent management, An empirical study, Wiesbaden 2012, Doctoral Thesis Techn. Univ. München 2011.

JEWKES JOHN/SAWERS DAVID/STILLERMAN RICHARD, The Sources of Invention, 2nd ed., New York 1969.

JONES ALISON/SUFRIN BRENDA/DUNNE NIAMH, Jones and Sufrin's EU Competition Law, Text, Cases, and Materials, 7th ed., Oxford 2019.

JUNG PETER, Die Zwangslizenz als Instrument der Wettbewerbspolitik, ZWeR 2004, 379 ff.

KADAR MASSIMILIANO, Article 102 and Exclusivity Rebates in a Post-Intel World: Lessons from the Qualcomm and Google Android Cases, Journal of European Competition Law & Practice 2019, 439 ff.

KALLAUGHER JOHN/SHER BRIAN, Rebates Revisited: Anti-competitive Effects and Exclusionary Abuse under Article 82, ECLR 2004, 263.

KÄLLER ANJA, Die Verweigerung einer immaterialgüterrechtlich geschützten Leistung und das Missbrauchsverbot des Article 82 EG, Die Anwendung europäischen Wettbewerbsrechts auf Immaterialgüterrechte, Baden-Baden 2006, Doctoral Thesis Univ. Freiburg i. Br. 2004.

KAMANN HANS-GEORG, § 3 Grundlagen der Rechtsdurchsetzung im System des europäischen und deutschen Kartellrechts, in: KAMANN HANS-GEORG/OHLHOFF STEFAN/VÖLCKER SVEN (EDS), Kartellverfahren und Kartellprozess, München 2017.

KANKANALA KALYAN C./NARASANI ARUN K./RADHAKRISHNAN VINITA, Indian Patent Law and Practice, New Delhi 2012.

KAPCZYNSKI AMY/PARK CHAN/SAMPAT BHAVEN, Polymorphs and Prodrugs and Salts (Oh My!): An Empirical Analysis of 'Secondary' Pharmaceutical Patents, PloS one 2012.

KARTTE WOLFGANG, Ein neues Leitbild für die Wettbewerbspolitik, Köln 1969.

KÄSEBERG THORSTEN, Intellectual Property, Antitrust and Cumulative Innovation in the EU and the US, Oxford 2012.

KASER MAX/KNÜTEL ROLF/LOHSSE SEBASTIAN, Römisches Privatrecht, Ein Studienbuch, 21st ed., München 2017.

KAYSEN CARL/TURNER DONALD F., Antitrust Policy: An Economic and Legal Analysis, Cambridge (MA) 1959.

KËLLEZI PRANVERA, Marchés pertinents et nature des relations concurrentielles dans le cadre de l'appréciation des accords de transfert de technologie, sic! 2005, 552 ff.

KEMPEL LEONIE, Die Anwendung von Article 102 AEUV auf geistiges Eigentum und Sacheigentum, Die Voraussetzungen des Kontrahierungszwangs nach Article 102 AEUV und der Essential-Facility-Doktrin unter besonderer Berücksichtigung der Unterschiede zwischen geistigem Eigentum und Sacheigentum, Frankfurt am Main 2011.

KESERU GYÖRGY M./MAKARA GERGELY M., Hit Discovery and Hit-to-Lead Approaches, Drug Discovery Today 2006, 741 ff.

KHAN ALFRED E., Standards for Antitrust Policy, Harvard Law Review 1953, 28 ff.

KIEFER MARIE LUISE/STEININGER CHRISTIAN, Medienökonomik, 3rd ed., München 2014.

KILLICK JAMES/JOURDAN JÉRÉMIE/PÊCHEUX PIERRE, The Servier Judgment: The General Court Annuls the Commission's Market Definition but Confirms the Illegality of Certain Patent Settlement Agreements, Journal of European Competition Law & Practice 2019, 25 ff.

KISS ALEXANDRE, Abuse of Rights, Max Planck Encyclopedia of Public International Law [MPEPIL] December 2006.

KJØLBYE LARS, Article 82 EC as Remedy to Patent System Imperfections: Fighting Fire with Fire?, World Competition 2009, 163 ff.

KLEIN THILO, SSNIP-Test oder Bedarfsmarktkonzept?, WUW, 169 ff.

KLEISSL KATHARINA, Lizenzkartellrecht in der amerikanischen und europäischen Rechtsordnung, Rechtsvergleichende Analyse des Spannungsverhältnisses zwischen geistigem Eigentum und Kartellrecht mit Schwerpunkt auf Technologietransfer-Vereinbarungen, Berlin 2008 (Diss Univ. Bayreuth 2008).

KLING MICHAEL/THOMAS STEFAN, Kartellrecht, München 2016.

KNIEPS GÜNTHER, Wettbewerbsökonomie, 3rd ed., Berlin, Heidelberg 2008.

KOBAK JAMES B., Running the Gauntlet: Antitrust and Intellectual Property on the Two Sides of the Atlantic, Antitrust Law Journal 1996, 341 ff.

KÖBLER GERHARD, Etymologisches Rechtswörterbuch, Tübingen 1995.

KÖHLER HELMUT/BORNKAMM JOACHIM (eds), Gesetz gegen den unlauteren Wettbewerb, Gesetz gegen den unlauteren Wettbewerb, Zugabeverordnung, Rabattgesetz und Nebengesetze, 22nd ed., München 2001 (cit. AUTHOR, in: KÖHLER/BORNKAMM, UWG Kommentar 2001, Article XY).

KÖHLER HELMUT/BORNKAMM JOACHIM/FEDDERSEN JÖRN (eds), Gesetz gegen den unlauteren Wettbewerb, Preisangabenverordnung, Unterlassungs-klagengesetz, Dienstleistungs-Informationspflichten-Verordnung, 38th ed., München 2020 (cit. AUTHOR, in: KÖHLER/BORNKAMM, UWG Kommentar 2020, Article XY).

KORTUM SAMUEL/LERNER JOSH, What Is Behind the Recent Surge in Patenting?, Research Policy 1999, 1 ff.

KRASSER RUDOLF/ANN CHRISTOPH, Patentrecht, Lehrbuch zum deutschen und europäischen Patentrecht und Gebrauchsmusterrecht, 7th ed., München 2016.

KRUGMAN PAUL R./WELLS ROBIN, Volkswirtschaftslehre, 2nd ed., Stuttgart 2017.

KÜNZLER ADRIAN, Effizienz oder Wettbewerbsfreiheit?, Zur Frage nach den Aufgaben des Rechts gegen private Wettbewerbsbeschränkungen, Tübingen 2012.

KURZ PETER, Weltgeschichte des Erfindungsschutzes, Erfinder und Patente im Spiegel der Zeiten; zum 100jährigen Jubiläum des Gesetzes betreffend die Patentanwälte vom 21. Mai 1900, Köln etc. 2000.

LAMPE RYAN/MOSER PETRA, Do Patent Pools Encourage Innovation?, Evidence from the 19th Century Sewing Machine Industry, The Journal of Economic History 2010, 898 ff.

LAMPING MATTHIAS, Patentschutz und Marktmacht, Köln 2010.

LANDES WILLIAM M./POSNER RICHARD A., Market Power in Antitrust Cases, Harvard Law Review 1980, 937 ff.

LANDES WILLIAM M./POSNER RICHARD A., The Economic Structure of Intellectual Property Law, Cambridge (MA) 2003.

LANGE MARKUS, Anspruchspolitik im Rahmen der Patentanmeldung, Wiesbaden 2006.

LANGINIER CORINNE, Are Patents Strategic Barriers to Entry?, Journal of Economics and Business 2004, 349 ff.

LAO MARINA, Reclaiming a Role for Intent Evidence in Monopolisation Analysis, American University Law Review 2004, 151 ff.

LEISTNER MATTHIAS, § 4 Wettbewerb, in: GLOY WOLFGANG/LOSCHELDER MICHAEL/ERDMANN WILLI (EDS), Handbuch des Wettbewerbsrechts, München 2010.

LEMLEY MARK A., Property, Intellectual Property, and Free Riding, Texas Law Review, 1031 ff.

LEMLEY MARK A., Intellectual Property Rights and Standard-Setting Organizations, SSRN Journal 2003.

LEMLEY MARK A./SHAPIRO CARL, Probabilistic Patents, Journal of Economic Perspectives 2005, 75 ff.

LENAERTS ANNEKATRIEN, The General Principle of the Prohibition of Abuse of Rights: A Critical Position on Its Role in a Codified European Contract Law, European Review of Private Law 2010, 1121 ff.

LENZ CARL OTTO/BORCHARDT KLAUS-DIETER/BITTERLICH JOACHIM (EDS), EU-Verträge Kommentar, EUV - AEUV - GRCh, 6th, Köln, Wien 2013 (cit. AUTHOR, in: LENZ ET AL., EUV - AEUV - GRCh, Article XY).

LERNER MAX, The Mind and Faith of Justice Holmes, His Speeches, Essays, Letters, and Judicial Opinions, London 2017.

LEVIN RICHARD G. ET AL., Appropriating the Returns form Industrial Research and Development, Special Issue on Microeconomics, Brookings Papers on Economic Activity, 783 ff.

LI JIE JACK, Blockbuster Drugs: The Rise and Decline of the Pharmaceutical Industry, New York 2014.

LICHTMAN DOUGLAS GARY, Patent Holdouts and the Standard-Setting Process, University Chicago Law and Economics, Olin Working Paper No 292 2006.

LIM DARYL, Patent Misuse and Antitrust: Rebirth or False Dawn?, Michigan Telecommunications and Technology Law Review 2014, 299 ff.

LIPSEY R.G./LANCASTER KELVIN, The General Theory of Second Best, The Review of Economic Studies 1956, 11 ff.

LOEWENHEIM ULRICH/MEESSEN KARL M./RIESENKAMPFF ALEXANDER/KERSTING CHRISTIAN/MEYER-LINDEMANN HANS JÜRGEN/ABLASSER-NEUHUBER ASTRID/BARON MICHAEL/ANWEILER JOCHEN (EDS), Kartellrecht, Kommentar, 3rd ed., München 2016 (cit. AUTHOR, in: LOEWENHEIM ET AL., Kommentar Kartellrecht, Article XY).

LOMBARDINO JOSEPH G./LOWE JOHN A., The Role of the Medicinal Chemist in Drug Discovery: Then and Now, Nature Reviews Drug Discovery 2004, 853 ff.

LOVDAHL GORMESEN LIZA, The Conflict Between Economic Freedom and Consumer Welfare in the Modernisation of Article 82 EC, European Competition Journal 2007, 329 ff.

LOWE PHILIP, DG Competition's Review of the Policy on Abuse of Dominance, in: HAWK BARRY E. (ED.), Annual Proceedings of the Fordham Corporate Law Institute International Antitrust Law & Policy, Huntington (NY) 2004, 163 ff.

LÜHRS PHILIPP MORITZ, Die Entstehung des Reichspatentgesetzes von 1877 und der Versuch eines europäischen Patentrechts von 1962 im Vergleich, Düsseldorf 2019, Doctoral Thesis Univ. Düsseldorf 2019.

MACDONALD STUART, When Means Become Ends: Considering the Impact of Patent Strategy on Innovation, Information Economics and Policy 2004, 135 ff.

MACHLUP FRITZ, Die wirtschaftlichen Grundlagen des Patentrechts – 1. Teil, GRUR Int. 1961, 373 ff.

MACHLUP FRITZ/PENROSE EDITH, The Patent Controversy in the Nineteenth Century, The Journal of Economic History 1950, 1 ff.

MANSFIELD EDWIN, Patents and Innovation: An Empirical Study, Management Science 1986, 173 ff.

MARTENET VINCENT/HEINEMANN ANDREAS, Droit de la concurrence, Genève etc. 2012.

MEIER MARTIN, Pleading for a 'Multiple Goal Approach' in European Competition Law, Outline of a Conciliatory Path Between the 'Freedom to Compete Approach' and the 'More Economic Approach', in: MATHIS KLAUS/TOR AVISHALOM (EDS), New Developments in Competition Law and Economics, Cham 2019.

MELÍCIAS MARIA JOÃO, The Use and Abuse of Intent Evidence in Antitrust Analysis, World Competition 2010, 569 ff.

MERDZO PAUL, Der Fall 'IMS Health' und das Spannungsverhältnis zwischen Nationalen Immaterialgüterrechten und dem europäischen Wettbewerbsrecht, ZEuS 2005, 135 ff.

MERGES ROBERT P./NELSON RICHARD R., On the Complex Economics of Patent Scope, Columbia Law Review 1990, 839 ff.

MESTMÄCKER ERNST-JOACHIM, Macht – Recht – Wirtschaftsverfassung, ZHR 1973, 97 ff.

MESTMÄCKER ERNST-JOACHIM, Der verwaltete Wettbewerb: Eine vergleichende Untersuchung über den Schutz von Freiheit und Lauterkeit im Wettbewerbsrecht, Tübingen 1984.

MESTMÄCKER ERNST-JOACHIM, Unternehmenskonzentrationen und Urheberrechte in der alten und 'neuen' Musikwirtschaft, ZUM 2001, 185 ff.

MESTMÄCKER ERNST-JOACHIM/SCHWEITZER HEIKE, Europäisches Wettbewerbsrecht, 3rd ed., München 2014.

MONTI GIORGIO, EC Competition Law: The Dominance of Economic Analysis?, in: ZÄCH ROGER/HEINEMANN ANDREAS/KELLERHALS ANDREAS (EDS), The Development of Competition Law, Cheltenham et al. 2010, 3 ff.

MORGAN STEVE ET AL., The Cost of Drug Development: A Systematic Review, Health Policy 2011, 4 ff.

MOTTA MASSIMO, Competition Policy, Theory and Practice, 12th ed., Cambridge 2009.

MÜLLER EVA-MARIA, Die Patentfähigkeit von Arzneimitteln: der gewerbliche Rechtsschutz für pharmazeutische, medizinische und biotechnologische Erfindungen, Berlin, Heidelberg 2003.

MÜLLER-GRAFF PETER-CHRISTIAN, Verfassungsziele der Europäischen Union, in: DAUSES MANFRED A./LUDWIGS MARKUS (EDS), Handbuch des EU-Wirtschaftsrechts, München 2019.

MURER ANGELIKA S./ZURMUEHLE SARAH E., Die Bedeutung digitaler Daten in der Fusionskontrolle anhand der Unternehmensübernahmen durch Google und Facebook, in: EPINEY ASTRID/HEHEMANN LENA/KERN MARKUS (EDS), Schweizerisches Jahrbuch für Europarecht 2014/2015, Zürich 2015, 455 ff.

NEUMANN MANFRED, Wettbewerbspolitik, Geschichte, Theorie und Praxis, Wiesbaden 2000.

NEVER HENNING, Meinungsfreiheit, Wettbewerb und Marktversagen im Rundfunk, Eine ökonomische Kritik der verfassungsrechtlich geforderten positiven Rundfunkordnung, Baden-Baden 2002, Doctoral Thesis Univ. Potsdamm 2001.

NIPPERDEY HANS CARL, Wettbewerb und Existenzvernichtung: eine Grundfrage des Wettbewerbsrechts, Berlin 1930.

O'DONOGHUE ROBERT/PADILLA ATILANO JORGE, The Law and Economics of Article 102 TFEU, 2nd ed., Oxford 2018.

OESCH MATTHIAS, Europarecht, Grundlagen, Institutionen, Verhältnis Schweiz-EU, 2nd ed., Bern 2019.

OPPENLÄNDER KARL HEINRICH, Patentschutz und Wettbewerb im Innovationsprozess, in: OPPENLÄNDER KARL HEINRICH (ED.), Patentwesen technischer Fortschritt und Wettbewerb, Berlin 1984, 47 ff.

OSTERRIETH CHRISTIAN, Patentrecht, 5th ed., München 2015.

ØSTERUD EIRIK, Identifying Exclusionary Abuses by Dominant Undertakings under EU Competition Law: The Spectrum of Tests, Alphen aan den Rijn 2010.

OSTI CRISTOFORO, What's in a Name: The Concept of Abuse in Sui Generis Abuses, in: PITRUZZELLA GIOVANNI/MUSCOLO GABRIELLA (EDS), Competition and Patent Law in the Pharmaceutical Sector, Alphen aan den Rijn 2016, 93 ff.

PACE LORENZO FEDERICO/SEIDEL KATJA, The Drafting and the Role of Regulation 17: A Hard-Fought Compromise, in: PATEL KIRAN KLAUS/SCHWEITZER HEIKE (EDS), The Historical Foundations of EU Competition Law, Oxford 2013, 54 ff.

PACÓN ANA MARIA, Was bringt TRIPS den Entwicklungsländern?, GRUR Int. 1995, 875 ff.

PASCHALL VALERIE, As Narrow as It Comes: The Hollensbury Spite House, Curbed 27 September 2013, https://dc.curbed.com/2013/9/27/10193488/as-narrow-as-it-comes-the-hollensbury-spite-house, accessed on 14 February 2020.

PAUL THOMAS, Behinderungsmissbrauch nach Article 82 EG und der 'More Economic Approach', Köln etc. 2008, Doctoral Thesis Univ. Bonn 2007/2008.

PECHSTEIN MATTHIAS/DRECHSLER CAROLA, § 7 Die Auslegung und Fortbildung des Primärrechts, in: RIESENHUBER KARL (ED.), Europäische Methodenlehre, Berlin 2014, 125 ff.

PÉREZ SIGFRIDO M. RAMÍREZ/VAN DE SCHEUR SEBASTIAN, The Evolution of the Law on Articles 85 and 86 EEC (Articles 101 and 102 TFEU), in: PATEL KIRAN KLAUS/SCHWEITZER HEIKE (EDS), The Historical Foundations of EU Competition Law, Oxford 2013, 19 ff.

PERGER LUDWIG/FATTINGER KARIN, Generika und Arzneimittelverschreibung, Schweiz Med Forum 2012, 237 ff.

PERINETTO PATRICK ACTIS, Intent and Competition Law Assessment: Useless or Useful Tool in the Quest for Legal Certainty?, European Competition Journal 2019, 153 ff.

PERITZ RUDOLPH J.R., Competition Policy in America, 1888-1992, History, Rhetoric, Law, New York 1996.

PETROVA ELINA, Innovation in the Pharmaceutical Industry: The Process of Drug Discovery and Development, in: DING MIN/ELIASHBERG JEHOSHUA/STREMERSCH STEFAN (EDS), Innovation and Marketing in the Pharmaceutical Industry, New York 2014, 19 ff.

PHILLIPS JEREMY, Trade Mark Law: A Practical Anatomy, Oxford 2003.

PICHT PETER, Standardsetzung und Patentmissbrauch, Schlagkraft und Entwicklungsbedard des europäischen Kartellrechts, GRUR Int. 2014, 1 ff.

PIEPER STEFAN ULRICH, Rechtsetzung und Vollzug des EG-Rechts, in: DAUSES MANFRED A./LUDWIGS MARKUS (EDS), Handbuch des EU-Wirtschaftsrechts, München 2019.

PIRES DE CARVALHO NUNO, The TRIPS Regime of Antitrust and Undisclosed Information, The Hague 2008 (cit. PIRES DE CARVALHO, The TRIPS Regime of Antitrust and Undisclosed Information).

PIRES DE CARVALHO NUNO, Current Trends in the Multilateral Evolution of Unfair Competition Law, in: DE WERRA JACQUES (ED.), Défis du droit de la concurrence déloyale, Genève 2014, 1 ff.

PIRES DE CARVALHO NUNO, The TRIPS Regime of Patents and Test Data, 4th, Alphen aan den Rijn 2014 (cit. PIRES DE CARVALHO, The TRIPS Regime of Patents and Test Data).

POOLEY JAMES, Was America's Industrial Revolution Based on Trade Secret Theft?, 5 July 2017, https://www.ipwatchdog.com/2017/07/05/americas-industrial-revolution-based-trade-secret-theft/id=85377/, accessed on 15 January 2020.

POSNER RICHARD A., The Chicago School of Antitrust Analysis, University of Pennsylvania Law Review 1979, 925 ff.

POSNER RICHARD A., Antitrust Law, 2nd ed., Chicago 2001.

PRASAD VINAY/MAILANKODY SHAM, Research and Development Spending to Bring a Single Cancer Drug to Market and Revenues after Approval, JAMA Internal Medicine 2017, 1569 ff.

PRETNAR BOJAN, Die ökonomische Auswirkung von Patenten in der wissensbasierten Marktwirtschaft, GRUR Int. 2004, 776 ff.

PRIES THORSTEN WILHELM, Kampfpreismissbrauch im ökonomisierten EG-Kartellrecht 2009.

RAASCH CHRISTINA, Der Patentauslauf von Pharmazeutika als Herausforderung beim Management des Produktlebenszyklus, 2nd ed., Wiesbaden 2010, Doctoral Thesis Univ. Nürnberg 2006.

RAHN GUNTRAM, Patentstrategien japanischer Unternehmen, GRUR Int., 377 ff.

RAISER LUDWIG, Missbrauch im Wirtschaftsrecht, JZ 1972, 732 ff.

RAUDA CHRISTIAN, Fallgruppen statt 'IMS Health' Zwangslizenzen an Urheberrechten im Rahmen des Article 82 EG, GRUR 2007, 1022 ff.

REIF EDUARD JOSEF, Der Begriff der Verwirkung der Grundrechte in Artikel 18 des Grundgesetztes, Unter besonderer Berücksichtigung der Lehre des Missbrauchs der Grundrechte, Bochum 1970 (Inauguraldissertation).

REINDL ANDREAS, The Magic of Magill: TV Program Guides as a Limit of Copyright Law?, IIC 1993, 60 ff.

REISS CHRISTOPH, Patente und Produktmarktwettbewerb, Der strategische Einsatz von Patenten im Wettbewerb jenseits der Innovationsförderung ; eine Untersuchung wettbewerbspolitisch relevanter Patentstrategien, Tübingen 2011, Doctoral Thesis Univ. Bayreuth 2010.

REULEN STEPHANIE, Strategiefähigkeit im Regulierungswettbewerb, Legislative, administrative und forensische Anpassungsprozesse im Zuge der Europäisierung des Markenschutzes, Wiesbaden 2010.

RICHTER CARSTEN, Der Schutzbereich von Wirkstoffpatenten, Soll und kann eine Umgehung über Prodrugs verhindert werden?, Köln 2016.

RIDDER CLAUDIA, Die Bedeutung von Zwangslizenzen im Rahmen des TRIPS-Abkommens, Heidelberg 2004.

RIDYARD DEREK, Compulsory Access under EC Competition Law: New Doctrine of 'Convenient Facilities' and the Case for Price Regulation, ECLR 2004, 669 ff.

RIESENHUBER KARL, § 10 Die Auslegung, in: RIESENHUBER KARL (ED.), Europäische Methodenlehre, Berlin 2014.

RIVETTE KEVIN G./KLINE DAVID, Discovering New Value in Intellectual Property, Harvard Business Review 2000, 54 ff.

RIVETTE KEVIN G./KLINE DAVID, Rembrandts in the Attic, Unlocking the Hidden Value of Patents, Boston (MA) 2000.

RIZIOTIS DIMITRIOS, Patent Misuse als Schnittstelle zwischen Patentrecht und Kartellrecht, Eine rechtsvergleichende Darstellung, GRUR Int. 2004, 367 ff.

RÖLLER LARS-HENDRIK/FRIEDERISZICK HANS W., Ökonomische Analyse in der EU Wettbewerbspolitik, Ein erstes Résumé, in: BAUDENBACHER CARL (ED.), Neueste Entwicklungen im europäischen und internationalen Kartellrecht, Basel 2007, 203 ff.

ROSS THOMAS W., The Evolution of Competition Law in Canada, Review of Industrial Organization, 1998, 1 ff.

ROUSSEVA EKATERINA, Modernizing by Eradicating: How the Commission's New Approach to Article 81 EC Dispenses with the Need to Apply Article 82 EC to Vertical Restraints, Common Market Law Review 2005, 587 ff.

RUFFNER MARKUS, Neue Wettbewerbstheorie und schweizerisches Kartellrecht, Möglichkeiten und Grenzen einer markt- und institutionentheoretischen Fundierung der Wettbewerbspolitik, Zürich 1990.

SACK ROLF, Zur Vereinbarkeit wettbewerbsbeschränkender Abreden in Lizenz- und Know-how-Verträgen mit europäischem und deutschem Kartellrecht, wrp 1999, 592 ff.

SÄCKER FRANZ JÜRGEN/RIXECKER ROLAND/OETKER HARTMUT/LIMPERG BETTINA (eds), Münchener Kommentar zum Bürgerlichen Gesetzbuch, Band 2, 8th ed.,

München 2019 (cit. AUTHOR, in: SÄCKER ET AL., Münchener Kommentar BGB, § XY).

SAMKALDEN IVO/DRUKER I.E., Legal Problems Relating to Article 86 of the Rome Treaty, Common Market Law Review 1966, 158 ff.

SAMPAT BHAVEN N./SHADLEN KENNETH C., TRIPS Implementation and Secondary Pharmaceutical Patenting in Brazil and India, SCID 2015, 228 ff.

SAMUELSON PAUL A., The Pure Theory of Public Expenditure, The Review of Economics and Statistics, 387 ff.

SANKARAN SRI KRISHNA, Patent Flooding in the United States and Japan, The Journal of Law and Technology 2000, 393 ff.

SCHECHTER ROGER E./THOMAS JOHN R., Intellectual Property, the Law of Copyrights, Patents and Trademarks, St. Paul (MN) 2003.

SCHERER FREDERIC M./ROSS DAVID, Industrial Market Structure and Economic Performance, 3rd ed., Boston (MA) 1990.

SCHEUER JOCHEN, Technologietransfer im Kartellrecht, Eine rechtsökonomische und rechtsvergleichende Perspektive 2009.

SCHLUEP WALTER R., Die Europaverträglichkeit des schweizerischen Lauterkeitsrecht, in: DUTOIT BERNARD (ED.), Un Droit européen de la concurrence déloyale en formation?, Geneva, New York 1994, 67 ff.

SCHMIDT ANDRÉ/VOIGT STEFAN, Der 'More Economic Approach' in der Missbrauchsaufsicht: Einige kritische Anmerkungen zu den Vorschlägen der Generaldirektion Wettbewerb, WUW 2006, 1097 ff.

SCHMIDT HEDVIG, Competition Law and IP Rights: Not So Complementary - Time for Re-alignment of the Goals?, World Competition 2019, 451 ff.

SCHMIDT INGO, More Economic Approach Versus Justitiabilität, WUW 2005, 877 ff.

SCHMIDT INGO/ENGELKE HEINZ, Marktzutrittsschranken und potentieller Wettbewerb, WiSt 1989, 399 ff.

SCHMIDT INGO/RITTALER JAN B., Die Chicago School of Antitrust Analysis, Wettbewerbstheoretische und -politische Analyse eines Credos, Baden-Baden 1986.

SCHMIDT KARSTEN/SCHWARK EBERHARD, Unternehmen, Recht und Wirtschaftsordnung, Festschrift für Peter Raisch, Köln etc. 1995 (cit. AUTHOR, in: SCHMIDT/SCHWARK, FS Raisch, Titel).

SCHMIDTCHEN DIETER, Die neue Wettbewerbspolitik auf dem Prüfstand, in: OBERENDER PETER (ED.), Effizienz und Wettbewerb, Berlin 2005a, 174 ff.

SCHMIDTCHEN DIETER, Effizienz als Leitbild der Wettbewerbspolitik: Für einen 'More Economic Approach', in: OBERENDER PETER (ED.), Effizienz und Wettbewerb, Berlin 2005b, 10 ff.

SCHUHMACHER FLORIAN, Altes und Neues zur Kampfpreisunterbietung, ZWeR 2007, 352 ff.

SCHULZE REINER/HOEREN THOMAS, Dokumente zum Europäischen Recht, Berlin, Heidelberg 2000.

SCHUMPETER JOSEPH A., Theorie der wirtschaftlichen Entwicklung, Eine Untersuchung über Unternehmergewinn, Kapital, Kredit, Zins und den Konjunkturzyklus, 9th ed., Berlin 2013.

SCHÜNEMANN WOLFGANG B., Der Beitrag der Ökonomik für das Europäische Lauterkeitsrecht, in: HILTY RETO M./HENNING-BODEWIG FRAUKE (EDS), Lauterkeitsrecht und Acquis Communautaire, Heidelberg 2009, 97 ff.

SCHWALBE ULRICH, Die Berücksichtigung von Effizienzgewinnen in der Fusionskontrolle - Ökonomisch Aspekte, in: OBERENDER PETER (ED.), Effizienz und Wettbewerb, Berlin 2005, 64 ff.

SCHWALBE ULRICH/ZIMMER DANIEL, Kartellrecht und Ökonomie, Moderne ökonomische Ansätze in der europäischen und deutschen Zusammenschlusskontrolle, 2nd ed., Frankfurt am Main 2011.

SCHWARZE JÜRGEN/BECKER ULRICH/HATJE ARMIN/SCHOO JOHANN (eds), EU-Kommentar, 4th ed., Baden-Baden, Wien, Basel 2019 (cit. AUTHOR, in: SCHWARZE ET AL., EU-Kommentar, Article XY).

SCHWEITZER HEIKE, The History, Interpretation and Underlying Principles of Section 2 Sherman Act and Article 82 EC European, in: EHLERMANN DIETER/MARQUIS MAL (EDS), European Competition Law Annual 2007, Oxford 2008, 119 ff.

SCHWEITZER HEIKE/PATEL KIRAN KLAUS, EU Competition Law in Historical Context: Continuity and Change in: PATEL KIRAN KLAUS/SCHWEITZER HEIKE (EDS), The Historical Foundations of EU Competition Law, Oxford 2013, 207 ff.

SCHWEND FRANZ, Der Leistungswettbewerb als ein geschütztes Rechtsgut des deutschen und französischen Wettbewerbsrechts?, Ein rechtsvergleichender Beitrag zu den Anforderungen des gemeinsamen Binnenmarktes, Frankfurt am Main 1991 (Doctoral Thesis Univ. Köln 1991).

SCOTCHMER SUZANNE, Innovation and Incentives, Cambridge (MA) Etc. 2006.

SCOTCHMER SUZANNE/GREEN JERRY, Novelty and Disclosure in Patent Law, The RAND Journal of Economics 1990, 131 ff.

SEDEF ARZU, Immaterialgüterrecht und Kartellrecht, in: WIEBE ANDREAS (ED.), Wettbewerbs- und Immaterialgüterrecht, Wien 2018, 523 ff.

SEITZ CLAUDIA, Klare Grenzlinie und Minenfeld: Die Marktmissbrauchskontrolle im Arzneimittelsektor nach dem AstraZeneca-Urteil des EuGH, EuZW 2013, 377 ff.

SEN RAJARSHI/RAMANUJAN ADARSH, Pruning the Evergreen Tree or Tripping Up over TRIPS?, Section 3(d) of the Indian Patents Act, 1970, IIC 2010, 170 ff.

SEUBA XAVIER, Human Rights and Intellectual Property Rights, in: CORREA CARLOS MARÍA/YUSUF ABDULQAWI (EDS), Intellectual Property and International Trade, Alphen aan den Rijn 2016, 465 ff.

SGANGA CATERINA/SCALZINI SILVIA, From Abuse of Rights to European Copyright Misuse: A New Doctrine for EU Copyright Law, IIC 2017, 405 ff.

SHAPIRO CARL, Navigating the Patent Thicket, Cross Licenses, Patent Pools, and Standard Setting, in: JAFFE ADAM B./LERNER JOSH/STERN SCOTT (EDS), Innovation Policy and the Economy, Cambridge, MA 2001, 119 ff.

SHAPIRO CARL, Antitrust Limits to Patent Settlements, RAND Journal of Economics 2003, 391 ff.

SIEBERT TILMAN/PRIES THORSTEN WILHELM, Kartellrechtliche Marktabgrenzung im Pharma-Bereich, PharmaR 2007, 147 ff.

SILVERMAN ARNOLD B., The Relationship Between Basic and Improvement Patents, JOM 1995, 50.

SINGER MARGARETE/STAUDER DIETER (eds), Substantive Patent Law: Preamble, Articles 1 to 89, 3rd ed., Köln 2003 (cit. AUTHOR, in: SINGER ET AL., EPC 2003, Article XY).

SINGER MARGARETE/STAUDER DIETER/LUGINBUEHL STEFAN (EDS), Europäisches Patentübereinkommen, Kommentar (Substantive Patent Law: Preamble, Articles 1 to 89), 8th ed., Köln 2019 (cit. AUTHOR, in: SINGER ET AL., EPC 2019, Article XY).

SONNEVEND PÀL, § 14 Eigentumsgarantie, in: GRABENWARTER CHRISTOPH (ED.), Europäischer Grundrechteschutz, Baden-Baden 2014, 527 ff.

SØRENSEN KARSTEN ENGSIG, Abuse of Rights in Community Law: A Principle of Substance or Merely Rhetoric?, Common Market Law Review 2006, 423 ff.

STIEF MARCO/BÜHLER DIRK, § 14 The Supplementary Protection Certificate, in: HAEDICKE MAXIMILIAN/TIMMANN HENRIK (EDS), Patent Law, München 2014.

STIEGER WERNER, § 12, in: BERTSCHINGER CHRISTOPH/GEISER THOMAS/MÜNCH PETER (EDS), Schweizerisches und europäisches Patentrecht, Basel, Genf, München 2002.

STIERLE MARTIN, Das nicht-praktizierte Patent, Tübingen 2018.

STIRNIMANN FRANZ XAVER, Urheberkartellrecht, Kartellrechtliche Verhaltenskontrolle von urheberrechtlichen Märkten in der Schweiz, Zürich 2004, Doctoral Thesis Univ. Zürich 2004.

STONE GEORGE, Development of Deep-tank Fermentation Pfizer Inc, 12 June 2008, https://www.acs.org/content/acs/en/education/whatischemistry/landmarks/penicillin.html, accessed on 12 February 2020.

STRAETMANS GERT, Misleading Practices, the Consumer Information Model and Consumer Protection, EuCML 2016, 199 ff.

STRAUS JOSEF, Implications of the TRIPS Agreement in the Field of Patent Law, in: BEIER FRIEDRICH-KARL/SCHRICKER GERHARD (EDS), From GATT to TRIPS: The Agreement on Trade-Related Aspects of Intellectual Property Rights, Munich 1996.

STRAUS JOSEF, Patentanmeldung als Missbrauch der marktbeherrschenden Stellung nach Article EGV Artikel 82 EGV?, GRUR Int. 2009, 93 ff.

STREINZ RUDOLF/MICHL WALTHER (EDS), EUV/AEUV, Vertrag über die Europäische Union, Vertrag über die Arbeitsweise der Europäischen Union, Charta der Grundrechte der Europäischen Union, 3rd ed., München 2018 (cit. AUTHOR, in: STREINZ/MICHL, EUV/AEUV/GrCh, Article XY).

STURMEY S.G., The Economic Development of Radio, London 1958.

SULLIVAN LAWRENCE A./GRIMES WARREN S./SAGERS CHRISTOPHER L., The Law of Antitrust: An Integrated Handbook, 3rd ed., St. Paul (MN) 2016.

SZYMAŃSKI PAWEŁ/MARKOWICZ MAGDALENA/MIKICIUK-OLASIK ELŻBIETA, Adaptation of High-Throughput Screening in Drug Discovery-Toxicological Screening Tests, International Journal of Molecular Sciences 2012, 427 ff.

TAYLOR DAVID, The Pharmaceutical Industry and the Future of Drug Development, in: HESTER RONALD E./HARRISON ROY M. (EDS), Pharmaceuticals in the Environment, Cambridge 2016, 1 ff.

TETENS JOUREN KRISITIN, Einfluss von Viagra (Sildenafil) auf die Blutflussparameter des lokal begrenzten Prostatakarzinoms, Kiel 2010, Doctoral Thesis Univ. Kiel, https://d-nb.info/1009573357/34, accessed on 14 February 2020.

THEUNE ULRICH, Die Beurteilung ausschließlicher Patentlizenzverträge nach Art. EWGVERTR Artikel 85 EWG-Vertrag, Erster Teil, GRUR Int. 1977, 63 ff.

THORELLI HANS B., The Federal Antitrust Policy, Origination of an American Tradition, Baltimore 1954.

THOUVENIN FLORENT, Funktionale Systematisierung von Wettbewerbsrecht (UWG) und Immaterialgüterrechten, Köln 2007, Doctoral Thesis Univ. Zürich.

THUMM NIKOLAUS A., Grundlagen des Geistigen Eigentums, in: HERREN JÜRG/MÜNCH PETER/WEINMANN CONRAD (EDS), Schweizer IP-Handbuch, Basel 2013.

THYRI PETER, Immaterialgüterrechte und Zugang zur wesentlichen Einrichtung, WUW 2005, 388 ff.

TIMMANN TOBIAS, Das Patentrecht im Lichte von Article 14 GG, Tübingen 2008, Doctoral Thesis Univ. Bayreuth 2008.

TOM WILLARD K./NEWBERG JOSHUA A., Antitrust and Intellectual Property: From Separate Spheres to Unified Field, Antitrust Journal 1997, 167 ff.

TORRISI SALVATORE/GAMBARDELLA ALFONSO/GIURI PAOLA/HARHOFF DIETMAR/HOISL KARIN, Used, Blocking and Sleeping Patents, Empirical Evidence from a Large-Scale Inventor Survey, Paper to Be Presented at DRUID15, Rome 15-17 June 2015, Research Policy 2016, 1374 ff.

TRIDIMAS TAKIS, The General Principles of EU Law, 3rd ed., Oxford 2016.

TROLLER KAMEN, Grundzüge des schweizerischen Immaterialgüterrechts, 2nd ed., Basel, Genf, München 2005.

TRÜEB HANS, Der Rechtsmissbrauch (Schikane) im modernen Recht: unter besonderer Berücksichtigung von Article 2.2 des schweiz. Zivilgesetzbuches, Bern 1909 (Doctoral Thesis Univ. Bern 1909).

TURNER DONALD F., The Scope of 'Attempt to Monopolize', New York 1975.

ULLRICH HANNS, Kooperative Forschung und Kartellrecht, Eine Kritik der Wettbewerbsaufsicht über FuE-Gemeinschaften in der USA, der EWG und der Bundesrepublik Deutschland, Heidelberg 1988.

ULLRICH HANNS, Lizenzkartellrecht auf dem Weg zur Mitte, GRUR Int. 1996, 555 ff.

ULLRICH HANNS, Antitrust Law Relating to High Technology Industries: A Case for or Against International Rules?, in: ZÄCH ROGER/CORREA CARLOS MARÍA (EDS), Towards WTO Competition Rules, Berne 1999, 261 ff.

ULLRICH HANNS, Grenzen des Rechtsschutzes, Technologieschutz zwischen Wettbewerbs- und Industriepolitik, in: SCHRICKER GERHARD/DREIER THOMAS/KUR ANNETTE (EDS), Geistiges Eigentum im Dienst der Innovation, Baden-Baden 2001, 83 ff.

ULLRICH HANNS, Strategic Patenting by the Pharmaceutical Industry: Towards a Concept of Abusive Practices of Protection, in: DREXL JOSEF/LEE NARI (EDS), Pharmaceutical Innovation, Competition and Patent Law, Cheltenham 2013, 241 ff.

ULMER PETER, Der Begriff 'Leistungswettbewerb' und seine Bedeutung für die Anwendung von GWB und UWG-Tatbeständen, GRUR 1977, 565 ff.

UNGER THOMAS, Innovation oder Scheininnovation, Das ist die Frage, Medizinische Klinik 2006, 257 ff.

VALLENDER KLAUS/HETTICH PETER/LEHNE JENS, Wirtschaftsfreiheit und begrenzte Staatsverantwortung, Grundzüge des Wirtschaftsverfassungs- und Wirtschaftsverwaltungsrecht, 4th ed., Bern 2006.

VAN DER VIJVER TJARDA, Article 102 TFEU: How to Claim the Application of Objective Justifications in the Case of Prima Facie Dominance Abuses ?, Journal of European Competition Law & Practice 2013, 121 ff.

VANZETTI ADRIANO, Kapitel 5: Italien, in: LANGE PAUL (ED.), Internationales Handbuch des Marken- und Kennzeichenrechts, München 2009.

VESALA JUHA, Misuse of Patent Application Procedures: A Case for Condemning Non-misleading Strategies?, in: BALLARDINI ROSA/BRUUN NIKLAS/NORRGÅRD MARCUS (EDS), Transitions in European Patent Law, Alphen aan den Rijn 2015, 269 ff.

VOLKMANN SEBASTIAN, Patenterwerb und Marktmachtmissbrauch, Eine Untersuchung missbräuchlicher Verhaltensweisen anhand der Rechtsprechung der europäischen Gerichte, Baden-Baden 2013, Doctoral Thesis Univ. Halle 2013.

VON BOGDANDY ARMIN/VILLARREAL PEDRO A., The Role of International Law in Vaccinating Against COVID-19: Appraising the COVAX Initiative, ZaöRV 2021, 89ff.

VON DANWITZ THOMAS, Eigentumsschutz in Europa und im Wirtschaftsvölkerrecht, in: VON DANWITZ THOMAS/DEPENHEUER OTTO/ENGEL CHRISTOPH (EDS), Bericht zur Lage des Eigentums, Berlin, Heidelberg 2002, 215 ff.

VON DER GROEBEN HANS, Deutschland und Europa in einem unruhigen Jahrhundert, Erlebnisse und Betrachtungen, 2nd ed., Baden-Baden 2014.

VON DER GROEBEN HANS/SCHWARZE JÜRGEN/HATJE ARMIN (eds), Europäisches Unionsrecht, Vertrag über die Europäische Union - Vertrag über die Arbeitsweise der Europäischen Union - Charta der Grundrechte der Europäischen Union, 7th ed., Baden-Baden 2015 (cit. AUTHOR, in: VON DER GROEBEN ET AL., Kommentar EU-Recht, Article XY).

VON WEISZÄCKER CARL CHRISTIAN, Marktzutrittsschranken, in: OBERENDER PETER (ED.), Effizienz und Wettbewerb, Berlin 2005, 43 ff.

VON WEISZÄCKER CARL CHRISTIAN, Konsumentenwohlfahrt und Wettbewerbsfreiheit: Über den tiefen Sinn des 'Economic Approach', WUW 2007, 1078 ff.

VOSSIUS CORINNA/VOSSIUS TILMAN/VOSSIUS VOLKER, Der Terfenadin-Verletzungsstreit; zum Standard der Neuheitsprüfung, GRUR 1994, 472 ff.

WALDBURGER ROBERT/SESTER PETER/PETER CHRISTOPH/BAER CHARLOTTE M., Law & Economics, Festschrift für Peter Nobel, Bern 2015 (cit. AUTHOR, in: WALDBURGER ET AL., FS Nobel, Titel).

WALSH JOHN P./ARORA ASHISH/COHEN WESLEY M., Research Tool Patenting and Licensing and Biomedical Innovation, in: MERRILL STEPHEN A./COHEN WESLEY MARC (EDS), Patents in the Knowledge-Based Economy, Washington, DC 2003, 285 ff.

WARSHOFSKY FRED, The Patent Wars: The Battle to Own the World's Technology, New York 1994.

WEBER ROLF H., Internationale Harmonisierungsansätze im Lauterkeitsrecht, sic! 1998, 158 ff.

WEBER ROLF H., Welches Lauterkeitsrecht braucht die Schweiz?, sic! 2012, 231 ff.

WEBER WALLER SPENCER, Antitrust and Social Networking, North Carolina Law Review 2012, 1771 ff.

WEILER FRANK, Grammatikalische Auslegung des vielsprachigen Unionsrechts, ZEuP 2010, 861 ff.

WERDEN GREGORY J., Identifying Exclusionary Conduct under Section 2: The 'No Economic Sense' Test, Antitrust Law Journal 2006, 413 ff.

WERMUTH CAMILLE GEORGES ET AL., The Practice of Medicinal Chemistry, 4th ed., Amsterdam 2015.

WERNICKE STEFAN, Das Intel-Urteil des EuG: ein Lehrstück dogmatischer Kontinuität, EuZW 2015, 19 ff.

WERTHEIMER ALBERT/LEVY RICHARD/O'CONNOR THOMAS, Too Many Drugs? The Clinical and Economic Value of Incremental Innovations, in: FARQUHAR IRINA/SUMMERS KENT/SORKIN ALAN L. (EDS), Investing in Health, Bingley (UK) 2001, 77 ff.

WHISH RICHARD/BAILEY DAVID, Competition Law, 9th ed., Oxford 2018.

WILD CLAUDIA/PUIG STEFAN, Analogpräparate:Marktstrategien der Arzneimittelhersteller wie der Arzneimitteleinkäufer am Beispiel nichtionischer (monomerer) Röntgenkontrastmittel, Gesundheitswesen 2004, 716 ff.

WOLFF CHRISTIAN, Zwangslizenzen im Immaterialgüterrecht, Göttingen 2005.

WOLFSON JEFFREY A., Patent Flooding in the Japanese Patent Office, Methods for Reducing Patent Flooding and Obtaining Effective Patent Protection, George Washington Journal of International Law and Economics 1993, 531 ff.

WURMNEST WOLFGANG, Marktmacht und Verdrängungsmissbrauch, Eine rechtsvergleichende Neubestimmung des Verhältnisses von Recht und Ökonomik in der Missbrauchsaufsicht über marktbeherrschende Unternehmen, 2nd ed., Tübingen 2012 (teilw.: Habil. Univ. Hamburg 2008-2009).

WURZER ALEXANDER/MÜLLER HEINZ, Patente steigern den Unternehmenswert, Die finanzielle Bewertung der Schutzrechte wird immer wichtiger, NZZ, 20 June 2007, https://www.ige.ch/fileadmin/user_upload/andere/Juristische_Infos/d/j401d.pdf, accessed on 27 April 2020.

WUTTKE JÜRGEN, Sicherung des Leistungswettbewerbs durch das Verbot der unbilligen Behinderung in § 26 Abs. 4 GWB, Köln, Berlin 1995, Doctoral Thesis Univ. Mainz 1994.

ZÄCH ROGER, Schweizerisches Kartellrecht, 2nd ed., Bern 2005.

ZÄCH ROGER/HEIZMANN RETO A., Grundzüge des Europäischen Wirtschaftsrechts, 2nd ed., Zürich 2005.

ZÄCH ROGER/KÜNZLER ADRIAN, Individualschutz und Institutionsschutz als Aufgaben des Kartellrechts, in: ZÄCH ROGER ET AL. (EDS), Individuum und Verband, Zürich 2006, 291 ff.

ZÄCH ROGER/KÜNZLER ADRIAN, Freedom to Compete or Consumer Welfare: The Goal of Competition Law According to Constitutional Law, in: ZÄCH ROGER/HEINEMANN ANDREAS/KELLERHALS ANDREAS (EDS), The Development of Competition Law, Cheltenham et al. 2010.

ZECH HERBERT, 'Defensive Patentstrategien' und technischer Fortschritt im Wettbewerbsrecht … Einsatz von Sperrpatenten als Behinderungsmissbrauch?, ZWeR 2011, 312 ff.

ZENKER STEFAN, Kartellrecht und Rechtsmissbrauch, Die Bedeutung des § 242 BGB als Instrument der Marktverhaltenskontrolle unterhalb kartellrechtlicher Aufgreifschwellen, Baden-Baden 2019, Doctoral Thesis Univ. München 2019.

ZHENG JUN, Judicial Review of Fines in EU Competition Law, Zürich Etc. 2015.

Table of Decisions

European Courts and European Commission

ADVOCATE GENERAL KARL ROEMER, *Parke, Davis & Co. v. Probel and Others*, C-24/67, 29 February 1968, ECLI:EU:C:1968:4 (cit.: AG ROEMER, *in: Parke/Davis*, C-24/67), 265

ADVOCATE GENERAL KARL ROEMER, *Europemballage Corporation and Continental Can Company Inc. v. Commission of the European Communities*, C-6/72, 21 November 1972, ECLI:EU:C:1972:101 (cit.: AG ROEMER, *in: Continental Can*, C-6/72), 187

ADVOCATE GENERAL HEINRICH KIRSCHNER, *Tetra Pak Rausing SA v. Commission*, T-51/89, 21 February 1990, ECLI:EU:T:1990:15 (cit.: AG KIRSCHNER, *in: TetraPak I*, T-51/89), 166

ADVOCATE GENERAL CLAUS CHRISTIAN GULMANN, *Radio Telefis Eireann (RTE) and Independent Television Publications Ltd (ITP) v. Commission*, Joined Cases C-241/91 P and C-242/91 P, 1 June 1994, ECLI:EU:C:1994:210 (cit. AG GULMANN, *in:* RTE *and ITP v. Commission*, Joined Cases C-241/91 P and C-242/91 P), 233

ADVOCATE GENERAL GIUSEPPE TESAURO, *Kefalas and Others v. Elliniko Dimosio and Organismos Oikonomikis Anasygkrotisis Epicheiriseon*, C-367/96, 4 February 1998, ECLI:EU:C:1998:41 (cit.: AG TESAURO, *in: Kefalas a.o.*, C-367/96), 222

ADVOCATE GENERAL FRANCIS JACOBS, *Oscar Bronner GmbH & Co. KG v. Mediaprint Zeitungs- und Zeitschriftenverlag GmbH*, C-7/97, 28 May 1998, ECLI:EU:C: 1998:264 (cit.: AG JACOBS, *in: Oscar Bronner*, C-7/97), 188

ADVOCATE GENERAL LUÍS MIGUEL POIARES PESSOA MADURO, *Halifax and Others*, C-255/02, 7 April 2005, ECLI:EU:C:2005:200 (cit.: AG MADURO, *in: Halifax and Others*, C-255/02), 228,

ADVOCATE GENERAL JULIANE KOKOTT, *British Airways v. Commission*, C-95/04, 23 February 2006, ECLI:EU:C:2006:133 (cit.: AG KOKOTT, *in: British Airways v. Commission*, C-95/04), 31

ADVOCATE GENERAL ANTONIO TIZZANO, *General Motors BV v. Commission*, C-551/03 P, 6 April 2006, ECLI:EU:C:2005:639 (cit.: AG TIZZANO, *in: General Motors*, C-551/03 P), 148

EUROPEAN COURT OF JUSTICE, *Industrial Diamond Supplies v. Luigi Riva*, C-43/77, 22 November 1977, ECLI:EU:C:1977:188 (cit.: ECJ, *Industrial Diamond Supplies v. Riva*, Case 43/77), 9

EUROPEAN COURT OF JUSTICE, *United Brands Company and United Brands Continentaal BV v. Commission of the European Communities*, C-27/76, 14 February 1978, ECLI:EU:C:1978:22 (cit.: ECJ, *United Brands*, C-27/76), 111, 118, 120, 188, 189

EUROPEAN COURT OF JUSTICE, *Hoffmann-La Roche & Co. AG v. Commission of the European Communities*, C-85/76, 13 February 1979, ECLI:EU:C:1979:36 (cit.: ECJ, *Hoffmann-La Roche v. Commission*, C-85/76), 57, 111, 115, 127, 131, 142, 182, 190, 191, 196, 199, 240

EUROPEAN COURT OF JUSTICE, *Liselotte Hauer v. Land Rheinland-Pfalz*, C-44/79, 13 December 1979, ECLI:EU:C:1979:290 (cit.: ECJ, *Hauer v. Land Rheinland-Pfalz*, C-44/79), 273

EUROPEAN COURT OF JUSTICE, *Regina v. Maurice Donald Henn and John Frederick Ernest Darby*, C-34/79, 14 December 1979, ECLI:EU:C:1979:295 (cit.: ECJ, *Henn and Darby*, C-34/79), 269

EUROPEAN COURT OF JUSTICE, *National Panasonic v. Commission*, C-136/79, 26 June 1980, ECLI:EU:C:1980:169 (cit.: ECJ, *National Panasonic v. Commission*, C-136/79), 7

EUROPEAN COURT OF JUSTICE, *NV L'Oréal and SA L'Oréal v. PVBA 'De Nieuwe AMCK'*, C-31/80, 11 December 1980, ECLI:EU:C:1980:289 (cit.: ECJ, *L'Oréal v. De Nieuwe AMCK*, C-31/80), 191

EUROPEAN COURT OF JUSTICE, *Merck & Co. Inc. v. Stephar BV and Petrus Stephanus Exler*, C-187/80, 14 July 1981, ECLI:EU:C:1981:180 (cit. ECJ, *Merck v. Stephar*, C-187/80), 56

EUROPEAN COURT OF JUSTICE, *Gaston Schul Douane Expediteur BV v. Inspecteur der Invoerrechten en Accijnzen, Roosendaal*, C-15/81, 5 May 1982, ECLI:EU:C: 1982:135 (cit.: ECJ, *Gaston Schul v. Inspecteur der Invoerrechten*, C-15/81), 181

EUROPEAN COURT OF JUSTICE, *NV Nederlandsche Banden Industrie Michelin v. Commission*, C-322/81, 9 November 1983, ECLI:EU:C:1983:313 (cit.: ECJ, *Michelin I*, C-322/81), 112, 117, 120, 191, 199, 201

EUROPEAN COURT OF JUSTICE, *Campus Oil Limited and others v. Minister for Industry and Energy and other*, C-72/83, 10 July 1984, ECLI:EU:C:1984:256 (cit.: ECJ, *Campus Oil*, C-72/83), 269

EUROPEAN COURT OF JUSTICE, *Windsurfing International Inc. v. Commission*, C-193/83, 25 February 1986, ECLI:EU:C:1986:75 (cit.: ECJ, *Windsurfing International v. Commission*, C-193/83), 52

EUROPEAN COURT OF JUSTICE, *Allen and Hanburys Ltd v. Generics (UK) Ltd.*, C-434/85, 3 March 1988, ECLI:EU:C:1988:109 (cit.: ECJ, *Allen & Hanburys v. Generics*, C-434/85), 52

EUROPEAN COURT OF JUSTICE, *SPRL Louis Erauw-Jacquery v. La Hesbignonne SC*, C-27/87, 19 April 1988, ECLI:EU:C:1988:183 (cit.: ECJ, *Erauw-Jacquery v. La Hesbignonne*, C-27/87), 51

French Courts

German Courts

Indian Courts

International Courts

Italian Courts

Spanish Courts

Swiss Courts

Bundesgericht, *H. v. Fachverband Elektroapparate für Haushalt und Gewerbe in der Schweiz (FEA)*, 120 II 76, 25 February 1994 (cit.: BGE 120 II 76), 36

Bundesgericht, *Kodak SA v. Jumbo-Markt AG*, 126 III 129, 7 December 1999 (cit.: BGE 126 III 129), 42

Bundesgericht, Limmi I, 4C.169/2004, 8 September 2004 (cit.: BGer 4C.169/2004), 87

Bundesgericht, *Gaba International AG v. Weko*, 143 II 297, 28 June 2016 (cit.: BGE 143 II 297), 210

Obergericht Thurgau, Limmi I, Z1.2002.2, 27 March 2003 (cit.: OG Thurgau, *Limmi I*, Z1.2002.2), 87

US Courts and Commissions

District Court District of Massachusetts, *Polaroid Corp. v. Eastman Kodak Co.*, 641 F. Supp. 828, 11 October 1986 (cit.: Diss. Mass., *Polaroid Corp. v. Eastman Kodak Co.*, 641 F. Supp. 828), 45, 92

District Court for the Southern District of New York, In Re Buspirone Patent Litigation, 185 F. Supp. 2d 340, 14 February 2002 (cit.: S.D.N.Y, *In Re Buspirone Patent Litigation*, 185 F. Supp. 2d 340), 81

Federal Trade Commission, FTC Accord in Ciba-Geigy/Sandoz Merger, 17 December 1996 (cit.: FTC, *Press Release Ciba-Geigy/Sandoz)*, 126

United States Court of Appeals for the District of Columbia Circuit, *United States v. Microsoft*, 253 F.3d 34, 28 June 2001 (cit.: D.C. Cir., *United States v. Microsoft*, 253 F.3d 34), 207

United States Court of Appeals for the Federal Circuit, In re Bose Corp., 91 USP.Q.2d 1938, 31 August 2009 (cit.: Fed. Cir., *In re Bose Corp.*, 91 USP.Q.2d 1938), 280

United States Court of Appeals, Federal Circuit, *Windsurfing Int'l Inc. v. AMF Inc.*, 782 F.2d 995, 28 January 1986 (cit.: Fed. Cir., *Windsurfing Int'l Inc. v. AMF Inc.*, 782 F.2d 995), 171

United States Court of Appeals, Federal Circuit, *Atari Games Corporation. and Tengen Inc. v. Nintendo of America Inc. and Nintendo Co., Ltd.*, 975 F.2d 832, 10 September 1992 (cit.: Fed. Cir., *Atari/Tengen v. Nintendo*, 975 F.2d 832), 49

United States Court of Appeals, Federal Circuit, *Mallinckrodt Inc v. Medipart Inc*, 976 F.2d 700, 24 September 1992 (cit.: Fed. Cir., *Mallinckrodt Inc v. Medipart Inc*, 976 F.2d 700), 170

United States Court of Appeals, Federal Circuit, *B. Braun Med. Inc. v. Abbott Labs*, 124 F.3d 1419, 8 September 1997 (cit.: Fed. Cir., *B. Braun Med. Inc. v. Abbott Labs*, 124 F.3d 1419), 170

United States Court of Appeals, Federal Circuit, *University of Rochester v. GD Seale & Co./Pfizer*, 358 F.3d 916, 13 February 2004 (cit.: Fed. Cir., *University of Rochester v. GD Seale & Co./Pfizer*, 358 F.3d 916), 99

United States Court of Appeals, Fourth Circuit, *Lasercomb America v. Reynolds*, 911 F.2d 970, 16 August 1990 (cit.: 4th Cir., *Lasercomb America v. Reynolds*, 911 F.2d 970), 170

UNITED STATES COURT OF APPEALS, SECOND CIRCUIT, *SCM Corp. v. Xerox Corp. v. Monitowoc Co.*, 645 F.2d 1195, 12 March 1981 (cit.: 2ND CIR., *SCM Corp. v. Xerox Corp. v. Monitowoc Co.*, 645 F.2d 1195), 135, 136

UNITED STATES COURT OF APPEALS, SEVENTH CIRCUIT, *Helene Curtis Industries Inc. v. Church and Dwight Co. Inc.*, 560 F.2d 1325, 7 August 1977 (cit.: 7TH CIR., *Helene Curtis Industries Inc. v. Church and Dwight Co. Inc.*, 560 F.2d 1325), 170

UNITED STATES COURT OF APPEALS, SEVENTH CIRCUIT, *A.A. Poultry Farms, Inc. v. Rose Acre Farms, Inc.*, 881 F.2d 1396, 4 August 1989 (cit.: 7TH CIR., *A.A. Poultry Farms, Inc. v. Rose Acre Farms, Inc.*, 881 F.2d 1396), 206, 208, 213

UNITED STATES COURT OF APPEALS, SIXTH CIRCUIT, *Conwood Co., LP. v. US Tobacco Co.*, 290 F.3d 768, 15 May 2002 (cit.: 6TH CIR., *Conwood Co., LP. v. US Tobacco Co.*, 290 F.3d 768), 207

UNITED STATES DISTRICT COURT FOR THE NORTHERN DISTRICT OF ILLINOIS, *Continental Automotive GmbH et al v. iBiquity Digital Corporation*, 14 C 1977, Memorandum Opinion and Order, 26 February 2015 (cit.: N.D. ILL., *Continental Automotive GmbH et al v. iBiquity Digital Corporation*, 14 C 1977), 170

UNITED STATES SUPREME COURT, *Swift & Co. v. United States*, 196 US 375, 30 January 1905 (cit.: UNITED STATES SUPREME COURT, *Swift & Co. v. United States*, 196 US 375), 290

UNITED STATES SUPREME COURT, *Bement v. National Harrow Co.*, 186 US 70, 19 May 1902 (cit.: UNITED STATES SUPREME COURT, *Bement v. National Harrow Co.*, 186 US 70), 47

UNITED STATES SUPREME COURT, *Standard Oil Co. of New Jersey v. United States*, 221 US 1, 15 May 1911 (cit.: UNITED STATES SUPREME COURT, *Standard Oil v. USA*, 221 US 1), 27, 237

UNITED STATES SUPREME COURT, *Standard Sanitary Mfg. Co. v. United States*, 226 US 20, 18 November 1912 (cit.: UNITED STATES SUPREME COURT, *Standard Sanitary Mfg. Co. v. USA*, 226 US 20), 47

UNITED STATES SUPREME COURT, *Motion Pictures Patents Co. v. Universal Film Mfg. Co.*, 243 US 502, 9 April 1919 (cit.: UNITED STATES SUPREME COURT, *Motion Pictures Patents Co. v. Universal Film Mfg. Co.*, 243 US 502), 47

UNITED STATES SUPREME COURT, *United States v. Colgate & Co.*, 250 US 300, 2 June 1919 (cit.: UNITED STATES SUPREME COURT, *USA v. Colgate & Co.*, 250 US 300), 188

UNITED STATES SUPREME COURT, *Crown Die & Tool Co. v. Nye Tool & Machine Works*, 261 US 24, 19 February 1923 (cit.: UNITED STATES SUPREME COURT, *Crown Die & Tool v. Nye Tool*, 261 US 24), 47

UNITED STATES SUPREME COURT, *FTC v. Raladam Co.*, 283 US 643, 25 May 1931 (cit.: UNITED STATES SUPREME COURT, *FTC v. Raladam Co.*, 283 US 643), 38

UNITED STATES SUPREME COURT, *Ethyl Gasoline Corp. v. United States*, 309 US 436, 25 March 1940 (cit.: UNITED STATES SUPREME COURT, *Ethyl Gasoline Corp. v. United States*, 309 US 436), 48

UNITED STATES SUPREME COURT, *Morton Salt Co. v. G.S. Suppiger Co.*, 314 US 488, 5 January 1942 (cit.: UNITED STATES SUPREME COURT, *Morton Salt Co. v. G.S. Suppiger Co.*, 314 US 488), 171

Materials

BAYER PHARMA A.G., Vom Molekül zum Medikament, Exkursion in die Arzneimittel-Forschung, Bayer Pharma Brochure 2014, https://docplayer.org/196686-Vom-molekuel-zum-medikament.html, accessed on 24 January 2020, 68

BOARDS OF APPEAL OF THE EUROPEAN PATENT OFFICE, Case Law of the Board of Appeal, https://www.epo.org/law-practice/case-law-appeals/case-law.html, accessed on 24 January 2020 (cit. BoA, Case Law), 270

Botschaft zu einem Bundesgesetz über Kartelle und andere Wettbewerbsbeschränkungen (Kartellgesetz, KG), BBl 1995 I 468, 23 November 1994 (cit. BBl 1995 I 468), 282

BUNDESRAT, Parallelimporte und Patentrecht, Bericht des Bundesrates, 8 May 2000, https://www.ige.ch/fileadmin/user_upload/andere/Juristische_Infos/d/j100_Parallelimporte_d.pdf, accessed on 8 February 2020 (cit. BUNDESRAT, *Bericht Parallelimporte und Patentrecht*), 51

COMITÉ INTERNATIONAL CRÉÉ PAR LA CONFÉRENCE DE MESSINA, Rapport, Des Chefs de Délégation aux Ministres des Affaires Etrangères, Bruxelles, 21 April 1956, https://www.cvce.eu/s/5t, accessed on 24 February 2020 (cit. COMITÉ INTERNATIONAL CRÉÉ PAR LA CONFÉRENCE DE MESSINA, *Spaak Report*), 176

Die Zeit, 'Ohne Wettbewerb kein freier Markt', 24 July 1952, https://www.zeit.de/1952/30/ohne-wettbewerb-kein-freier-markt, accessed on 27 April 2020, 26

EUROPEAN COMMISSION, XXVIth Report on Competition Policy 1996, Luxembourg 1997 (cit. EC, *Report on Competition Policy 1996*), 22

EUROPEAN COMMISSION, Commission Notice, on the definition of relevant market for the purpose of Community competition law, 9 December 1997 (cit. EC, *Commission Notice on the definition of relevant market*), 115–117, 120

EUROPEAN COMMISSION, XXVIIth Report on Competition Policy 1997, Luxembourg 1998 (cit. EC, *Report on Competition Policy 1997*), 182

EUROPEAN COMMISSION, White Paper, On Modernisation of Rules Implementing Articles 85 and 86 of the EC Treaty, 28 April 1999, http://europa.eu/documents/comm/white_papers/pdf/com99_101_en.pdf, accessed on 4 February 2020 (cit. EC, *White Paper*), 28, 29, 185, 186

EUROPEAN COMMISSION, Press Release, EMI and Time Warner withdraw their notification to the Commission, IP/00/1122, 14 June 2000 (cit.: EC, *Press Release, EMI/Time Warner,* IP/00/1122), 120

EUROPEAN COMMISSION, Guidelines on market analysis and the assessment of significant market power, under the community regulatory framework for electronic communications networks and services 11 July 2002 (cit. EC, *Guidelines on market analysis 2002*), 118

EUROPEAN COMMISSION, Guidelines on the assessment of horizontal mergers, under the Council Regulation on the control of concentrations between undertakings 5 February 2004 (cit. EC, *Guidelines on the assessment of horizontal mergers*), 131, 205

EUROPEAN COMMISSION, Communication from the Commission, A pro-active Competition Policy for a Competitive Europe, 20 April 2004 (cit. EC, *Communication pro-active Competition Policy*), 184

EUROPEAN COMMISSION, DG Competition Discussion Paper, on the application of Article 82 of the Treaty to exclusionary abuses, December 2005 (cit. EC, *DG Competition discussion paper*), 29–32, 112, 119, 197

EUROPEAN COMMISSION, Communication, Enhancing the Patent System in Europe, 3 April 2007 (cit. EC, *Communication Enhancing the Patent System in Europe*), 42

EUROPEAN COMMISSION, Pharmaceutical Sector Inquiry, Final Report 2009 (cit. EC, *Sector Inquiry, Final Report*), 11, 45, 59–61, 63, 65, 75, 82, 83, 95, 99, 104, 107, 149, 259, 287

EUROPEAN COMMISSION, Communication, Guidance on the Commission's enforcement priorities in applying Article 82 of the EC Treaty to abusive exclusionary conduct by dominant undertakings, 24 February 2009 (cit. EC, *Guidance Paper*), 30–32, 111, 112, 130, 131, 164, 182–184, 188, 189, 192–197, 206, 209, 213

EUROPEAN COMMISSION, Communication, Guidelines on the applicability of Article 101 of the Treaty on the Functioning of the European Union to horizontal co-operation agreements, 14 January 2011 (cit. EC, *Guidelines on the applicability of Article 101*), 126

EUROPEAN COMMISSION, Press Release, Antitrust: Commission welcomes improved market entry for lung disease treatment, IP/11/842, 6 July 2011 (cit.: EC, *Press Release, Boehringer Ingelheim v. Almirall,* IP/11/842), 154, 165

EUROPEAN COMMISSION, Guidelines on the application of Article 101 of the Treaty on the Functioning of the European Union to technology transfer agreements, 28 March 2014 (cit. EC, *Technology Transfer Guidelines*), 122

EUROPEAN COMMISSION, Press Release, Fair Taxation: The Commission sets out next steps to increase tax transparency and tackle tax abuse 5 July 2016 (cit. EC, *Press Release, Fair Taxation*), 178

EUROPEAN COMMISSION, Press Release, Antitrust: Commission fines Servier and five generic companies for curbing entry of cheaper versions of cardiovascular medicine, IP/14/799 (cit.: EC, *Press Release, Commission fines Servier,* IP/14/799), 161, 165

EUROPEAN COMMISSION, Communication, Guidelines on market analysis and the assessment of significant market power under the EU regulatory framework for electronic communications networks and services 27 April 2018 (cit. EC, *Guidelines on market analysis 2018*), 116, 118, 119

EUROPEAN FEDERATION OF PHARMACEUTICAL INDUSTRIES AND ASSOCIATIONS, The Pharmaceutical Industry in Figures, Key Data 2018, https://www.efpia.eu/media/361960/efpia-pharmafigures2018_v07-hq.pdf, accessed on 5 July 2018, 68

EUROPEAN MEDICINES AGENCY, Guidelines for the Investigation of Bioequivalence, 20 January 2010, https://www.ema.europa.eu/en/documents/scientific-guideline/guideline-investigation-bioequivalence-rev1_en.pdf, accessed on 28 July 2020, 62

EUROPEAN MEDICINES AGENCY, Withdrawal of pain medicine flupirtine endorsed 23 March 2018, http://www.ema.europa.eu/docs/en_GB/document_library/Referrals_document/Flupirtine-31/Position_provided_by_CMDh/WC500248611.pdf, accessed on 9 February 2020, 70

EUROPEAN PATENT OFFICE, Compulsory licensing in Europe, A country-by-country overview, 2018 http://documents.epo.org/projects/babylon/eponot.nsf/0/8509F913B768D063C1258382004FC677/$File/compulsory_licensing_in_europe_en.pdf, accessed on 28 July 2020 (cit. EPO, *Compulsory licensing in Europe*), 106

EUROPEAN PATENT OFFICE, Guidelines for Examination in the European Patent Office November 2019, http://documents.epo.org/projects/babylon/eponet.nsf/0/8654640290C2DBE7C12584A4004D2D9A/$File/epo_guidelines_for_examination_2019_hyperlinked_en.pdf, accessed on 18 February 2020 (cit. EPO, *Guidelines for Examination*), 71, 72, 271

EUROPEAN PATENT OFFICE, National Law Relating to the EPC, 20 October 2019, http://documents.epo.org/projects/babylon/eponet.nsf/0/14EA57040E061C6EC125806D005921BF/$File/national_law_relating_to_the_EPC_13th_edition_de.pdf, accessed on 20 January 2020 (EPO, *National Law Relating to the EPC*), 252

FEDERAL TRADE COMMISSION, To Promote Innovation: The Proper Balance of Competition and Patent Law and Policy (A Report by the Federal Trade Commission) October, https://www.ftc.gov/sites/default/files/documents/reports/promote-innovation-proper-balance-competition-and-patent-law-and-policy/innovationrpt.pdf, accessed on 14 February 2020 (cit. FTC, *Report: To Promote Innovation*), 86, 97, 107, 287, 288

GAMBARDELLA ALFONSO/GIURI PAOLA/MARIANI MYRIAM, The Value of European Patents, Evidence from a Survey of European Inventors (The Final Report of the PatVal EU Project) January, https://pdfs.semanticscholar.org/7d07/1c3a54224e6abca0c0cd4c5ee21fd06b03cf.pdf, accessed on 29 January 2020, 3

GIURI PAOLA/ HIRSCH DENISE/ SZEPANOWSKA-KOZLOWSKA KRYSTYNA/ SELHOFER HANNES/ TEMPLE LANG JOHN/ THUMM NIKOLAUS, Report of the Expert Group on patent aggregation, Luxembourg 2015, https://ec.europa.eu/research/innovation-union/pdf/expert-groups/report_of_the_expert_group_on_patent_aggregation_-_2015.pdf, accessed on 29 January 2020 (cit. GIURI ET AL.), 3

International Association for the Protection of Intellectual Property (AIPPI), AIPPI's position paper on the waiver for certain provisions of the TRIPS agreement for the prevention, containment and treatment of COVID-19 proposed by some countries within the WTO, 12 May 2021, https://aippi.org/wp-content/uploads/2021/05/AIPPI-Position-Paper-on-WTO-Waiver_12May2021.pdf, accessed on 12 May 2021 (cit. AIPPI, Position Paper on the waiver of certain provisions under the TRIPS), 302

INTERPHARMA, Pharma-Markt Schweiz, Ausgabe 2019, Basel, Interpharma ph 2019, https://www.interpharma.ch/wp-content/uploads/2020/02/ly_iph.01.19.002_-_pharmamarkt_schweiz_2019_d_web-komprimiert.pdf, accessed on 1 April 2020, 64

KHEMANI R. SHYAM/SHAPIRO DANIEL M., Glossary of Industrial Organisation Economics and Competition Law 1993, http://www.oecd.org/regreform/sectors/2376087.pdf, accessed on 31 July 2019, 23, 33

KROES NEELIE, Consumer welfare: more than a slogan, Speech delivered at conference 'Competition and Consumers in the 21st century' in Brussels, 21 October 2009, https://ec.europa.eu/commission/presscorner/detail/en/SPEECH_09_486, accessed on 1 April 2020, 32

Mémorandum sur la Concentration dans le Marché Commun, Revue trimestrielle de droit européen, Revue trimestrielle de droit européen 1966, 186

MONTI MARIO, European Competition Policy : Quo Vadis?, Speech delivered at XX. International Forum on European Competition Policy in Brussel 10 April 2003, https://europa.eu/rapid/press-release_SPEECH-03-195_en.htm?locale=de, accessed on 4 February 2020, 28

ORGANISATION FOR ECONOMIC CO-OPERATION AND DEVELOPMENT, Patents and Innovation, Trends and Policy Challenges 2004, https://www.oecd-ilibrary.org/science-and-technology/patents-and-innovation_9789264026728-en, accessed on 14 February 2020, 85

ORGANISATION FOR ECONOMIC CO-OPERATION AND DEVELOPMENT, Policy Roundtables, Competition on the Merits 2005, https://www.oecd.org/competition/abuse/35911017.pdf, accessed on 1 April 2020, 199–201

ORGANISATION FOR ECONOMIC CO-OPERATION AND DEVELOPMENT, Policy Roundtables, Licensing of IP Rights and Competition Law, Background Note by the Secretariat, 6 June 2019, https://one.oecd.org/document/DAF/COMP(2019)3/en/pdf, accessed on 27 August 2021 (cit. OECD, Licensing of IP Rights and Competition Law, Background Note), 14

SWITZERLAND, Communication delivered in the Multilateral Trade Negotiations of the Uruguay Round 14 May 1990, https://www.wto.org/gatt_docs/English/SULPDF/92100157.pdf, accessed on 1 April 2020 (cit. SWITZERLAND, *Communication*), 275

TEGERNSEE GROUP, Consolidated Report on the Tegernsee User Consultation, on Substantive Patent Law Harmonization May, http://documents.epo.org/projects/babylon/eponet.nsf/0/C3407F28C924DA5CC1257CD80036DB61/$File/Tegernsee_user_consultation_consolidated_report_en.pdf, accessed on 1 April 2020, 252, 254

US DEPARTMENT OF JUSTICE/FEDERAL TRADE COMMISSION, Antitrust Guidelines for the Licensing of Intellectual Property 12 January 2017, https://www.justice.gov/atr/IPguidelines/download, accessed on 18 February 2020, 28, 50, 116, 117, 122, 126

UK COMPETITION COMMISSION/OFFICE OF FAIR TRADING, Merger Assessment Guidelines September, https://assets.publishing.service.gov.uk/government/uploads/system/uploads/attachment_data/file/284449/OFT1254.pdf, accessed on 31 July 2019, 19

VERBAND DER FORSCHENDEN ARZNEIMITTELHERSTELLER, Statistics 2015, Die Arzneimittelindustrie in Deutschland 2015, https://www.vfa.de/de/presse/publikationen, accessed on 17 June 2018, 69

WORLD HEALTH ORGANIZATION, Definition of a pharmaceutical ingredient, Revised Draft for Comment 2011, https://www.who.int/medicines/areas/quality_safety/quality_assurance/DefinitionAPI-QAS11-426Rev1-08082011.pdf, accessed on 1 April 2020 (cit. WHO, *Definition of a pharmaceutical ingredient*), 155

WORLD HEALTH ORGANIZATION, Promoting access to medical technologies and innovation, Intersections between public health, intellectual property and trade, Geneva 2013, https://www.wto.org/english/rese/bookspe/pamtiwhowipowtoweb13e.pdf, accessed on 1 April 2020 (cit. WHO, *Promoting access to medical technologies and innovation*), 64, 65

Index

G

I

L

M

O

P

R

S

T

U

INTERNATIONAL COMPETITION LAW SERIES

1. Ignacio De Leon, *Latin American Competition Law and Policy: A Policy in Search of Identity*, 2001 (ISBN 90-411-1542-0).
2. Wim Dejonghe & Wouter Van de Voorde (eds), *M & A in Belgium*, 2001 (ISBN 90-411-1594-3).
3. Yang-Ching Chao, Gee San, Changfa Lo & Jiming Ho (eds), *International and Comparative Competition Law and Policies*, 2001 (ISBN 90-411-1643-5).
4. Martin Mendelsohn & Stephen Rose, *Guide to the EC Block Exemption for Vertical Agreements*, 2002 (ISBN 90-411-9813-X).
5. Clifford A. Jones & Mitsuo Matsushita (eds), *Competition Policy in the Global Trading System: Perspectives from the EU, Japan and the USA*, 2002 (ISBN 90-411-1758-X).
6. Christian Koenig, Andreas Bartosch, Jens-Daniel Braun & Marion Romes (eds), *EC Competition and Telecommunications Law*. Second Edition, 2009 (ISBN 978-90-411-2564-4).
7. Jürgen Basedow (ed.), *Limits and Control of Competition with a View to International Harmonization*, 2002 (ISBN 90-411-1967-1).
8. Maureen Brunt, Economic Essays on Australian and New Zealand Competition Law, 2003 (ISBN 90-411-1991-4).
9. Ky P. Ewing, Jr., *Competition Rules for the 21st Century: Principles from America's Experience*, Second Edition, 2006 (ISBN 90-411-2477-2).
10. Joseph Wilson, *Globalization and the Limits of National Merger Control Laws*, 2003 (ISBN 90-411-1996-5).
11. Peter Verloop & Valérie Landes (eds), *Merger Control in Europe: EU, Member States and Accession States*, Fourth Edition, 2003 (ISBN 90-411-2056-4).
12. Themistoklis K. Giannakopoulos, *Safeguarding Companies' Rights in Competition and Anti-dumping/Anti-subsidies Proceedings*, Second Edition, 2011 (ISBN 978-90-411-3404-2).
13. Marjorie Holmes & Lesley Davey (eds), *A Practical Guide to National Competition Rules across Europe*, Second Edition, 2007 (ISBN 978-90- 411-2607-8).
14. Sigrid Stroux, *US and EU Oligopoly Control*, 2004 (ISBN 90-411-2296-6).
15. Tzong-Leh Hwang and Chiyuan Chen (eds), *The Future Development of Competition Framework*, 2004 (ISBN 90-411-2305-9).

16. Phedon Nicolaides, Mihalis Kekelekis and Maria Kleis, *State Aid Policy in the European Community: Principles and Practice,* Second Edition, 2008 (ISBN 978-90-411-2754-9).
17. Doris Hildebrand, *Economic Analyses of Vertical Agreements: A Self- Assessment*, 2005 (ISBN 90-411-2328-8).
18. Frauke Henning-Bodewig, *Unfair Competition Law: European Union and Member States*, 2005 (ISBN 90-411-2329-6).
19. Duarte Brito & Margarida Catalão-Lopes, *Mergers and Acquisitions: The Industrial Organization Perspective,* 2006 (ISBN 90-411-2451-9).
20. Nikos Th. Nikolinakos, *EU Competition Law and Regulation in the Converging Telecommunications, Media and IT Sectors*, 2006 (ISBN 90-411- 2469-1).
21. Mihalis Kekelekis, *The EC Merger Control Regulation: Rights of Defence. A Critical Analysis of DG COMP Practice and Community Courts' Jurisprudence,* 2006 (ISBN 90-411-2553-1).
22. Mark R. Joelson, *An International Antitrust Primer: A Guide to the Operation of United States, European Union and Other Key Competition Laws in the Global Economy*, Third Edition, 2006 (ISBN 90-411-2468-3).
23. Themistoklis K. Giannakopoulos, *A Concise Guide to the EU Anti-dumping/ Anti-subsidies Procedures*, 2006 (ISBN 90-411-2464-0).
24. George Cumming, Brad Spitz & Ruth Janal, *Civil Procedure Used for Enforcement of EC Competition Law by the English, French and German Civil Courts,* 2007 (ISBN 978-90-411-2471-5).
25. Jürgen Basedow (ed.), *Private Enforcement of EC Competition Law,* 2007 (ISBN 978-90-411-2613-9).
26. Jung Wook Cho, *Innovation and Competition in the Digital Network Economy: A Legal and Economic Assessment on Multi-tying Practices and Network Effects*, 2007 (ISBN 978-90-411-2574-3).
27. Akira Inoue, *Japanese Antitrust Law Manual: Law, Cases and Interpretation of the Japanese Antimonopoly Act*, 2007 (ISBN 978-90-411-2627-6).
28. René Barents, *Directory of EC Case Law on Competition,* 2007 (ISBN 978-90-411-2656-6).
29. Paul F. Nemitz (ed.), *The Effective Application of EU State Aid Procedures: The Role of National Law and Practice,* 2007 (ISBN 978-90-411-2657-3).
30. Jurian Langer, *Tying and Bundling as a Leveraging Concern under EC Competition Law,* 2007 (ISBN 978-90-411-2575-0).
31. Abel M. Mateus & Teresa Moreira (eds), *Competition Law and Economics – Advances in Competition Policy and Antitrust Enforcement*, 2007 (ISBN 978-90-411-2632-0).
32. Alberto Santa Maria, *Competition and State Aid: An Analysis of the EC Practice,* 2007 (ISBN 978-90-411-2617-7).
33. Barry J. Rodger (ed.), *Article 234 and Competition Law: An Analysis,* 2007 (ISBN 978-90-411-2605-4).

34. Alla Pozdnakova, *Liner Shipping and EU Competition Law,* 2008 (ISBN 978-90-411-2717-4).
35. Milena Stoyanova, *Competition Problems in Liberalized Telecommunications: Regulatory Solutions to Promote Effective Competition*, 2008 (ISBN 978-90-411-2736-5).
36. *EC State Aid Law/Le Droit des Aides d'Etat dans la CE. Liber Amicorum Francisco Santaolalla Gadea*, 2008 (ISBN 978-90-411-2774-7).
37. René Barents, *Directory of EU Case Law on State Aids,* Third Edition, 2019 (ISBN 978-94-035-1101-6).
38. Ignacio De Leon, *An Institutional Assessment of Antitrust Policy: The Latin American Experience*, 2009 (ISBN 978-90-411-2478-4).
39. Doris Hildebrand, *The Role of Economic Analysis in EU Competition Law: The European School*, Fourth Edition, 2016 (ISBN 978-90-411-6245-8).
40. Eugène Buttigieg, *Competition Law: Safeguarding the Consumer Interest. A Comparative Analysis of US Antitrust Law and EC Competition Law*, 2009 (ISBN 978-90-411-3119-5).
41. Ioannis Lianos & Ioannis Kokkoris (eds), *The Reform of EC Competition Law: New Challenges,* 2010 (ISBN 978-90-411-2692-4).
42. George Cumming & Mirjam Freudenthal, *Civil Procedure in EU Competition Cases before the English and Dutch Courts*, 2010 (ISBN 978-90-411-3192-8).
43. A.E. Rodriguez & Ashok Menon, *The Limits of Competition Policy: The Shortcomings of Antitrust in Developing and Reforming Economies*, 2010 (ISBN 978-90-411-3177-5).
44. Mika Oinonen, *Does EU Merger Control Discriminate against Small Market Companies? Diagnosing the Argument with Conclusions*, 2010 (ISBN 978-90-411-3261-1).
45. Eirik Østerud, *Identifying Exclusionary Abuses by Dominant Undertakings under EU Competition Law: The Spectrum of Tests*, 2010 (ISBN 978-90-411-3271-0).
46. Marco Botta, *Merger Control Regimes in Emerging Economies: A Case Study on Brazil and Argentina*, 2011 (ISBN 978-90-411-3402-8).
47. Jürgen Basedow & Wolfgang Wurmnest (eds), *Structure and Effects in EU Competition Law: Studies on Exclusionary Conduct and State Aid*, 2011 (ISBN 978-90-411-3174-4).
48. George Cumming (ed.), *Merger Decisions and the Rules of Procedure of the European Community Courts*, 2012 (ISBN 978-90-411-3671-8).
49. Eduardo Molan Gaban & Juliana Oliveira Domingues (eds), *Antitrust Law in Brazil: Fighting Cartels,* 2012 (ISBN 978-90-411-3670-1).
50. Giandonato Caggiano, Gabriella Muscolo & Marina Tavassi (eds), *Competition Law and Intellectual Property: A European Perspective,* 2012 (ISBN 978-90-411-3447-9).
51. Ben Van Rompuy, *Economic Efficiency: The Sole Concern of Modern Antitrust Policy? Non-efficiency Considerations under Article 101 TFEU*, 2012 (ISBN 978-90-411-3870-5).

52. Liyang Hou, *Competition Law and Regulation of the EU Electronic Communications Sector: A Comparative Legal Approach*, 2012 (ISBN 978-90-411-4047-0).
53. Barry Rodger, *Landmark Cases in Competition Law: Around the World in Fourteen Stories*, 2012 (ISBN 978-90-411-3843-9).
54. Andreas Scordamaglia-Tousis, *EU Cartel Enforcement: Reconciling Effective Public Enforcement with Fundamental Rights*, 2013 (ISBN 978-90-411-4758-5).
55. Bernardo Cortese (ed.), *EU Competition Law: Between Public and Private Enforcement*, 2014 (ISBN 978-90-411-4677-9).
56. Barry Rodger (ed.), *Competition Law: Comparative Private Enforcement and Collective Redress across the EU*, 2014 (ISBN 978-90-411-4559-8).
57. Nada Ina Pauer, *The Single Economic Entity Doctrine and Corporate Group Responsibility in European Antitrust Law*, 2014 (ISBN 978-90-411-5262-6).
58. Urška Petrovčič, *Competition Law and Standard Essential Patents: A Transatlantic Perspective*, 2014 (ISBN 978-90-411-4960-2).
59. David Telyas, *The Interface between Competition Law, Patents and Technical Standards*, 2014 (ISBN 978-90-411-5418-7).
60. Katerina Maniadaki, *EU Competition Law, Regulation and the Internet: The Case of Net Neutrality*, 2014 (ISBN 978-90-411-4140-8).
61. Horacio Vedia Jerez, *Competition Law Enforcement and Compliance across the World: A Comparative Review*, 2015 (ISBN 978-90-411-5815-4).
62. Kadir Baş, *The Substantive Appraisal of Joint Ventures under the EU Merger Control Regime*, 2015 (ISBN 978-90-411-5816-1).
63. Alberto Santa Maria, *Competition and State Aid: An Analysis of the EU Practice*, Second Edition, 2015 (ISBN 978-90-411-5818-5).
64. Lúcio Tomé Feteira, *The Interplay between European and National Competition Law after Regulation 1/2003: "United (Should) We Stand?"*, 2016 (ISBN 978-90-411-5663-1).
65. Giovanni Pitruzzella & Gabriella Muscolo (eds), *Competition and Patent Law in the Pharmaceutical Sector: An International Perspective*, 2016 (ISBN 978-90-411-5927-4).
66. Małgorzata Cyndecka, *The Market Economy Investor Test in EU State Aid Law: Applicability and Application*, 2016 (ISBN 978-90-411-6102-4).
67. Damiano Canapa, *Trademarks and Brands in Merger Control: An Analysis of the European and Swiss Legal Orders*, 2016 (ISBN 978-90-411-6717-0).
68. Inge Graef, *EU Competition Law, Data Protection and Online Platforms: Data as Essential Facility*, 2016 (ISBN 978-90-411-8324-8).
69. Anders Jessen, *Exclusionary Abuse after the* Post Danmark I *Case: The Role of the Effects-Based Approach under Article 102 TFEU*, 2017 (ISBN 978-90-411-8996-7).
70. Baskaran Balasingham, *The EU Leniency Policy: Reconciling Effectiveness and Fairness*, 2017 (ISBN 978-90-411-8479-5).
71. Eugene Stuart & Iana Roginska-Green, *Sixty Years of EU State Aid Law and Policy: Analysis and Assessment*, 2018 (ISBN 978-90-411-8869-4).

72. Anna Renata Pisarkiewicz, *Margin Squeeze in the Electronic Communications Sector: Critical Analysis of the Decisional Practice and Case Law*, 2018 (ISBN 978-90-411-6246-5).
73. Ploykaew Porananond, *Competition Law in the ASEAN Countries: Regional Law and National Systems*, 2018 (ISBN 978-90-411-9102-1).
74. Corinne Ruechardt, *EU State Aid Control of Infrastructure Funding*, 2018 (ISBN 978-90-411-9099-4).
75. Amalia Athanasiadou, *Patent Settlements in the Pharmaceutical Industry under US Antitrust and EU Competition Law*, 2018 (ISBN 978-94-035-0113-0).
76. Miroslava Marinova, *Fidelity Rebates in Competition Law: Application of the 'As Efficient Competitor' Test*, 2018 (ISBN 978-94-035-0570-1).
77. Gabriella Muscolo & Marina Tavassi, *The Interplay Between Competition Law and Intellectual Property: An International Perspective*, 2019 (ISBN 978-90-411-8687-4).
78. Fevzi Toksoy, Bahadir Balki & Hanna Stakheyeva, *Merger Control in the EU and Turkey: A Comparative Guide*, 2019 (ISBN 978-94-035-0934-1).
79. Paulo Burnier da Silveira & William Evan Kovacic (eds), *Global Competition Enforcement: New Players, New Challenges*, 2019 (ISBN 978-94-035-0283-0).
80. Giovanna Massarotto, *Antitrust Settlements: How a Simple Agreement Can Drive the Economy*, 2019 (ISBN 978-94-035-1133-7).
81. Marc Veenbrink, *Criminal Law Principles and the Enforcement of EU and National Competition Law: A Silent Takeover?*, 2020 (ISBN 978-94-035-1434-5).
82. Ferdinand Wollenschläger, Wolfgang Wurmnest & Thomas M.J. Möllers (eds), *Private Enforcement of European Competition and State Aid Law: Current Challenges and the Way Forward*, 2020 (ISBN 978-94-035-0281-6).
83. Jorge Marcos Ramos, *Firm Dominance in EU Competition Law: The Competitive Process and the Origins of Market Power*, 2020 (ISBN 978-94-035-2030-8).
84. Ingrid Margrethe Halvorsen Barlund, *Leniency in EU Competition Law*, 2020 (ISBN 978-94-035-1722-3).
85. Jan Blockx, Mens Rea *in EU Antitrust Law: When Intentions Matter*, 2020 (ISBN 978-94-035-2353-8).
86. Maria Wasastjerna, *Competition, Data and Privacy in the Digital Economy: Towards a Privacy Dimension in Competition Policy?*, 2020 (ISBN 978-94-035-2220-3).
87. Maria Fernanda Caporale Madi, *Regulating Vertical Agreements: A Comparative Law and Economics Review of the EU and Brazil*, 2020 (ISBN 978-94-035-2650-8).
88. Martin Gassler, *Information Exchange Between Competitors in EU Competition Law*, 2021 (ISBN 978-94-035-3183-0).

89. Andrea Biondi, Gabriella Muscolo & Renato Nazzini (eds), *After the Damages Directive: Policy and Practice in the EU Member States and the United Kingdom*, 2022 (ISBN 978-94-035-1302-7).
90. Angelika S. Murer, *Blocking Patents in European Competition Law: The Implications of the Concept of Abuse*, 2022 (ISBN 978-94-035-3814-3).